BLITZKRIEG

In the early days of World War II, the German army seemed invincible, driving wedge after wedge into Poland, France, Scandinavia and the Low Countries. Europe rapidly learned the meaning of the word "Blitzkrieg." Those early German victories were partly the result of surprise, but they were also the result of the Nazis' highly sophisticated use of tank warfare . . .

PANZER BATTLES

provides an unparalleled look at the conception and use of German armor in World War II. Maj. Gen. Von Mellenthin was a member of the German General Staff and was present at most of the major armed clashes—in the desert, in Russia, and in the final defense of Germany. Combining dynamic military maps, detailed first-hand narrative and astute strategic and tactical analysis, this campaign-by-campaign and battle-by-battle account is a classic study of one of the most important aspects of 20th-century warfare.

PANZER BATTLES

A Study of
the Employment of Armor
in the Second World War

Major General
F. W. von Mellenthin

Translated by H. Betzler
Edited by L. C. F. Turner

BALLANTINE BOOKS • NEW YORK

Preface

THIS BOOK IS based on my experiences during World War II. As an officer of the German General Staff I took part in some of the greatest campaigns in Africa, Russia, and the West, and came into close contact with many of Germany's outstanding soldiers. For over a year I served on the personal staff of Field Marshal Rommel.

Perhaps I may be permitted to strike a personal note, and explain why I have ventured to make this contribution to the increasing flood of war literature. When the war broke out I was a captain on the staff of Third Army Corps in the invasion of Poland, and when it ended I was a major general and chief of staff of Fifth Panzer Army in the Ruhr pocket. Apart from brief intervals of illness I was on active service during the whole war and held operational appointments in Poland, France, the Balkans, the Western Desert, Russia, Poland again, France again, and finally in the Ardennes and the Rhineland. I was present at many critical battles; I met some heroic and brilliant soldiers; and I have seen tanks in action under all conditions of war, from the snowbound forests of Russia to the endless plains of the Western Desert.

In preparing this book I have received generous aid from brother officers in the German Army. In particular I am deeply indebted to my former commander, General Balck, for putting his personal papers at my disposal; they have proved invaluable, especially with regard to the fighting in Russia. I am very grateful to my friend Colonel Dingler of the German General Staff for allowing me to quote freely

v

from his narrative of the Stalingrad operations, and I must thank Lieutenant General von Natzmer and my brother General Horst von Mellenthin, for providing important documents relating to the Red Army.

I have endeavored to give an objective account of the campaigns in which I took part. Although this book is written from the German point of view, I have not confined myself to German sources. Some excellent British and American histories have been published, and I have made full use of them. With the material now available it should be possible to attempt a serious assessment of the military events of 1939–45. I feel confident that soldiers of all nations are now anxious to establish the facts about World War II, and to avoid conclusions based on individual prejudice or patriotic sentiment. This I have attempted to do.

F. W. VON MELLENTHIN

Johannesburg, South Africa

Contents

PART FOUR: *Campaign in the West*

Maps

Introduction

I WAS BORN ON 30 August 1904, in the old German trading city of Breslau, situated in the heart of our beautiful province of Silesia.

Winston Churchill has related how he attended the German military maneuvers of 1908, and was presented to His Imperial Majesty the Kaiser Wilhelm II. The Kaiser greeted him with the remark: "A fair country this Silesia, well worth fighting for." Today Silesia belongs to Poland, and some of the greatest names in German history and tradition —Leuthen, Liegnitz, Katzbach—have been obliterated from the map of Europe. The fate of Silesia is shared by Pomerania, whence my father's family originally came and where the Mellenthins were established in 1225.

My father, Paul Henning von Mellenthin, was a lieutenant colonel of artillery, and was killed in action on the Western Front on 29 June 1918. I was his third son. The family of my mother Orlinda, née von Waldenburg, derived from Silesia and Brandenburg; her great-grandfather was Prince August of Prussia, a nephew of Frederick the Great. My mother was my guiding star in times of peace and war, and after my father's early death she shouldered the entire burden of bringing up and educating her three sons. She passed away in August, 1950, a few weeks before I left for South Africa.

At Breslau I attended the Real-Gymnasium, and after graduation I enlisted in the Seventh Cavalry Regiment on 1 April 1924. This regiment was stationed at Breslau, and drew its traditions from the famous White Cuirassiers of the Imperial Army. All my life I have had a passion for horses and I look back on my eleven years' service in the cavalry as the happiest period of my life. But my first four years in the army were spent under hard conditions, for at that period it took several years to qualify for commissioned rank. I enlisted as a private and remained so for eighteen months before I was promoted to corporal. In 1926 I attended the Infantry School at Ohrdruf, and then went to the Cavalry School at Hanover, where we received a most rigorous training in tactics and horsemanship.

On 1 February 1928 I was commissioned as a lieutenant—a promotion of which I felt extremely proud. During the days of the Reichswehr of one hundred thousand men, only four thousand officer posts were available in the whole army; the process of selection was strict, for the commander in chief, General von Seekt, was determined that his officers should be a *corps d'élite*. I served as a regimental officer with a cavalry squadron until 1935 and indulged my love of racing and steeplechasing to the full.

On 2 March 1932 I married Ingeborg, née von Aulock, daughter of Major von Aulock and Nona, née Malcomess. My wife's grandfather emigrated to South Africa in 1868, where his family is firmly established in the Eastern Province —a member of the house was a senator in the Union Parliament. Thanks to an inheritance from her grandfather which my wife received at the end of World War II, we were able to emigrate to South Africa, after we had lost all our estates and possessions in eastern Germany. We have two sons and three daughters.

Originally I had no ambition to become a staff officer, for I loved regimental life and was perfectly happy to remain in the Seventh Cavalry. Unfortunately my commanding officer, Colonel Count S——, shared my aversion to office work; he asserted that I displayed a tactical flair during training exercises, and detailed me to prepare all operational papers for submission to divisional headquarters. Division approved of the papers, and the Count approved of my work. On 1 October 1935 I was ordered to report to the War Academy at Berlin for training as a General Staff officer.

The staff course at the War Academy lasted for two years. During the first year, training was restricted to the regimental level, and, in the second year, we were taught the handling of divisions and larger formations. I look back on that course with regret—it was my last carefree period as an officer. Lectures were confined to the morning, and the afternoons were free for study or more pleasant occupations. Prewar Berlin was a most attractive city and offered all that could be desired as regards theatres, sport, music, and social life.

In the autumn of 1937 I qualified at the War Academy and was appointed to the staff of the third Corps in Berlin. My commander was General von Witzleben, who later commanded First Army in the French campaign; he was then promoted to field marshal and appointed Commander in Chief West, but in January, 1942, he went into retirement. Witzleben played a leading role in the conspiracy of 20 July 1944, and was hanged by the Gestapo. I was very pleased to serve under this distinguished soldier, who commanded the respect and affection of all his staff.

My post as a staff captain of the Berlin corps involved me in much work relating to state receptions and military parades. I helped to organize various Führer parades, as well as ceremonies in honor of Mussolini and Prince Paul of Yugoslavia. I was always very happy to see the last of these V.I.P.'s; all staff officers will recall the feeling of relief when a ceremonial parade goes off without a hitch.

Of greater interest was my work in connection with counter-espionage in the Berlin Military District and with the security of our armament factories in the area. An elegant Polish officer called Sosnowski had caused a flutter in high quarters by disguising himself as a racehorse owner and then getting introductions to lady secretaries at the War Office, from whom he obtained valuable secrets. It was my responsibility to see that such incidents did not recur!

During the 1930's the question of mechanizing the German Army came very much to the fore. The Versailles Treaty had prohibited Germany from possessing any modern arms or equipment, and we were not allowed a single tank. I well remember how as young soldiers we were taught with

wooden guns and dummy weapons. In 1930 our motorized
troops consisted of a few obsolete armored reconnaissance
vehicles and some motorcycle companies, but by 1932 a
motorized formation with dummy tanks was taking part in
maneuvers. It demonstrated beyond any doubt the role which
armor would play in modern war.

The driving force behind these developments was Colonel
Heinz Guderian, who for many years was chief of staff of the
Inspectorate for Motorized Troops. It is customary to say
that the German Army derived its conceptions of armored
warfare from the British military writers, Liddell Hart and
General Fuller. I would be the last to deny the stimulating
effect of their work, yet it is a fact that by 1929 German
tactical theory had progressed beyond that of Great Britain
and indeed was basically similar to the doctrine which we
practiced with such effect in World War II. The following
extract from General Guderian's *Panzer Leader* is significant:

In this year, 1929, I became convinced that tanks working
on their own or in conjunction with infantry could never
achieve decisive importance [*sic*]. My historical studies, the
exercises carried out in England and our own experiences with
mock-ups had persuaded me that tanks would never be able
to produce their full effect *until the other weapons on whose
support they must inevitably rely*[1] were brought up to their
standard of speed and of cross-country performance. In such
a formation of all arms, the tanks must play the primary role,
the other weapons being subordinated to the requirements of
the armour. It would be wrong to include tanks in infantry
divisions: what was needed were armoured divisions which
would include all the supporting arms needed to allow the
tanks to fight with full effect.[2]

This armored theory of Guderian provided the essential
foundation on which Germany's panzer armies were built
up. There are those who sneer at military theory and talk
contemptuously of "chairborne officers," but the history of
the last twenty years has demonstrated the vital importance
of clear thinking and farsighted planning. Naturally the theo-

---

[1] My italics.
[2] Heinz Guderian, *Panzer Leader* (London, Michael Joseph, 1952), 24.

rist must be closely allied to practical realities—Guderian is a brilliant example—but without his preliminary work all practical development will ultimately fail. British experts did indeed appreciate that tanks had a great part to play in the wars of the future—this had been foreshadowed by the battles of Cambrai and Amiens[3]—but they did not stress sufficiently the need for cooperation of all arms within the armored division.

The result was that Britain was about ten years behind Germany in the development of tank tactics. Field Marshal Lord Wilson of Libya has described his efforts to train the 7th Armored Division in Egypt in 1939–40 and says:

In the training of the armoured divison, I stressed the need of full co-operation of all arms in battle. One had to check a pernicious doctrine which had grown up in recent years, aided by certain civilian writers, that tank units were capable of winning an action without the assistance of the other arms. . . . The chief agents in debunking this and many other fallacies of our pre-war pundits were the Germans.[4]

In spite of warnings by Liddell Hart on the need for cooperation between tanks and guns, British theories of armored warfare tended to swing in favor of the "all-tank" concept, which, as Field Marshal Wilson points out, had such a mischievous effect in the British Army. It was not until late in 1942 that the British began to practice close cooperation between the tanks and artillery in their armored divisions.

The development of our tank arm undoubtedly owed much to Adolf Hitler. Guderian's proposals for mechanization met with considerable opposition from influential generals, although General Baron von Fritsch, the commander in chief of the army, was inclined to favor them. Hitler was keenly interested; he not only acquired a remarkable knowledge of the technical problems of motorization and armor, but showed that he was receptive to Guderian's strategic and

[3] As General von Zwehl remarked: "Germany was not defeated by the genius of Marshal Foch, but by General Tank."

[4] Henry M. Wilson, *Eight Years Overseas, 1939–47* (London, Hutchinson, 1950), 28.

tactical ideas. In July, 1934, an Armored Troops Command was established with Guderian as chief of staff, and from then on progress was rapid. Hitler stimulated interest by attending the trials of new tanks, and his government did everything possible to build up our motor industry and develop trunk roads. This was of vital importance, because from the technical point of view the German motor industry had a great deal of leeway to make up.

In March, 1935, Germany formally denounced the military clauses of the Treaty of Versailles, and that year the first three panzer divisions were established. My own cavalry regiment was among those selected for conversion to armor. As passionate cavalrymen we all felt rather sore at having to bid farewell to our horses, but we were determined to maintain the great traditions of Seidlitz and Ziethen and pass them on to the new armored corps. We were proud of the fact that the panzer divisions were mainly composed of former cavalry regiments.

Between 1935 and 1937 a tense struggle was fought out within the German General Staff regarding the future role of armor in battle. General Beck, the chief of staff, wished to follow the French doctrine and tie down the tanks to close support of the infantry. This pernicious theory, which proved so fatal to France in the summer of 1940, was successfully combated by Guderian, Blomberg, and Fritsch. By 1937 we had begun to form panzer corps, composed of a panzer division and a motorized infantry division; Guderian looked further ahead and foresaw the creation of tank armies.

Meanwhile the political situation was growing increasingly tense. There were many aspects of the internal policy of Nazism which were disliked by professional soldiers, but General von Seekt, the creator of the Reichswehr, had adopted the principle that the army should remain aloof from political affairs, and his view was generally accepted. No German officer liked the antics of the "brown men," and their attempts to play at soldiers aroused laughter and contempt.[5]

---

[5] *Editor's note.* A few words on the S.S. and the S.A. may prove of value to the reader. In 1923 the S.A. (Sturm Abteilung) was organized as a bodyguard for the Nazi leaders. Of this the S.S. (Schutzstaffel or Elite Guard), distinguishable from the brown-shirted S.A. troopers by

But Hitler did not swamp the army with the S.A.; on the contrary he accepted general conscription and the exclusive control of the army by the General Staff. Moreover his great successes in the field of foreign policy, and particularly the decision to rearm, were welcomed by the whole German nation. The revival of Germany as a Great Power was hailed with enthusiasm by the officer corps.

This does not mean that we wanted war. The General Staff tried hard to restrain Hitler, but its position was weakened when he occupied the Rhineland in direct opposition to their advice. In 1938 the General Staff was strongly opposed to any action in Czechoslovakia which might lead to a European war, but the weakness of Chamberlain and Daladier encouraged Hitler to attempt new adventures. I am well aware that the German General Staff is regarded with great suspicion abroad, and that my comments on our reluctance to wage war will be received with skepticism. Therefore I cannot do better than quote the words of Cyril Falls, one of Britain's leading military writers, who until recently was Chichele Professor of the History of War at the University of Oxford. He says:

We in this country do consider ourselves up to a certain point entitled to reproach the German General Staff for having set its face towards war in 1914. Sometimes we make the same charge about the year 1939, but I agree with Herr Görlitz that in this case it cannot be justified. You can indict Hitler, the Nazi state and party, even the German nation. But the General Staff did not want war with France and

---

its black shirts, formed a small part. In 1929 Himmler took charge of the S.S., and rebuilt and enlarged it along racial lines. In 1933 the S.S. was divided into three major groups: nonspecialized troopers, troopers for special guard duty, and the S.S.-Verfügungstruppe, troops at the disposal of the Party chiefs. From the last group were developed the Waffen-S.S., Elite Guard troops organized and fully-equipped as crack military units. Although units of the Waffen-S.S. served alongside army formations, and were under the operational orders of the General Staff, they were not part of the German Army, and and did not come under army discipline.

The S.A. were reduced in power after the execution of their leader, Ernst Röhm, in 1934, but were given a significant military and political role by Hitler in 1937.

Britain, and after it had become engaged in war with them it did not want war with Russia.[6]

The peaceful solution of the Sudeten crisis in October, 1938, was a great relief to the army. I was then serving as Ic[7] of the third Corps; our headquarters was situated near Hirschberg in Silesia. As a result of the Munich agreement we were able to move peacefully into Sudetenland, and as we marched past the formidable Czech fortifications everyone felt relieved that bloody fighting had been avoided, fighting in which the chief victims would have been the Sudeten Germans. Our soldiers received a touching reception in every village and were greeted with flags and flowers.

For a few weeks I was liaison officer to Konrad Henlein, the leader of the Sudeten Germans. I learned much about the difficulties of these frontier Germans, who had been suppressed culturally and economically. Faith in Hitler's leadership had grown immeasurably, but with the annexation of Bohemia in March, 1939, the international situation became increasingly critical. I was then back in Berlin and had my hands full in preparing the gigantic military parade in honor of Hitler's fiftieth birthday. This parade was designed as a military demonstration and a display of power; the marching columns were headed by color parties bearing all the battle standards of the Wehrmacht.

I longed to get away from this sort of life—I was tired of running a military circus, and wanted to return to the troops. Arrangements were made for my attachment for a year to Panzer Regiment 5,[8] and I was told to report on 1 October 1939. But soon the Polish crisis overshadowed everything, and I was immersed in the details of operational staff work.

In spite of the military preparations along the eastern frontier and the increasing tension in our relations with Britain and France, we still hoped that our demand for Danzig—a purely German city—would not lead to a world conflagration. Presented at a different time and in a different

[6] Walter Görlitz, *The German General Staff* (London, Hollis & Carter, 1953), *ix*.
[7] Chief Intelligence Officer.
[8] Afterwards part of Rommel's famous 21st Panzer Division.

manner the demand for Danzig would have been perfectly justified. Coming as it did—immediately after the annexation of Czechoslovakia—the demand was bound to arouse the gravest concern in London and Paris. In 1945, when a prisoner of war, I was told by General Geyr von Schweppenburg, the former military attaché in London, that Hitler was convinced that an invasion of Poland would not lead to war with the Western powers. He ignored the warning of his military attaché that Great Britain would declare war, and thought that his Non-Aggression Pact with Russia had clinched the matter.

During the last days of August, 1939, the long convoys of the 3rd Corps rumbled through the streets of Berlin and headed for the Polish frontier. Everyone was quiet and serious; we all realized that for good or ill Germany was crossing the Rubicon. There was no trace of the jubilant crowds whom I had seen in 1914 as a boy of ten. Civilians or soldiers—nobody felt any elation or enthusiasm. But determined to do his duty to the very last, the German soldier marched on.

PANZER BATTLES

PART ONE

Poland, France, and the Balkans

1: *The Polish Campaign*

THE GERMAN ARMY entered Poland at 0445 hours on 1 September 1939; the advance of the ground forces was preceded by devastating attacks by the Luftwaffe on Polish airfields, railway junctions, and mobilization centers. From the beginning of the offensive we had complete air superiority and the deployment of the Polish forces was seriously hampered in consequence. Our mechanized columns raced over the border and soon made deep penetrations into Polish territory.

It is not my purpose to discuss this campaign in detail, for the German superiority was so marked that the operations have no special interest for the student of strategy and tactics. I propose therefore to summarize the reasons for our success and to give only a brief outline of my own experiences during the campaign.

In size, the Polish Army was impressive and appeared to justify the claim of the Polish government and press that Poland had now become a Great Power. On paper the Poles could muster thirty first-line divisions, ten reserve divisions, and eleven cavalry brigades. But, as I have observed, the Polish mobilization was gravely affected by the attacks of the Luftwaffe, and even those formations which did mobilize found their power of movement seriously restricted and their supply system breaking down. With only a few hundred modern aircraft, and inadequate antiaircraft artillery, the Polish forces were unable to bring their numerical strength into action. Moreover, with their inadequate firepower and

3

obsolete equipment, the Polish divisions were really only comparable with German regimental groups. The Poles had only a few tanks and armored cars, their antitank artillery was totally insufficient, and, like the Italians, much of their equipment dated from World War I. Their best formations were undoubtedly their cavalry brigades, which fought with magnificent gallantry—on one occasion they charged our panzers with drawn sabers. But all the dash and bravery which the Poles frequently displayed could not compensate for the lack of modern arms and serious tactical training.

A heavy responsibility rests with the Polish military clique for the condition of the army in 1939. The state of their arms and equipment may have been influenced by economic factors, but there can be no excuse for their failure to appreciate the influence of firepower on modern tactics.

The same intellectual weakness was shown in the field of strategy. In fairness to the Poles, they may well have hoped that the French Army and the Royal Air Force would tie down considerable German forces in the west, but even so their plans were lacking in a sense of reality. A cautious attitude was fully justified by their inferiority in every arm, and by the configuration of the frontier, which made large areas indefensible. But so far from attempting to gain time by large-scale strategic withdrawals, the Polish Command held Poznia and the Polish Corridor in strength, attempted to deploy all their available forces on a front of eight hundred miles from Lithuania to the Carpathians, and even formed a special assault group for an invasion of East Prussia. Thus the Polish High Command succeeded in thoroughly splitting up and dispersing all their available forces.

Into these Polish dispositions the German plan fitted like a glove. We attacked Poland with forty-four divisions and two thousand aircraft. Only a minimum force was left to hold the West Wall, which was still far from complete. Virtually the entire striking force of the Wehrmacht was flung across the Polish frontier, in the confident expectation of gaining a rapid and easy victory. (See map on page 6.)

Army Group North (Colonel General von Bock) comprised the Third and Fourth Armies, of which the Fourth faced Danzig and the Polish Corridor, while the Third was poised

in East Prussia for a thrust towards Warsaw. The task of the
Fourth Army was to overrun the Corridor and join hands
with the Third in an advance on the Polish capital.

Army Group South (Colonel General von Rundstedt), comprising the Eighth, Tenth, and Fourteenth Armies, was based
in Silesia and Slovakia. This Group also was to advance in
the general direction of Warsaw, and provide the second
arm of a giant pincer movement which was designed to entrap the Polish forces in Poznia and indeed in all their territory west of the Vistula. The two army groups were only
connected by light containing forces which faced towards
Posen and covered the main road to Berlin. This conception
of a weak center with two powerful attacking wings was
traditional in German strategy. and found its roots in Count
von Schlieffen's classic study of Hannibal's victory at Cannae.

The German forces included six panzer divisions and four
light divisions. Each panzer division had one panzer brigade
and one rifle brigade. The panzer brigade consisted of two
regiments with 125 tanks each, and the rifle brigade had
two rifle regiments and a motorcycle battalion. The light
divisions had two rifle regiments, each of three battalions,
and one tank detachment (*Abteilung*).[1]

In this campaign the quality of our matériel left much to
be desired. We had only a few Mark IV's with low-velocity
75-mm guns, some Mark III's carrying the unsatisfactory 37-
mm,[2] and the bulk of our armored strength was made up
of Mark II's carrying only a heavy machine gun. Moreover
both armored strategy and tactics were still in an experimen-
tal stage. Fortunately General Guderian was in command of
the mechanized divisions operating with Army Group North;
from detailed study and experiment before the war he had
gained a profound insight into the possibilities of the tank
and, what was equally important, into the need for combined
action by tanks, artillery, and infantry within the panzer division.

Guderain foresaw the ultimate creation of panzer armies,
and in this campaign he handled the two panzer divisions

---

[1] The establishment of the light divisions did not prove satisfactory
and after the campaign they were converted to panzer divisions.

[2] A gun appreciably inferior to the British 2-pounder.

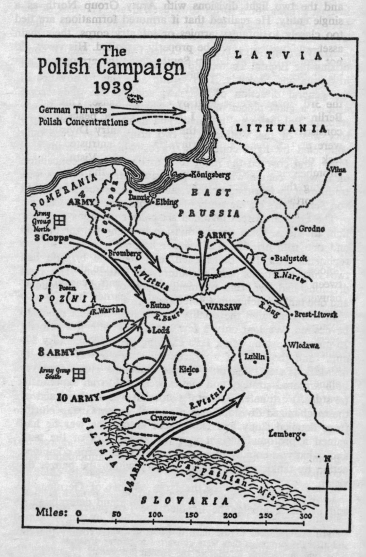

The Polish Campaign 1939

German Thrusts
Polish Concentrations

LATVIA

LITHUANIA

Vilna

Königsberg

EAST PRUSSIA

Grodno

POMERANIA
4 ARMY

Danzig Elbing

Army Group North
3 Corps

Białystok

3 ARMY

R. Narew

Bromberg

R. Vistula

Posen

POZNIA

R. Warthe

Kutno

R. Bzura

WARSAW

R. Bug

Brest-Litovsk

Łódź

Włodawa

8 ARMY

Army Group South

Kielce

Lublin

10 ARMY

R. Vistula

SILESIA

Cracow

Lemberg

N

14 ARMY

Carpathian Mts.

SLOVAKIA

Miles: 0   50   100   150   200   250   300

and the two light divisions with Army Group North as a single entity. He realized that if armored formations are tied too closely to infantry armies or infantry corps, their main asset—mobility—cannot be properly exploited. His views did not prevail in Army Group South where the armor was split up and dispersed among the various armies and corps.

When the campaign opened I was intelligence officer (Ic) of the 3rd Corps, commanded by General Haase. This was the Berlin Corps with which I had served in peacetime, and consisted of the 50th and the 208th Infantry Divisions. We were part of the Fourth Army, and were entrusted with the task of advancing from Pomerania to the Vistula east of Bromberg and cutting the line of retreat of the Polish troops holding the Corridor. Guderian's 19th Corps advanced on our northern flank, and he achieved such rapid and spectacular success that the resistance on our front crumbled away. Even during the first days of the invasion we took hundreds of prisoners with negligible losses.

Nevertheless, the operations were of considerable value in "blooding" our troops and teaching them the difference between real war with live ammunition and peacetime maneuvers. Very early in the campaign I learned how "jumpy" even a well-trained unit can be under war conditions. A low-flying aircraft circled over corps battle headquarters and everyone let fly with whatever he could grab. An air-liaison officer ran about trying to stop the fusillade and shouting to the excited soldiery that this was a German command plane—one of the good old *Fieseler Störche*. Soon afterwards the aircraft landed, and out stepped the Luftwaffe general responsible for our close air support. He failed to appreciate the joke.

On 5 September the spearhead of our corps approached Bromberg, where no serious opposition was anticipated. I accompanied the leading troops, who were eager to enter the town and bring relief to the large number of Germans living there. But we were met with a fierce and determined resistance by the Polish rearguard, assisted by many armed civilians. After we broke into the town, we found that the Poles had slaughtered in cold blood hundreds of our compatriots living in Bromberg. Their dead bodies littered the streets.

Meanwhile the German armies were advancing along the whole front. By 7 September Army Group South had entered Cracow and was approaching Kielce and Lodz, the Polish Corridor had been broken through, and the Third and Fourth Armies had joined hands. The bulk of Fourth Army advanced on Warsaw along the right bank of the Vistula, but on 11 September the 3rd Corps was put under Eighth Army and ordered to move west of the Vistula through Kutno. I was ordered to fly in a Storch to the battle headquarters of Eighth Army somewhere near Lodz, report on our situation, and ask for orders.

We took off in clear weather, flew over our advancing spearheads, then crossed a wide belt of Polish territory, where we could see the roads packed with dense columns of troops and civilians fleeing eastwards, and then entered a zone where we might expect to see the vanguards of Eighth Army. I have always regarded aircraft with a certain skepticism, and it did not surprise me when the engine started to give trouble while we were over an area of uncertain ownership. There was nothing for it but to make an emergency landing, and as the pilot and I stepped out of the machine we saw not far away groups of men in olive-green uniforms—definitely Poles. Just as we were about to let rip with our machine-pistols we heard German commands—they were an advance detachment of "Organization Todt,"[3] and were employed in repairing bridges and roads.

After reporting to the commander of the Eighth Army, I was put in the picture by the chief of staff, General Felber. He told me that Eighth Army had just overcome a serious crisis on its northern flank. Thirtieth Infantry Division, which had been holding a wide front on the River Bzura, was attacked by superior Polish forces withdrawing from Poznia towards Warsaw. This group of four infantry divisions and two cavalry brigades was assisted by other Polish units crammed in the area west of Warsaw. To avoid a serious reverse, Eighth Army was compelled to suspend its advance

---

[3] Labor force.

on Warsaw and come to the rescue of the 30th Division. The Polish attacks had been repulsed and Eighth Army was now launching its own attack across the Bzura to encircle and destroy the very considerable Polish forces in the Kutno Area. Third Corps was to close the gap on the west.

During that week we tightened the ring around Kutno and beat off desperate break-out attempts by the encircled Poles. The situation was comparable in many ways with the encirclement of the Russians at Tannenberg in 1914. On 19 September the remnants of nineteen Polish divisions and three cavalry brigades, totalling one hundred thousand men, surrendered to Eighth Army.

That day virtually saw the end of the Polish Campaign. Guderian's Panzer Corps, dashing forward far in advance of the infantry formations of Army Group North, had crossed the Narew, and on 14 September had breached the fortifications of Brest-Litovsk. On 17 September Guderian made contact with the armored spearheads of Army Group South, at Wlodawa on the River Bug. Thus the pincer movement was completed, and we had succeeded in surrounding almost the entire Polish Army. The various pockets remained to be cleared up, and the tenacious defense of Warsaw continued until 27 September.

In conformity with the agreement signed in Moscow on 26 August, Russian troops entered Poland on 17 September, and our troops abandoned Brest-Litovsk and Lemberg and retired to the prearranged boundary line. Dazzling though the Polish victory had been, many of us had misgivings about this vast extension of Soviet power towards the west.

2: *The Conquest of France*

In the West

EVEN BEFORE THE end of the Polish Campaign, the 3rd
Corps was transferred to the West, and at the beginning of
October we arrived in the sector north of Trèves. My second
brother, who in peacetime was a high-ranking officer in the
forestry department, was serving as a platoon commander
in a reserve division near Saarbrücken, and I was able to
visit him. This gave me an opportunity of inspecting the
famous West Wall, or Siegfried Line, at first hand.

I soon realized what a gamble the Polish Campaign had
been, and the grave risks which were run by our High Command. The second-class troops holding the Wall were badly
equipped and inadequately trained, and the defenses were
far from being the impregnable fortifications pictured by
our propaganda. Concrete protection of more than three
feet was rare, and as a whole the positions were by no means
proof against heavy caliber shelling. Few of the strongpoints
were sited to fire in enfilade and most of them could have
been shot to pieces by direct fire, without the slightest risk
to the attackers. The West Wall had been built in such a
hurry that many of the positions were sited on forward
slopes. The antitank obstacles were of trivial significance,
and the more I looked at the defenses the less I could understand the completely passive attitude of the French.

Apart from sending some local patrols into the outlying
areas (very "outlying") of Saarbrücken, the French had kept

very quiet and left the West Wall alone. This negative attitude was bound to affect the fighting morale of their troops, and was calculated to do much more harm than our propaganda, effective though it was.

When Hitler's peace proposals were rejected in October, 1939, his immediate reaction was to force the issue by launching another blitzkrieg. He feared that with every month of delay the Allies would grow stronger; moreover, no one really believed that our pact with Russia would last. Already she had followed up her advance into Poland with the occupation of the Baltic States; in November the Red Army attacked Finland. The menacing shadow in the East was an added inducement to seek victory in the West.

It was originally planned to launch our offensive in November, but bad weather grounded the Luftwaffe and forced repeated postponements of D day. The army spent the winter in carrying out intensive training and in large-scale maneuvers. I was transferred to the 297th Infantry Division as chief of staff (Ia); the division trained in the Posen area in bitterly cold weather. We continued our maneuvers and fieldfiring exercises in temperatures of twenty to thirty degrees below freezing point, and training from platoon to divisional level never knew any interruption.

In March, 1940, the division was inspected by the famous General von Manstein, then corps commander, who actually designed the plan of attack in the West which was to lead to such undreamed-of success.[1] Manstein had the best brain in the German General Staff, but his manner was blunt; he said what he thought and did not attempt to disguise his opinions even when they were not flattering to his superiors. In consequence he had been "put into cold storage" and was allotted a relatively minor part in the campaign which he had so brilliantly conceived.

My own experience of the French campaign was confined to Lorraine, and I did not take part in the great drive across northern France to the English Channel. Nevertheless I

---

[1] I am aware that the British official history, *The War in France and Flanders 1939–1940*, minimizes Manstein's influence, but in my view the evidence of Guderian and other officers is decisive. Liddell Hart also takes the view that Manstein was the originator of the plan.

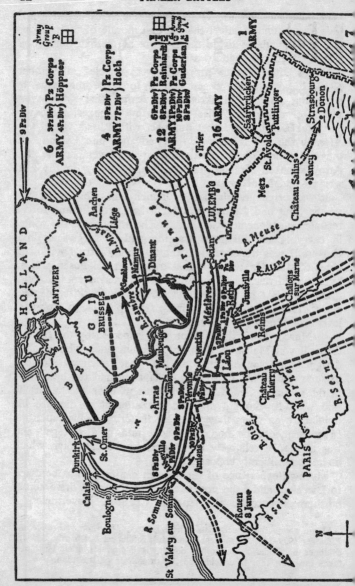

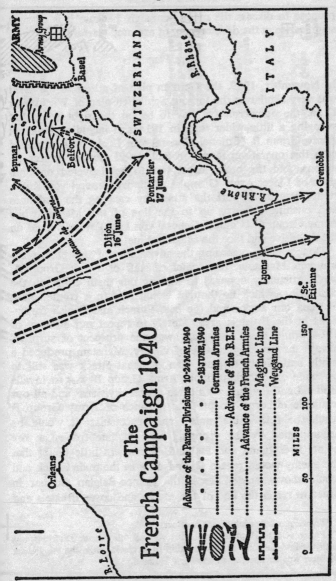

The
French Campaign 1940

Advance of the Panzer Divisions 10-24 MAY, 1940
                                     5-18 JUNE, 1940
German Armies
Advance of the B.E.F.
Advance of the French Armies
Maginot Line
Weygand Line

MILES

0   50   100   150

propose to discuss the main campaign, because it is of such significance in the development of armored warfare.

The Plan

In November, 1939, the German plan of attack in the West was very similar to the famous Schlieffen plan of World War I, i.e. the *Schwerpunkt*[2] was to be on the right wing, but swinging a little wider than in 1914 and including Holland. Army Group B (Colonel General von Bock) was entrusted with this operation; it was to include all our ten panzer divisions, and the main thrust was to be delivered on both sides of Liége. Army Group A (Colonel General von Rundstedt) was to support the attack by crossing the Ardennes and pushing infantry up to the line of the Meuse, while Army Group C (Colonel General von Leeb) was to stand on the defensive and face the Maginot Line.

Doubts arose regarding the advisability of this plan. General von Manstein, then chief of staff of Army Group A, was particularly opposed to making our main effort on the right wing, which he thought would lead to a frontal clash between our armor and the best French and British formations in the Brussels area. Merely to repeat our strategy of 1914 would mean throwing away the prospect of surprise, always the surest guarantee of victory. Manstein produced a subtle and highly original plan. A great attack was still to be made on our right flank, Army Group B was to invade Holland and Belgium with three panzer divisions[3] and all our available airborne troops. The advance of Army Group B would be formidable, noisy, and spectacular; it would be accompanied by the dropping of parachute troops at key points in Belgium and Holland. There was little doubt that the enemy would regard this advance as the main attack and would move rapidly across the Franco-Belgian frontier in order to reach the line of the Meuse and cover Brussels and

[2] *Schwerpunkt:* point of main effort.
[3] Panzer Corps Höppner with the 3rd and 4th Panzer Divisions was to thrust into Belgium in the direction of Brussels, while the 9th Panzer Division was to operate in southern Holland.

Antwerp. The more they committed themselves to this sector, the more certain would be their ruin.

The decisive role was to be given to Army Group A. This was to comprise three armies—the Fourth, Twelfth, and Sixteenth—and Panzergruppe Kleist. Fourth Army, which included Hoth's Panzer Corps,[4] was to advance south of the Meuse and force a crossing at Dinant. The main thrust was to be delivered on the front of our Twelfth Army by Panzergruppe Kleist. This comprised Reinhardt's Panzer Corps (the 6th and 8th Panzer Divisions), Guderian's Panzer Corps (1st, 2nd, and 10th Panzer Divisions) and Wietersheim's Motorized Corps (five motorized divisions). They were to cross the difficult terrain of the Ardennes—very unsuitable tank country and presumably inadequately guarded—and force the crossing of the Meuse at Sedan. They were then to sweep rapidly west and push far behind the flank and rear of the enemy's forces in Belgium. Their left flank was to be covered initially by Sixteenth Army.

Such was the plan adopted by the German High Command, on the advice and inspiration of Manstein. It must be admitted that Manstein's proposals met with considerable opposition, and the scales were only tilted in their favor by a curious incident. In January, 1940, a German courier aircraft lost its way and landed in Belgian territory. The officer on board had a copy of the original plan in his pocket, and we could not be certain whether it had been destroyed. Therefore it was decided to adopt Manstein's plan, to which Hitler was particularly attracted because of its originality and daring.

Sedan

At 0535 on 10 May 1940 the spearheads of the German Army crossed the frontiers of Belgium, Luxembourg, and Holland. As in Poland we enjoyed the advantage of air superiority, but no attempt was made to interfere with the British and French columns streaming into Belgium and southern Holland. The German High Command was delighted

---

[4] The 5th and 7th Panzer Divisions.

to see the enemy responding to our offensive in the exact manner which we desired and predicted.

The key to the offensive rested with Panzergruppe Kleist which plunged into the wooded hills of the Ardennes and headed for the Meuse. I must emphasize that the German victories of May, 1940, were due primarily to skillful application of the two great principles of war—surprise and concentration. The German Army was actually inferior to the Allied armies, not only in numbers of divisions but particularly in numbers of tanks. While the combined Franco-British forces had about 4,000 tanks, the German Army could field only 2,800. Nor did we have any real advantage in quality. The Allied tanks, and especially the British Matilda, had stronger armor than our own, while the 37-mm gun on our Mark III—the principal German fighting tank—was inferior to the British 2-pounder. But the decisive factor was that for the breakthrough between Sedan and Namur we had massed seven of our ten panzer divisions, of which five were concentrated in the Sedan sector. The Allied military leaders, and particularly the French, still thought in terms of the linear tactics of World War I, and split up their armor among the infantry divisions. The British 1st Armored Division had not yet arrived in France, and the setting up of four French armored divisions was only in the initial stage. Nor did the French contemplate using their armored divisions in mass. By dispersing their armor along the whole front from the Swiss frontier to the English Channel, the French High Command played into our hands and have only themselves to blame for the catastrophe which was to follow.[5]

Panzergruppe Kleist met no resistance in Luxembourg, and in the Ardennes the opposition of French cavalry and Belgian chasseurs was rapidly broken. The terrain was undoubtedly difficult, but carefully planned traffic control and farsighted staff work smoothed the approach march of armored divisions and motorized columns moving in echelons

[5] Three French mechanized cavalry divisions, each with about 200 tanks, took part in the advance into Belgium. The four French armored divisions each had about 150 tanks. The average strength of a panzer division at this time was about 260 tanks.

sixty miles deep. The enemy was unprepared for a massive thrust in this sector, his weak opposition was brushed aside, and on the evening of 12 May the advance guard of Panzer Corps Guderian had reached the Meuse and occupied the town of Sedan. Kleist decided to force a crossing of the Meuse on the afternoon of the 13th with the leading elements of the Panzer Corps. Infantry divisions would have been more suitable, but it was vital to take advantage of the enemy's confusion and give him no opportunity to regain his balance. Very powerful Luftwaffe formations were available to support the crossing.

I am fortunate in possessing a firsthand account of the battle written by the commander of the 1st Rifle Regiment of the 1st Panzer Division, Lieutenant Colonel Balck.[6] On the evening of 12 May his regiment had reached the Meuse south of Floing and stood ready to attack. Officers and men knew exactly what was expected of them; for months they had practiced this attack and studied maps and photographs of the terrain. Our Intelligence had obtained exact details of the French positions even down to the individual bunkers.

Nevertheless on the morning of 13 May the situation seemed ominous to the staff of the 1st Rifle Regiment. The French artillery was alert and the slightest movement attracted fire. The German artillery was held up on congested roads and could not get into position in time, and neither the engineers nor the bulk of their equipment had reached the river. Fortunately the transport carrying the collapsible rubber boats had reached the Rifle Regiment, although the troops had to handle this equipment without help from the engineers.[7] Colonel Balck sent a liaison officer to corps headquarters to request maximum Luftwaffe support and to point out that the attack could not hope to succeed unless the French artillery was eliminated. The enemy's fire was making all movement impossible.

---

[6] Later General of Panzer Troops; a corps commander in Russia, an army commander in Poland and Hungary, and an army group commander in the West.

[7] This illustrates the importance of infantry receiving thorough and versatile training in the work of other arms—as was the case with the 1st Rifle Regiment.

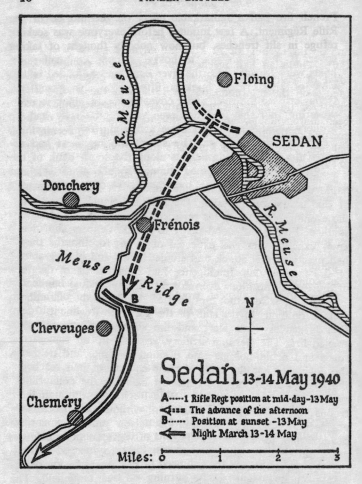

Sedań 13-14 May 1940

A ····· 1 Rifle Regt position at mid-day-13 May
◄ ·=== The advance of the afternoon
B ····· Position at sunset -13 May
◄━━━ Night March 13-14 May

Miles: 0   1   2   3

At about noon the Luftwaffe began its attack, using up to a thousand aircraft in dense formations. The Stuka onslaught completely silenced the French artillery which never recovered from the blow. Colonel Balck has the impression that the crews deserted their batteries and could not be induced to go back to the guns. The complete cessation of

French fire had a remarkable effect on the morale of the Rifle Regiment. A few minutes before everyone was seeking refuge in slit trenches, but now nobody thought of taking cover. It was impossible to hold the men. The collapsible boats were driven up to the river bank and offloaded in full view of the French bunkers fifty yards away, and the troops crossed the river under cover of an air attack so overpowering that they did not even notice that they had no artillery support whatever. Once across the river everything went like clockwork, and by sunset the regiment had secured the commanding heights along the south bank of the Meuse. The French seemed stunned by the air attack and their resistance was feeble; moreover every unit under Balck's command had practiced and rehearsed its role for months.

That evening Colonel Balck decided to enlarge the bridgehead and push on to Chémery, more than six miles south of the Meuse. It was a very bold decision. Neither artillery, armor nor antitank guns had yet come forward, and bridgebuilding over the Meuse was proceeding slowly in the face of continuous and determined air attacks. But Balck feared that a small bridgehead would be easily sealed off and, in spite of the exhaustion of his men, he decided to push deep into French territory. After a night march of six miles Chémery was occupied without opposition.

The morning of 14 May brought the crisis which Balck had deliberately courted; a French armored brigade counterattacked with the support of low-flying aircraft. Fortunately the French found it difficult to improvise such an attack at short notice; their tanks moved slowly and clumsily and by the time they got into action, our antitank guns were arriving, as were the first elements of the 1st Panzer Brigade. The action was short and sharp; although the French attacked courageously they showed little skill, and soon nearly fifty of their tanks were burning on the battlefield. The signal arrangements in the French armored brigade were poor, and the up-to-date wireless equipment of our armored units gave them a clear advantage in maneuver. The obsolete French aircraft suffered heavily from the machine gun fire of the Rifle Regiment.

During the battle—and also during the crossing of the

Meuse the previous day—General Guderian was well forward and Balck was able to consult him in person.

The Battle of Sedan has an important place in the development of armored warfare. At that time it was customary to draw a sharp distinction between rifle units and armored units. This theory proved unsound. Had Colonel Balck had tanks under his command during the Meuse crossing, things would have been much easier. It would have been possible to ferry single tanks across the river, and there would have been no need to send the troops forward without any tank support on the night 13/14 May. If the French had counterattacked more promptly the position of the Rifle Regiment would have been very critical, but at the time it was thought to be unwise to attach tanks to the infantry—the panzer brigade was to be kept intact for the decisive thrust. From Sedan onwards armor and infantry were used in mixed battle groups. These *Kampfgruppen* embodied a principle as old as war itself—the concentration of all arms at the same time in the same area.

The French resistance along the Meuse now collapsed. Their positions on the river bank were held by second-line troops with few antitank guns, and their morale seemed to go to pieces under dive-bombing. To the north of Mézières General Reinhardt's two panzer divisions crossed the Meuse at several places, and Hoth's Panzer Corps took the French completely by surprise at Dinant. On 14 May Guderian's Panzer Corps enlarged the bridgehead south and west of Sedan and beat off various counterattacks by the French 3rd Armored Division. The fighting here was very stubborn, and the most important heights changed hands several times.

On 15 May the German High Command developed "nerves" and forbade any further advance by the panzer corps until the infantry divisions of the Twelfth Army, which were plodding along behind Panzergruppe Kleist, were ready to take over protection of the southern flank. But the commanders of the panzer corps and panzer divisions, judging the situation at the front, saw clearly that a gigantic victory was in the offing if only the westward drive was kept going and the enemy was allowed no time to develop countermeasures. In view of their strong protests, permission was given to "enlarge the bridgeheads," and on 16 May Panzer-gruppe Kleist broke clean through the French front west of the Meuse and set out on its drive to the sea.

The Debacle

While the French center was being pierced at Sedan a violent tank battle developed in Belgium on 13 and 14 May. Höppner's Panzer Corps advancing north of the Meuse ran into French armored forces of superior strength near Gembloux. But with their thorough training and excellent signals service Höppner's panzers outmaneuvered the French and drove them back across the Dyle. Höppner was ordered to avoid a direct thrust at Brussels, and make his main effort along the line of the Sambre in order to keep close touch with the panzer corps advancing south of the river.

Guderian's drive along the line of the Somme developed with astonishing speed. By the evening of the 18th he was in St. Quentin, on the 19th he crossed the old Somme battlefield, and by the 20th his vanguard had reached Abbeville and the English Channel—the Allied armies had been cut in two. Such a rapid advance involved grave risks, and there was much anxiety about the security of the southern flank. Tenth Panzer Division, Wietersheim's Motorized Corps, and the infantry divisions of Sixteenth Army were successively committed to building up a defensive line along the Aisne and the Somme. The crisis came on 19 May when the French 4th Armored Division under General de Gaulle counterattacked at Laon and was severely repulsed. It was typical of French strategy to throw away their armor in this piecemeal fashion —their 3rd Armored Division had been flung away at Sedan on 14/15 May, and their 4th Armored Division suffered the same fate at Laon on the 19th. Even after our initial breakthrough at Sedan the French would still have had a fighting chance if their High Command had not lost its head and had refrained from counterattacks until all available armor had been assembled for a decisive blow.[8]

Strongly pressed by Army Group B, the Allied forces in

[8] General Charles de Gaulle, *The Call to Honour* (London, Collins, 1955), 40–48.

Belgium had fallen back from Brussels to the line of the
Scheldt, with their southern flank at Arras only twenty-five
miles from Péronne, on the banks of the Somme. If the
Allies could close the gap Arras–Péronne they would cut off
our panzer divisions which had penetrated to the sea. On 20
May Lord Gort, the commander of the British Expeditionary
Force, issued orders for a local counterattack at Arras to be
carried out on the 21st; attempts were also made to enlist
French support in a larger operation to close the vital gap.[9]
The French declared that they could not attack until the 22nd,
but units of the British 50th Division and 1st Army Tank
Brigade went into action south of Arras on the morning of
the 21st. The forces employed were too small to achieve
any decisive result, but they did inflict severe casualties on
Rommel's 7th Panzer Division. Our 37-mm antitank gun was
too light to stop the heavy British Matilda tanks, and it was
only by committing all his artillery, and particularly the
heavy 88-mm antiaircraft guns, that Rommel brought the British thrust to a halt.

South of the Somme nothing happened at all—the French
troops assembling for counterattack were subjected to continuous bombing by the Luftwaffe. The British official history
remarks[10] that "At this most critical juncture the French High
Command proved unable to exercise effective control." There
were many conferences, discussions, and directives, but little
or no positive action. Our Fourth Army struck back, captured Arras, and pushed the British farther north. The situation of the Allies in Belgium and northern France soon became catastrophic.

Guderian advanced northwards from Abbeville and on 22
May attacked Boulogne; Reinhardt's Panzer Corps moving on
his flank captured St. Omer on the 23rd. Thus the leading
panzer divisions were only eighteen miles from Dunkirk, and
were much nearer to the port than the bulk of the Anglo-
French forces in Belgium. On the evening of 23 May General
von Rundstedt, the commander of Army Group A, ordered
his panzer divisions to close up on the 24th along the line of

---

[9] See *The War in France and Flanders 1939–1940*, 87 *et seq.*
[10] *Op. cit.,* 103.

the canal between St. Omer and Béthune. General von Brauchitsch, commander in chief of the army, considered that the operations against the Allied armies in the north should be directed by a single commander and, moreover, that the encircling attacks against them should continue without respite. Accordingly he ordered on 24 May that Rundstedt's Fourth Army, which included all the panzer divisions of Army Group A, should come under command of General von Bock's Army Group B, which was attacking the Allied salient from the east. On 24 May Hitler visited von Rundstedt's HQ. and countermanded the orders of Brauchitsch.[11] On his departure Rundstedt issued a directive which read: "By the Führer's orders . . . the general line Lens–Béthune–Aire–St. Omer–Gravelines (canal line) will not be passed." When Hitler ordered Rundstedt to resume the attack on the 26th it was too late to achieve decisive results, and the British were able to execute a fighting withdrawal to the Dunkirk beaches.[12]

But if Dunkirk was not the triumph which the German Army was entitled to expect, it was none the less a crushing defeat for the Allies. In Belgium, the French Army had sacrificed most of its armored and motorized formations, and was left with barely sixty divisions to hold the long front from the Swiss Frontier to the English Channel. The British Expeditionary Force had lost all its guns, tanks, and transport, and little support could now be given to the French on the line of the Somme.[13] At the end of May our panzer divisions

[11] *Editor's note.* The British official history seems to lay excessive stress on Rundstedt's influence, for the documents quoted by Major Ellis show that Hitler's intervention was significant and important. Even if it be granted that Hitler's decision to countermand the orders of Brauchitsch, the army commander in chief, was taken on Rundstedt's advice, yet the responsibility was Hitler's. Major Ellis disputes the significance of the "halt order," but it is probable that the last word on this subject has yet to be spoken. French documents have not been examined.

[12] See the British official history, pp. 346–50. On 25 May a British patrol ambushed a German staff car on the Ypres front, and captured army documents on the highest level. As the British history shows (p. 148), this incident was of vital importance, for it led Lord Gort to move two divisions to the northern flank and so secure his withdrawal to the sea.

[13] Only the 51st (Highland) Division and the 1st Armored Division were available.

began to move southwards, and preparations were made to mount a new offensive as rapidly as possible against the so-called Weygand Line.[14]

The plan of the German High Command for the last phase of the French campaign envisaged three main attacks. Army Group B with six panzer divisions was to break through between the Oise and the sea and advance to the lower Seine in the area of Rouen. A few days later Army Group A with four panzer divisions was to attack on both sides of Rethel and penetrate deep into France with the Plateau de Langres as its objective. When these attacks were well under way, Army Group C was to assault the Maginot Line and aim at a breakthrough between Metz and the Rhine.

At the beginning of June the German armor was grouped as follows. Panzer Corps Hoth, with the 5th and 7th Panzer Divisions, was in the Abbeville sector, under command of Fourth Army. Panzergruppe Kleist stood between Amiens and Péronne, with Panzer Corps Wietersheim (9th and 10th Panzer Divisons) and Panzer Corps Höppner (3rd and 4th Panzer Divisions). The panzer divisions in the Rethel area formed a new Panzergruppe under Guderian—Panzer Corps Schmidt (1st and 2nd Panzer Divisions and 29th Motorized Division) and Panzer Corps Reinhardt (6th and 8th Panzer Divisions and the 20th Motorized Division).

Early in June the enemy weakened his armor still further by some ill-advised attacks on our bridgeheads at Abbeville and Amiens. On 5 June Army Group B opened its attack, and Hoth's Panzer Corps penetrated deeply into the hostile positions. The enemy was unable to hold us in the Abbeville bridgehead, and the 7th Panzer Division under General Erwin Rommel drove rapidly towards the Seine. By 8 June he was in Rouen, and taking advantage of the complete confusion of the enemy he swung round towards the sea and cut off the British Highland Division and considerable French forces at St. Valéry.

Farther east, however, the German offensive did not go so smoothly. Panzergruppe Kleist tried in vain to break out of the bridgeheads at Amiens and Péronne; the French troops in

[14] On 20 May General Weygand, formerly chief of staff to Marshal Foch, took over command from the unfortunate General Gamelin.

this sector fought with extreme stubbornness and inflicted considerable losses. On 9 June Army Group A launched its offensive; the first objective was to secure bridgeheads south of the Aisne. The task was entrusted to the infantry of Twelfth Army, and although they failed to force a crossing near Rethel they did secure three bridgeheads west of the town. On the night of 9/10 June a bridge was built, and the tanks of Schmidt's Panzer Corps crossed the Aisne. There was fierce fighting on 10 June; the country was difficult with numerous villages and woods which were strongly held by the French. These were left to the rifle regiments, while the panzer units bypassed opposition and pushed as far south as they could. On the afternoon of the 10th French reserves, including a newly formed armored division, counterattacked from Juniville against the flank of our panzers, and were driven off after a tank battle lasting two hours. During the night 10/11 June Guderian moved Panzer Corps Reinhardt into the bridgehead, which was now twelve miles deep. On 11 June Reinhardt beat off several counterattacks by French armored and mechanized brigades.

The success of Guderian and the failure of von Kleist were the result of a difference in methods. The attacks of the latter from the Amiens and Péronne bridgeheads demonstrate that it is quite useless to throw armor against well-prepared defensive positions, manned by an enemy who expects an attack and is determined to repulse it. In contrast Guderian's tanks were not committed until the infantry had made a substantial penetration across the Aisne.

After Kleist's repulse on the Somme, the German High Command showed its versatility by switching his Panzergruppe to the Laon area. Here Kleist met with immediate success, and thrusting forward against slight opposition his vanguard reached the Marne at Château Thierry on 11 June. The following day Guderian's tanks reached the river at Châlons. Eight panzer divisions, firmly controlled and directed, were thrusting forward on both sides of Reims and the enemy had nothing to stop them.

In contrast to 1914, the possession of Paris had no influence on strategic decisions. The city was no longer a great fortress from which a reserve army might sally out and attack our communications. The French High Command declared Paris an open city, and the German High Command virtually ignored the place in its calculations—the entry of German troops on 14 June was a mere incident in the campaign. Meanwhile, Hoth's Panzer Corps was thrusting into Normandy and Brittany, Kleist's Panzergruppe was directed towards the Plateau de Langres and the valley of the Rhône, and Guderian's Panzergruppe swung eastwards into Lorraine in order to take the Maginot Line in the rear.

On 14 June the Maginot Line was penetrated south of Saarbrücken by the First Army, under Army Group C. French resistance dissolved along the whole front, and the pace of the German advance was only limited by the distance the panzer divisions could cover in a day—the infantry formations were left far behind along the dusty roads. On 16 June Kleist's tanks rattled into Dijon, and on the 17th Guderian's spearhead reached the Swiss frontier at Pontarlier and completed the envelopment of the French armies in Alsace and Lorraine. On 18 June Hitler and Mussolini met at Munich to discuss the French request for an armistice.

The closing stages of the campaign, with German tanks penetrating to Cherbourg, Brest, and Lyons, are strongly reminiscent of the French cavalry pursuit after Jena, which flooded over the plains of north Germany. The position of our panzers at the end of the campaign was very similar to that outlined by Murat in his message to Napoleon in November, 1806: "Sire, the fighting is over, because there are no combatants left."

In Lorraine

As I have already explained, my own part in this campaign was limited to the fighting in Lorraine, where I served as chief of staff (Ia) of the 197th Infantry Division. It formed part of the First German Army which on 14 June attacked the famous Maginot Line at Puttlinger, south of Saarbrücken. I had a good opportunity of seeing the battle at first hand, although in our division only the artillery and an engineer battalion were engaged in the actual breakthrough.

The Maginot Line was widely believed to be impregnable,

and for all I know there may still be those who think that the fortifications could have resisted any attack. It may be of interest to point out that the Maginot defenses were breached in a few hours by a normal infantry attack, without any tank support whatever. The German infantry advanced under cover of a heavy air and artillery bombardment in which lavish use was made of smoke shell. They soon found that many of the French strongpoints were not proof against shells or bombs, and moreover, a large number of positions had not been sited for all-round defense and were easy to attack from the blind side with grenades and flamethrowers. The Maginot Line lacked depth, and taken as a whole the position was far inferior to many defense systems developed later in the war. In modern war it is in any case unsound to rely on static defense, but as far as the Maginot Line was concerned the fortifications had only a moderate local value.

After the breakthrough the 197th Infantry Division followed up the retreating enemy by forced marches—the troops gladly submitted to tramping thirty-five miles a day as everyone wanted "to be there." On reaching Château-Salins we were ordered to turn left and advance into the Vosges Mountains, with Donon, the highest peak in the northern Vosges, as our objective. At dawn on 22 June we passed through the front of a division which had been pinned down with heavy losses and fought our way forward through densely wooded hills. The enemy had blocked the roads by felling trees, and his artillery, snipers, and machine guns took full advantage of the excellent cover. In slow, bitter fighting our division fought its way towards Donon, and at nightfall on the 22nd was only a mile from the summit.

On the evening of 22 June I received a telephone call from Colonel Speidel,[15] the corps chief of staff, who informed me that the French Third, Fifth, and Eighth Armies in Alsace-Lorraine had capitulated unconditionally. He directed that a *parlementaire* should be sent to the enemy to arrange a cease-fire. At dawn on the 23rd our intelligence officer made contact with the French troops on our front, and during the morning I travelled with the divisional commander, General

---

[15] Later lieutenant general, and in 1944 Rommel's chief of staff in Normandy.

Meyer-Rabingen, to the headquarters of the French 43rd Corps. Passing through our forward positions, we had to drive over half a mile before we reached the French outposts—they had already removed the road blocks. French troops "fell in" and saluted in true peacetime fashion. French military police in short leather jackets gave permission to proceed, and French guards presented arms. We arrived at the villa "*Chez nous*," where General Lescanne had his headquarters. The corps commander was a man of about sixty; he received us surrounded by his staff. The old man was clearly at the end of his tether, but he was polite—the terms of the surrender were quietly discussed as between officers and gentlemen. Lescanne and his officers were accorded full military honors.

On 24 June a communiqué from the Führer's headquarters announced that the enemy surrounded in the Vosges Mountains had surrendered at Donon. The communiqué reported the capture of 22,000 prisoners, including a corps commander and three divisional commanders, together with twelve artillery battalions and a vast quantity of stores and equipment.

Conclusions

What were the causes of the rapid collapse of France? I have already dealt with most of them in my account of the operations, but it may be of value to touch again on the salient points. Although political and moral factors were undoubtedly of great significance, I shall confine myself to the purely military aspect of the collapse.

There is little doubt that the German armor, brilliantly supported by the Luftwaffe, decided the campaign. This opinion does not belittle our infantry divisions whose quality was to be fully proved in the terrible campaigns in Russia. But in the blitzkrieg in France they had little opportunity to demonstrate their prowess.

The whole campaign hinged on the employment of armor, and was essentially a clash of principles between two rival schools. The Allied military leaders thought in terms of World War I and split their armor in fairly even proportions along the entire front, although their best divisions took part in the advance into Belgium. Our panzer leaders believed that armor should be used in mass, with the result that we had two panzer corps and one motorized corps with the *Schwerpunkt* at Sedan. Our theory of tank warfare was far from being a secret to the Allies. Writing in 1938 Max Werner pointed out that "German military theory sees only one use for the tank—its concentrated employment in great masses."[16] The French and British generals not only refused to accept our theory, but failed to make adequate dispositions to meet it.

Even after our breakthrough on the Meuse the French generals seemed to be unable to concentrate their armor, and on the field of battle French tank tactics were far too rigid and formal. Our panzer corps and divisions not only had the advantage of excellent training and communications, but the commanders at every level fully appreciated that panzer troops must be commanded from the front. Thus they were able to take immediate advantage of the rapid changes and opportunities which armored warfare brings.

Perhaps I should stress that although we attached the greatest importance to armor, we realized that tanks cannot operate without the close support of motorized infantry and artillery. Our panzer division was a balanced force of all arms —that was a lesson which the British did not learn until well into 1942.

The skillful use of surprise was a very important factor in our success. Rather than forfeit the opportunity of surprise, von Kleist forced the crossing of the Meuse on 13 May without waiting for his artillery; the successful co-operation between the Luftwaffe and the panzer corps on this occasion was duplicated later on during the pursuit in central and southern France. Time and again the rapid movements and flexible handling of our panzers bewildered the enemy. The use of our parachute troops in Holland also illustrates the paralyzing effect of a surprise blow.

The German High Command comes out well from the campaign, and in general its strategic handling of the armor was bold and confident. There were only two serious flaws in the conduct of our High Command—the order to the

[16] *The Military Strength of the Powers* (London, Gollancz, 1939).

panzers to mark time after the forming of the Sedan bridge-head, and the particularly tragic decision to halt the panzer divisions when they had Dunkirk at their mercy.

To sum up: The Battle for France was won by the German Wehrmacht because it reintroduced into warfare the decisive factor of mobility. It achieved mobility by the combination of firepower, concentration, and surprise, together with expert handling of the latest modern arms—Luftwaffe, parachutists, and armor. The series of disasters in subsequent years must not be allowed to obscure the fact that in 1940 the German General Staff achieved a military masterpiece, worthy to rank beside the greatest campaigns of the greatest generals in history. It was not our fault that the fruits of this tremendous triumph were wantonly thrown away.

3: The Balkan Campaign

Interlude

FOR THE GERMAN ARMY the summer of 1940 was the happiest of the war. We had gained a series of victories unprecedented since the days of Napoleon; Versailles had been avenged, and we could look forward to the prospect of a secure and glorious peace. Our occupation forces in France and the Netherlands settled down to the calm routine of peacetime soldiering. Riding parties and hunting expeditions were arranged, and there was talk that our families might be allowed to join us.

The High Command actually made preparations to disband a large number of divisions, and important armament contracts were cancelled. Our dreams were rudely shaken when Britain rejected Hitler's offers, and Churchill announced his country's unshakable determination to continue the war. Operation *Sea Lion* was hurriedly improvised, and the Luftwaffe set about the task of winning air superiority over the Narrow Seas. Our air force had done brilliantly in the blitzkrieg in France, but it had been designed mainly to support ground operations. It soon became clear that the Luftwaffe was not strong enough to maintain weeks of hard fighting against the R.A.F., with its superior radar equipment, and as our losses mounted the prospect of crossing the Channel faded away.

During the summer months I had a good opportunity of studying conditions in France and Holland. On the conclusion of the campaign my division was transferred to the Breda area, where the polite though reserved behavior of the German troops made an excellent impression on the Dutch. I was accommodated in the house of a former Dutch Colonial officer, and I look back with gratitude to those quiet weeks in his hospitable and cultured home. It is a matter of regret that Gestapo officers and party officials soon raised a barrier between the occupation troops and the civil population; their complete lack of consideration and ruthless conduct alienated many potential friends. Unfortunately these officials lacked culture and education—the foundation of successful work in a foreign country.

After a few weeks in Holland I was transferred to the headquarters of First Army in Lorraine, with the appointment of Ic (Staff Officer Intelligence). We had excellent quarters in the old Gothic castle at Nancy, and I was overjoyed to serve under my old corps commander of Berlin days, Field Marshal von Witzleben, then commanding First Army.

My duties brought me into contact with many Frenchmen in prominent positions in politics and commerce. I found a genuine desire to co-operate on the basis of a United Europe, built up on the principle of absolute equality. This spirit of co-operation was furthered and encouraged by the well-disciplined and affable attitude of the German occupation troops. But Hitler could not make up his mind about adopting a clear-cut policy of moderation towards France. For instance we were not permitted to let French refugees from the area north of the Somme return to their homes, and the whole of northern France and Belgium was placed under a single military government. We could see the idea of a "Greater Flanders" behind this measure.

During the autumn of 1940 the general staff of First Army worked out plans for a rapid occupation of the rest of France. Apart from friction with the Pétain regime, these plans were connected with a proposed advance through Spain with a view to capturing Gibraltar. But Franco did not regard Britain's position as hopeless, and with great diplomatic skill kept Hilter at arm's length.

During November, 1940, I spent a few days in Rome as the guest of the Genova Regiment, an old and distinguished cavalry unit. There I found an atmosphere of profound peace.

The Italian cavalry officers were most hospitable, and took me to their famous jumping school at Tor de Quinto. They asked whether I would like to try a few jumps, and when I assented produced a magnificent thoroughbred. I fancied, however, that they watched my preparations with skeptical eyes, and indeed they could hardly be blamed for not expecting much in the equestrian sphere from a German staff officer. I did not mention my years of cavalry experience and the 150 races in which I had ridden, and I was delighted to see their surprise when I cleared all the jumps successfully.

During my stay in Italy I was able to discuss the situation with General von Rintelen, our very able military attaché in Rome, whom I was to meet again on several occasions when I was serving on Rommel's staff. The picture he painted was a depressing one. In North Africa Graziani's offensive had come to a complete standstill, and there seemed to be a lack of drive and determination behind his whole campaign. Mussolini's attack on Greece in October, 1940, had been launched with forces which were deplorably insufficient. After only a week's fighting, the Greeks had gained the initiative, and the Italian troops in Albania were soon in a very critical position.

The developments in Greece were most unwelcome to the German High Command. British forces had obtained the right to land in Greece and the vital Rumanian oilfields at Ploesti—of such importance to the Wehrmacht—were now in range of R.A.F. bombers. So far it had been our policy to keep the Balkans out of the war, but at the beginning of December the High Command was forced to prepare for operations in Greece.

In January, 1941, I returned to the headquarters of First Army at Nancy. There I was informed by Colonel Röhricht, the chief of staff, that the conversations between Hitler and Molotov, held at Berlin in November, had ended in a complete fiasco. Instead of entering the Tripartite Pact as Hitler had hoped, Molotov was said to have used blackmailing tactics and to have submitted impossible demands regarding Rumania, Bulgaria, and Turkey. Hitler's answer was to order the Wehrmacht to make preparations for Operation *Barbarossa*— the invasion of Russia. D day was finally fixed for 22 June

1941—rather late in the year, but it was necessary to eliminate Greece first and then withdraw the panzer divisions from the Balkans to Russia.

The German High Command planned to overrun Greece by the beginning of April, and in January, 1941, German forces began to assemble in Rumania. Both Rumania and Hungary had joined the Tripartite Pact some months before, and Bulgaria also became a member on 1 March. German troops at once entered Bulgaria, a development which put Yugoslavia in an unenviable strategic position. Accordingly, the government of Prince Paul decided on 20 March to join the Tripartite Pact, but on 27 March the *coup d'état* of General Simovic resulted in a complete reversal of policy. Hitler thereupon ordered an invasion of Yugoslavia, to proceed simultaneously with the attack on Greece.

The Invasion of Yugoslavia

At the end of March, 1941, I was appointed Ic (Staff Officer Intelligence) to the Second Army, then assembling in southern Austria between Klagenfurt and Graz. After a nonstop journey through Bavaria, I reached Graz and reported myself to the army commander, General von Weichs, and his chief of staff, Colonel von Witzleben. I was at once put in the picture.

The Yugoslav Army was disposed in three groups. Army Group I, based on Zagreb, was facing us across the frontier; Army Group II was covering the approaches from Hungary; and Army Group III, with the bulk of their troops, was disposed along the borders of Rumania, Bulgaria, and Albania. The strategic position of the Yugoslavs was most unfavorable, and when hostilities began they had only succeeded in mobilizing two-thirds of their twenty-eight divisions and three cavalry divisions. They lacked modern equipment, there was no armor at all, and the air force possessed only three hundred machines.

The military weakness of Yugoslavia was accentuated by political, religious, and racial divisons. Apart from the two main groups, the Serbs and the Croats, there were millions of Slovenes, Germans, and Italians, each with separate national aspirations. Only the Serbs were really hostile to us, and our propaganda took the line of offering liberation to the other races, and particularly the Croats. At army headquarters we had a Propaganda Company, working under my supervision and staffed by various language experts. We learned that the formations facing us were chiefly Croatian, of whom only about a third of the personnel on paper had obeyed the mobilization order. The Propaganda Company worked at top speed, preparing pamphlets and loudspeaker records to put our opponents in a receptive mood for surrender.

The German invasion plan was as follows: The Second Army was to advance on Zagreb, and thence into the Bosnian highlands towards Sarajevo; simultaneously an armored assault group was to thrust at Belgrade through Hungary. The main attack was to come from Bulgaria, where our Twelfth Army and Panzergruppe Kleist had been assembled. Kleist was to advance through Niš and attack Belgrade from the south, while Twelfth Army was to move simultaneously into northern Greece and southern Serbia. As the deployment of Second Army was not yet complete, Twelfth Army began operation on 6 April. Our advance from the north began on the 8th.

Twelfth Army pushed forward rapidly, and entered Skoplje on 10 April. A panzer division swung off to the southwest and soon made contact with the Italians in Albania, while the left wing of Twelfth Army swept victoriously into Greece. Meanwhile Kleist's tanks had smashed right through the Yugoslav positions on the first day of the offensive. Kleist entered Niš on 9 April, and disregarding the Yugoslav forces on his flank —they had been thrown into complete confusion—his panzers made a daring thrust along the Morava valley towards Belgrade. By 11 April the Panzer Group was only sixty miles from the capital.

Forty-sixth Panzer Corps of Second Army swept down on Belgrade from the northwest, and made rapid progress against negligible resistance. This corps was opposed mainly by Croats, who had been so influenced by our propaganda that some units mutinied and greeted us as "liberators." The main body of the 46th Panzer Corps entered Belgrade on 12 April, while another panzer division from this corps occupied Zagreb and was received enthusiastically by the population. Simultaneously the infantry divisions of Second Army ad-

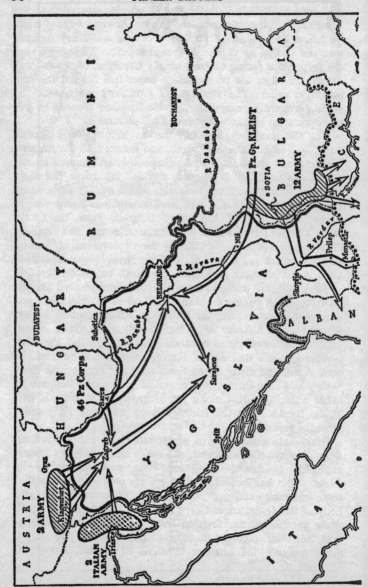

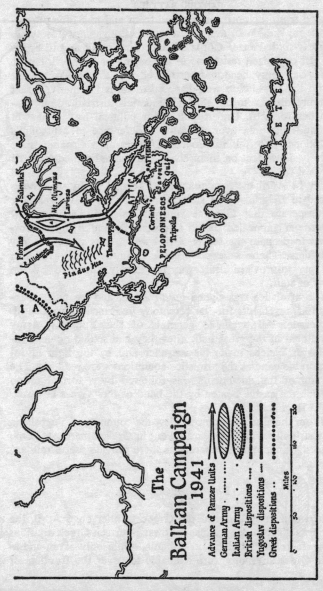

The
Balkan Campaign
1941

Advance of Panzer Units
German Army
Italian Army
British dispositions
Yugoslav dispositions
Greek dispositions

Miles
5   50   100   150   200

vanced from the north on a broad front and met little opposition from the Yugoslavs, whose units were rapidly dissolving.

Forty-sixth Panzer Corps advanced on Sarajevo and broke the last organized resistance of the enemy of 13 April. On 11 April our army headquarters moved into Zagreb, where we found the population well-disposed towards Germany, a fact undoubtedly due to the efficient Imperial-Austrian administration before 1914. Unfortunately our political leaders saw fit to hand this area over to Italy, in deference to Mussolini's ambitions. The Italians proceeded to set up a Croatian state entirely dependent on themselves, and soon alienated some of our best friends.

On 14 April the headquarters of Second Army was transferred to Belgrade. The situation of the Yugoslavs was now so desperate that General Simovic resigned, and the new government appealed for an armistice. Second Army was ordered to prepare the terms, a task which was placed on my shoulders. There were no precedents immediately available, but my improvised draft was fortunately approved by the chief of staff.

The armistice was signed on 17 April, and we made elaborate arrangements for the ceremony in Prince Paul's beautiful castle. All available generals of the Yugoslav Army assembled in the great hall; after they had settled down General von Weichs made his entrance and by the light of innumerable candles the armistice conditions were read out. The signing of the documents was followed by a formal tattoo outside the castle, beaten by the band of the "Gross Deutschland" Regiment.

From the German point of view the conquest of Yugoslavia was virtually a military parade, but in Greece there was some hard fighting, and the operations there provide useful military lessons.

The Greek Campaign

When our troops crossed the Greek frontier on 6 April, the enemy's dispositions were as follows: Fourteen Greek divisions were facing the Italians in Albania, while only seven-and-a-half Greek divisions were available to cover the frontiers of

Yugoslavia and Bulgaria. Of the latter, three-and-a-half divisions were holding the so-called Metaxas Line between the Struma valley and the Turkish border. two divisions were in position between the Struma and the Vardar, and two divisions were west of the Vardar trying to cover the assembly of British forces along the Aliakmon river. These comprised the 2nd New Zealand Division, the 6th Australian Divison, and a British armored brigade, all under command of General Maitland Wilson.

Of all British enterprises during the war, the expedition to Greece seems to me the most difficult to justify on purely military grounds. The Greeks had fought well in Albania, but they had suffered heavily during the winter campaign, and were certainly in no condition to resist a full-scale offensive by the Wehrmacht. The British forces sent to their support—while they deprived Wavell of an excellent opportunity of getting to Tripoli—were a mere drop in the ocean by the standards of continental warfare. In retrospect it seems incredible that the British planners should have thought that four Commonwealth divisions[1] could maintain a prolonged resistance in Greece against the unlimited resources of the Wehrmacht. On this point I fully endorse Major General de Guingand's criticisms in *Operation Victory*.[2]

Actually the British position became hopeless before their troops were seriously engaged. On 6 April our Twelfth Army crossed the frontier with ten divisions, including two panzer divisions. On 7 April the Metaxas Line was breached at several points and on 9 April the 2nd Panzer Division occupied Salonika and cut off all Greek troops east of the Struma. By 10 April the right wing of Twelfth Army had overrun southern Serbia, and crossed the frontier south of Monastir. Greek resistance in this sector was speedily broken, and our advance continued through Florina towards the Pindus mountains, and threatened to entrap all the Greek divisions on the Albanian front. On 13 April the Greeks began to withdraw

---

[1] The Australian 7th Division and a Polish brigade were intended for Greece, but were held back because of Rommel's advance in Cyrenaica.

[2] Francis de Guingand, *Operation Victory* (London, Hodder & Stoughton, 1947).

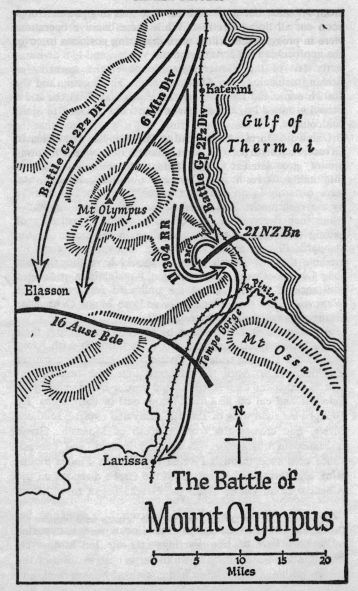

Katerini

Gulf of
Thermai

Battle Gp 2Pz Div

6 Mtn Div

Battle Gp 2Pz Div

Mt Olympus

II/304. RR

21 NZ Bn

Elasson

16 Aust Bde

R. Pinios

Tempe Gorge

Mt Ossa

Larissa

N

The Battle of
Mount Olympus

0   5   10   15   20
Miles

from Albania, but they were too late and our panzer troops soon cut all lines of retreat. While these decisive operations were in progress the British were preparing positions to cover the approaches to Mount Olympus.

By 16 April it had become clear to all concerned that nothing could save the Greek Army from disaster, and the British command gave orders for a withdrawal to the Thermopylae Line. The Greek government was anxious to spare the country unnecessary suffering, and it was agreed that the British would form a bridgehead at Thermopylae and endeavor to embark their troops. The rearguard actions which followed are of great interest to the student of armored warfare in mountainous terrain, and I propose to consider them in detail. (See map on page 40.)

After the capture of Salonika, General Böhme, the commander of our 18th Corps, was ordered to advance on both sides of Mount Olympus and capture Larissa, thus cutting off the retreat of the British and Greek forces in central Macedonia. General Böhme decided to deploy the 2nd Panzer Division and the 6th Mountain Division, and made the following dispositions.

On the right flank a battle group of the 2nd Panzer Division was to advance north of Mount Olympus towards Elasson, where an Australian force was in position. On the left flank another battle group of this division was to advance along the line of the railway between the mountain and the sea, and endeavor to break through the Tempe Gorge towards Larissa. In the center the 6th Mountain Division was to advance directly over Mount Olympus and come down on the rear of the enemy forces in the Tempe Gorge. For the account of what followed, I am indebted to the reports of General Balck, then commanding Panzer Regiment 3 of the 2nd Panzer Division.

On 15 April Balck took over command of the left-flanking battle group of 2nd Panzer. The battle group had advanced through Katerini and was halted before a ridge stretching between Mount Olympus and the sea. Enemy forces supported by artillery were holding the ridge and our 2nd Motorcycle Battalion had been pinned down in dense bush in front of the British positions. The enemy had concealed himself well, and our supporting artillery was unable to locate targets.[3] German reinforcements were moving up—the Ist Battalion of Panzer Regiment 3, IInd Battalion of Rifle Regiment 304, and an engineer company. The deeply broken ground, covered with thick bush, was quite unsuitable for armor; the tanks were road-bound, and reconnaissance revealed that the road was mined.

After a thorough personal reconnaissance, Balck decided that the only hope of success was a wide outflanking movement by the infantry. The terrain on the slopes of Mount Olympus was extremely difficult, even for foot soldiers, but for that reason it was unlikely to be well-guarded by the enemy. Accordingly the tanks were ordered to demonstrate, and under cover of their fire the 2nd Motorcycle Battalion was drawn out of the line, and was sent off—without transport—on a wide flanking move. They were followed by IInd Battalion of Rifle Regiment 304, which swung still farther to the right and made a night march of incredible difficulty across unknown ground covered with bush and boulders, and cut by deep gullies. Only an engineer company was left to protect our guns and tanks during the hours of darkness.

The morning of 16 April showed that the thorough training and splendid physical condition of our riflemen had produced results. Movements, indicating a withdrawal, were noted in front and Balck at once ordered his tanks to push forward—regardless of terrain—and engage the enemy. While our motorcycle troops attacked the left flank of the New Zealanders, our riflemen had swung right round in rear of their position and had taken them completely by surprise. The enemy fled to the south, leaving behind heavy weapons, transport, and equipment.

Pursuit was out of the question as the riflemen were exhausted by the night march, and for the time being it was impossible to move tanks and vehicles along the atrocious cart track which served as a road. Some men, who were still strong enough, were sent off to reconnoiter towards the east-

---

[3] The position was held by the 21st Battalion of the 2nd New Zealand Division, supported by an artillery troop and some engineers. We afterwards learned that they had been given no antitank weapons as the terrain was regarded as unsuitable for armor.

ern entrance of the Tempe Gorge, while the engineers began blasting on a large scale to open a way for the tanks.

By noon on 17 April two panzer companies had reached the entrance to Tempe, a very narrow gorge with high vertical mountain walls on either side and the Pinios River rushing in a formidable torrent down the middle. On the northern bank of the river ran the Salonika-Athens railway line, and on the southern bank there was a road—inaccessible as yet, for there were no bridges, and bridging equipment had not arrived.

A panzer company felt its way cautiously along the railway line; the troops were warned that in no circumstances must they bunch together in this narrow pass, where a few shells from the British guns would have wrought havoc among them. At first the move along the permanent way went smoothly; the first tunnel was intact but the second had been blown in the middle, and the tanks could go no farther. Recce parties found a point where the Pinios was divided by an island, and it was just possible that tanks might cross under their own power.

Balck decided to risk one tank in the attempt. It got through. Two more crossed successfully but the crossing was a hazardous and difficult process. Each tank took between half an hour and an hour to cross the river; some got water in their engines and were not recoverable. Nevertheless the first three tanks advanced along the road and ran up against a demolition covered by Australians. They had no antitank guns and fled when they saw the tanks. Parties from the Rifle Regiment were sent forward to repair the road, and although the enemy shelled the valley heavily on the night 17/18 April there were few casualties.

The passage of the Pinios continued day and night, and by the afternoon of 18 April Balck had assembled a tank battalion and a rifle battalion at the western entrance to the gorge. No wheeled vehicles had been able to get through, but four 100-mm guns drawn by tractors had got across the river. To a man of Balck's temperament it was enough, and he flung these troops at the Australians covering the western entrance to Tempe Gorge.

The Australian 16th Brigade was holding the approaches to Larissa; they were under pressure from the 6th Mountain

Division thrusting across the massif of Mount Olympus, and from the right-flanking battle group of the 2nd Panzer Division at Elasson. Balck's advance across terrain regarded as impassable decided the issue, and his tanks soon broke into open country and advanced rapidly on Larissa until darkness compelled a halt. The Australians withdrew during the night, and at dawn on 19 April Balck's battle group entered Larissa.

A British Intelligence report, which fell into our hands, commented as follows: "The German Panzer Regiment 3 knows no going difficulties and negotiates terrain which was regarded as absolutely safe against armor."[4] Apart from this aspect, Balck's success is to be ascribed to his boldness in separating his infantry from their transport and sending them off on wide-flanking moves, which should really have been entrusted to trained mountain troops. Balck pointed out in his report that his tanks and tractors were the only vehicles able to negotiate such immensely difficult terrain, and drew the conclusion that all wheeled transport should be eliminated from the panzer division, and even the supply vehicles should be tracked or half-tracked.[5] He stated that it was virtually impossible to evacuate casualties or bring gasoline up to the forward troops until Larissa was occupied, although some barrels for fuel were sent across the Pinios on boats and then transferred to oxen and donkeys. Fortunately, as soon as Larissa airfield was occupied, the High Command dispatched several fuel-carrying aircraft there to enable the advance to continue.

The Greek campaign now moved rapidly to a close. On 16 April German panzer troops, advancing from Macedonia, reached the passes through the Pindus mountains and cut off the retreat of the Greek divisions withdrawing from Albania. Their continued resistance became pointless and on 23 April a capitulation was signed in Salonika.

---

[4] *The Other Side of the Hill* (Wellington, 1952), 8. This official New Zealand pamphlet says of Balck's operations around Mount Olympus: "Seldom in war were tanks forced through such difficult country, or had foot soldiers, already with over 500 kilometres marching behind them, pushed forward so rapidly under such punishing conditions; it was a record of which any soldier could be proud."

[5] This was a lesson which became bitterly apparent in Russia.

However we did not succeed in capturing the British Expeditionary Force. The terrain was most unsuitable for armored movement, and the British rearguards, in the Mount Olympus area and later in the Thermopylae position, were handled with skill. The capture of the Isthmus of Corinth by German parachute troops was a spectacular success, but it failed to prevent the British evacuating some 43,000 troops from Attica and the Peloponnesus. The British lost some 12,-000 killed, wounded, and prisoners, and their shipping losses were high, but they got the bulk of their troops away in spite of heavy air attacks. The units of the Royal Navy based on Alexandria threw themselves into the fray regardless of loss, and these embarkations, carried out in the face of overwhelming German air superiority, constitute a remarkable achievement.

A New Assignment

Meanwhile I remained at Belgrade with the staff of General von Weichs, who had by that time been appointed head of the military government in Yugoslavia. We entered into discussions with the staff of the Italian Second Army on the question of boundary lines between the areas of German and Italian administration. The Italians were allotted Croatia with Zagreb and the entire Dalmatian coast—truly a remarkable political victory in view of the very modest part played by the Italians in the Yugoslav campaign.[6]

German administration, although not always popular, was at least efficient. Italian rule, on the other hand, was regarded as a humiliation by the Balkan nations, chiefly because the Italian Army was held in such contempt. This undoubtedly furthered the growth of the partisan movement.

At the end of April General von Wiechs accompanied his personal staff on a very pleasant tour of inspection in Prince Paul's special train. We went through Niš and Skoplje down to Salonika. In Belgrade the buildings and the racial features of some of the people provided plenty of evidence of the long period of Turkish rule, but in Skoplje we really felt

----

[6] Their Second Army made a very slow and cautious advance from the Trieste sector towards the southeast.

we were in the Orient, when we saw the numerous mosques, with the men in fezzes and the women veiled. A refreshing swim in the Aegean, and the sight of Mount Olympus, made us forget the war for a while.

At the beginning of May I was ordered to take over as the head of the German liaison staff with the Italian Second Army at Fiume. My driver and I drove without an escort across country which a few months later was aflame with partisan warfare. At Fiume I reported to the commander of the Italian Second Army, General Ambrosio, who became commander in chief of the Italian Army on Mussolini's resignation. During the following weeks I went on maneuvers with the Italians and got to know them very well. I was surprised at their obsolete arms and equipment, and I noted the very low standard of training among their junior officers. The human material differed vastly in quality, and in contrast with the troops from southern Italy the Alpini Divisions made an excellent impression. After one field exercise General Ambrosio travelled alone with me to the Heroes Cemetery on the Isonzo, where German and Italian soldiers of World War I lie buried. He expressed the hope that we would never fight each other again.

This interesting spell with the Italians, broken by excursions along the wonderful Dalmatian coast and many a refreshing dip in the "Blue Adriatic," lasted until the end of May, when I was ordered to report to Munich immediately. I had been appointed Ic (Staff Officer Intelligence) on the staff of Panzergruppe Afrika, which was being formed in Bavaria. In a powerful Mercedes, I rushed through Venice, Bolzano, and Innsbruck to Munich. In Venice, while dining at a hotel, I surprised the Italians by having my driver at the same table. While normally officers and other ranks took their meals separately, it was a matter of course for us to eat together on occasions like this when officer and private were all on their own. In contrast to 1918 the inner knowledge that officers and men belonged together was never shaken, and even in 1945 there were no signs of a rot in the German Army.

From Innsbruck I ventured on a short visit to Mittenwald, where my wife and our five children had come to live to get away from the bombing of Berlin.

In Munich I found Lieutenant Colonel Westphal, chief operations officer (Ia) of Panzergruppe Afrika. Within a few days the staff had assembled, all feeling a little strange in our new tropical uniforms. On 10 June Westphal and I travelled to Rome by rail, where we met Major General Gause, the chief of staff. General von Rintelen gave us the North African picture, and the next day we flew in an Italian aircraft to Sicily, and on to Tripoli.

During this flight it was brought home to us that the Mediterranean was not exactly a "Mare Nostrum." On several occasions British fighters appeared over the horizon and forced our aircraft to fly at sea level to avoid detection.

In Tripoli we spent the night in an elegant hotel, although the unaccustomed tropical heat was very trying and kept us awake. But in any case luxury hotels were now to be only a memory—tents and armored vehicles took their place. The Western Desert had caught us, and for a long time did not release its grip.

PART TWO

The Western Desert

4: *At Rommel's Headquarters*

Rommel

IN THE SUMMER of 1938 I was serving on the staff of the
3rd Army Corps in Berlin. I had come straight from the War
Academy as a youthful cavalry captain to my first staff
appointment. One day a colonel entered my office—stocky,
alert, full of health and energy, and wearing the coveted
Pour le Mérite[1] at his throat. It was purely a routine call—
Colonel Erwin Rommel, recently appointed to supervise the
military training of the Hitler Youth, had dropped in to
discuss some minor problems of administration and discipline
in the Berlin area. It was my first glimpse of a commander
with whom I was to be thrown into very close contact during
fifteen bitter months of African warfare, and whom I was to
learn to love and honor as one of the outstanding generals
of our time, the Seidlitz of the panzer corps, and perhaps the
most daring and thrustful commander in German military
history.

Even in 1938 Rommel's reputation stood high in the German Army—his brilliant leadership as a regimental officer in
World War I foreshadowed his subsequent successes in High
Command. He had recently attracted Hitler's attention by
publishing a valuable textbook on infantry tactics, and his
appointment to supervise the military training of the Hitler

---

[1] The German equivalent of the Victoria Cross in World War I.

51

Youth was obviously a steppingstone to important commands. I learned later that Rommel was far from happy in
his appointment and quarreled continually with Baldur von
Schirach, the Reichs Youth Leader. This man had never
been a soldier himself, and had the idea that youth should be
led by youth, with the result—as Rommel put it—that
Schnoesels[2] of sixteen commanded their *Standarten*[3] in big,
shining Mercedes cars as though they were corps commanders. Anyhow, Rommel soon relinquished his task, and
Schirach's impossible attitude was the reason.

I arrived in Africa in June, 1941, as a member of the
Panzergruppe staff, which had been formed in Germany, and then moved bodily to Libya to provide Rommel
with a large operational headquarters. Hitherto Rommel
had merely been commander of the Deutsche Afrika Korps
(D.A.K.); his great victories in April, 1941, had brought
him increased responsibilities and it was essential for him to
have an adequate staff. At first Rommel himself did not see
matters in that light, and I shall never forget his reserved
and frigid manner when he received us at Gambut. We were
all very much officers of the General Staff, and yet we were
all obviously new to African conditions. As a fighting soldier,
Rommel looked at us with a skeptical eye; moreover he had
never been on the General Staff himself and was clearly uneasy that we might attempt to supervise and even supersede
him. In his memoirs Rommel says:

One day General Gause arrived in Africa with a large staff.
He had been ordered to examine the possibilities of employ-
ing large forces in Africa and to prepare for an offensive
against Egypt. Although General Gause had been given clear
orders from O.K.W. [Oberkommando Wehrmacht] not to
place himself under my command, he did so nevertheless,
after I had told him that I alone had been given the command
of all German troops in Africa.[4]

In actual fact there was never any question of our chal-
lenging Rommel's right to command; we had come to Africa

---

[2] I.e. young and silly asses.
[3] *Lit.* formations, roughly equivalent to an army regiment.
[4] *Krieg ohne Hass* (Heidenheim, Heidenheimer Zeitung, 1950), 54.

to serve him and he soon realized that he could not command a large army without our help.

When we arrived in Africa the military situation was as follows: After the collapse of Graziani's army before Wavell's offensive, the German High Command had to intervene in Africa, and in February and March, 1941, the 5th Light Division (later called the 21st Panzer Division) was sent to Libya. Fifteenth Panzer Division was to follow, but Rommel did not wait for its arrival, and, disregarding the protests of the Italian Comando Superiore, he attacked at the end of March. Breaking out of the bottleneck at Mersa Brega, Rommel took the British completely by surprise and overwhelmed their forces in western Cyrenaica. On 4 April German armored cars entered Benghazi, and Rommel drove his troops onward. Usually he travelled in his Storch—a small aircraft which could land on a tennis court. It is recorded that during this advance he flew over a company which had halted for no apparent reason, and dropped a message: "Unless you get going at once I shall come down. Rommel."

Rommel recaptured Cyrenaica by advancing across the desert through the old fort of Mechili, where several generals and more than two thousand men were taken prisoner. This advance bypassed the "Cyrenaican bulge" and the mountains of Jebel el Akdar—a feature which cannot be held against an attack from the east or west, because the attacker can always take the shorter route across the desert. By 10 April Bardia had been taken and the Egyptian frontier crossed at Sollum; Tobruk held out and repulsed determined assaults in April and May, but nevertheless weak German forces had reconquered almost the whole of Cyrenaica in twelve days.

This dazzling victory put a new complexion on the African war, but after the failure of his attack on Tobruk on 3 May, Rommel had to stand on the defensive. Towards the end of May Wavell attacked our positions around Capuzzo and Halfaya and was beaten off; in mid-June he launched a more ambitious operation under the code-name of *Battleaxe*. This led to heavy armored fighting around Capuzzo and Sidi Omar—the Afrika Korps suffered serious tank losses but under Rommel's resolute leadership turned the tables on the 7th Armored Division[5] and gained a notable victory. This was followed by a long lull in the Western Desert, and no serious battles were fought between June and November.

Before I describe the great battles of *Crusader* and Gazala, and our triumphant advance through Tobruk to Alamein—a period which includes some of the most dramatic and revealing episodes in the history of armored warfare —I propose to give my impressions of Rommel and of life at his headquarters. I shall also say something about the general conditions of the desert war.

Rommel was not an easy man to serve; he spared those around him as little as he spared himself. An iron constitution and nerves of steel were needed to work with Rommel, but I must emphasize that although Rommel was sometimes embarrassingly outspoken with senior commanders, yet once he was convinced of the efficiency and loyalty of those in his immediate entourage, he never had a harsh word for them.[6]

Rommel had some strange ideas on the principles of staff work. A particularly irksome characteristic was his interference in details which should have been the responsibility of the chief of staff. As a rule Rommel expected his chief of staff to accompany him on his visits to the front—which frequently meant into the very forefront of the battle. This was contrary to the accepted general staff principle, that the chief of staff is the deputy of the commander in chief during the latter's absence. But Rommel liked to have his principal adviser always at his elbow, and if he became a casualty, well—he could always be replaced.[7]

During critical periods the absence of Rommel and his chief of staff sometimes lasted not only for a day, but for several days. This threw a heavy responsibility on the junior

[5] The most famous British armored formation of the war, with the insignia of the "desert rat."

[6] *Editor's note.* On occasion Rommel did not mince his words. When I asked General von Mellenthin what he thought of Mr. James Mason's performance in the film *The Desert Fox*, he smiled before replying, "Altogether too polite."

[7] During the fighting in the "Cauldron" on 30 May–1 June 1942 both General Gause, the chief of staff, and Colonel Westphal, the Ia, were wounded.

staff officers, and particularly on the Ia (Chief of Operations Section). We accepted it gladly, because we knew that Rommel would always back up any decisions we felt compelled to make. The most critical absence was at the height of the *Crusader* battle in November, 1941, when Westphal as Ia, and myself as Ic, were left in complete control of Panzergruppe headquarters from 23 to 28 November. Westphal felt compelled to countermand one of Rommel's most important orders, and on his return the commander in chief showed his magnanimity by endorsing Westphal's action, although it was in direct contradiction to his earlier commands.[8]

During the period August–November, 1941, I got to know Rommel very well. Although there was a lull on the front, this did not imply any respite for the staff or the troops. Rommel worked feverishly at improving his positions on the frontier, and a most formidable mine barrier grew up between Sidi Omar and Sollum. He also threw himself into preparations for the capture of Tobruk. During these so-called quiet weeks Rommel would appear as early as 5 A.M. at the A.C.V. (armored command vehicle) of his Ia to study the latest situation reports. Then he would give orders to his staff, and accompanied by a staff officer he would travel to the front—Sollum or Tobruk—where he usually spent the whole day.

Normally it is the staff officer who does the guiding, but Rommel had an incredible sense for direction and terrain and did his own navigation. During his visits to the front he saw everything and nothing escaped him. When a gun was inadequately camouflaged, when mines were laid in insufficient number, or when a standing patrol did not have enough ammunition, Rommel would see to it. Everywhere he convinced himself personally that his orders were being carried out. While very popular with young soldiers and N.C.O.'s with whom he cracked many a joke, he could become most outspoken and very offensive to commanders of troops if he did not approve of their measures. After such one-sided discussion he was, however, quite prepared to listen to the arguments of the accompanying staff officer in de-

[8] Westphal had cancelled the orders directing the 21st Panzer Division to pursue into Egypt, and had recalled the division to Bardia.

fense of the unlucky victim, and when his reproaches had been unjustified Rommel got things square again during his next visit.

Rommel's vitality was something to marvel at; he usually spent the whole day on such inspections—regardless of the scorching heat which during the summer months sometimes reached 110 degrees in the shade. Lunch consisted of a few sandwiches eaten in the car, with a mouthful of tea from a bottle. Dinner in the evening was no less Spartan; Rommel usually dined by himself or in the company of a few of his closest staff officers. During dinner he allowed himself one glass of wine. For himself and his staff Rommel insisted on the same rations as the troops. In North Africa this was not always a suitable diet; for months we had no fresh vegetables and lived only on tinned stuff; moreover, the water was always brackish even in coffee or tea. We had many casualties from what the English call "gyppo tummy," and I myself had to leave Africa in September 1942 with amoebic dysentery.

Rommel was not always the stern commander, and when he chose to relax he could be a delightful companion. *The Rommel Papers* contain the following extract from a letter to his wife:

10 Sept. 1941. I went out shooting last evening with Major von Mellenthin and Lieutenant Schmidt [A.D.C.]. It was most exciting. Finally I got a running gazelle from the car. We had the liver for dinner and it was delicious.[9]

My impressions of Rommel as a general in the field will appear in the subsequent chapters. He was in my opinion the ideal commander for desert warfare. His custom of "leading from the front" occasionally told against him; decisions affecting the army as a whole were sometimes influenced unduly by purely local successes or failures. On the other hand by going himself to the danger spot—and he had an uncanny faculty for appearing at the right place at the right time—he was able to adapt his plans to new situations, and in the fluid conditions of the Western Desert this was a

---

[9] (London, Collins, 1953), 150.

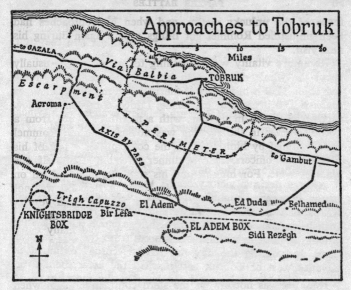

Approaches to Tobruk

factor of supreme importance. In planning an operation he was thoughtful and thorough; in taking a decision in the field he was swift and audacious—shrewdly assessing the chances of some daring stroke in the ebb and flow of battle. What I admired most were his courage and resourcefulness, and his invincible determination under the most adverse circumstances. These qualities were shown in his brilliant riposte towards Agedabia in January, 1942, which surprised and routed the victorious Eighth Army; in his coolness in the "Cauldron" during the following June when defeat stared us in the face—the prelude to his greatest victory; and in the iron resolution with which he held on at Alamein in July, 1942, when reserves and ammunition were almost exhausted.

Between Rommel and his troops there was that mutual understanding which cannot be explained and analyzed, but which is a gift of the gods. The Afrika Korps followed Rommel wherever he led, however hard he drove them—it was always the same Afrika Korps with the same three divisions

—at Sidi Rezegh, at Agedabia, at Knightsbridge, and at El Alamein. The men knew that Rommel was the last man that Rommel spared; they saw him in their midst and they felt, "this is our leader."

A Typical Day

It may be of interest if I give a detailed account of a typical day at Rommel's headquarters during a great battle. The period I have chosen is the twenty-four hours between 1800 hours on 15 June and 1800 hours on 16 June 1942. The general situation on that day was as follows.

After a decisive victory on 12 June in the great armored battle between Knightsbridge and El Adem, the Afrika Korps had thrust northwards and on 13 June broke the British resistance in the Knightsbridge area. On 14 June Ritchie decided to withdraw his forces from the Gazala positions, and during the day the Afrika Korps continued its advance west of Tobruk and reached the escarpment overlooking the Via Balbia and the sea. On the morning of 15 June Rommel decided that it was too late to cut off the main body of the 1st S.A. Division, which was retiring from Gazala along the Via Balbia to Tobruk. He ordered the 15th Panzer Division to descend the escarpment and reach the sea in order to cut off the South African rearguards, but he detached 21st Panzer on a wide sweep towards El Adem where the 29th Indian Brigade was holding a well-fortified box. In Rommel's view it was vital to give the British no chance to build up a new front south of Tobruk, and accordingly 21st Panzer and 90th Light were ordered to capture El Adem and Belhamed and then drive on through Gambut to isolate the Fortress of Tobruk on the east. This is the background of the twenty-four hours which I shall now describe.

It is 1815 hours at the army battle headquarters at Bir Lefa. Colonel General Rommel (C. in C.) and the chief of staff, Colonel Bayerlein, are back from a journey to the front and enter my A.C.V.[10] With me is Oberleutnant Voss.

[10] I took over the post of Ia when Colonel Westphal was wounded on 1 June.

The C. in C., coming from the sector of the 15th Panzer Division (Via Balbia), says that although part of the rearguard of the 1st S.A. Division has been captured, the bulk of the Gazala formations have got away; therefore the 21st Panzer Division was ordered at noon to pursue the enemy by swinging east of Tobruk.

I report on the situation: 21st Panzer Division with foremost elements is in the area west of Ed Duda, where strong enemy defensive fire is being encountered from the fortified positions of Ed Duda and Belhamed. Messages from 90th Light say that although local penetrations have been made in the east and west sectors of the El Adem Box, enemy resistance is on the whole unbroken. The three German reconnaissance units report that in the area south and southeast of El Adem they have thrown back enemy reconnaissance forces. Italian 20th (Motorized) Corps is assembling around Knightsbridge, Italian 10th and 21st Corps are moving east through the Gazala position.

Enemy situation. The enemy has succeeded in evading our pincer movement and is escaping from the Gazala position. These forces (1st S.A. Division and the 50th British Division) and the armored brigades—no longer fit for battle— of the 1st and 7th Armored Divisions are assembling on the Libyan-Egyptian frontier; air reconnaissance confirms continuous movements from Tobruk eastwards; wireless intercept has confirmed that the 1st S.A. Division and the 50th Division together with the two armored divisions are on the frontier.[11] Therefore in the Tobruk zone we can reckon on the 2nd S.A. Division only, with the 11th and 29th Indian Brigades in the outer approaches of the fortress.

C. in C.: "It is my intention to take Tobruk by a *coup de main*. For this purpose the outlying area of Tobruk, south and east of the Fortress, must be gained without delay, and the British Eighth Army pressed away farther to the east.

"The following are my orders for 16 June" (Rommel sketches his intentions in a few lines on the operation map):

"D.A.K. with the 21st Panzer Division will take Ed Duda and Belhamed. Fifteenth Panzer Division at present west of

---

[11] This was not entirely correct, but the reports are given as I made them at the time.

Tobruk will be relieved by Italians—for the time being by Trieste—and will go to the El Adem area. Panzer Division Ariete will cover the southern flank in the area southwest of El Adem. Ninetieth Light will take the El Adem box, Italian 10th Corps will move up to invest Tobruk on the southwest, and Italian 20th Corps will invest the fortress on the west.

"Fliegerführer Afrika will be requested to make his main effort on 16 June in the El Adem-Ed Duda area."

(All these orders were sent over the air to the various corps concerned as independent orders; during those days no formal army orders were issued, with the exception of the army order for the attack on Tobruk issued on 18 June.)

At 1930 hours the C. in C. takes supper in his caravan and invites the chief of staff and me to share it with him. (Usually Rommel took his meals alone or with his A.D.C.) Private conversation is limited to reminiscences of garrison life in Wiener Neustadt, and of skiing, for which Rommel had a great enthusiasm. Soon, however, the talk reverts to Tobruk. For Rommel there is only one thought—the capture of Tobruk. The attack is to proceed exactly as was planned in November, 1941, i.e. from the southeast. The chief of staff weighs our prospects and assesses the reactions of the enemy, but stops when he sees that Rommel has fallen asleep in his chair. Nature claims its own even from this hard man, who has been moving about on the battlefield since five o'clock in the morning.

Until midnight the evening reports of the various corps keep coming in; they are collated by Oberleutnant Voss and a summary is sent by wireless to O.K.H.;[12] simultaneously the Italian Liaison staff with the Panzerarmee receives a summary to pass on to the Italian Comando Supremo in Rome.

16 June 0430 hours. Ordonnanz officer No. 1 marks up the morning reports on the operations map.

0450 hours. C. in C. comes to the A.C.V. of the Ia. I report on the morning situation.

Major General Krause, commander of the army artillery, is summoned and ordered to concentrate the bulk of the

---

[12] Oberkommando des Heeres, i.e. The Army High Command in Berlin.

artillery by noon in support of the attack of 90th Light. A discussion follows between the C. in C. and the commander of the army engineers, Colonel Hecker, who is ordered to reconnoiter the minefields on the southeastern approaches of Tobruk.

The IIa (Administrative Officer), Colonel Schulte-Heuthaus, is ordered to recce a new army battle headquarters in the area immediately to the northwest of El Adem.

At 0600 hours the C. in C. with the chief of staff leave for the battle headquarters of 90th Light. It is his intention to proceed from there to the battle headquarters of the Afrika Korps and then to 21st Panzer; he is accompanied by several wireless links capable of listening in to the army signals traffic and of establishing direct contact with all corps and divisions.

At 0845 hours D.A.K. signals that the 21st Panzer Division has captured the strongpoint of Ed Duda.

From 0900 hours there is lively enemy fighter-bomber activity above the areas of Afrika Korps and 90th Light. Several low-level attacks are made on army battle headquarters.

At 1015 hours Major Otto, quartermaster general of the army, calls on me and is briefed on the situation and the proposed attack on Tobruk. He complains that during the past week the shipping space for German supplies has been considerably cut down by the Italian High Command in favor of the Italian Panzer Division Littorio which is being shipped to Africa. Therefore the supply situation is most critical, particularly the fuel position. (This was greatly improved on the following days when vast quantities of gasoline were captured around Gambut.)

At 1030 hours the Wireless Intercept Company reports on an enemy wireless conversation in clear between the 29th Indian Brigade and the 7th Armored Division according to which the garrison of the El Adem Box is preparing to break out during the night 16/17 June. The information is immediately passed on to Rommel and the 90th Light.

1130 hours. A signal is intercepted from the C. in C. to 90th Light: "Discontinue attack at once. Invest El Adem Box securely. Army artillery to increase fire on box."

1130 hours. Major Zolling, the Ic, discusses the position with me. There is further confirmation that the bulk of Eighth Army has withdrawn as far as the frontier. The fact that the 2nd S.A. Division has been left in Tobruk leads to the conclusion that the Fortress is to be defended.

1215 hours. Colonel Büchting, the army signals officer, reports that the new battle headquarters will be ready to function from 1530 hours as far as signals are concerned.

1240 hours. General Count Barbasetti, the commander of the Italian Liaison Staff, discusses the situation with me. He reports that Panzer Division Littorio is en route and that its advanced elements will reach the Gazala area that night. But the Italian High Command has not yet given approval for the division to take part in operations.

1250 hours. A wireless report from the 21st Italian Corps says that all units of the 15th Panzer Division in the coastal area have been relieved.

1315 hours to 1350 hours. Several reports are received from Italian Panzer Division Ariete, and Reconnaissance Units 3 and 580 to the effect that all harassing attacks by the 7th Motor Brigade have been repulsed south and southeast of El Adem.

1500 hours. I move to the new battle headquarters with No. 1 Operations Section. En route we are under artillery fire from the south and endure several low-level air attacks.

(Ic with No. 2 Operations Section remains with the old battle headquarters until I report that the new headquarters has opened.)

1545 hours. I reach the new battle headquarters and find that the C. in C. has arrived before me.

1615 hours. There is a discussion between the C. in C. and Field Marshal Kesselring in my A.C.V. Rommel reports on the situation and explains his intention to attack Tobruk from the southeast. Kesselring promises to support this attack with all aircraft at his disposal. He explains that on 15 June, and also today, his formations were unable to support the Panzerarmee as they have been operating against a British convoy en route for Malta.

1815 hours. Sidi Rezegh has been captured by the 21st Panzer Division.

1900 hours. I report on the situation. C. in C. gives the following orders for 17 June: "To continue the mopping up of the outer defenses of Tobruk, to complete the investment of the Fortress, and to hold off enemy forces on the east and south."

Arms and Armament

As Rommel himself says in his memoirs:

North Africa may well have been the theatre in which the war was waged in its most modern guise. . . . It was only in the desert that the principles of armored warfare as they were taught in theory before the war could be fully applied and thoroughly developed. It was only in the desert that real tank battles were fought by large-scale formations.[13]

The terrific armored battles in the Western Desert cannot be understood without some reference to the weapons and equipment on both sides. Contrary to the generally accepted view, the German tanks did not have any advantage in quality over their opponents, and in numbers we were always inferior. In the *Crusader* offensive of November, 1941, the British attacked with 748 tanks, of which there were 213 Matildas and Valentines, 220 Crusaders, 150 cruisers of earlier model than the Crusader, and 165 American Stuarts. To meet this attack the Panzergruppe had 249 German and 146 Italian tanks.[14] The Italian tanks, with their inadequate armor, and low-velocity 47-mm guns, were decidedly inferior to all categories of tank on the British side, and moreover they were mechanically unreliable.

Of the German tanks, 70 were Mark II's, which only mounted a heavy machine gun, and could therefore play no part in a tank battle, except as reconnaissance vehicles. The bulk of our strength consisted of 35 Mark IV's and 139 Mark III's (we also had five British Matildas, of which we thought highly). The Mark IV acquired an awe-inspiring rep-

---

[13] *Krieg ohne Hass*, 118.
[14] I have omitted the Italian L3's and the British Mark VI B's from this calculation. They only carried machine guns, were lightly armored and quite useless.

utation among the British, mainly because it mounted a 75-mm gun. This, however, was a low-velocity weapon of poor penetrating power, and although we did use our Mark IV's in tank fighting, they were of more value in firing high explosive shells in support of infantry.[15] The Mark III used by the Panzergruppe in the *Crusader* battle only mounted a low-velocity 50-mm gun, which British experts now admit had no advantage over their 2-pounder.[16] Nor did we have any advantage in thickness of armor. The British heavy infantry tanks—Matilda and Valentine—completely outclassed us in this respect, and even the Crusaders and Stuarts were better protected than our Mark III. For example the maximum basic armor of the Mark III in the *Crusader* battle was 30 mm, while the Crusader nose and hull fronts were protected by 47 mm, and the Stuart had 44 mm protection there.[17]

To what then are we to ascribe the brilliant successes of the Afrika Korps? To my mind, our victories depended on three factors—the superior quality of our antitank guns, our systematic practice of the principle of *Co-operation-of-Arms*, and—last but not least—our tactical methods. While the British restricted their 3.7-in antiaircraft gun (a very powerful weapon) to an antiaircraft role, we employed our 88-mm gun to shoot at tanks as well as airplanes. In November, 1941, we only had thirty-five 88's, but moving in close touch with our panzers these guns did terrific execution

[15] From June, 1942, we began to receive the Mark IV Special with high-velocity 75-mm gun. This was a very good tank, far superior to its predecessor. Similarly in May, 1942, we began to receive Mark III Specials with the high-velocity 50-mm gun. They were excellent tanks.

[16] See the interesting articles by Colonel R. M. P. Carver in the *Royal Armoured Corps Journal*.

[17] The armor of our Mark III's and IV's was virtually doubled in 1942 as a result of our experiences in Russia.

In 1941 the very weak sides of the Mark IV were strengthened by bolting on additional armor, and the fronts of the driver's and auxiliary machine gunner's compartments in the Marks III and IV were reinforced in a similar way. These changes were not of great significance. It was not until 1942 that we began to receive new models of the Marks III and IV, protected by special face-hardened armor. This gave our panzers an advantage in quality in the counterattack on January, 1942, but with the arrival of the Grant tank in May, 1942, the balance of armored strength again tilted in favor of Eighth Army.

among the British tanks. Moreover, our high-velocity 50-mm antitank gun was far superior to the British 2-pounder, and batteries of these guns always accompanied our tanks in action. Our field artillery, also, was trained to co-operate with the panzers. In short, a German panzer division was a highly flexible formation of all arms, which always relied on artillery in attack or defense. In contrast the British regarded the antitank gun as a defensive weapon, and they failed to make adequate use of their powerful field artillery, which should have been taught to eliminate our antitank guns.

Our panzer tactics had been evolved by General Guderian during the prewar years, but Rommel thoroughly understood Guderian's principles and adapted them to desert conditions. Their value was fully proved in the great battle which began on 18 November 1941.[18]

---

[18] Although generally inferior in numbers of tanks, our tactical leadership usually succeeded in concentrating superior numbers of tanks and guns at the decisive point (i.e. the *Schwerpunkt*).

5: *Sidi Rezegh*

BETWEEN 19 AND 23 November 1941 the Eighth Army and the Panzergruppe Afrika were engaged in an armored battle which has a unique place in the history of war. There has never been a battle fought at such an extreme pace and with such bewildering vicissitudes of fortune. More than a thousand tanks, supported by large numbers of aircraft and guns, were committed to a whirlwind battle fought on ground which allowed complete freedom of maneuver and were handled by commanders who were prepared to throw in their last reserves to achieve victory. The situation changed with such rapidity that it was difficult to keep track of the movements of one's own troops, let alone those of the enemy. The dust clouds raised by charging tanks and moving columns added to the obscurity, and, as Auchinleck says, "at times the fog of war literally descended on the battlefield."[1]

This battle made tremendous demands on generalship and staff work, and for this reason I believe it deserves very careful study today. We are likely to learn far more from these great "maneuver battles" of the desert, than from the later campaigns of the war in which the issue was decided by weight of numbers and weapons. Accordingly I propose to deal with this battle in detail, but before doing so I shall sketch the strategic background.

[1] Field Marshal Sir C. J. E. Auchinleck, *Dispatch* (London, H.M. Stationery Office).

66

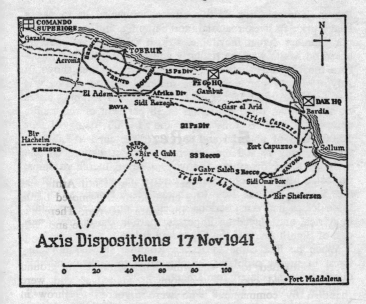

Axis Dispositions 17 Nov 1941

The Strategic Background

During the late summer and autumn of 1941 all German planning in North Africa was conditioned by the problems of supply. Both the German and Italian High Commands appreciated that no great results could be achieved in Africa until Rommel had eliminated Tobruk; he was ordered in July to prepare for an attack on the Fortress and he hoped he would be able to launch his assault in September. But continual sinkings on the supply route to Africa forced us to postpone the assault from month to month, until the date was finally fixed for 21 November.

Our communications between Europe and Africa were dominated by the British possession of Malta. I have no hesitation in saying that this island exercised a decisive influence on the course of the desert war. This fact was appreciated by Grand Admiral Raeder in April, 1941, when he strongly urged Hitler to capture Malta before attacking

Russia. The rejection of this advice compelled us to pay a heavy price in lives, material, and shipping, and indeed made our ultimate defeat inevitable. British warships and aircraft based on Malta were particularly active during the period before the *Crusader* battles, as the following figures show. In July, 1941, 17 per cent of the material sent to Africa was lost, and in August 35 per cent. In September shipping losses on the African route had risen to 38 per cent of the traffic, comprising 49,000 tons sunk and 14,000 damaged. Of 50,000 tons of material and supplies dispatched to Libya in October, only 18,500 tons reached their destination. On the night of 8/9 November a convoy of seven merchant ships, protected by Italian cruisers and destroyers, was wiped out by the British without loss to themselves.[2] Needless to say these losses had most serious effects on our supply position in Africa, and played an important part in the ultimate success of Eighth Army in the *Crusader* battle.[3]

When he first came to Africa Rommel showed little interest in supply problems, but he came to realize that this question was absolutely fundamental.

While we were standing impotently outside the Fortress of Tobruk waiting for the supplies and reinforcements without which we could not attack, the British forces in the Middle East were increasing vastly in strength. Auchinleck was able

[2] *Editor's note.* According to Winston Churchill, *The Grand Alliance* (London, Cassell, 1950), 492, the British ships were of the Malta-based "Force K." According to S. Roskill, *The War at Sea, 1939–1945* (London, H. M. Stationery Office, 1954), the convoy consisted of seven ships totalling 39,000 tons; it was escorted by six destroyers with two heavy cruisers and four destroyers in support. "Force K" consisted of the light cruisers *Aurora* and *Penelope* with two destroyers; they sank the whole convoy and a destroyer, and damaged another destroyer.

Count Galeazzo Ciano commented in his diary that the affair was "inexplicable," and added: "This morning Mussolini was depressed and indignant." See *Ciano's Diary 1939–1943* (London, W. Heinemann, 1947), 395.

[3] Even when our supplies did reach Africa, it was no easy matter to move them to the front, because of the great distances involved. It was 700 miles from Tripoli to Benghazi, 300 from Benghazi to Tobruk, yet another 350 from Tobruk to Alamein. When we were at Alamein many of our supplies had to be hauled 1,400 miles from Tripoli.

to go ahead with preparations for a great offensive to sweep us out of Cyrenaica, and to base his plans on the assumption that the main military effort of the British Empire was to be made in the Middle East. At Panzergruppe headquarters we were well aware of what was coming and as Staff Officer Intelligence I was responsible for drawing up detailed appreciations of the enemy's strength and intentions.

In the middle of October I issued an appreciation for distribution to all units, in which I emphasized the likelihood of a large-scale British offensive in the near future. For weeks our air reconnaissance kept reporting on the construction of a railway line from Mersa Matruh towards the frontier, while in September our very efficient Wireless Intercept Service established that the 1st S.A. Division and the 2nd N.Z. Division had moved up to Matruh from the Nile Delta. Long range air reconnaissance confirmed that numerous convoys were en route through the Red Sea towards the Suez Canal.

These developments put us in an extremely difficult position. Most of our troubles would be solved by taking Tobruk, and by 26 October Rommel felt strong enough to formulate his plan of attack and issue his orders. Our preparations would be complete by 15 November, but the attack could not be made before 20 November on account of the moon. There was a real danger that Eighth Army would attack first, or strike when our forces were deeply embedded in the Fortress, in which case our position would be very critical.

Moreover, Rommel was deeply troubled by the attitude of the Italians. Rommel's nominal superior, General Bastico, the Italian commander in chief in North Africa, was convinced that the British were planning an offensive, and he said that "the enemy attack will not be merely diversionary but a heavy offensive aimed at forcing a final decision." Bastico believed that it would be simultaneous with our assault on Tobruk, and accordingly he was very anxious for Rommel to cancel his plans for attacking the Fortress. Rommel would not hear of it, and on broad grounds I think he was right. There are always elements of risk in war, and to cancel our Tobruk plans, and stand tamely on the defensive, would

mean renouncing the initiative to the enemy. The capture of
Tobruk would immensely strengthen our position, and Rommel was prepared to run the risks which such a venture
involved.

To allay the fears of the Italians and prevent interference
with his plans, Rommel instructed his staff to adopt a confident tone in all discussions with Italian officers, and in
November—as the date of our attack drew nearer—I deliberately minimized the possibilities of a British offensive
whenever I spoke to our allies. When he visited Rome in
November, Rommel assumed the same attitude in conversation with Ugo Cavellero, the Italian chief of staff. In his
memoirs Cavallero says:

I asked Rommel whether it was possible that the enemy
might make a large-scale enveloping attack. Rommel regarded
this possibility as extremely unlikely, as the enemy would be
afraid of having his line of withdrawal cut by the Italo-
German divisions. He only foresaw an action with small
forces on the side of the enemy, with the enemy air force in
support.[4]

Similarly the Italian official history makes the following
statement:

The German intelligence service for reasons not easy to
explain opposed the idea that the British contemplated an
offensive and attributed the information received by our intelligence service to "an excessive Latin nervousness." On
11 November the head of the German intelligence service
[i.e. myself, as Ic] in a discussion with an Italian liaison
officer, who talked to him about the coming British offensive,
remarked: "Major Revetria [head of Italian intelligence] is
much too nervous. Tell him not to worry, because the British
won't attack."[5]

Actually we were very perturbed about the possibility
of a British offensive, and Rommel took comprehensive measures to meet it. Our positions on the frontier stretched for

[4] *Comando Supremo* (Bologna, Capelli, 1948), 150.
[5] Ferruccio Manzetti, *Seconda Offensiva Britannica in Africa* (Rome,
Historical Section, Italian General Staff, 1949), 41.

twenty-five miles from Sollum to Sidi Omar; they were covered by thick minebelts, and were defended by battalions of the Savona Division reinforced by German detachments with 88-mm guns. These positions ensured that any British offensive must make a wide sweep into the desert, and expose a long line of communications to our counterattack.

After long consideration Rommel decided that he could not commit the 21st Panzer Division to the attack on Tobruk, and this formation was placed south of Gambut ready to deal with any British attempt to interfere with our plans. Rommel took this step because our intelligence reports showed that a British offensive was extremely likely. Fifteenth Panzer Division and the newly formed Afrika Division were to attack Tobruk, but 15th Panzer had to make its plans on the assumption that it might be withdrawn at twenty-four hours' notice to support 21st Panzer. Moreover the Italian Armored Corps was to hold Bir Hacheim and Bir el Gubi and cover the approaches to Tobruk from the south.[6]

Two German reconnaissance units, 3 and 33, held the gap between Bir el Gubi and Sidi Omar, and our air patrols penetrated far across the frontier. The bulk of the enemy's strength was in the Matruh area, and in an appreciation which I issued on 11 November I said: "A serious attack to relieve Tobruk cannot be expected until the main force from the Mersa Matruh–El Daba area arrives in the assembly area near the Sollum front." I estimated that if the British reacted to our attack on Tobruk by launching an offensive, then they would require three days before they could intervene seriously in the Tobruk sector. In the meantime we hoped to capture the Fortress.

The Armored Clash

On 16 Nobember the artillery of the 15th Panzer Division began to move into position on the southeastern sector of

---

[6] This corps consisted of the Ariete Armored Division and the Trieste Motorized Division. It was commanded by General Gambara, Bastico's chief of staff, and was not under Rommel's command. But after discussions with Rommel on 29 October Gambara agreed to put Trieste at Bir Hacheim and Ariete at Bir el Gubi. Rommel said to Gambara, "This takes a great load off my mind."

Tobruk, and the units of Afrika Division[7] got ready to attack the Fortress. Heavy storms blew up during the day, and for the next twenty-four hours Cyrenaica was swept by rain of unprecedented intensity. Bridges were carried away, roads became rivers, and all our airfields were under water. For days it was impossible for any aircraft to take off, and our air reconnaissance was reduced to nothing.[8]

On 15 November our Wireless Intercept Service had reported that the 1st S.A. Division seemed to be moving west from Mersa Matruh, and these reports were confirmed on the 16th. On 17 November General von Ravenstein, the commander of the 21st Panzer Division, decided to strengthen our reconnaissance screen with an antitank company, and that evening our Intelligence Diary reported: "Complete English wireless silence."[9]

On the morning of 18 November we again noted that the British maintained, "almost complete wireless silence," and that air reconnaissance on our side was impossible, with "landing grounds a sea of mud and water running high in the wadis." But from midday onwards we began to pick up reports from the recce screen of 21st Panzer; there was clearly much patrol activity on the British side with large numbers of armored cars pressing northwards towards the Trigh el Abd. Rommel believed it was merely a reconnaissance in force, and throughout the day the Panzergruppe headquarters was engaged in preparations for the attack on Tobruk.

That evening General Cruewell, the commander of the Afrika Korps, came to see Rommel. He explained that von Ravenstein was uneasy and wanted to move a strong battle group towards Gabr Saleh on the morning of the 19th. Cruewell told Rommel that he had warned 15th Panzer to be ready to move from the Tobruk area to the support of 21st Panzer south of Gambut. Rommel was irritated by Cruewell's

---

[7] Later the 90th Light Division. Largely composed of ex-members of the French Foreign Legion, it was poorly equipped in November, 1941, and most of its heavy weapons were still in Naples.

[8] During the *Crusader* battles our air force was heavily outnumbered.

[9] On the night of 17/18 November British Commandos attacked our quartermaster general's headquarters at Beda Littorio, in the belief that Rommel was there. As is well known, this ill-conceived undertaking ended in tragedy.

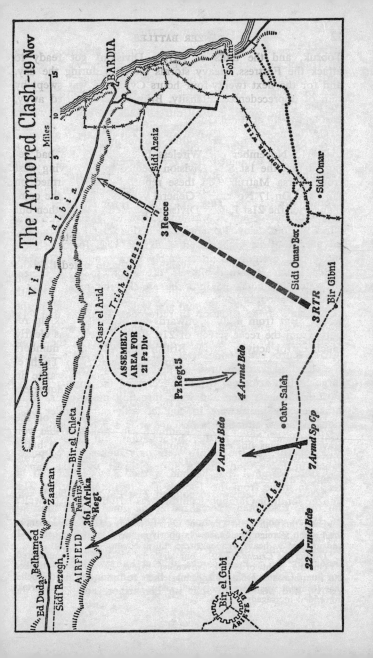

The Armored Clash—19 Nov

BARDIA

Sollum

Sidi Azeiz

Sidi Omar

Sidi Omar Box

3 Recce

Via Balbia

Gasr el Arid

Trigh Capuzzo

ASSEMBLY AREA FOR 21 Pz Div

3 RTR

Bir Gibni

Pz Regt 5

4 Armd Bde

Gabr Saleh

Gambut

Sidi Rezegh

Bir el Chleta

AIRFIELD

Point 175

361 Afrika Regt

7 Armd Bde

7 Armd Sp Gp

Trigh el Abd

Ed Duda

Belhamed

Zaafran

22 Armd Bde

Bir el Gubi

ARIETE

Miles
0   5   10   15

attitude; he was reluctant to give up his cherished attack on Tobruk and said, "We must not lose our nerves." He forbade the movement of a battle group to Gabr Saleh, "for fear of discouraging the enemy too soon." Nevertheless he warned the Italian Corps to maintain "increased vigilance" east and south of Bir el Gubi.

On the morning of 19 November Cruewell again appeared at the headquarters at Gambut and had a long discussion with Rommel. He explained that the position was serious; our reconnaissance units had been driven across the Trigh el Abd by strong enemy tank forces, which were thrusting vigorously northwards. This was not a reconnaissance but a major offensive, and it was imperative to take countermeasures without delay. Rommel agreed that 21st Panzer should advance towards Gabr Saleh, and that 15th Panzer should move that evening to an assembly area south of Gambut. After lunch Rommel himself drove off to 21st Panzer to watch his tanks go into the attack—the great armored battle was about to begin.

Looking at the situation in retrospect, I realize that 21st Panzer was committed too hastily, and that it would have been better for the division to avoid battle until the whole Afrika Korps could concentrate. At midday on 19 November the situation was obscure—all that we really knew was that large British armored forces had crossed the frontier in the Fort Maddalena area and were thrusting northwards, while other enemy units were in contact with our frontier positions. When a situation is obscure, it is a good rule to concentrate and await further information, but Rommel was still hopeful that the British were only making a reconnaissance in force, and that a strong thrust by 21st Panzer would fling them back.

Actually the decision to commit 21st Panzer to battle was far more risky than we realized at the time. On the morning of 19 November the whole of the 7th Armored Division was grouped in the Gabr Saleh area, and if this force had remained concentrated it could have inflicted a very serious defeat on the isolated forces of 21st Panzer. But mercifully for us, General Cunningham, the commander of Eighth Army, had decided to split up his armor, and during the

day the various formations of the 7th Armored Division
went off in different directions.[10] Twenty-second Armored
Brigade went to attack the Italians at Bir el Gubi—where it
suffered a severe repulse—the 7th Armored Brigade thrust
north to Sidi Rezegh airfield and was followed by the Divisional Support Group.[11] Only the 4th Armored Brigade
was left at Gabr Saleh, with the task of keeping touch with
the left flank of the British 13th Corps (the 2nd N.Z. Division, the 4th Indian Division, and the 1st Army Tank Brigade) which was closing in on our frontier positions.

Afrika Korps ordered 21st Panzer to attack with a battle
group, consisting of Panzer Regiment 5 reinforced by twelve
field guns and four 88-mm's. The force was led by the regimental commander, Colonel Stephan, a bold and resolute
officer who was killed later in the campaign. At about 1530
hours he ran into strong British tank forces about five miles
northeast of Gabr Saleh, and in a fierce action which lasted
until dark he drove the British across the Trigh el Abd. Our
losses were slight—two Mark III's and a Mark II—while
twenty-three British tanks were knocked out.[12]

On the evening of 19 November the situation was still far
from clear at Panzergruppe headquarters. During the afternoon British tanks and South African armored cars had
seized Sidi Rezegh airfield, which was virtually unguarded.
Ariete claimed to have knocked out about fifty British tanks
at Bir el Gubi—they had charged headlong at the Italian defenses—and another strong enemy group was reported to
have chased our Reconnaissance Unit 3 across the Trigh

[10] General Cunningham's original intention was to move the 7th
Armored Division to Gabr Saleh, and then wait for Rommel's reaction. This was not a very good plan; nevertheless, had Cunningham
adhered to it, he might have won a brilliant victory. Seventh Armored
Division was the spearhead of the 30th Corps, which also included the
1st S.A. Division and the 22nd Guards Brigade.

[11] Commanded by Brigadier Campbell. The Support Group had thirty-
six 2-pounder antitank guns, and thirty-six 25-pounders.

[12] These were all Stuarts. Fourth Armored Brigade had only two
regiments in action; another—the 3rd Royal Tanks—had chased Reconnaissance Unit 3 across the Trigh Capuzzo, and could not get back in
time. Fourth Armored Brigade had two batteries of artillery, but only
one of them seems to have been engaged.

Capuzzo near Sidi Azeiz. There were also reports of enemy forces moving westwards from Giarabub.[13]

On the evening of 19 November General von Ravenstein reported to Cruewell by telephone. He suggested that both panzer divisions should be concentrated, but that no large-scale operation should be undertaken until we had a clearer picture of the enemy's dispositions and intentions. His caution was fully justified, for the whole course of the battle depended on Rommel or Cruewell taking the correct decision. Colonel Bayerlein, Cruewell's chief of staff, rang up Panzergruppe headquarters and asked what he should do. Rommel gave Cruewell a free hand, and ordered him to "destroy the enemy battle groups in the Bardia–Tobruk–Sidi Omar area before they can offer any serious threat to Tobruk."

Cruewell appreciated that he was faced with three main groups—the force at Gabr Saleh which had been engaged by Colonel Stephan, the force pushing directly towards Tobruk via Sidi Rezegh, and the force on the eastern flank which had chased Reconnaissance Unit 3 across the Trigh Capuzzo.

Cruewell decided to concentrate towards Sidi Omar, with a view to destroying the group which was threatening Reconnaissance Unit 3. But this enemy group had no existence —on the afternoon of 19 November the 3rd Royal Tanks had been operating in this area, but had now retired and joined the 4th Armored Brigade. Nevertheless on 20 November the whole Afrika Korps moved eastwards on Sidi Azeiz and spent most of the day chasing an imaginary enemy. Twenty-first Panzer finally ran out of gasoline and was left stranded in the desert, about six miles north of Sidi Omar Box. Frantic appeals arrived at Panzergruppe headquarters, asking for gasoline to be flown in by air. All we could do was

---

[13] This was the 29th Indian Brigade with the 6th and 7th S.A. Armored Car Regiments. Known as E Force, this group was supposed to give the impression that a strong armored formation was moving across the desert towards Benghazi. The operations of E. Force certainly made us uneasy, but Rommel was so busy elsewhere that he could not divert forces to deal with it. Giarabub is about eighty miles south of Fort Maddalena.

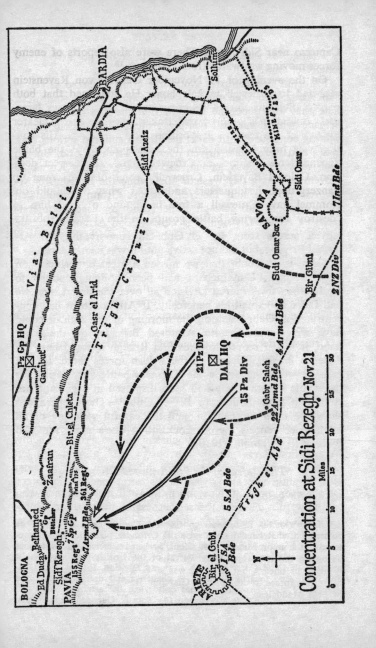

Concentration at Sidi Rezegh—Nov 21

to arrange for gasoline convoys and these did not arrive until
long after dark.

Fifteenth Panzer drove along the Trigh Capuzzo as far as
Sidi Azeiz, and then made a wide sweep to the southwest.
Late that afternoon the division ran into the 4th Armored
Brigade which was still waiting around Gabr Saleh. Heavy
fighting continued until dark; the British suffered serious tank
losses and were again driven over the Trigh el Abd. But no
decisive success was gained, and for the Afrika Korps 20
November was a day wasted. Meanwhile the British 7th Armoured Brigade and the 7th Support Group consolidated
their grip on Sidi Rezegh airfield and repulsed counterattacks by Afrika Division. The British 22nd Armored Brigade
moved across from Bir el Gubi to support the 4th Armored Brigade, but did not arrive until it was nearly dark.

There is no doubt that we missed a great opportunity on
20 November. Cunningham had been obliging enough to
scatter the 7th Armored Division all over the desert, and we
had failed to exploit his generosity. If Afrika Korps had concentrated at Gabr Saleh on the morning of the 20th, it could
have wiped out the 4th Armored Brigade; on the other
hand, if it had moved towards Sidi Rezegh it could have inflicted a crushing defeat on the British forces there. In that
case we would have won the *Crusader* battle very easily, for
the whole Eighth Army had been dispersed in a gigantic arc
stretching from Sollum to Bir el Gubi.[14] These operations
show the need for caution, and the careful weighing of all
intelligence reports, before committing one's main armored
force in a great mobile battle.

The Defeat of the 7th Armored Division

On the evening of 20 November Cruewell met Rommel, who
was now fully alive to the seriousness of his position. Rom-

[14] *Editor's note.* In fairness to General Cunningham, it should be
pointed out that he did not devise the *Crusader* plan, but had it presented to him by Middle East G.H.Q., when he arrived in September
from East Africa. The radical defect of the British plan was that it
required the 30th Corps (the 7th Armored Division, the 1st S.A. Division, and 22nd Guards Brigade) to challenge and defeat the armored
strength of the Panzergruppe, and only when the armored battle had
been won were the 13th Corps and the Tobruk Garrison to intervene.

mel decided that on the 21st the Afrika Korps should move towards Sidi Rezegh, "to attack and destroy the enemy force which has advanced on Tobruk." At 0400 on the 21st Rommel sent a signal to Cruewell stressing that "the situation in this whole theatre is very critical," and that the Afrika Korps "must get going in good time."

These orders, however, were not too easy to execute, for 15th and 21st Panzer had first to break contact with the British 4th and 22nd Armored Brigades in the Gabr Saleh area. The Afrika Korps formed strong rearguards supported by 88 mm's and antitank guns, and these inflicted heavy losses on the British when they tried to interfere with the northward movement. Nevertheless some British tanks did break into our motorized columns, and set a number of trucks on fire. By noon both British brigades had broken off the pursuit and paused to refuel.

While the rearguards were holding off the British pursuit, the tanks of 15th and 21st Panzer, with artillery in close support, advanced rapidly towards Sidi Rezegh. The commander of the 7th Armored Brigade decided to leave the 6th Royal Tanks with the Support Group on Sidi Rezegh airfield, and took the 7th Hussars and the 2nd Royal Tanks to meet the advancing panzers. This was typical of British tactics at this time—their commanders would not concentrate tanks and guns for a co-ordinated battle. By 1000 hours most of the tanks of the 7th Hussars were on fire, and 15th and 21st Panzer had reached the high ground overlooking Sidi Rezegh airfield from the south.

The Afrika Korps then attempted to overrun Sidi Rezegh airfield by launching attacks from the southeast. These attacks failed, partly because of a serious shortage of ammunition, and partly owing to the magnificent resistance of the 7th Support Group, brilliantly commanded by Brigadier Campbell. The British artillery was the best trained and best commanded element in the British Army, and the quality of these gunners was fully proved in the desperate fighting at Sidi Rezegh on 21 November. Towards evening the 4th Armored Brigade advanced from the southeast against the rear of the Afrika Korps and was stopped by an antitank screen; the 22nd Armored Brigade swung round to the southwest and engaged the left flank of the 15th Panzer Division.

Rommel took no part in this battle. At dawn on the 21st the Tobruk garrison—the 70th British Division and the 32nd Army Tank Brigade—made a sortie on the southeast of the perimeter and after savage fighting broke through units of Afrika and Bologna Divisions holding that sector. Our situation was extremely serious and Rommel himself hurried to the danger point. He took command of Reconnaissance Unit 3, strengthened by 88-mm guns, and led it personally against the enemy. Several British tanks were knocked out, and the sortie brought to a halt.

Meanwhile ominous reports came in from the frontier area. The New Zealand Division was on the march, and on the afternoon of the 21st it thrust behind our frontier fortresses and crossed the Trigh Capuzzo on both sides of Sidi Azeiz. This brought them dangerously close to Panzergruppe headquarters at Gambut, and Rommel ordered us to move to El Adem during the night.

On the evening of the 21st Rommel sent a signal to Cruewell and ordered him to prevent the Tobruk garrison from making a junction with the British 30th Corps (the 7th Armored Division, the 1st S.A. Division, and the 22nd Guards Brigade). For this purpose the bulk of Afrika Division was put under Cruewell's command.

In spite of the failure to expel the 7th Support Group from Sidi Rezegh airfield, the Afrika Korps was in a favorable position on the evening of 21 November. The corps held a central position between the Support Group and the British 4th and the 22nd Armored Brigades, and could attack each of these groups in turn. But in a discussion with General Neumann-Silkow, the commander of 15th Panzer, on the afternoon of the 21st, Cruewell announced that he intended to gain "complete freedom of maneuver," and that he would move the Afrika Korps eastwards during the night and regroup in the Gambut area.[15] Cruewell received Rommel's

---

[15] Neumann-Silkow strongly disagreed, and said that the situation could best be cleared up "by a swift thrust by the 8th and 5th Panzer Regiments." By moving the Afrika Korps towards Gambut, Cruewell hoped to gain a favorable opportunity to strike the British in flank.

orders at 2240 hours, and modified his own plan accordingly. Fifteenth Panzer was to move away from the battlefield and regroup south of Gambut, but 21st Panzer was to move north, descend the escarpment overlooking the Trigh Capuzzo, and assemble in the Belhamed area. The effect of these orders was to enable the British to concentrate the 7th Armored Division—for the first time since 19 November. Moreover the two divisions of the Afrika Korps would now be separated by about eighteen miles.

The bulk of the panzer divisions withdrew during the night from the battlefield south of Sidi Rezegh airfield, but the rearguards were brought to action by the British on the morning of 22 November. Once again our antitank guns and 88-mm's proved their value, and the British tanks were unable to get to close quarters. The rearguards joined their divisions during the morning and early afternoon—15th Panzer lay south of Gambut and 21st Panzer between Belhamed and Zaafran. By midday the 4th and 22nd Armored Brigades were in close touch with the 7th Support Group and the remnants of the 7th Armored Brigade on Sidi Rezegh airfield. The British position was now very favorable—the 7th Armored Division had concentrated its brigades, and still had about 180 tanks fit for action. First S.A. Division had been ordered to concentrate at Sidi Rezegh, and the 5th S.A. Brigade was already in the area, under orders to clear the southern escarpment west of Pt. 178.[16] During the afternoon of the 22nd the 6th N.Z. Brigade began to move along the Trigh Capuzzo towards Sidi Rezegh. The sortie of the Tobruk Garrison on 21 November had been checked, but was far from broken. If the 7th Armored Division could have resisted our attacks on the afternoon of 22 November, the balance of force at Sidi Rezegh would have turned heavily against us. (See map on page 82.)

At about midday Rommel went to see von Ravenstein and decided on a bold and aggressive plan, which turned the tables on the British. The infantry and the bulk of the artillery of 21st Panzer were ordered to attack the Sidi Rezegh escarpment from the north, while Panzer Regiment

[16] Held by part of Infantry Regiment 155.

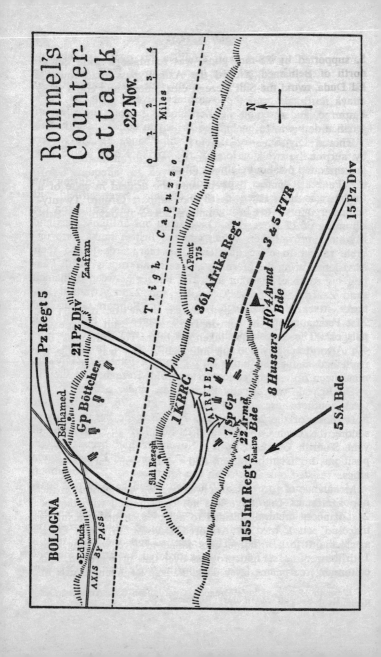

Rommel's Counter-attack

22 Nov.

0 1 2 3 4
Miles

N

BOLOGNA

•Ed Duda

AXIS BY PASS

Belhamed

Gp Böttcher

Pz Regt 5

21 Pz Div

Zaafran

Sidi Rezegh

1 KRRC

AIRFIELD

7 Sp Gp

22 Armd Bde
△ Point 178

155 Inf Regt

Trigh Capuzzo

△ Point 175

361 Afrika Regt

HQ 4 Armd Bde

3 & 5 RTR

8 Hussars

15 Pz Div

5 SA Bde

5, supported by 88-mm guns, was to make a wide detour north of Belhamed, ascend the Axis Bypass road towards Ed Duda, avoid the Sidi Rezegh escarpment, and come in to attack the airfield from the west. The heavy artillery of the Panzergruppe was concentrated at Belhamed and kept up a terrific bombardment in support of 21st Panzer.

This attack appears to have taken the British completely by surprise; they had a large number of armored cars[17] but these do not seem to have conveyed any adequate warning. Panzer Regiment 5 swept onto the airfield in spite of a furious fire from the guns of the Support Group. Twenty-second Armored Brigade counterattacked through the British gun positions, but for some reason the 4th Armored Brigade hung back. The 88-mm's and the antitank guns on both escarpments inflicted severe losses on the 22nd Armored Brigade, which eventually withdrew with a loss of half its strength. First King's Royal Rifle Corps were holding the northern escarpment above Sidi Rezegh tomb; German tanks attacked this battalion in rear while the infantry of 21st Panzer assaulted them in front. As a result the greater part of the battalion was taken prisoner. Towards dusk the 4th Armored Brigade came into action, but was unable to retrieve the situation and 21st Panzer held its positions on the northern escarpment and west of the airfield.

The commander of the 7th Armored Division, General Gott, decided that the airfield was untenable; as darkness fell he withdrew his battered forces to new positions south of the southern escarpment. During the afternoon the 3rd Transvaal Scottish of the 5th S.A. Brigade had attacked our positions around Pt. 178 and had suffered considerable casualties.

Meanwhile the 15th Panzer was coming into action on the opposite flank. This move was not co-ordinated with that of 21st Panzer; Cruewell decided to advance on his own initiative and attack the 7th Armored Division in flank. Once again the British armored cars failed to give warning; the 15th Panzer made rapid progress over flat, firm ground, and continued to advance after dark. Panzer Regiment 8 was in

---

[17] Eleventh Hussars, King's Dragoon Guards, 4th S.A. Armored Car Regiment.

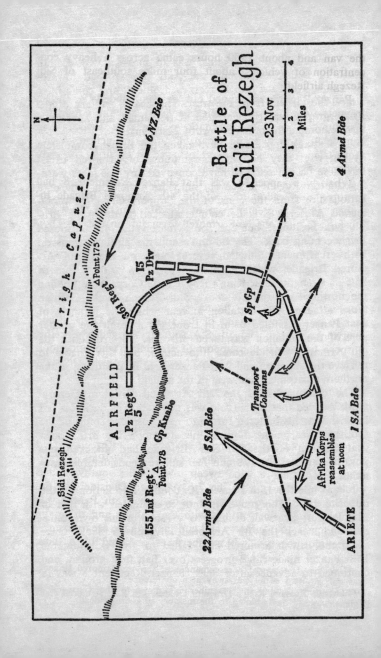

Battle of Sidi Rezegh

23 Nov

Miles

0 1 2 3 4

6 NZ Bde

Trigh Capuzzo

△ Point 175

361 Regt.

15 Pz Div

Pz Regt 5

AIRFIELD

155 Inf Regt. △ Point 178 Gp Knabe

Sidi Rezegh

7 Sp Gp

Transport Columns

5 SA Bde

22 Armd Bde

Afrika Korps reassembles at noon

1 SA Bde

4 Armd Bde

ARIETE

the van and about 1900 hours came across a heavy concentration of vehicles, about four miles southeast of Sidi Rezegh airfield.

Panzer Regiment 8 fanned out and surrounded the British leaguer; the tanks shone their headlights and the commanders jumped out with automatic pistols. The British were completely surprised and incapable of taking action. A few tanks tried to escape and were at once set on fire—the glare of flames made the battlefield as bright as day.

What had happened was that Panzer Regiment 8 had captured the headquarters of the 4th Armored Brigade together with the greater part of the 8th Hussars. It was a crushing blow to the best armored formation in the 7th Division.[18] The Afrika Korps had won a spectacular victory and was again in command of the battlefield.

The Sunday of the Dead

For 23 November[19] Rommel planned a concentrated attack to smash the remnants of the 7th Armored Division and overwhelm the 1st and 5th S.A. Infantry Brigades. For this purpose he gained the support of Gambara, who undertook to advance northeast from Bir el Gubi with Ariete Division, while the 15th and 21st Panzer drove the British towards the Italians. Rommel ordered Afrika Korps to "encircle the enemy and destroy them."

The Panzergruppe order arrived too late for Cruewell to act upon it; he left the infantry and artillery of the 21st Panzer to hold the escarpment south of Sidi Rezegh airfield and he ordered the 15th Panzer, reinforced by Panzer Regiment 5, to make a wide sweep towards the southwest and circle across the rear of the 7th Armored Division and the 5th S.A. Brigade. On meeting Ariete, the 15th Panzer was to make a combined attack with the Italians and drive the British against our infantry and guns holding the escarpment.

The morning of 23 November was obscured by a thick

---

[18] Brigadier Gatehouse, the commander of the 4th Armored Brigade, was not captured as he was away at a conference.
[19] The third Sunday in November is known to the Germans as *Totensonntag*, a day devoted to the memory of German dead.

mist, but when this lifted Cruewell ordered the advance to
begin and the long columns of tanks, lorries, and guns rumbled off to the south. Before long they came across "vast
supply columns" interspersed with guns and tanks. Fifteenth
Panzer swung west, and threw the British into the greatest
confusion. The transport of the 7th Armored Division and
the 5th S.A. Brigade stampeded across the desert, and General Neumann-Silkow suggested to Cruewell that the southward move should be abandoned; 15th Panzer would take
advantage of the enemy's confusion and attack the main
body of the 5th S.A. Brigade, sweeping it against the
escarpment. Cruewell admitted that the prospect was
"tempting" but he believed that the co-operation of Ariete
was essential. Accordingly the action was broken off and
15th Panzer moved southwest to join hands with Ariete. Panzer Regiment 5 had been slow in starting and did not over-
take 15th Panzer until about midday.

There is no doubt that we missed an opportunity here,
and that it would have been better to continue the attack
before the South Africans and British could co-ordinate their
defense. As it was the South Africans took advantage of the
respite to move most of their artillery to the southern flank
of the 5th Brigade; their western flank was protected by a
composite regiment of the 22nd Armored Brigade, and their
eastern flank by the remnants of the Support Group.[20]
However, the move of 15th Panzer did prevent the 1st
S.A. Brigade from coming up from the south and joining
their countrymen.

Rommel left Panzergruppe headquarters early on the 23rd
with the intention of joining the Afrika Korps. He was prevented from doing so by the advance of the 6th N.Z. Brigade from the east. This brigade advanced during the night
22/23 November, and at dawn on the 23rd surprised and
captured the main headquarters of the Afrika Korps near
Bir Chleta. They then pressed forward towards Pt. 175 and
launched a most dangerous attack on our 361st Afrika
Regiment which was holding the eastern approaches to Sidi
Rezegh airfield. Rommel himself was drawn into the fray,

[20] At about noon the 26th N.Z. Battalion took up a position about
two miles east of the South Africans.

and was unable to join Cruewell and the main body of the Afrika Korps.

Cruewell launched his attack on the 5th S.A. Brigade at 1500 hours. He had drawn up his tanks in long lines, and he ordered the infantry to follow in their lorries. When all was ready the order was given to charge, and tanks, lorries, and guns rushed headlong at the enemy.[21] An attack of this sort was an innovation in German tactics—it certainly proved a costly experiment. The South Africans were overwhelmed after a most determined resistance, in which they were gallantly supported by the tanks of the 22nd Armored Brigade. But our motorized infantry suffered heavy casualties—most of their officers and N.C.O.'s were killed and wounded—while the panzer regiments lost 70 tanks out of 150. This was our highest daily loss in the *Crusader* battle, and gravely weakened our armored strength.

In spite of our losses, the evening of 23 November found us in a favorable position, and we could claim to have won the Battle of Sidi Rezegh. The tank strength of the 7th Armored Division had been reduced to a shadow, the 5th S.A. Brigade had been destroyed, and the Tobruk sortie had been contained. On the evening of 23 November Rommel came back to Panzergruppe headquarters to announce his plans and issue his orders. He was in a jubilant mood, and there can be no doubt that this was one of the most critical moments of the desert war.

---

[21] Ariete, on the left flank, played virtually no part in this attack.

6: Rommel's Defeat and Recovery

The Thrust to the Wire

THE BATTLE OF 23 November ended with the Afrika Korps in a state of great confusion, and in the words of General Bayerlein, "the wide area south of Sidi Rezegh had become a sea of dust, fire, and smoke."[1] He comments that when darkness fell, "hundreds of burning vehicles, tanks, and guns lit up the battlefield," and says that, "not until midnight was it possible to gauge the results of the battle, to organize the formations, to assess losses and gains, and to appreciate the general situation." Indeed no cool or accurate appraisal was possible under such conditions. The Afrika Korps had suffered very heavy losses, whose severity was not known at Panzergruppe headquarters for many days to come. On 24 November we had fewer than one hundred tanks fit for battle, and the rifle regiments had been decimated by the South African fire.

Unfortunately Rommel overestimated his success and believed that the moment had come to launch a general pursuit. Rommel had been away from his headquarters all day, engaged in fighting the 6th N.Z. Brigade near Pt. 175, and his knowledge of the situation south of Sidi Rezegh was necessarily limited. He had, however, seen the South African transport on fire, and he had picked up garbled reports about the so-called "battle of annihilation." When he came

[1] Rommel, *Krieg ohne Hass*, 76.

back to El Adem that night he was in a state of excited exultation, and at once began to issue orders which changed the whole character of the *Crusader* battle. In a signal which he dispatched to Berlin about midnight, Rommel said: "Intention for 24 November: *a*) To complete destruction 7th Armored Division. *b*) To advance with elements of forces towards Sidi Omar with a view to attacking enemy on Sollum front."

At Panzergruppe headquarters I had reliable reports of the advance of the main body of the 2nd N.Z. Division along the Trigh Capuzzo; moreover, the situation on the Tobruk front was very menacing. Westphal and I pointed out to Rommel that it would be dangerous to move the Afrika Korps far from Tobruk and that we would be forfeiting an excellent opportunity of destroying the N.Z. Division, which was coming up piecemeal. Indeed it is my conviction that if we had kept the Afrika Korps in the Sidi Rezegh area, we would have won the *Crusader* battle. The Eighth Army had a fatal practice of committing its forces in succession, and we could have destroyed them one after the other. It is true, however, that Rommel's advance to the Wire gravely disturbed General Cunningham and nearly stampeded Eighth Army into a headlong flight.

At no time did I hear Rommel express any interest in the supply dumps of Eighth Army. We knew of their location from captured documents, but Rommel's aim was not to attack the British supplies, but to destroy their field army. To do this he planned to cut the line of retreat of the 30th Corps, and drive the 4th Indian Division into the Sollum minefields. In any case I am very doubtful whether the destruction of some supply dumps would have brought the British offensive to an end. The British excelled in the organization of supplies, and their resources were unlimited.

Early on the morning of 24 November Rommel and Gause left Panzergruppe headquarters, and Westphal as Ia was left as the senior officer at Panzergruppe headquarters. We did not realize that this absence would last for several days and that we would only have the vaguest idea of where Rommel was or what he was doing. It is in periods such as this that sound staff training proves its value; the officers of the German General Staff were not mere clerks or mouth-pieces of their commanders, but were trained to accept responsibility for grave decisions and were respected accordingly. In contrast the British fighting commanders tend to look down on the staff, and the British show a curious reluctance to appoint capable staff officers to operational commands.

At about 1030 hours on the 24th, Rommel put himself at the head of the 21st Panzer Division and drove off at a furious pace. Late that afternoon he reached the Wire, with the whole Afrika Korps stretched out behind him over forty miles of desert, and the 7th Armored Division and the 1st S.A. Division stampeding in all directions. Rommel's bold move had thrown the 30th Corps into complete disorder, and according to British accounts General Cunningham wanted to retire at once into Egypt.[2]. But very fortunately for the British, General Auchinleck had arrived at Eighth Army headquarters; he disagreed with Cunningham, and ordered the continuation of the offensive. This was certainly one of the great decisions of the war; Auchinleck's fighting spirit and shrewd strategic insight had saved the *Crusader* battle and much else besides.[3]

Rommel had formed an incorrect impression of the situation on the Sollum front. Only one Indian brigade, the 7th, was actually there,[4] and this brigade had just captured Sidi Omar, where it was protected by our own minefields. On the night 24/25 November Rommel and Cruewell, with their immediate staffs, got themselves hopelessly lost on the Egyptian side of the Wire and had to camp down in the midst of British gun positions and columns. They escaped by a miracle, but Rommel's decisions on the morning of the 25th were taken hastily and with inadequate knowledge of the enemy's dispositions. Panzer Regiment 5 was flung at Sidi Omar and lost half its strength in vain attacks on the 7th

---

[2] See Major de Guingand's graphic description in *Operation Victory*, 98.

[3] On 26 November Cunningham was replaced by Ritchie.

[4] Eleventh Indian Brigade was below the escarpment near Buq Buq, and the 5th Indian Brigade was around the British railhead near Sofafi. (See map on page 91).

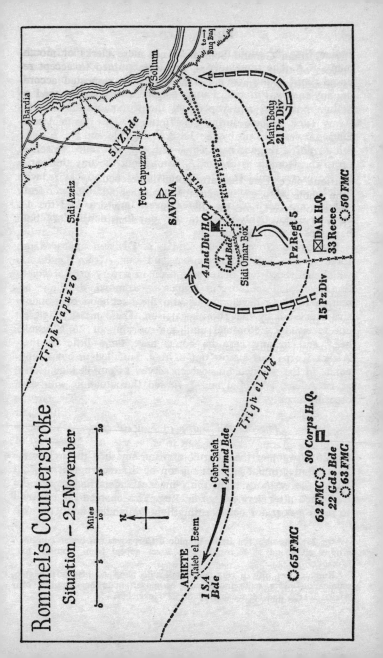

Rommel's Counterstroke

Situation – 25 November

Miles
0   5   10   15   20

N

to Buq Buq →

Bardia

Sollum

5 NZ Bde

Sidi Aziz

Fort Capuzzo

SAVONA

Trigh Capuzzo

WIRE

MINE FIELDS

Main Body
21 Pz Div

4 Ind Div H.Q.

Ind Bde

Sidi Omar Box

Pz Regt 5

DAK H.Q.
33 Recce

50 FMC

15 Pz Div

Trigh el Abd

ARIETE
•Taieb el Esem

•Gabr Saleh
4 Armd Bde

1 S A
Bde

30 Corps H.Q.

62 FMC

22 Gds Bde

63 FMC

65 FMC

Indian Brigade, supported by the 1st and 25th Field Regiments R.A. The remainder of the 21st Panzer Division wandered about in the area south of Halfaya Pass, without meeting any enemy. Fifteenth Panzer formed a cordon, west of the Sollum positions, and wiped out the workshops of the 1st Army Tank Brigade during the afternoon. The Italian Ariete Division was held up by the 1st S.A. Brigade and the British 4th Armored Brigade near Taieb el Esem, and failed to come up to the frontier as ordered.[5] Throughout the day the Afrika Korps was subjected to uninterrupted air attacks, which inflicted serious casualties, the more so as the Sollum front was beyond reach of our fighter cover. In short, 25 November was a thoroughly unsatisfactory day in which we suffered heavy losses for little result.

During 25 November the 2nd N.Z. Division appeared in force in the Sidi Rezegh area, and our Afrika Division, which had been left there, was soon in a very critical position. Westphal sent urgent signals to Rommel, drawing attention to these developments and the likelihood of a massive break-out by the Tobruk garrison. These messages were not received by Rommel until the morning of 26 November,[6] and in any case he could have done little as the Afrika Korps was almost out of fuel. Huddled in our overcoats, in the wooden huts which served as our headquarters at El Adem, Westphal and I viewed the situation with increasing anxiety.

The Second Battle of Sidi Rezegh

On 26 November the Tobruk garrison smashed through our lines of investment and got on top of the escarpment at Ed Duda; the previous night the New Zealanders had captured Belhamed after very savage fighting. This enabled the enemy to form a corridor between the New Zealanders and Tobruk

---

[5] On 23 November the Italian Armored Corps was put under Panzergruppe command as a result of a direct appeal from Rommel to Mussolini.

[6] Rommel had only a very small staff with him, and his signal communications were quite inadequate. Moreover, main headquarters of Afrika Korps had been captured on 23 November.

and he proceeded to consolidate his positions at Belhamed and Ed Duda with artillery and heavy tanks.

In this crisis Westphal—unable to contact Rommel or Afrika Korps headquarters—took the responsibility of sending a signal direct to 21st Panzer; he cancelled all pursuit orders and ordered the division to move towards Tobruk with a view to attacking the rear of the New Zealanders. Twenty-first Panzer passed north of the Sollum minefields and on the evening of 26 November attacked and overran positions of the 5th N.Z. Brigade near Fort Capuzzo, where contact was made with 15th Panzer. This division had concentrated towards Bardia in order to replenish fuel and ammunition.

In spite of the very critical situation around Tobruk, Rommel persisted in his operations on the Sollum front. On 27 November he did order 21st Panzer to move towards Tobruk, but 15th Panzer was told to advance south from Bardia and destroy the enemy forces on the line Sidi Omar–Capuzzo. Early on the morning of the 27th, Panzer Regiment 8 surprised the headquarters of the 5th N.Z. Brigade at Sidi Azeiz; the brigade commander, eight hundred prisoners, six guns, and a great quantity of baggage were captured by 15th Panzer. Satisfied with this notable success, Rommel decided to leave the Sollum front and ordered 15th Panzer to press westwards towards Tobruk.

Thus on 27 November Rommel renewed the Battle of Sidi Rezegh, but under conditions which were far less propitious than three days before. The New Zealanders had made a firm junction with the Tobruk garrison, and our forces in that quarter were gravely weakened. The Afrika Korps had accomplished nothing decisive on the frontier and was only a fraction of the magnificent force which had entered the battle on the 18th. The British armor had been given a respite; many tanks had been salvaged, large tank reserves had been sent up from Egypt, and the 4th and 22nd Armored Brigades were again formidable fighting formations. The Royal Air Force dominated the battlefield, and our unprotected columns were repeatedly hit.

On the afternoon of 27 November 15th Panzer won an important victory over the 4th and 22nd Armored Brigades in the area of Bir el Chleta.[7] Twenty-first Panzer had been held up on the Via Balbia, but now swung south to join 15th Panzer on the Trigh Capuzzo. Although our panzer divisions were much weakened, they were concentrated, while the British forces were widely scattered and poorly co-ordinated.

On the evening of 27 November Rommel reached Gambut and succeeded in making direct wireless contact with our headquarters at El Adem. Westphal explained that the Tobruk front was on the verge of collapse and that he had had great difficulty in preventing the Italian commanders from ordering a general withdrawal.[8] The commander in chief was now fully enlightened about the dangers of his situation, but with characteristic pugnacity he sought to turn defeat into victory, and made preparations to attack and destroy the 2nd N.Z. Division. On the morning of the 28th he flew to El Adem where he was in a better position to co-ordinate the battle as a whole. His arrival was a tremendous relief to us, and particularly to Westphal, who as a lieutenant colonel had had to handle senior Italian corps commanders.

There was no heavy fighting on 28 November. Fifteenth Panzer, advancing from the east, fought its way to the Sidi Rezegh escarpment and repulsed British armor pressing up to Sidi Rezegh from the south. On the evening of 28 November General Cruewell ordered the Afrika Korps to attack next day and drive the New Zealanders into Tobruk. Twenty-first Panzer was to attack through Zaafran towards Belhamed, 15th Panzer through Sidi Rezegh towards Ed Duda, while Ariete was to cover the southern flank. These intentions were reported to us by wireless.

Rommel was opposed to Cruewell's plan and wanted the Afrika Korps to cut the New Zealanders off from Tobruk, and not to drive them into the Fortress. Accordingly at midday on the 29th Cruewell ordered 15th Panzer to make a de-

---

[7] *Editor's note.* Tactically the fighting was in favor of the British, but at nightfall the two armored brigades withdrew south to leaguer, and so gave the Germans free passage along the Trigh Capuzzo.

[8] It should be noted that the Italian troops in the Tobruk area, and particularly Trieste Division, fought extremely well during this period.

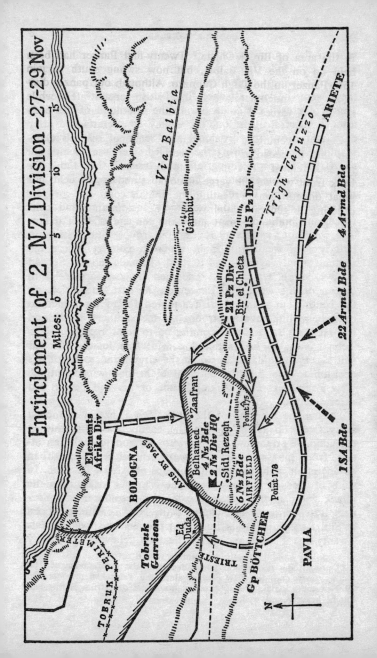

Encirclement of 2 NZ Division — 27-29 Nov

Miles: 0 5 10 15

Via Balbia

Elements Afrika Div

BOLOGNA

AXIS BY-PASS

Tobruk Garrison

TOBRUK PERIMETER

Ed Duda

TRIESTE

GP BÖTTCHER

PAVIA

Belhamed
Zaafran
4 NZ Bde
2 NZ Div HQ
Sidi Rezegh
6 NZ Bde
AIRFIELD
Point 178

Point 175

Bir el Chleta

21 Pz Div

15 Pz Div

Gambut

Trigh Capuzzo

ARIETE

4 Armd Bde

22 Armd Bde

1 SA Bde

N

tour to the southwest of Sidi Rezegh and then advance to
attack Ed Duda from the southwest. Twenty-first Panzer
and Ariete were unable to play the role assigned to them, for
they were heavily attacked by British armor.[9] Fifteenth
Panzer captured Ed Duda during the afternoon of the 29th
after a bitter struggle, but the enemy counterattacked after
dark and drove the divisional rifle regiment off this commanding position. During the day Rommel went personally
to Afrika Korps headquarters and insisted that the New
Zealand Division should be destroyed in the open field and
not be driven into Tobruk.

The situation was now extremely complicated and confused, and both sides were almost at the end of their tether.
The conditions were very severe; the troops were fighting in
bitterly cold weather, and in waterless country where the
normal supply system had virtually broken down. Second
N.Z. Division was almost encircled by our armor—15th
Panzer on the west, 21st Panzer on the east, and Ariete on
the south—but strong British armored forces threatened to
overwhelm our covering troops on the southern flank, and
the 1st S.A. Brigade was coming up to reinforce them. The
Tobruk garrison had suffered considerable losses, but was
still a very formidable force. In the circumstances Rommel's
decision to continue the battle until he had wiped out the
New Zealanders is a striking proof of his will power and
determination.

During the morning of the 30th 15th Panzer was moved
away from Ed Duda—where the enemy was obviously in
considerable strength—and got into position to make an attack from the south on the escarpment at Sidi Rezegh, in
co-operation with mixed battle groups of Afrika Division. In
spite of pleas for a postponement Rommel insisted on the
attack going in that afternoon, and his resolution was justified. By evening we had captured the New Zealand positions
at Sidi Rezegh, with six hundred prisoners and twelve guns.
Twenty-first Panzer and Ariete beat off relieving attacks by

---

[9] During the day General von Ravenstein, the commander of 21st
Panzer, drove into the New Zealand lines and was taken prisoner. On
29 November Ariete was put under command of Afrika Korps and
fought bravely and well.

the British armor from the south and southeast, and that night the 1st S.A. Brigade made a tentative attack near Pt. 175 which was easily repulsed.[10]

Our success on 30 November made the position of the New Zealanders untenable, and on 1 December General Freyberg, their indomitable commander, gave orders for a break-out to the southeast. Assisted by the 4th Armored Brigade, he managed to extricate part of his division, although during the day we captured another thousand prisoners and twenty-six guns. Seventh Armored Division, the 2nd N.Z. Division, and the 1st S.A. Brigade now broke away from the Sidi Rezegh area and moved south to regroup. Tobruk was again isolated, and on paper we seemed to have won the *Crusader* battle. But the price paid was too heavy; the Panzergruppe had been worn down, and it soon became clear that only one course remained—a general retreat from Cyrenaica.

The Withdrawal from Cyrenaica

It was characteristic of Rommel that he was reluctant to accept the hard facts of the situation. Indeed on 3 and 4 December he ordered detachments of the Afrika Korps to advance on Bardia; his aim was to bring supplies to that fortress, and he still hoped to drive the enemy forces on the Sollum front into the minefields. But the bulk of the Afrika Korps had to remain in the Sidi Rezegh area to reorganize, and in consequence the detachments were too weak to relieve Bardia and had to return. On the morning of 4 December 21st Panzer tried to capture Ed Duda, where the Tobruk garrison was strongly entrenched. This attack broke down.

On 4 December we received reports of the concentration of the 4th Indian Division at Bir el Gubi—the 2nd S.A. Division relieved them on the Sollum front—and strong enemy columns were reported in the area of Bir Hacheim and

---

[10] *Editor's note.* Brigadier "Dan" Pienaar, the South African commander, was understandably cautious after the experience of the 5th S.A. Brigade at Sidi Rezegh. Moreover, the brigades of the 7th Armored Division were handled with similar caution.

El Adem. Indeed that day our own headquarters at El Adem was harassed by armored cars and artillery advancing from the south. The supply position was causing grave anxiety, and we were at a hopeless disadvantage in the air. Accordingly Rommel decided on 4 December that the investment of Tobruk could not be maintained, and that we must fall back to a new line running southwest of the Fortress.

It was no easy matter to extricate our troops and material on the eastern sector of Tobruk, and to cover the withdrawal the Afrika Korps advanced towards Bir el Gubi on 5 December. In confused fighting between 5 and 7 December the Afrika Korps held its ground against very superior British forces—principally the 7th Armored Division and the 4th Indian Division—and gained time for a further retirement to a line running south of Gazala.[11] On the night 7/8 December the Afrika Korps broke away from the enemy and fell back to cover the southern flank of the Gazala position. On 9 December Afrika Division[12] was sent off to Agedabia, one hundred miles south of Benghazi, in order to protect that area against the 29th Indian Brigade, which had captured Jalo and was threatening to cut our line of communication with Tripoli. At this stage Rommel still hoped to hold Eighth Army on the Gazala Line.

The battle of Gazala began on 11 December and continued until the 15th. Although the British attacks were repulsed, it became clear that the fighting power of the Italians had decreased to an alarming degree; we were in danger of exhausting our last stocks of ammunition, and were in no condition to meet a strong armored thrust around the southern flank. On 15 December Rommel held a conference with Field Marshal Kesselring, whom Hitler had recently appointed as Commander in Chief South,[13] General Cavallero, the Italian chief of staff, and General Bastico, the commander in chief in North Africa.

The discussions were exceedingly lively. Rommel pointed out his difficulties and losses, and said that he must with-

---

[11] This line had been fortified by the Italians earlier in the year.
[12] Renamed the 90th Light Division on 15 December.
[13] Kesselring had no operational authority over Rommel, but was responsible for his supplies and air support.

draw from Cyrenaica and reorganize his army in the Mersa Brega bottleneck. To the Italian generals this announcement came like a bolt from the blue, and even Kesselring was taken aback. Bastico broke out in angry criticism, and formally forbade any further retreat. Finally Rommel got his way, but not before the two generals had indulged in much undignified recrimination.

The withdrawal was carried out with great skill, under cover of strong rearguards. The Royal Air Force was our principal enemy, for the Eighth Army had been fought to a standstill. Rommel's main anxiety was that the enemy would make a strong armored thrust across the desert and get astride our line of retreat; however, this threat did not develop. The arrival of 15th Panzer south of Benghazi on the evening of 20 December was a great relief to Rommel and orders were now given to concentrate on the Agedabia position. Very fortunately a tank transport got into Benghazi on 17 December, and brought up the strength of 15th Panzer to forty tanks.

On 23 December leading elements of the 7th Armored Division tried to cut the Via Balbia between Benghazi and Agedabia. The British had split up their armor in various columns, separated by wide intervals, and 15th Panzer was able to beat them in detail. On 24 December we evacuated Benghazi.

On 26 December the British advanced against our positions at Agedabia. The Afrika Korps now had seventy tanks and the enemy's initial attacks were easily held. British armored forces tried to envelop the Agedabia positions by an attack from the southeast, but Afrika Korps made a most effective counterattack on 28 December, destroyed a large number of tanks, and drove the British in confusion from the battlefield. Our supply position was now much easier, and we were receiving increased air support. Seventh Armored Division was in poor shape; it had lost most of its experienced tank crews and was in great need of rest and reorganization. In fact Rommel did not have to withdraw from Agedabia to Mersa Brega; nevertheless he did so on the night 5/6 January. Events were to show that this was a wise decision.

Rommel's Counterattack

On 11 January 1942 the Panzergruppe concentrated in the Mersa Brega position; in spite of the heavy losses of the past seven weeks Rommel's strategic position was not unfavorable.[14] Luftflotte 2 had been transferred from the Russian front to Sicily and Italy, and was able to challenge British air superiority and give a large measure of close support. The supply position had greatly improved; on 18 December and 5 January two convoys crossed to Africa under the escort of Italian battleships and brought considerable stocks of fuel and ammunition—moreover the arrival of four panzer companies greatly increased the hitting power of the Afrika Korps. Kesselring subjected Malta to a terrific battering from the air, and the effect was shown by a sharp fall in the total of sinkings on the sea lanes to Tripoli.

In contrast the Eighth Army was now stretched out on a long line of communications and was still engaged in subduing our positions on the frontier. Bardia did not fall until 2 January, and Halfaya held out nearly a fortnight longer. These operations absorbed the 2nd S.A. Division, as well as British medium artillery and heavy tank units, and the delay in opening Halfaya Pass imposed an additional strain on the British supply system.

On 12 January a discussion took place at Panzergruppe headquarters, and I was asked for a detailed appreciation. Thanks to the excellent work of our Wireless Intercept Company I was able to give a fairly clear pciture of the British situation and dispositions, and to draw attention to the opportunity of delivering an effective counterstroke. The tough and experienced 7th Armored Division had been so mauled in the preceding weeks that it had been withdrawn into the area south of Tobruk, and in its place near Agedabia stood the 1st Armored Division, which was entirely new to desert conditions, and had only recently come out from England. It appeared that the 4th Indian

---

[14] *Editor's note.* This was accounted for in part by the loss to the British of "Force K" in mid-December. See Churchill, *The Grand Alliance,* 512.

Division was still in the Benghazi area with some elements advanced as far as Agedabia.[15] Information on the 1st S.A. Division, the 2nd N.Z. Division, and the 70th British Division was far from clear, but they were certainly not in the forward area.

My calculations showed that the Panzergruppe would enjoy a certain superiority in western Cyrenaica until 25 January; thereafter the balance would be restored and swing in favor of the British.[16] The Mersa Brega position had some serious defects as Rommel himself had noted when flying over the front, and on the whole it seemed dangerous to remain on the defensive and allow the enemy to gather strength. Certainly the Italian divisions could not stand up to the strain of another heavy defensive battle.

Rommel was fully sensible of these arguments; however, he was somewhat doubtful whether our transport was adequate for an offensive. When satisfied on this point he threw all his energy into the preparations, but insisted that the attack would not succeed unless it came as a complete surprise to the enemy. He decided not to report his intentions to the Italian Comando Superiore in North Africa, nor did he inform the German High Command. The regrouping of our forces was carried out in short night marches; all reconnaissance—particularly by tanks—was forbidden and tanks behind the front were camouflaged as lorries. Movements of motor vehicles towards the front were forbidden in daylight.[17] The commander of the Afrika Korps was not informed of the plan until 16 January, and his divisional commanders were given their tasks verbally on the 19th. Zero hour was to be 1830 on the 21st.

On the night of 20/21 January the village of Mersa Bre-

---

[15] Actually the 201st Guards Brigade was near Agedabia, in advance of the 4th Indian Division. We now know from Auchinleck's *Dispatch* (p. 349) that the 4th Indian Division was unable to move up from Benghazi owing to supply difficulties.

[16] 117 German and 79 Italian tanks were available for the counterattack. According to Auchinleck's *Dispatch* (p. 351) the 1st Armored Division had 150 tanks.

[17] The German Army has always excelled in security preparations of this kind; for example the success of our great attacks on the Western Front between March and May, 1918, was due to similar measures.

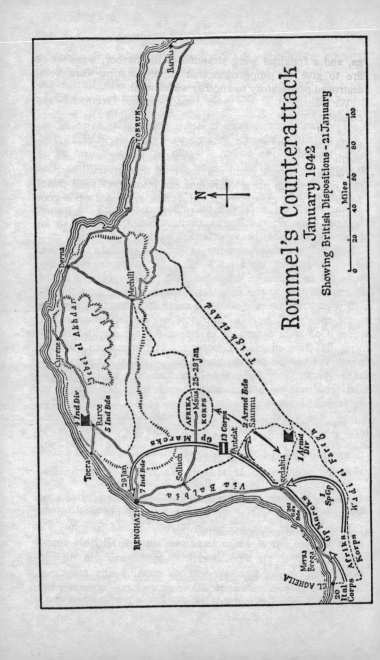

Rommel's Counterattack
January 1942

Showing British Dispositions – 21 January

ga, and a freighter lying stranded in the harbor, were set on fire to give the impression that supply dumps were being destroyed preparatory to another withdrawal.

We advanced in two main assault groups. Group Marcks, consisting of mobile elements of the 90th Light Division and some tanks of 21st Panzer, moved along the Via Balbia, while the Afrika Korps advanced through the desert to the north of the Wadi el Faregh. At first all went well and the Afrika Korps made rapid progress over firm ground, but later that morning the panzer divisions ran into heavy sand dunes, which not only caused great delays but also used up a good deal of gasoline. However, the leading tanks captured some British guns and many motor vehicles, which had got bogged down in the sand while trying to escape our advance. On the northern flank Group Marcks drove back weak enemy covering forces but was delayed by swamps on both sides of the road.

On the evening of 21 January air reconnaissance and wireless intercept indicated that the British were withdrawing in a northeasterly direction and that the bulk of 1st Armored Division was concentrating east and southeast of Agedabia. The enemy had been taken completely by surprise; on the other hand our panzer regiments were immobilized for lack of gasoline. Rommel decided to place himself at the head of Group Marcks and advance with every available man towards Agedabia; at all costs the enemy must be given no chance to pull himself together, even if this meant leaving most of our tanks behind. These operations show Rommel at his best—swift, audacious, and flexible in his plans.

Driving along the Via Balbia against weak resistance, Group Marcks entered Agedabia at 1100 hours on the 22nd. Rommel himself was at the head of the column and ordered the advance to continue towards Antelat and Saunnu. The spearhead of Group Marcks drove through British supply columns and threw them into wild confusion, and we captured many motor vehicles without meeting any resistance. Antelat was reached at 1530, and without stopping the column swept on to Saunnu regardless of the coming night.

At 1930 Saunnu fell after a short struggle, and Group
Marcks camped as best it could, surrounded by the enemy,
and very uncertain of its situation. The spearhead of 15th
Panzer reached Antelat after dark; both panzer divisions
attempted to close up but were delayed by traffic jams.

During the night 22/23 January Rommel issued orders
which he hoped would enable us to surround the 1st Armored Division, which appeared to be cut off to the east
of Agedabia. The Italian Armored Corps was to hold the
Agedabia area, the Afrika Korps was to try and establish
a cordon along the line Agedabia–Antelat–Saunnu, and
Group Marcks was to move southeast of Saunnu, and endeav-
or to close the ring on the eastern flank.

It was an ambitious plan, and was only partially successful. Owing to a serious lapse in staff work at Afrika Korps
headquarters, Saunnu was not occupied by 21st Panzer after
the departure of Group Marcks, and the enemy took advantage of this gap to extricate the bulk of the 1st Armored
Division. We did succeed in knocking out a considerable
number of tanks and guns, but the operations proved yet
again how difficult it is to encircle armored formations in
the desert by establishing a cordon. Unfortunately it was
not realized on the 24th that the bulk of the enemy had
escaped and much time was wasted in sweeping an enemy
battlefield.

On the evening of 24 January Rommel decided to advance
to Msus on the 25th and complete the destruction of the
1st Armored Division. On the right flank 21st Panzer met
little opposition, but six miles northwest of Saunnu 15th
Panzer ran into very superior tank forces. These were overwhelmed by Panzer Regiment 8, closely supported by antitank guns and artillery; it soon became apparent that the
British tank units had no battle experience and they were
completely demoralized by the onslaught of 15th Panzer. At
times the pursuit attained a speed of fifteen miles an hour,
and the British columns fled madly over the desert in one of
the most extraordinary routs of the war. After covering
fifty miles in under four hours 15th Panzer reached Msus
airfield at 1100, overwhelming numerous supply columns,

and capturing twelve aircraft ready to take off. Further exploitation was impossible as the division was out of fuel, but 96 tanks, 38 guns, and 190 lorries were the booty of the day.

These operations decided the campaign in western Cyrenaica, and Rommel was tempted to exploit his success by advancing to Mechili and thus cutting off the units of the 4th Indian Division in the Benghazi area and farther north. A move across the open desert, south of the "Green Mountain" of the Jebel el Akhdar, had proved most fruitful in 1941 and after their crushing defeat the enemy's armored forces hardly seemed in a position to hold such an advance. Rommel simply did not have the gasoline for a massive thrust towards Mechili, and very reluctantly he gave up the idea. Meanwhile Cavallero, the Italian chief of staff, had arrived in Africa, and attempted to forbid any further advance; he even refused Rommel the right to dispose of the Italian 10th and 21st Corps, and ordered them to remain at Mersa Brega.

Rommel insisted on pushing on to Benghazi. He ordered the Afrika Korps to feint in the direction of Mechili—a move which completely misled Ritchie, who concentrated his armor to meet it. Then taking personal command of Group Marcks, Rommel executed a brilliant march through pouring rain and over very difficult ground to attack Benghazi from the east. Once again the British were surprised and on 29 January Rommel entered the town, after capturing a thousand prisoners from the 4th Indian Division.[18] This success brought Rommel promotion to colonel general. Ironically enough, Mussolini's signal authorizing an advance to Benghazi reached Rommel when he was entering the place.

General Ritchie, the commander of Eighth Army, was

---

[18] *Editor's note.* Seventh Indian Brigade was nearly trapped in Benghazi, but under the determined leadership of Brigadier Briggs broke out to the southeast. Auchinleck and Ritchie had insisted on holding Benghazi, despite the strong objections of General Godwin-Austen, commanding the 13th Corps, and General Tuker, commanding the 4th Indian Division. See Compton Mackenzie, *Eastern Epic* (London, Chatto & Windus, 1951), I, 294.

now very glad to withdraw his forces to Gazala and give up the whole of the Cyrenaican bulge. The Panzerarmee was too weak to do more than follow up, and on 6 February our advance came to a halt before the Gazala position.

7: *The Gazala Battles*

The Preliminaries

IN MARCH, 1942, Rommel flew to Hitler's headquarters to discuss future operations in the African theater. On the whole the visit gave him little cause for satisfaction; the High Command was engrossed in preparations for the summer offensive in Russia, and the conquest of Egypt had only a small place in their calculations. In particular Halder, the chief of the Army General Staff, adopted a disapproving attitude towards Rommel's proposals. Hitler was friendly, but made it clear that no major reinforcements would be available for Libya.

Nevertheless the German Supreme Command now understood that something would have to be done about Malta. Grand Admiral Raeder had always appreciated its significance and he now persuaded Hitler to co-operate with the Italians in taking the island. General Cavallero had been pressing strongly for a combined Italo-German attack, and Hitler agreed to let him have a German parachute division. The landing, known as Operation *Hercules,* was to take place during the full-moon period in June, and as a preliminary Field Marshal Kesselring was ordered to soften up Malta by continuous air attacks. More than two thousand tons of bombs were dropped on Malta in March, and nearly seven thousand in April—these terrific attacks compelled the British to withdraw their submarine flotilla, and also

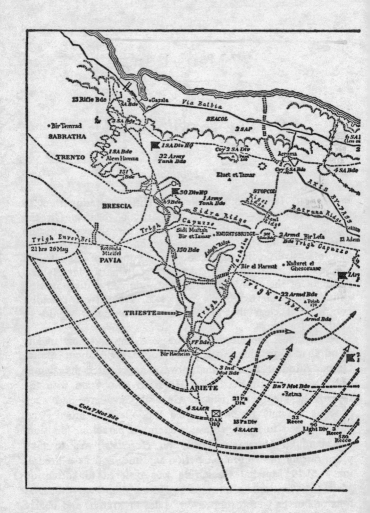

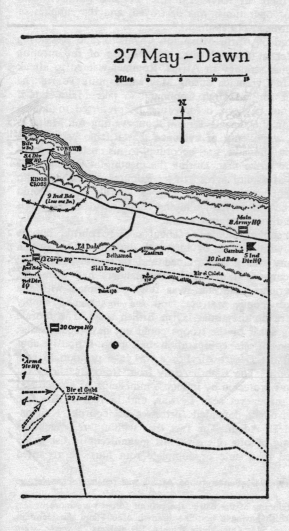

27 May – Dawn

Miles 0 5 10 15

N

eliminated their air force. For the moment Malta's value, as a base of operations, was destroyed, and the supplies of the Panzerarmee were assured.[1]

At the end of April, Mussolini, Cavallero, and Kesselring visited Hitler at Obersalzberg; the purpose of the meeting was to discuss strategy in Africa. Rommel wanted to attack the British in Cyrenaica during May and capture Tobruk; he was anxious for the High Command to take Malta, but if this could not be done before June he preferred to launch his attack on the Gazala Line without waiting for Malta to fall. There was plenty of evidence that Ritchie was getting ready for an offensive, and according to his custom Rommel was eager to strike first. During the meeting at Obersalzberg Hitler and Mussolini agreed to let Rommel attack, but with the important proviso that as soon as Tobruk fell he should stand on the defensive, while the main effort of the Axis forces were directed against Malta.

Rommel spoke confidently about taking Tobruk, but he was faced with a task of immense difficulty. The British Eighth Army was a well-trained and thoroughly organized force; its corps and divisional commanders had plenty of desert experience; the staff was fully acquainted with the problems of mobile warfare, and the signals and supply services were on the usual lavish British scale. The morale and fighting spirit of the troops could not have been better; the question of air co-operation had been seriously considered and the Desert Air Force was in a position to give strong support.[2] The Eighth Army front from Gazala to Bir Hacheim was protected by immense minefields, of a scale and complexity never yet seen in war, and in rear of the line were the strongly defended fortresses of Tobruk, Knightsbridge, and El Adem. The fact that within three weeks of the launching of our offensive this magnificent British army was reduced to a state of complete rout must be regarded

[1] In January, 1942, Panzergruppe Afrika was renamed Panzerarmee Afrika.

[2] At the beginning of the battle, the two air forces were more or less equal, the British having a first-line strength of 604 and the Germans and Italians of 542. Our Messerschmitt 109 fighters, however, were superior to the Hurricanes and Kittyhawks of the Desert Air Force.

as one of the greatest achievements in German military annals.

The British defeats cannot be ascribed to any inferiority in numbers or equipment. The British infantry divisions were much stronger and better equipped than their counterparts in the Italian 10th and 21st Corps, and although less mobile than our 90th Light were far superior in numbers and hitting power. Auchinleck admits that the British had a great superiority in field artillery and says "Numerically the Eighth Army undoubtedly had a considerable superiority" in tanks, and a "much larger reserve of tanks to draw on than the enemy." To oppose the 333 German and 228 Italian tanks, the British armor had a first-line strength of 700 tanks, while their superiority in armored cars was about ten to one.

Moreover the Eighth Army now had about 200 American Grant tanks, mounting a 75-mm gun. These outclassed the 220 Mark III's which made up the bulk of our armored strength, and the only tanks we had to compete with them were 19 Mark III Specials with high-velocity 50-mm guns.[3] Even in antitank artillery the British position was much improved with the arrival of the 6-pounder, a weapon superior to our 50-mm, although somewhat inferior to the Russian 76-mm which Rommel was now receiving. In this arm, however, the balance was tilted heavily in our favor by the 88-mm, and by the reluctance of the British to use their 3.7-in A.A. gun in a similar role.

Perhaps, fortunately, we underestimated the British strength, for had we known the full facts even Rommel might have balked at an attack on such a greatly superior enemy.[4] Owing to the excellent wireless security of the British, and their great superiority in armored cars, it was

[3] The Panzerarmee also had four Mark IV Specials but these had no ammunition at the beginning of the battle. From June onwards this excellent tank began to arrive in increasing numbers. The British tank expert, Colonel R. M. P. Carver, has said of the Gazala battle. "The idea that we were out-gunned and out-armoured in this battle cannot hold water." (*Royal Armoured Corps Journal*, April, 1951.)

[4] Contrary to a statement in Rommel's *Krieg ohne Hass* (p. 130), we did know that the British were receiving Grant tanks, about which our Intelligence appreciation of 20 May included a full description.

very difficult for us to assess their numbers and dispositions. We did not know that the 22nd Armored Brigade and the 32nd Army Tank Brigade were close behind the Gazala Line, nor were we aware of the existence of the Knightsbridge Box held by the 201st Guards Brigade. Twenty-ninth Indian Brigade at Bir el Gubi and the 3rd Indian Motor Brigade southeast of Bir Hacheim had also escaped our attention, and it was not realized that the main Gazala minebelt had been extended from the Trigh el Abd as far south as Bir Hacheim. Our lack of information is a tribute to the security and camouflage of Eighth Army.

Only in very rare cases can an army obtain a complete picture of the enemy's situation before an attack is launched, even when reconnaissance has been detailed and thorough. Wireless silence, misleading information from agents, standing patrols, and defensive screens by land and air, make reconnaissance difficult. Therefore offensive plans must be flexible, and once the attack has begun commanders and troops must be ready to adapt themselves to rapidly changing situations. In principle, estimates of enemy dispositions only hold good until the first clash—as the great Moltke said, "No plan survives contact with the enemy."

Rommel decided on a bold and relatively simple plan. The German 15th Rifle Brigade,[5] and the Italian 10th and 21st Corps, were to advance directly against the Gazala Line and assault the front by the 1st S.A. and the 50th British Divisions. The Axis formations on this front were to be commanded by General Cruewell, and were to be known as "Group Cruewell"; I was appointed as Ia to the group. The main striking force was to be led by Rommel in person, and consisted of Afrika Korps (now commanded by General Walter Nehring), the Italian 20th Corps (Ariete Armored Division and Trieste Motorized Division), and the 90th Light Division; the striking force was to make a rapid night march, advance round the Gazala Line to the Acroma area, and then attack the British forces from the rear. Ninetieth Light and the reconnaissance units were to advance to El Adem and cause disruption on the British supply routes.

[5] Two regimental groups of the 90th Light Division.

At first Rommel thought it would be possible to capture Bir Hacheim during the initial advance, and the thrustline of the Afrika Korps was drawn to pass through the place. In the final version of the plan, known to us as *Case Venezia*, the Afrika Korps and 90th Light were directed well south of Bir Hacheim, but Ariete on the northern flank was to move close to the strongpoint and make an attempt to capture it. Events were to show that our attitude towards Bir Hacheim was far too casual, and that the capture of the place was a *sine qua non* for any successful operation behind the Gazala Line. Once our main armored forces had gone round, Bir Hacheim was in a position to serve as a base for attacks on our supply convoys, and in fact it did so very effectively. In my opinion both 90th Light and the Italian Armored Corps should have attacked Bir Hacheim on the first day of the assault, with strong Luftwaffe support.

The question arises whether Rommel's plan was unsound or overdaring. It is arguable that he should have made an attack in the center of the Gazala Line, along the Trigh el Abd or Trigh Capuzzo. Such an attack, however, would have run into the 1st and 7th Armored Divisions, fighting under the protection of dense minefields and supported by artillery in well-defended boxes. I am rather surprised that such an eminent soldier as Field Marshal Auchinleck should have suggested to Ritchie (in a letter dated 20 May) that this was the most probable line of our advance, for in my opinion such an attack would have had no chance whatever. Rommel's only hope of victory lay in mobile warfare, where the excellent training of his troops and commanders might enable him to outmaneuver the British and concentrate superior forces against isolated detachments. It is certainly arguable, however, that Rommel should have limited his enveloping movement to gaining the line Naduret el Ghesceuasc–Bir el Harmat, instead of ordering his panzer divisions to reach the Acroma area on the first day. This overambitious objective caused our striking force to be split up over a wide area, and presented the British with excellent opportunities for a counterattack. It was a mistake to send 90th Light and our reconnaissance units as far away as El

Adem; it is true that they caused considerable confusion in the British rear areas but they were too weak to achieve decisive results, and dispersed our striking force.

The Eighth Army was divided into two corps—the 13th commanded by General Gott, and the 30th commanded by General Norrie. Thirteenth Corps controlled the 1st S.A. and the 50th British Divisions holding the northern sector of the Gazala Line, the 2nd S.A. Division and the 9th Indian Brigade in Tobruk, and the El Adem Box (held by a battalion of the 9th Indian Brigade). First and 32nd Army Tank Brigades were under command of this corps, and were in close support of the northern sector of the Gazala Line.

Thirtieth Corps commanded the 1st Armored Division (the 2nd and 22nd Armored Brigades and the 201st Guards Brigade), the 7th Armored Division (the 4th Armored Brigade and the 7th Motor Brigade), the 1st Free French Brigade holding Bir Hacheim, the 29th Indian Brigade holding Bir el Gubi, and the 3rd Indian Brigade, which came up just before the battle to establish a new box southeast of Bir Hacheim. Two hundred and first Guards Brigade was ordered to hold the Knightsbridge Box, and the 7th Motor Brigade, in addition to forming a reconnaissance screen to the west of Bir Hacheim, established a box at Retma.

First Armored Division was grouped astride the Trigh Cupuzzo, and the 7th Armored Division was farther south, ready to deal with a thrust round Bir Hacheim. These dispositions conformed to a sound principle of armored warfare, namely, never to put armored divisions under the command of infantry formations holding defensive positions but to leave them free for a concentrated counterattack. Unfortunately for the British, however, they had allowed the 201st Guards Brigade to get tied up in the defense of the Knightsbridge Box, and throughout the battle this brigade was unable to support the 1st Armored Division in the field and was tied down to a static role. Seventh Motor Brigade was certainly mobile, but its effectiveness was nullified by splitting up the brigade in independent columns which never co-operated with the divisional armor on the battlefield. A motor brigade is an integral part of an armored division and its existence is only justified if it works in close co-operation with the armored brigades.

Auchinleck's letter of 20 May indicated to Ritchie that our attack would probably be delivered along the Trigh Capuzzo; however, he did not discount the possibility of a turning movement round Bir Hacheim, and the letter contained some excellent advice. The commander in chief warned Ritchie to concentrate both armored divisions astride the Trigh Capuzzo, and said:

It does not look from the map as if this would be too far north to meet the main attack should it come round the southern flank. . . . I consider it to be of the highest importance that you should not break up the organization of either of the armoured divisions. They have been trained to fight as divisions, I hope, and fight as divisions they should. Norrie must handle them as a corps commander, and thus be able to take advantage of the flexibility which the fact of having two formations gives to him.[6]

There was much to be said for Auchinleck's proposal, for a concentration of the two British armored divisions between Knightsbridge and Bir el Harmat would have enabled the 30th Corps to deal very effectively with a thrust along the Trigh Capuzzo or a turning movement round Bir Hacheim. Alternatively, the 7th Armored Division might have been placed at Bir el Gubi ready to take the turning movement of the Afrika Korps in flank, while the 1st Armored Division fought a delaying action to the east of Bir el Harmat. The alternative solution looks attractive, but I am inclined to doubt whether the standard of training in the British armored divisions was adequate for such a maneuver. In the circumstances the Eighth Army would have done well to adopt the simple and thoroughly sound solution suggested by Auchinleck.

Ritchie, however, did not follow this advice, with the result that on 27 May his armored brigades were committed to battle one after the other, and neither corps nor divisional headquarters had any control over the fighting.

[6] Auchinleck, *Dispatch,* 391.

The Assault

During 26 May our armored forces moved to a concentration area east of Rotonda Segnali; morale was superb and even the dense dust storms raised by the khamsin were welcome, for they helped to conceal our movements. That afternoon Group Cruewell advanced against the Gazala Line, and opened a heavy bombardment of the South African and British positions—we wished to convey the impression that the great offensive was coming in that sector.

After dark Rommel put himself at the head of the Afrika Korps, and taking advantage of the bright moonlight the great march began. The move of this column of several thousand vehicles had been prepared in minute detail; compass bearings, distances, and speeds had been carefully calculated; dim lights concealed in gasoline tins indicated the line of march, and with the smoothness of a well-oiled machine the regiments of the Afrika Korps swept on to their refuelling-point southeast of Bir Hacheim. Rommel says in his memoirs that he was in a state of "high tension" when his vehicles took the road, and indeed the whole Afrika Korps was thirsting for battle and confident of victory.

At the time the Afrika Korps thought it had taken the British completely by surprise, for there was no sign of their reconnaissance troops. We know now, however, that the 4th S.A. Armored Car Regiment was keeping the move under close observation, and was signalling detailed reports to the 7th Motor Brigade and Headquarters 7th Armored Division. These reports seem to have had little effect, for when our panzers attacked at dawn they met no organized opposition.

On the left flank Ariete overwhelmed the 3rd Indian Motor Brigade, and on the right 90th Light and the reconnaissance units swept over the Retma Box, which was only partly manned by the 7th Motor Brigade. Fifteenth Panzer in the center caught the 4th Armored Brigade while still deploying for battle; the headquarters of the 7th Armored

Division was captured on the move[7] and the divisional supply echelons were overrun or dispersed. It is true that 15th Panzer suffered severe losses in the fighting with the 4th Armored Brigade and were glad when 21st Panzer came up on their left flank, but on the British side the 8th Hussars were destroyed as a fighting unit, and the 3rd Royal Tanks lost sixteen Grants. We had in fact inflicted a shattering defeat on the famous 7th Armored Division, which made off as best it could towards Bir el Gubi and El Adem. Ninetieth Light and the reconnaissance units followed in hot pursuit.

The British failure was due purely and simply to the inability of their command to concentrate and co-ordinate the armored and motorized brigades. But the 1st Armored Division did little better. At 0845, the 22nd Armored Brigade (then in position ten miles south of the Trigh Capuzzo) was ordered to move south—it would have been better if it had retired north to join the 2nd Armored Brigade on the Trigh Capuzzo. Twenty-second Armored Brigade was caught on the move by the Afrika Korps and was severely handled in a concentric attack by the 15th and 21st Panzer Divisions. The rearguard, however, inflicted heavy casualties on our panzers, and it became clear that the Grant tank was a far more formidable fighting vehicle than any the Afrika Korps had yet encountered.

At this stage Rommel thought that the battle was won; he congratulated Nehring and ordered him to press on, but in fact there were some unpleasant surprises in store. At noon the Afrika Korps was attacked by the 2nd Armored Brigade when trying to cross the Trigh Capuzzo east of Knightsbridge; 1st Army Tank Brigade entered the battle west of Knightsbridge and the assault of these two brigades, unco-ordinated though it was, disrupted the advance and brought Rommel close to defeat.

The Grants and Matildas charged home recklessly—our tanks took a severe hammering, one rifle battalion suffered such losses that it had to be disbanded, and the supply col-

---

[7] General Messervy, the divisional commander, was taken prisoner, but concealed his identity and escaped the next day. He had commanded the 1st Armored Division during the January disaster.

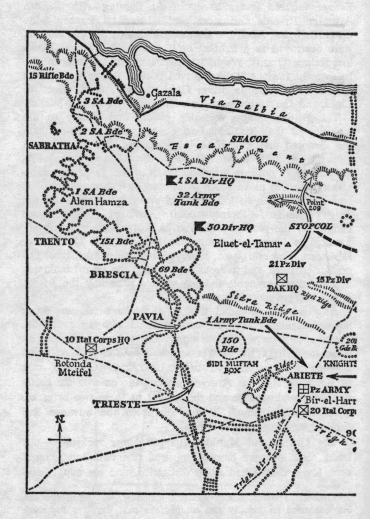

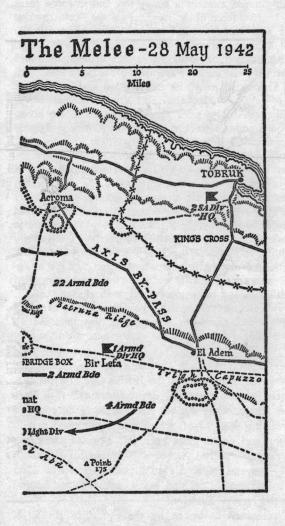

The Melee–28 May 1942

0   5   10   20   25
Miles

TOBRUK

Acroma

2 SA Div HQ

KINGS CROSS

AXIS BY-PASS

22 Armd Bde

Batruna Ridge

1 Armd Div HQ

El Adem

...de
...BRIDGE BOX   Bir Leta
2 Armd Bde

Trigh Capuzzo

nat
HQ   4 Armd Bde

) Light Div

...l Aba   ▲ Point 175

umns were cut off from the panzer divisions. It is true that
our antitank gunners exacted a heavy toll, but in some cases
the British tanks forced their way up to the very muzzles
of the guns and wiped out the crews. When night fell the
15th and 21st Panzer Divisions "hedgehogged" between Rigel
Ridge and Bir Lefa; their position was very critical, for more
than a third of the tanks were out of action, and 15th
Panzer had almost exhausted its ammunition and fuel. Ariete
had failed to take Bir Hacheim, and leaguered near Bir el
Harmat. Ninetieth Light, after reaching the El Adem crossroads, had been counterattacked by the 4th Armored Brigade
and was forced to "hedgehog" south of El Adem.

The supply route of the Panzerarmee was completely ex-
posed to British light forces based on Bir Hacheim and Bir el
Gubi, and in spite of the initial reverses of the day, Eighth
Army was in a position to win a crushing victory.

On 28 May Ritchie should have concentrated his armored
forces in order to destroy the Afrika Korps by a concentric
counterattack. Admittedly the British armor had lost heavily
in the fighting on the 27th, but the 32nd Army Tank
Brigade with 100 heavy infantry tanks had not been engaged—this was a situation in which a fresh and untouched
tank formation could have intervened with decisive effect.
The main thing, however, was to co-ordinate the armored
brigades and direct them on a common objective. At all
costs Ritchie should have kept his armor across our supply
routes.

The operations on the 28th furnish a striking example of
the breakdown of command on the British side. Twenty-second Armored Brigade spent the day "observing" 15th Panzer on Rigel Ridge, while the 4th Armored Brigade confined
itself to harassing 90th Light, which was well-provided with
antitank guns and could have been left alone. First Army
Tank Brigade and the 2nd Armored Brigade operated south
of Knightsbridge and inflicted casualties on Ariete; the 32nd
Army Tank Brigade did nothing at all and remained behind
the front of the 1st S.A. Division.

Rommel remained unshaken by the events of the 27th,
and on the 28th he ordered the Afrika Korps to resume the

northward advance. Fifteenth Panzer had no gasoline and could not move, but 21st Panzer routed a British column north of Rigel Ridge and reached the escarpment overlooking the Via Balbia. Rommel himself was not with the Afrika Korps during the day; his headquarters were at Bir el Harmat and British tanks blocked the way when he tried to get through to Rigel Ridge. During his absence Panzerarmee headquarters was dispersed by British armor, and the supply columns tried in vain to find a safe route across the Trigh Capuzzo.

During this phase I was at Cruewell's headquarters west of Gazala; we received an urgent appeal from Panzerarmee to breach the Gazala Line and join hands with the Italian 20th Corps near Bir el Harmat. The warm reception which our probing attacks had met with on 27 and 28 May did not promise success; nevertheless Cruewell ordered a large-scale attack by the Sabratha Division against the South African front on the 29th. The Italians moved up during the night and at dawn delivered a determined attack on the South African positions near Alam Hamza. They were received by a terrific fire, the minefields could not be pierced, and four hundred men were cut off by the South African barrage and taken prisoner.

On the morning of the 29th the position of the Afrika Korps was becoming desperate, but the situation was saved by Rommel's personal leadership. Taking command of the supply columns he led them through a gap he had observed the previous evening and brought them safely to 15th Panzer at Rigel Ridge. Rommel now set up his battle headquarters with the Afrika Korps, and struck fiercely at the 2nd Armored Brigade which was moving west from Knightsbridge and trying to drive a wedge between Ariete to the South of the Trigh Capuzzo and the two panzer divisions to the north.

The battle which followed was one of the most critical of the campaign; a British account describes it as "probably the stiffest day's fighting of all," and goes on to say, "the Grants were shooting magnificently and time after time

brought the squat black Mark III's and IV's to a standstill."[8]
Twenty-second Armored Brigade came up to assist the
2nd Armored Brigade, but very fortunately for us the
4th Armored Brigade remained in Corps reserve near El
Adem until the late afternoon, when it moved towards Bir
el Harmat to skirmish with 90th Light. A hot wind and
whirling sandstorms added to the strain on the tank crews,
and by evening both sides were glad to call off the battle.
In spite of considerable casualties in the panzer divisions,
the day ended in our favor, for 90th Light, Ariete, and the
Afrika Korps were now in close contact. The British armor had suffered heavily—once again their command failed
to co-ordinate the tank brigades.

But the supply factor continued to dominate the situation. Although Rommel had led convoys through to the
Afrika Korps on the morning of the 29th, it had become
clear that the supply route round Bir Hacheim was far too
long and precarious. On the evening of 29 May the Afrika
Korps was almost out of ammunition and many vehicles
had empty gasoline tanks; it was impossible to continue
the original plan of attacking the Gazala Line from the rear.
Rommel decided to retire towards Sidi Muftah, clear a gap
in the British minefields, and re-open direct communication
with Group Cruewell and the main line of supply. This did
not mean that Rommel regarded the battle as lost. On the
contrary, his stubborn and courageous personality was at its
best in such a situation. He was prepared to make a limited
withdrawal, but once his supplies were assured Rommel intended to sally forth again and seek a decisive victory over
the Eighth Army.

The "Cauldron"

On 29 May General Cruewell was shot down while flying
over the Gazala positions to visit the Italian 10th Corps; his
capture by the British left me in temporary control of
group headquarters. Very fortunately Field Marshal Kessel-

---

[8] Joan Bright, *Ninth Queen's Royal Lancers, 1936–1945: The Story
of an Armoured Regiment in Battle* (Aldershot, Gale & Polden, 1951),
73.

ring arrived—he wanted to know how the battle was going
—and I asked him to take command of the group until
Rommel could make other arrangements. Kesselring was
amused, and remarked that as a field marshal he could
hardly take orders from Colonel General Rommel. But I
pointed out that it would not suit us to have an Italian general
in command of Group Cruewell at such a critical juncture,
and Kesselring agreed to take the command for a few
days.[9] It was one of the few occasions in the war when I
was brought into close contact with this great German
soldier, whose conduct of the Italian campaign will always be regarded as a masterpiece of defensive strategy.

Although Group Cruewell's attacks on the South African
front had been foiled, the Italian 10th Corps succeeded in
opening gaps through the minefields in the area of the Trigh
Capuzzo. The British 50th Division was stretched out on too
wide a front, and there was a fifteen-mile gap between the
150th Brigade at Sidi Muftah and the Free French at Bir
Hacheim; thus many sectors of the British "mine marshes"
were uncovered by fire. In designing the Gazala Line the
British Command had neglected the elementary tactical
principle that "a minefield by itself means nothing; it is the
fire that covers a minefield which counts." The gaps made
by the Italians were to be of great value to Rommel when
he withdrew to the Sidi Muftah area on 30 May.

On the afternoon of 30 May, Rommel himself drove
through the minefield to confer with Kesselring and Hitler's
personal adjutant, Major von Below. The situation of the
Panzerarmee was still very critical, for the 150th Brigade
was strongly entrenched at Sidi Muftah, and was keeping
the minefield gaps under continuous artillery fire. Rommel
believed that the British would at once launch a full-scale
armored attack, and in view of the grave shortage of ammunition in the Afrika Korps we would have been hard put
to repulse it. On the morning of the 30th, General Lumsden,
the commander of the 1st Armored Division, did order an
attack by the 2nd and 22nd Armored Brigades, but after
suffering casualties from 88-mm and antitank guns, the Brit-

[9] Albert Kesselring, *Soldat Bis Zum Letzten Tag* (Bonn, Athenäum-
Verlag, 1953), 171.

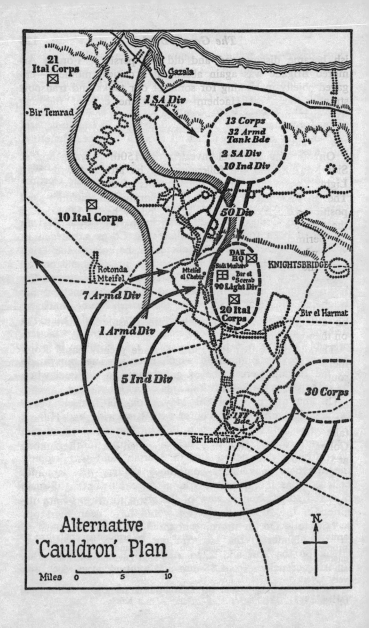

21 Ital Corps

Gazala

1 SA Div

•Bir Temrad

13 Corps
32 Armd Tank Bde
2 SA Div
10 Ind Div

10 Ital Corps

50 Div

Rotonda
Mteifel

DAK
HQ
Sidi Muftah

Mteifel
el Chebir

Bir el
Scerab
90 Light Div

KNIGHTSBRIDGE

7 Armd Div

Bir el Harmat

1 Armd Div

20 Ital Corps

5 Ind Div

30 Corps

1 FF
Bde

Bir Hacheim

Alternative
'Cauldron' Plan

Miles 0   5   10

N

ish became discouraged and did not persist.[10] Fourth Armored Brigade was again absent at a critical moment—engaged chiefly in looking for some of our tanks and transport stranded near Bir Hacheim—and at the end of the day Rommel had formed quite a strong front on the Aslagh and Sidra ridges, to enclose the area afterwards known as the "Cauldron."

On 30 May Rommel invested the 150th Brigade box at Sidi Muftah, and the following day he attacked with 90th Light, Trieste, and strong detachments of the Afrika Korps. The British infantry resisted stubbornly in skilfully sited positions and were gallantly supported by heavy Matildas of the 44th Royal Tank Regiment. The actual breakthrough into the perimeter was led by Rommel in person; he went forward when the infantry of 21st Panzer were held up and took over the leading platoon. By 1 June the brigade had expended its ammunition and resistance collapsed; we took three thousand prisoners and 124 guns of all types. While this desperate contest was in progress Eighth Army made no attempt to interfere, apart from spasmodic air attacks on the minefield gaps.

The elimination of the 150th Brigade greatly eased Rommel's position, and on 2 June he sent 90th Light and Trieste southwards to attack Bir Hacheim. Warned by the failure of his initial attack Rommel had decided to follow a methodical plan and eat up the Eighth Army positions one by one. At this stage I was ordered to return to his headquarters and take over as Ia (Chief Operations Officer) from Lieutenant Colonel Westphal, who had been wounded during the fighting at Sidi Muftah.[11]

Between 2 and 5 June we invested Bir Hacheim and prepared ourselves for the British attack, which to us seemed to be very long in coming. Before actually dealing with the

[10] Colonel R. M. P. Carver, one of the leading British experts on armored warfare, has said of this attack: "The armour generally had no proper tactics of attack, based on location and destruction of the enemy. In this case the whole of 1 Armoured Division was held at bay all day by rearguards based on 88-mm anti-tank guns, which were very vulnerable to H.E. fire."

[11] Gause, the chief of staff, was also wounded there, and was replaced by Bayerlein, the chief of staff of the Afrika Korps.

great battle of the "Cauldron," I propose to consider the courses open to the British; my excuse for doing so is that the military situation at Gazala at the beginning of June, 1942, was one of the most interesting in my experience.

On 2 June, after the destruction of the 150th Brigade, General Ritchie signalled to Auchinleck; he said he was "much distressed" at this event but that he considered his situation was "favorable" and "getting better daily." In reply Auchinleck said that he regarded with "some misgiving" Rommel's ability to exploit "a broad and deep wedge in the middle of your position." The commander in chief warned Ritchie that he was losing the initiative, and urged the need for a large-scale attack from the northern sector of the Gazala Line, with a view to piercing the front held by Group Cruewell and reaching Bir Temrad. Eighth Army considered this plan, and contemplated that the 5th Indian Division would pass through the South African front and thrust westwards along the coast. If such an advance had reached Tmimi it would have gravely embarrassed the communications of the Panzerarmee and might have forced Rommel to withdraw from the "Cauldron." But from the British point of view the plan involved the risk that Rommel might react by bursting out of the "Cauldron," and the thrusting towards their principal supply dumps at Belhamed-Gambut; alternatively he might thrust north and get across the Via Balbia in rear of the Gazala Line.

On the while I am inclined to think that a large-scale British offensive towards Tmimi would have been too risky in view of Rommel's commanding position in the "Cauldron." A rather similar maneuver led to the destruction of the Austro-Russian army at Austerlitz.

Another possibility was to attempt a double-envelopment of our "Cauldron" positions. I suggest that the 1st and 7th Armored Divisions, with the 5th Indian Division, would pass south of Bir Hacheim and attack the "Cauldron" from the rear, while the 13th Corps would attack from the north with the 32nd Army Tank Brigade, as well as the 2nd S.A. Division, and the 10th Indian Division (brought up from the frontier area). (See map on page 124.) It is quite true

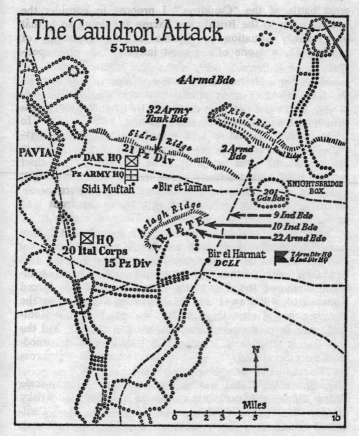

The 'Cauldron' Attack
5 June

4 Armd Bde

32 Army
Tank Bde

Sidra Ridge

Rigel Ridge

PAVIA

DAK HQ 21 Pz Div

2 Armd Bde

Rigel Ridge

Pz ARMY HQ

Sidi Muftah

Bir et Tamar

KNIGHTSBRIDGE BOX

201 Gds Bde

Aslagh Ridge

ARIETE

9 Ind Bde

10 Ind Bde

22 Armd Bde

HQ
20 Ital Corps
15 Pz Div

Bir el Harmat
DCLI

7 Armd Div HQ
5 Ind Div HQ

N

Miles
0 1 2 3 4 5 10

that the Afrika Korps could have reacted by going for
Tobruk or Belhamed, but in that case the Panzerarmee
would have been hopelessly divided and Eighth Army could
have annihilated Group Cruewell, before turning back to
deal with the Afrika Korps.

This is one of those plans which look very risky on paper
and are therefore avoided by cautious generals, but if it
could have been boldly and resolutely applied I think it
would have smashed the Panzerarmee. As a preliminary it

would have been necessary to accumulate reserve stocks of
gasoline and ammunition in the 50th Division area—these
could have been used by the British armored divisions if
Rommel had cut their communications by moving on
Tobruk or Belhamed. Such is the plan which I would rec-
ommend for a German army in the position of Eighth Army
in June, 1942. I must admit, however, that at the time
Eighth Army did not have the flexibility or ability to regroup
which such a plan would demand.

The third possibility was a concentric attack on the
"Cauldron" to eliminate the Afrika Korps by frontal attack.
This was the plan actually adopted by the British; it
would have been perfectly sound if the attack had been
made in adequate force. But instead of throwing in every
available tank and gun, the Eighth Army attacked with
about half its available troops.

After long discussions with his corps and divisional commanders, Ritchie decided to attack the northern flank of
our salient with the 32nd Army Tank Brigade, and the eastern flank with the 9th and 10th Indian Brigades and the
22nd Armored Brigade. Tenth Indian Brigade was to advance during the night 4/5 June and breach the positions
held by Ariete on Aslagh Ridge, the 22nd Armored Brigade was to pass through and capture Sidi Muftah, and the
9th Indian Brigade was ordered to follow up and consolidate the ground won.[12]

The command arrangements on the British side were pecu-
liar. Thirteenth Corps was to command the attack on the
Sidra Ridge, and the 30th Corps the one on the Aslagh
Ridge. Fifth Indian Division was to command during the
actual breach of Ariete's positions, the 7th Armored Division would take over during the advance of the 22nd Armored Brigade, and the 5th Indian Division would resume
command when the 9th Indian Brigade moved up. For this
purpose General Messervy (the 7th Armored Division) and
General Briggs (the 5th Indian Division) established a

---

[12] See J. A. I. Agar-Hamilton and L. C. F. Turner, *Crisis in the
Desert, May–July, 1942* (New York, Oxford University Press, 1952).
There is a very illuminating account of the "Cauldron" battle in this
official South African publication.

combined headquarters. The tactical details have been severely criticized by Brigadier Fletcher, the commander of the 9th Indian Brigade, who says:

Battalions were expected to advance in the dark, over ground they did not know, to an assembly area, the centre of which was marked by a barrel; to do a further advance to a point east of B. 100; where they were to be joined by a battery of a regiment which they did not know (it had arrived from Iraq two days previously) and by a squadron of the 4 R.T.R. which [would have] already been in action in the dark.[13]

On broad grounds the British were quite correct to use infantry to make the initial breach for the armor;[14] but in this case it was essential for a corps commander to keep strict control over the two divisions taking part in the battle. Moreover it is a mistake to commit an armored formation too early in a breakthrough battle; in that case the armor will get mixed up with the infantry, with consequent confusion and loss of control. This is exactly what happened on 5 June.

On 4 June Rommel decided that Afrika Korps should undertake an operation on 5 June to salvage some abandoned tanks in the Bir el Harmat area. For this purpose 15th Panzer opened up gaps in the minefields to the southwest of Bir el Harmat on the night of 4/5 June; this was a great stroke of luck for us and had an important effect on the battle.

In accepting the plan of attack on the "Cauldron," General Auchinleck had stressed the need for close co-operation between infantry and tanks, and also for thorough reconnaissance. Ritchie replied that there had been "Plenty of time for recce," and on the night of 4 June he signalled that the commanders concerned were "full of beans and happy."[15]

[13] Antony Brett-James, *Ball of Fire: The Fifth Indian Division in the Second World War* (Gale & Polden, 1952), 183.

[14] That is on the 30th Corps front. Thirteenth Corps sent the 32nd Army Tank Brigade into the attack with virtually no infantry or artillery support.

[15] Agar-Hamilton, *Crisis in the Desert*, 42.

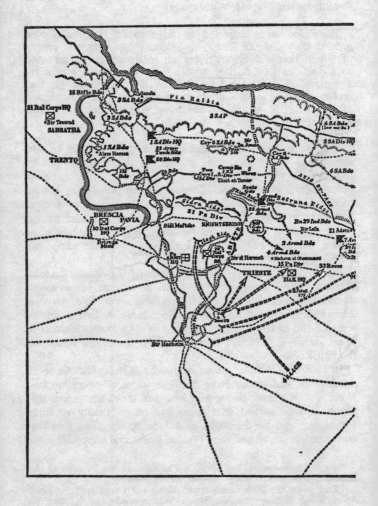

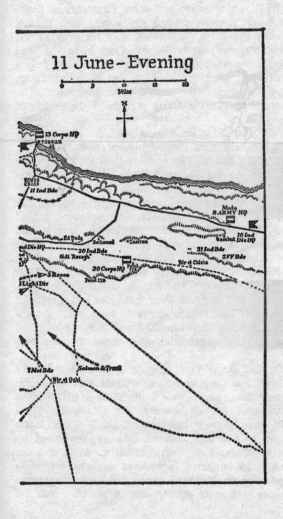

11 June – Evening

At 0250 on 5 June four regiments of artillery opened a bombardment in support of the 10th Indian Brigade; the volume of fire was impressive and from Panzerarmee headquarters we could see the eastern sky ablaze with flashes. This, then, was the British offensive, and we awaited the first reports with some anxiety. We need not have disturbed ourselves. Ariete signalled that the British shells were falling well short of their positions, and in fact the preliminary bombardment was completely wasted on empty desert. The artillery overture provided a fitting prelude to the events of the day.

At dawn the British realized their mistake, and a determined attack was made on the infantry of Ariete Division, holding the Aslagh Ridge. The Italians gave way, the ridge was cleared, and the 9th Indian Brigade and the 22nd Armored Brigade went forward to drive us out of the "Cauldron." The British tanks were received with a terrific fire from our antitank guns and artillery, and withdrew behind Bir et Tamar after suffering considerable losses. German and Italian tanks counterattacked and inflicted heavy casualties on the 2nd Highland Light Infantry and the 2nd West Yorkshire Regiment, who were attempting to establish "boxes" in the "Cauldron." The British armor made no attempt to protect and support their infantry, and Brigadier Fletcher comments that "there seems to have been a complete misunderstanding between 22Armd Bde and 9 Ind Inf Bde as to the capabilities and tasks of the two brigades."[16]

Meanwhile 32nd Army Tank Brigade attacked 21st Panzer on Sidra Ridge. For some reason this attack was supported by only twelve guns, and it was brought to a halt with a loss of fifty tanks out of seventy. An attack on Sidra Ridge would have gravely embarrassed us if it had been made at night by a strong force of infantry, supported by the full weight of the 13th Corps' artillery. As it was the heavy British tanks lumbered forward in daylight, providing perfect targets for our antitank guns, and ending up on a minefield where they were simply shot to pieces. From the tactical point of view this was one of the most ridiculous attacks of the campaign.

By midday it was clear that the British offensive had been held and that the attacking troops had suffered serious losses. Rommel was not the man to remain satisfied with a passive defense, and that afternoon he launched one of the most brilliant counterattacks of his career. While 21st Panzer thrust southeastwards towards Bir et Tamar, 15th Panzer emerged from the gap in the minefields near Bir el Harmat and struck at the flank and rear of the troops holding the Aslagh Ridge. Rommel himself accompanied the southern attack, which overwhelmed the single battalion which the British had placed as a flank guard, and overran the combined headquarters of Generals Messervy and Briggs.[17] To add to the enemy's confusion the Luftwaffe heavily bombed the area west of the Knightsbridge Box.

The result was that on the night 5/6 June we formed a ring round the 10th Indian Brigade on the Aslagh Ridge, the Support Group of the 22nd Armored Brigade to the north of them, and four regiments of field artillery which had been brought up behind the Indians. The only hope for the British was a vigorous counterattack by the 2nd, 4th, and 22nd Armored Brigades, but this never developed. To judge from British accounts their armor spent 6 June moving backwards and forwards in accordance with contradictory orders and it was certainly unable to interfere with our operations around Aslagh Ridge. Tenth Indian Brigade and the British artillery made a brave resistance, but at the end of the day the Afrika Korps alone had captured 3,100 prisoners, 96 guns, and 37 antitank guns. Tenth Indian Brigade had been wiped out, the 9th Indian Brigade had been roughly handled, and well over 100 tanks had been lost. Four regiments of field artillery simply disappeared.

In spite of this brilliant success, Rommel decided to eliminate Bir Hacheim before bursting out of the "Cauldron" to complete the defeat of Eighth Army. A strong detachment of 15th Panzer was moved southwards on 8 June to support 90th Light and Trieste, who were making slow prog-

---

[17] The British left flank was covered by the 1st Duke of Cornwall's Light Infantry, who had no armor or artillery in support.

ress in the face of very determined French resistance. Heavy
Stuka bombardments prepared the way for a successful attack on 9 June by infantry of 15th Panzer; they captured
Pt. 186 overlooking the main French position, and on the
night 10/11 June the French garrison felt compelled to
break out. Some British officers have insinuated that French
morale gave way, but in the whole course of the desert war
we never encountered a more heroic and well-sustained defense.

The way was now clear for a decisive advance into the
area Knightsbridge–El Adem.

The Battle of Knightsbridge

In spite of the tremendous blows which Rommel had inflicted in the "Cauldron," the balance of force was still in
Ritchie's favor, and from the British point of view the
battle was far from being lost. A line of defended posts,
protected by minefields, had been built up to the north of
the "Cauldron"; the 201st Guards Brigade was firmly established in the Knightsbridge Box, and the 29th Indian Brigade was holding a strong position at El Adem. On 11
June Ritchie still disposed 250 cruiser and 80 infantry
tanks, while the Afrika Korps had 160 tanks and Ariete
and Trieste about 70. Our infantry units had suffered
heavily in the fighting and 90 Light Division was reduced
to a thousand men. It was still possible for the British
to hold Rommel, and then rebuild their strength. Already
British light forces and armored cars were attacking our
communications west of the Gazala minefields and were scor-
ing significant successes against supply convoys.

Rommel's plan was as follows. While 21st Panzer demonstrated against the British positions hemming in the "Cauldron" on the north, 15th Panzer was to swing northeast-
wards towards El Adem, with 90th Light on their right
and Trieste on their left flank. This was really a reversion
to the original plan of 27 May; it would not have succeeded
if the British command had not made serious mistakes.

The new advance began on the afternoon of 11 June.
By nightfall 15th Panzer had reached the area of Naduret

el Ghesceuasc; 90th Light and the two armored reconnaissance units were south of the El Adem Box. Our Wireless
Intercept Service—a very important factor in Rommel's
victories—reported that "4th Armored Brigade has refused
to carry out an attack to the southeast."[18] Rommel was
delighted to hear that the British were contemplating such
a move; he ordered 15th Panzer to stand on the defensive
on 12 June, while 21st Panzer advanced south of the Knightsbridge Box to take the British armor in the rear.

The battle of 12 June was slow to develop. Fifteenth
Panzer was anticipating a British attack, while on their side
the 2nd and 4th Armored Brigades were waiting for definite
orders.[19] Finally General Nehring ordered 15th Panzer to
attack, and taking advantage of the sand haze our antitank
gunners brought effective fire to bear on the British tanks.
At noon Rommel judged that the battle was ripe, and
ordered 21st Panzer to advance into the open flank of the
7th Armored Division. This move met with immediate
success, and soon our Wireless Intercept reported that the
British tanks were "calling for help."

Twenty-second Armored Bridgade advanced from the
north to extricate their comrades, and suffered heavy losses
at the hands of 21st Panzer and Trieste. Under the converg-
ing pressure of the two Panzer divisions, the 2nd and 4th
Armored Brigades gave way; the retreat of the 4th Armored Brigade became a rout, and as the sun was setting it
was driven headlong over the Raml escarpment. Second and
22nd Armored Brigades withdrew towards the Knightsbridge Box under continual pressure from our panzers; in
that area a desperate battle continued until dark. In the fight-

[18] In fact General Messervy, the commander of the 7th Armored
Division, wanted to concentrate his division (the 2nd and 4th Armored
Brigades) at El Gubi to operate against the flank of the German
advance.

[19] Actually a serious dispute had arisen between General Messervy
and his two brigadiers. The former wanted to advance to Bir el Gubi,
the latter were opposed to it. (*See* Agar-Hamilton, *Crisis in the Desert,*
64.) Messervy decided to go back to his headquarters to consult
Ritchie, and was nearly captured by 90th Light which was advancing
north of the El Adem Box. He had to make a long detour, and as a
result command on the British side broke down.

ing on 12 June the British lost 120 tanks—the Gazala
Battle had been decided.

On 13 June the two panzer divisions advanced against
Rigel Ridge, which was held by the Scots Guards, supported by South African field and antitank artillery. After a
very stubborn defense the ridge was overrun, and weak relieving attacks by the British armor were beaten off. The
Knightsbridge Box was now isolated, and the Guards Brigade broke out on the night 13/14 June.

On the morning of 14 June Ritchie accepted that the
battle was lost and decided to abandon the Gazala Line.
Even before he was aware of the retreat, Rommel had
ordered the Afrika Korps to thrust towards the Via Balbia and cut off the Gazala divisions. During the day a furious
battle developed near Eluet et Tamar, where South African
and British infantry,[20] supported by the remains of the
armor, succeeded in holding up our advance until the late
afternoon, when 15th Panzer broke through to reach Bu
Amaia near the escarpment. But by then darkness had fall-
en, and the withdrawal of the 1st S.A. Division was well under way.

On the 14th our reconnaissance aircraft had reported
much traffic on the Via Balbia and every sign of a hurried
withdrawal, so that Rommel was well aware of the need for
reaching the coast road as rapidly as possible.[21] He issued
the most urgent orders to the Afrika Korps to descend the
escarpment during the night and cut off the South African
retreat, but his orders were virtually ignored. The fact is
that the Afrika Korps had reached the end of its tether
after the terrific fighting of the past three weeks; it was
impossible to rouse the men. On the morning of 15 June,
15th Panzer descended the escarpment and cut off the
South African rearguards, but the bulk of the division escaped. Most of the British 50th Division succeeded in breaking out through the front of the Italian 10th Corps, and
passing south of Bir Hacheim reached the frontier.

[20] First Worcesters and a composite battalion of the 1st S.A. Division.
[21] On 14 June most of Rommel's supporting aircraft were attacking a
Malta convoy; thus the retreat of the 1st S.A. Division was not effectively hampered from the air.

Looking at the operations 11–15 June in retrospect, it seems surprising that after the capture of Bir Hacheim Rommel again reverted to what was essentially his original plan —a fanwise advance with his right wing directed at El Adem. In both cases he failed to achieve his object—the envelopment of the troops in the Gazala Line—because his forces were spread out too widely. Ninetieth Light was too weak to take the El Adem Box and was not available to support the Afrika Korps in the critical fighting. After the defeat of the British armor on 12 June, the Afrika Korps was ordered to thrust northwards and cut the Via Balbia, while the Italian 20th Corps was given unimportant covering tasks south of Knightsbridge. Had all five German-Italian armored and motorized divisions been used in the thrust towards the Via Balbia, they would have been able to prevent the bulk of the Gazala forces slipping away. After three weeks of bitter fighting the Afrika Korps alone could not muster the necessary momentum and driving power.

On the morning of 15 June Rommel ordered 21st Panzer to advance to El Adem and support 90th Light in that area. The battle of Gazala had been won, and the bulk of Eighth Army was in full retreat to the frontier; Tobruk remained to be subdued and it appeared that Ritchie was determined to hold the Fortress. Rommel was resolved to give the Eighth Army no time to regroup; he decided to thrust towards Gambut, isolate Tobruk, and then take the Fortress by storm. He was on the eve of the crowning victory of his career.

8: Tobruk to Alamein

The Fall of Tobruk

THE BATTLE OF GAZALA can be said to have ended at about midday on 15 June; Eighth Army was then in full retreat to the frontier, and the Panzerarmee was closing in on the outer defenses of Tobruk. On the evening of 15 June another battle began, which is best described as the struggle for the Tobruk–El Adem line.

The researches of South African military historians, which have been set out in great detail in *Crisis in the Desert*, show that General Auchinleck was entirely opposed to another siege of Tobruk on the same lines as that of 1941. He rightly appreciated that conditions had completely changed, that the defenses of the Fortress had seriously deteriorated, and that the Panzerarmee could deliver a much more formidable attack than those of April/May, 1941.[1] In any case the Royal Navy had made it clear that they would not be prepared to supply Tobruk in the event of another siege. Accordingly, when Auchinleck authorized Ritchie to abandon Gazala on 14 June, he ordered that the Eighth Army should regroup on the Tobruk–El Adem line; in particular he insisted that El Adem was of vital importance to a successful defense of Tobruk. Auchinleck

[1] Superior even to the attack which Rommel was planning in November 1941. Twenty-first Panzer would not have been available for the November attack, and the Tobruk defenses were much stronger at that time.

138

urged Ritchie to bring "maximum force into play in El Adem area"; and added significantly: "I look to you to spare nothing to achieve this. We must emulate the enemy's speed in thought and action and I wish you to impress this as strongly as possible on *all* commanders."[2]

Rommel's appreciation was exactly similar to that of Auchinleck. When he stood on the escarpment above the Via Balbia on the morning of 15 June and saw that the greater part of the 1st S.A. Division had escaped from his clutches, Rommel realized at once that he must swing his *Schwerpunkt* round towards El Adem and knock away what we called the "cornerstones of Tobruk." In armored warfare speed is of decisive importance—a point which Auchinleck fully understood—and the operations of the next two days show Rommel concentrating an overwhelming force in the El Adem area and completely forestalling Eighth Army, whose slow and cumbersome methods were quite out of place in such a battle. The events of 15–17 June decided the fate of Tobruk, which Auchinleck well knew could not be held as an isolated fortress against the full weight of the Panzerarmee.[3]

On 15 June the 90th Light Division advanced against El Adem, then held by two battalions of the 29th Indian Brigade. Twenty-first Panzer arrived from the Acroma area in the late afternoon and overwhelmed a box at B. 650 on the Batruna escarpment, where the remaining battalion of the 29th Brigade had been placed to block the Axis Bypass road.[4] This was a promising beginning to the new battle, and in his orders for 16 June Rommel told 21st Panzer to push on to Sidi Rezegh and Belhamed; 90th Light supported by our army artillery was to attack the El Adem box; Ariete and the three reconnaissance units were to guard the southern flank against British relieving forces,

[2] Agar-Hamilton, *Crisis in the Desert*, 102.
[3] *Editor's note.* Churchill thought it could, and his signals on the subject gravely embarrassed Auchinleck and prevented his ordering a break-out of the Tobruk garrison while there was still time. By the summer of 1942 Tobruk had ceased to be a fortress or a harbor, it had become a name and like Verdun in World War I its retention became a matter of prestige rather than strategy.
[4] Seven hundred prisoners were take from 3/12 Frontier Force Rifles.

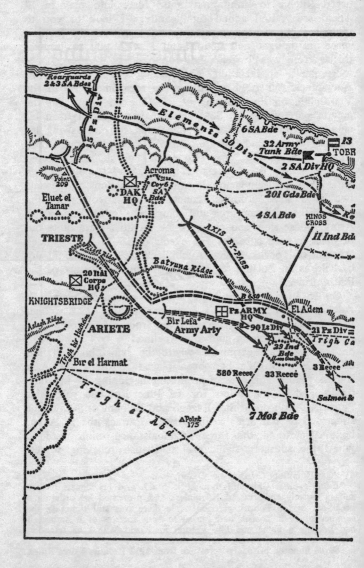

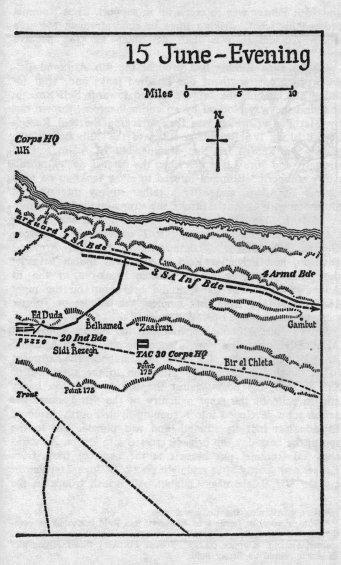

15 June – Evening

Miles 0 ⎯⎯ 5 ⎯⎯ 10

N

Corps HQ
.UK

arguard 1 S A Bde

3 S A Inf Bde   4 Armd Bde

Ed Duda
Belhamed   Zaafran   Gambut

Fuzzo ⎯⎯ 20 Ind Bde
Sidi Rezegh   TAC 30 Corps HQ   Bir el Chleta
Point
175

Point 178

Trout

and 15th Panzer was to come up in support. Thus Rommel ordered his whole striking force to concentrate in the area which Auchinleck was then describing as "the decisive spot."

On 16 June Ritchie had brought the 4th Armored Brigade up to a strength of one hundred tanks and, after refitting at Gambut, the brigade moved towards Sidi Rezegh. It found the way blocked by an antitank screen, thrown out by 21st Panzer which was then attacking the Sidi Rezegh box, held by 1/6 Rajputana Rifles of the 20th Indian Brigade.[5] Sidi Rezegh fell that evening, but El Adem resisted strongly, and 90th Light described the defense as "extraordinarily stubborn." Rommel refused to allow tanks to be used against El Adem, and after a rather stormy meeting that afternoon with Colonel Marcks, the strong-minded commander of 90th Light, he agreed to call off the attack. During the day we were intercepting R/T conversations between General Messervy, the commander of the 7th Armored Division, and Brigadier Reid of the 29th Indian Brigade; they were arranging for a possible break-out of the El Adem garrison. The garrison did break out on the night 16/17 June, and from that moment the defense of Tobruk ceased to be a serious operation of war.[6]

On 17 June Rommel concentrated the Afrika Korps and Ariete Division with a view to knocking out the 4th Armored Brigade and opening the way to Gambut. The armored battle developed during the afternoon to the southeast of Sidi Rezegh; the odds against the British were too heavy and in spite of the great gallantry of the 9th Lancers the action soon developed into a running fight. Fourth Armored Brigade lost half its strength and was pursued far to the south; the next day the brigade crossed into Egypt. As darkness fell Rommel put himself at the head of the Afrika Korps, and shortly after midnight on 17/18 June 21st Panzer cut the Via Balbia near Gambut. All British troops in the

[5] Then garrisoning the Belhamed area.

[6] *Editor's note.* In fairness to Messervy and Reid it should be mentioned that permission to break out was given by Ritchie, who had assured General Klopper (G.O.C. Tobruk Fortress) that morning that El Adem would be firmly held.

area were in full flight to the east; some efforts had been made to demolish the supply dumps but we captured enormous quantities of gasoline and rations, and a good deal of transport.[7]

Twentieth Indian Brigade was still at Belhamed and in the circumstances a cool strategist would have ordered this formation to withdraw quietly into Tobruk, where it would have provided a most welcome reinforcement for the 11th Indian Brigade holding the southeastern sector. Instead Ritchie ordered the 20th Indian Brigade to break through to the frontier; on the morning of 18 June it ran into the Afrika Korps near Gambut and "Disappeared from Eighth Army's Order of Battle."

By the evening of 18 June Tobruk was completely invested; the Italian 21st Corps lay to the west, their 10th Corps to the south, and Trieste and the German reconnaissance units to the southeast and east. The Afrika Korps and Ariete lay in the Gambut area and Rommel decided not to bring them up until the night before the attack. Our operation order was issued on 18 June and embodied a relatively simple plan. A Stuka and artillery bombardment was to be concentrated against the sector of the 11th Indian Brigade at 0520 on 20 June; Group Menny[8] would penetrate gaps made by engineers in the perimeter minefield during the previous night, and would then make a breach on a narrow front in the line of bunkers and concrete positions behind the antitank ditch.[9] Engineers would then lay bridges across the ditch, and the tanks would pour through the breach into the Fortress. The plan was very flexible—as such plans should be—and there was no attempt to lay down rigid objectives and boundary lines. Arrangements were made for close air support and Kesselring promised to provide additional aircraft from Europe. The whole Panzerarmee artillery took up positions on the heights to the east of El Adem, and we were astonished to find that the British had been obliging

[7] The Panzerarmee's battle report for 18 June says that "supply dumps of extraordinary size—fuel, ammunition, and rations—were found in the area around Gambut, which we at once used for our own supply."

[8] Infantry units under Colonel Menny.

[9] Actually in the sector held by 2/5 Mahratta Battalion.

enough to leave the dumps of artillery ammunition, which we had placed there for that very purpose in November, 1941.[10]

On 19 June 90th Light Division moved eastwards and found that the enemy had abandoned Bardia. Our reconnaissance units patrolled the wide area between Bardia and Bir el Gubi; only light British forces were encountered and it was clear that Ritchie would not make any serious attempt to interfere with our attack on Tobruk. That evening the Afrika Korps began moving from Gambut towards its concentration area to the southeast of the Fortress; the move had been carefully prepared and was carried out without a hitch. At 0330 on 20 June, 21st Panzer reported that it was "fully prepared and ready for the attack on Tobruk."

At 0500 I stood with Rommel on the escarpment to the northeast of El Adem; battle headquarters had been set up there and when daylight came we had excellent observation as far as the Tobruk perimeter. Promptly at 0520 the Stukas flew over. Kesselring had been as good as his word and sent hundreds of bombers in dense formations; they dived on to the perimeter in one of the most spectacular attacks I have ever seen. A great cloud of dust and smoke rose from the sector under attack, and while our bombs crashed on to the defenses, the entire German and Italian army artillery joined in with a tremendous and well co-ordinated fire. The combined weight of the artillery and bombing was terrific, and as we soon realized had a crushing effect on the morale of the Mahratta battalion in that sector. The Stukas kept it up all day, flying back to the airfields at Gazala and El Adem, replenishing with bombs, and then returning to the fray. On this occasion the air force bombing was directed through the Operations Section of army headquarters, with very fruitful results.

After a time the assault engineers released orange smoke

---

[10] Tobruk was defended by the 2nd S.A. Division (the 4th and 6th Infantry Brigades), the 11th Indian Brigade, the 201st Guards Brigade (in reserve on the Pilastrino Ridge), and the 32nd Army Tank Brigade (52 Matildas and Valentines). The tanks were mostly in the King's Cross and Pilastrino areas, ready for mobile counterattack. There were three regiments of field and two of medium artillery, and about 70 antitank guns distributed among various units. Major General H. B. Klopper, G.O.C. the 2nd S.A. Division, was the Fortress commander.

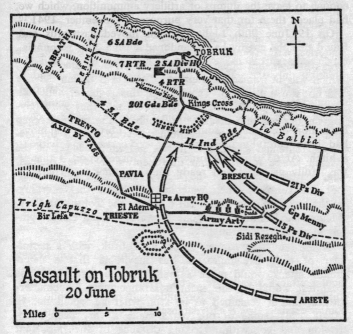

Assault on Tobruk
20 June

Miles 0 5 10

as a signal that the range should be lengthened, and at 0635 the report came back that the wire had been cut in front of Strong Point 69. Group Menny, and the infantry of the Afrika Korps, now attacked the forward line of bunkers and made rapid progress against feeble resistance. At 0703 Group Menny reported that a whole company of Indians had been taken prisoner, and by 0745 a wide breach had been made and about ten strong points had been taken. Bridges were laid across the antitank ditch and the way was prepared for the tanks to enter the perimeter.

The weak resistance of the defenders was due primarily to the bombardment, and paradoxically to the excellent concrete shelters built by the Italians. Under the crushing weight of bombs and shells the Indians were driven below ground, where they were relatively secure, but could not bring any fire to bear on our attacking troops, who followed closely behind the barrage.[11] Another important factor was the weakness of the defenders' artillery fire. There seems to have been a complete lack of co-ordination of the various batteries; a few South African guns were firing during the breakthrough, but apparently the 25th Field Regiment R.A., which was in immediate support of the 11th Indian Brigade did not fire until 0745. The guns of this regiment had been sited in an antitank role, and it appears that they were relying on the medium artillery to bombard the perimeter gap and the German troops assembling beyond it. But the mediums remained silent, and it was not until 0845 that the Afrika Korps reported that the enemy's fire was "increasing," particularly that of the "heavy calibers." I well remember our surprise, when watching the battle that morning, at the small volume of fire put down by the Tobruk artillery. Meanwhile Rommel had gone forward to take direct command of the breakthrough.

Against a "ring fortress" such as Tobruk, with a perimeter of thirty-five miles, it was inevitable that a determined attack would make a breach in the defenses.[12] The real test would be the enemy's arrangements for counterattack, and it remained to be seen what he would do. In April, 1941, some of our tanks made a very deep penetration and got within striking distance of the important road junction of King's Cross; they were then brilliantly counterattacked by British tanks and mobile artillery, and were driven out of the perimeter with heavy loss. This was not likely to happen in June, 1942, for we had over 200 tanks, of which 125 were German. Our armor was employed in mass, and air and artillery liaison officers traveled with the leading tanks to ensure the closest support. Even so, a well co-ordinated counterattack could have caused us considerable trouble, although I do not think that the garrison could have made a prolonged defense, as the inner mine-

---

[11] As frequently happened in 1914–18 when troops were caught in dugouts.

[12] In principle armor should not be used in attacks on fortresses, but "ring fortresses" like Tobruk provide an exception. Once the armor gets through the breach and smashes the counterattack, it can play havoc within the perimeter.

fields had fallen into decay—or had been stripped of their contents—and were no longer a serious obstacle. Actually a counterattack never developed because the British forces came up piecemeal and without any unified command. A counterattack plan should have been drafted before our attack, and a senior commander should have been put in charge.[13]

By 0930 the German tanks had crossed the antitank ditch and were fanning out inside the perimeter. General Nehring, the commander of the Afrika Korps, moved with the 15th Panzer Division,[14] while General von Bismarck, the thrustful commander of 21st Panzer, travelled in a motorcycle sidecar among his leading tanks. He personally reconnoitered the inner minefields and showed the way to the panzers. Rommel himself was also close behind the advance and ready to take over at a critical moment. I stress this element of personal leadership, because British and South African accounts show that no senior officer of the 2nd S.A. Division, the 32nd Army Tank Brigade, or the 201st Guards Brigade ever went near King's Cross—the defending troops fought with great gallantry but "without leadership or direction."

At 1100 hours 15th Panzer claimed the destruction of fifteen tanks and the capture of 150 prisoners; by noon both divisions had reached the line of the inner minefield where they met determined resistance from some British tanks and various artillery batteries.[15] A violent battle devel-

---

[13] *Editor's note.* At 0700 on 20 June General Klopper ordered that a battalion of tanks and two companies of Coldstream Guards should counterattack. For a variety of reasons the 4th Royal Tanks did not reach King's Cross until 0930, and were then thrown into the battle without waiting for the Guards and their 6-pounder antitank guns. Later a squadron of the 7th Royal Tanks arrived, and then the remaining squadron of that regiment. The tanks cannot be said to have counterattacked; they reached the line of the inner minefield and were overwhelmed by the advance of the Afrika Korps. The Guards never left the King's Cross area.

[14] The former commander, General von Vaerst, had been wounded in the Gazala battles and Colonel Crasemann had taken over.

[15] Twenty-fifth Field Regiment R.A. reinforced by D Troop of the 5th S.A. Field Battery. Second S.A. Field Battery, which lay fairly close to the perimeter, had already been destroyed.

oped, in the course of which our tanks eliminated the enemy's gunners by machinegun fire, and then swept over
their positions. By 1400 the Afrika Korps had reached the
escarpment north of King's Cross, and Rommel himself drove
up in his big command vehicle to direct the next thrust.[16]

For practical purposes the Battle of Tobruk was now over,
and it only remained to exploit the victory and mop up the
various sectors of the Fortress. During the afternoon 21st
Panzer descended the escarpment and advanced against
Tobruk harbor; the main opposition came from a British
heavy antiaircraft battery which was finally captured by
some of our antiaircraft troops, fighting under Rommel's
personal supervision. The battery had knocked out several
tanks, and showed what the British might have done had
they used their 3.7-in A.A. gun as we used our 88. As dusk
was falling 21st Panzer fought its way into Tobruk town—
now enveloped in the thick smoke of burning dumps—and
opened fire from the quay on British naval craft seeking to
break out to the open sea. Several vessels were sunk or set
on fire.

Fifteenth Panzer Division advanced against the Guards
Brigade on Pilastrino Ridge; they overwhelmed 1st Sher-
wood Foresters and most of the 3rd Coldstream Guards,
and also captured the Brigade headquarters. After having
taken a large number of prisoners they withdrew to leaguer
around King's Cross—we had done enough for the day. By
nightfall it was obvious that Tobruk was in its death throes
and Rommel was able to send off a triumphant signal to
Berlin. Our losses during the day had been very small and
out of all proportion to those of the enemy.

The only possible course open to the Tobruk garrison on
night 20/21 June was to break out from a Fortress
which had become a death trap. Admittedly we had captured or destroyed great quantities of transport, but enough
remained to enable many troops to escape. Apparently
General Klopper wanted to break out, but he could get no
clear directive from Eighth Army headquarters and met with

---

[16] Incidentally Ariete was still held up at the antitank ditch by the
2nd Cameron Highlanders.

great opposition from some of his subordinates.[17] Nothing was done, and at dawn on 21 June the western sector of Tobruk was in a state of chaos, the situation being complicated by the presence of large numbers of disorganized base and supply troops who had fled from the eastern sector the previous day. Shortly after dawn on 21 June the white flag was hoisted over General Klopper's headquarters, and 33,000 prisoners fell into our hands at a single stroke.[18] In spite of demolitions, numerous dumps full of food, gasoline, clothing, and ammunition were found intact, and many guns, vehicles, and tanks swelled the booty of the Panzerarmee.

On the evening of 21 June Rommel heard over the radio that he had been promoted field marshal—a fitting reward, for in the words of the South African official account: "The capture of Tobruk crowned what was probably the most spectacular series of victories ever gained over a British army."[19]

The Invasion of Egypt

At 0945 on 21 June Rommel issued a signal to all troops of the Panzerarmee: "Fortress of Tobruk has capitulated. All units will reassemble and prepare for further advance." That afternoon 21st Panzer was hurried off along the road to Gambut, the first step in the invasion of Egypt.

A grave decision had to be made now. In the original plan agreed upon between Hitler and Mussolini at the end of April, it was laid down that after Rommel had taken Tobruk, the Panzerarmee would stand on the defensive on the Egyptian frontier, and that all available aircraft and shipping would then be diverted to the attack on Malta. With the fall of the island our communications would be secure, and an advance to the Nile could follow. On 21 June Field Marshal Kesselring flew to Africa, and I was pres-

---

[17] Klopper and some of his staff moved to H.Q. of the 6th S.A. Brigade on the evening of 20 June.

[18] Second Camerons continued to resist until the evening of 21 June, and only surrendered because the rest of the Fortress had done so. Only a few hundred troops succeeded in escaping from Tobruk.

[19] Agar-Hamilton, *Crisis in the Desert*, 222.

ent at his conference with Rommel in our command vehicle. Rommel insisted that he must follow up his victory without waiting for an attack on Malta, but Kesselring pointed out that an advance into Egypt could not succeed without full support from the Luftwaffe. If this were given, the Luftwaffe would not be available for operations against Malta, and should the island recover, Rommel's communications would be in serious jeopardy. Kesselring maintained that the only sound course was to stick to the original plan, and postpone an invasion of Egypt until Malta had fallen.

Rommel disagreed emphatically and the discussions became exceedingly lively. He admitted that the Panzerarmee had suffered heavily in the Gazala battles, but maintained that Eighth Army was in far worse plight and we now had a unique opportunity for a thrust to the Suez Canal. A delay of even a few weeks would give the enemy time to move up new forces and prevent any further advance. The two commanders failed to reach agreement, and before leaving Kesselring made no secret of his intention to withdraw his air units to Sicily.

Rommel had made up his mind irrevocably. The vanguard of the Afrika Korps was already on its way to the frontier, and on the evening of the 21st Rommel sent off a personal liaison officer to put his views before Hitler. He also signalled to Rome, and assured the Duce that "the state and morale of the troops, the present supply position owing to captured dumps, and the present weakness of the enemy, permit our pursuing him into the depths of the Egyptian area." Rommel carried the day with Hitler, in spite of the reasoned and powerful objections of the Italian General Staff, the German Naval Staff, Field Marshal Kesselring, and also General von Rintelen, the German military attaché in Rome. Hitler signalled to Mussolini that, "it is only once in a lifetime that the Goddess of Victory smiles," and the fateful decision was made to postpone the Malta attack until September, and throw everything behind Rommel's invasion of Egypt.

Was the decision correct? There can be no absolute answer to such a question. We undoubtedly came very

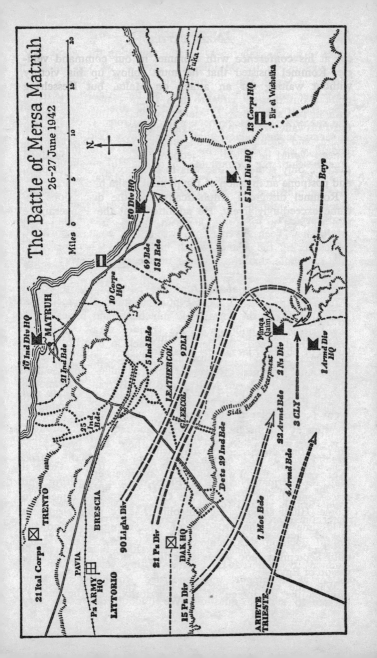

The Battle of Mersa Matruh
26–27 June 1942

close to conquering the Delta and upsetting the whole British position in the Middle East, for we won a smashing victory at Mersa Matruh, and with a little luck we might well have hustled Eighth Army out of the Alamein position. The fact remains, however, that the attempt failed, and the subsequent consequences were disastrous. Looking back, it seems understandable that Rommel as a field commander should wish to remain on the heels of a fleeing enemy. But the Supreme Command—or rather Hitler—should have appreciated the strategic importance of Malta and its decisive significance in the Mediterranean. It was for the Supreme Command to assert itself on a strategic question and refuse to allow an advance to the Suez Canal until Malta had been taken. Thus we lost a great opportunity of capturing the island, which had been so hammered by the Luftwaffe that the chances of success were very promising.

On the evening of 23 June the advance guard of the Afrika Korps crossed the Egyptian frontier. Rommel's aim was to outflank the formidable minefields and boxes which the British had built up in the frontier area, but in fact Ritchie had already decided to fall back to Matruh. During the next twenty-four hours our advance guard made a sensational advance of over a hundred miles and reached the coast road between Matruh and Sidi Barrani. The morale of the troops was high and the victories of the past month went far to balance the strain and exhaustion of incessant fighting at the height of a desert summer. Tank strength, however, was ominously low, for there had been many breakdowns in the march from Tobruk, and the Afrika Korps entered Egypt with only forty-four panzers.

Our advance on 24/25 June met with little interference from British ground forces, but was exposed to heavy and determined attacks by the Desert Air Force; the pace of the advance was outstripping our available fighter cover and we had to pay a heavy toll in casualties; indeed from the moment we entered Egypt the writing was on the wall as far as air support was concerned. Rommel never again enjoyed the advantage of air superiority, and the enemy's air forces grew with terrifying strength. It was the beginning of a process which was to alter the whole balance of the war, and which reached its culmination in the annihilating battles of Mortain and Falaise.

On the evening of 25 June our reconnaissance units reached the outer defenses of Mersa Matruh, and Rommel declared his intention of attacking next day. There was no time for serious reconnaissance and we entered on the battle with only the vaguest idea of the British dispositions.

The western approaches of Mersa Matruh were covered by dense minefields to a distance of fifteen miles from the sea. In this area we assumed that the Eighth Army had four divisions (the 50th British, the 2nd N.Z., and the 5th and 10th Indian) and that their left flank was covered by the 1st Armored Division in position between the main minefields and the Sidi Hamza escarpment. Rommel's aim was to encircle the infantry divisions around Matruh, and accordingly his first object was to drive off the 1st Armored Division. The Afrika Korps was entrusted with this task; 21st Panzer was to advance between the escarpment and the main minefield, while 15th Panzer was to move south of the escarpment. Ninetieth Light was to thrust on the left flank of 21st Panzer and cut the coast road to the east of Mersa Matruh; the Italian 10th and 21st Corps were to contain the western face of Matruh Fortress, and their Armored Corps —which had not yet come up—was to move south of the escarpment in support of 15th Panzer.

But the actual British dispositions were very different from those envisaged by Rommel. Tenth Corps was in the Matruh area, with the 50th British Division and the 10th Indian Division under command. Thirteenth Corps was grouped on the southern side of the Sidi Hamza escarpment; it comprised the 2nd N.Z. Division, which had just come up from Syria, and the 1st Armored Division, now brought up to a strength of 159 tanks, of which 60 were Grants.[20] The ten-mile gap between the Sidi Hamza escarpment and the main Matruh minefields was covered by a thin minefield and

---

[20] The Afrika Korps entered the battle with sixty tanks.

protected by two weak columns, Gleecol and Leathercol.[21]
In short, Eighth Army had two very strong wings, and a
weak center.

One might think that the Eighth Army dispositions were
designed as a deliberate trap for Rommel, but this was far
from being the case. It appears that General Auchinleck,
who had taken over from Ritchie, could not decide whether or not to make a determined stand at Mersa Matruh,
and his dispositions were designed to protect his army from
envelopment, rather than as a means of destroying the
enemy. It is true that Auchinleck told General Gott, commanding the 13th Corps, and General Holmes, commanding the 10th Corps, that "the strongest possible resistance"
was to be offered, and that if "one corps or part of it has
to give ground the other is immediately . . . to take advantage of it by rapidly and boldly attacking the enemy in
flank." This was an admirable idea, but unfortunately for
the British, both corps commanders were left with the impression that they were to withdraw rather than run the
risk of envelopment. A battle cannot be fought in this
fashion; if Auchinleck did not feel strong enough to fight
at Matruh he should have gone back to Alamein. If he did
not want to fight at Matruh—and his forces were ample for
a successful defense—then he should not have given his
subordinates the idea that this was only a delaying action.
As a result of Auchinleck's hesitation, the British not only
lost a great opportunity of destroying the Panzerarmee but
suffered a serious defeat, which might easily have turned
into an irretrievable disaster. I stress this point, for to the
student of generalship there are few battles so instructive
as Mersa Matruh.

Our advance began on the afternoon of the 26th, and
purely by chance it struck the British at their weakest point
—the thin minefield between the escarpment and main Matruh minefields. Ninetieth Light penetrated the minefield with

---

[21] Each consisting of two platoons of infantry and a battery of field
and antitank artillery. They formed part of the 29th Indian Brigade
which had been split up into columns and "battle groups." A cynical
South African staff officer has described a battle group as "a brigade
group which has been twice overrun by tanks."

ease, and annihilated Leathercol, while 21st Panzer routed Gleecol. At one stroke the British center had been pierced, and the way was open for a deep thrust on the following day.

At dawn on 27 June 90th Light annihilated the 9th Durham Light Infantry, which for some reason had been told to take up a position seventeen miles south of Matruh.[22] Ninetieth Light reported the capture of three hundred prisoners, but was pinned down by artillery fire, and was unable to advance until the Afrika Korps came up on the south. During the morning 21st Panzer moved across the front of the 2nd N.Z. Division at Minqa Qaim, and under cover of an artillery duel worked round the New Zealanders and attacked their eastern flank. In any circumstances this would have been a risky maneuver, but it appears still more dangerous when one considers that 21st Panzer had only twenty-three tanks and about six hundred very tired infantry. Rommel himself accompanied 21st Panzer; he did not realize that the British had a whole corps around Minqa Qaim, and thought he had only to deal with the 1st Armored Division. Very fortunately the British armor failed to cooperate closely with the New Zealanders, and for most of the day was quite content to block the advance of 15th Panzer south of the escarpment.

By the evening of 27 June 21st Panzer was in a most dangerous position. The division could make no headway in its attacks on the New Zealanders (although it did scatter their main transport park), and was in danger of being cut in two. A British armored regiment, the Bays, threatened 21st Panzer on the east, and another tank force, the 3rd County of London Yeomanry, attacked from the west. Moreover, the division was hopelessly separated from 15th Panzer (whose eastward advance was blocked by the 22nd Armored Brigade) and was very short of ammunition and fuel.[23]

On the afternoon of the 27th Rommel went to 90th Light and under his supervision the division swung round the

[22] A typical example of Eighth Army's craving for dispersion.

[23] *Editor's note.* General Lumsden afterwards said of 21st Panzer on the 27th, "we should have obliterated the lot."

southern flank of the 10th Corps, and shortly after dark cut the coast road some twenty miles east of Mersa Matruh. All this was undoubtedly very disturbing to the British commanders, but if they had kept their heads they should have realized that it was the Panzerarmee which was in greater danger of destruction. Ninetieth Light with only about 1,600 men was on the coast road about fifteen miles away from the nearest troops of the Afrika Korps, and was hardly capable of tackling the British 10th Corps, which it had "cut off" so impudently. Twenty-first Panzer lay isolated to the east of Minqa Qaim, and was at the mercy of the 2nd N.Z. Division and the 1st Armored Division. Fifteenth Panzer and the Italian Armored Corps were too weak to cut through the 13th Corps and rescue 21st Panzer, while the Italian 10th and 21st Corps were badly scattered to the west and south of Mersa Matruh. Admittedly Rommel was supremely confident, for he issued orders at 1722 that 21st Panzer should "stand by in the late evening to pursue the enemy in the direction of Fuka." All this shows that Rommel had a complete contempt for the enemy, and no idea of the perils of his position.

Marshal Foch once remarked that "a battle lost is a battle which one thinks one has lost," and this saying applies exactly to the situation in the Mersa Matruh area on 27 June. That afternoon General Gott decided that in view of "enemy southward move against N.Z. eastern flank, he did not feel it safe to stay in area Sidi Hamza–Minqa Qaim," and accordingly he ordered the 2nd N.Z. Division and the 1st Armored Division to withdraw to the Fuka Line. Gott was undoubtedly influenced by Auchinleck's insistence that no part of Eighth Army was to be cut off, and that the decisive battle need not be fought in the Matruh area. Unfortunately for the British there was a serious breakdown in their signal communications, and it was not until 0430 on 28 June that the 10th Corps in Matruh was aware that the 13th Corps was in full retreat to Fuka.[24]

On the night 27/28 June the 1st Armored Division withdrew south of 21st Panzer, but the New Zealanders broke

[24] *Editor's note.* Field Marshal Wilson afterwards remarked: "13th Corps just disappeared and left 10 Corps up the pole."

clean through that hard-pressed division, and inflicted very serious losses on our infantry in bitter hand-to-hand fighting.[25] Yet we got off very lightly, when one considers that concerted attacks by the greatly superior British forces could have terminated the existence of Panzerarmee Afrika.

On 28 June 90th Light and the Italian divisions invested Mersa Matruh, and got ready to storm the fortress, while the Afrika Korps continued the eastward advance to Fuka. On the evening of the 28th 21st Panzer reached the escarpment overlooking Fuka and overwhelmed the remnants of the 29th Indian Brigade, besides capturing two trainloads of bombs and much transport.

On the night 28/29 June the 10th Corps broke out of Matruh. This enterprise led to violent clashes in the dark between the British columns and our investing troops, and although the enemy lost heavily we were unable to prevent the bulk of their troops getting through. One British column was unkind enough to choose a route through Panzerarmee battle headquarters. These things do happen in desert warfare, and it was for this reason that we had formed a special army headquarters *Kampfstaffel*. But so severe was the fighting that staff officers had to take a hand, and I have vivid recollections of firing a submachine gun during the melee. Rommel does not exaggerate when he says that "the confusion reigning on that night can scarcely be imagined."[26]

On the morning of 29 June 90th Light entered Mersa Matruh, while 21st Panzer intercepted some British columns near Fuka and captured another 1,600 prisoners. In the Battle of Mersa Matruh we took 8,000 prisoners, together with many guns and vehicles, and great quantities of war material. Fiftieth Division and the 10th Indian Division were so disorganized that they could play little part in the first critical fighting at Alamein, while the New Zealand Division

---

[25] The Afrika Korps War Diary remarked: "During these operations violations of international law, such as slaughter of wounded etc. occurred." See Brigadier George Clifton's comments in *The Happy Hunted* (London, Cassell, 1952), 224.

[26] *Krieg ohne Hass*, 171. Rommel refers to the New Zealanders breaking through his headquarters, but this is a mistake. There were no New Zealanders with the 10th Corps.

was also badly shaken. Rommel may have been lucky, but Mersa Matruh was certainly a brilliant German victory, and gave us great hopes of "bouncing" Eighth Army out of the Alamein Line.

Repulse at Alamein

Staff officers might profitably consider whether Rommel was wise to push on to Alamein immediately after his victory at Mersa Matruh. In principle it is always correct to keep on the heels of a fleeing enemy, and yet it is arguable that we would have fared better if Rommel had halted for a few days. The troops were desperately in need of sleep and rest and would have been greatly refreshed by a brief halt; our air force would have had a chance to catch up, and we would have been stronger in tanks and better off for ammunition. It should be remembered that at Alamein we had to encounter formations which had had plenty of time to rest and reorganize. First S.A. Division had been in the Alamein positions for about a week, while the 6th N.Z. Brigade and the 18th Indian Brigade had as yet played no part in the battle. The Afrika Korps and 90th Light, now very weak and utterly exhausted, were compelled to tackle fortifications manned by resolute troops in good physical condition.[27]

On the afternoon of 29 June 90th Light took the coast road from Matruh to El Daba, with the Italian 21st Corps and Littorio Division following as best they could. After dark 90th Light pushed through El Daba and, driving on amidst burning supply dumps, the division camped for the night about fifteen miles west of the El Alamein Box. It would have been well if the Afrika Korps had also taken the relatively easy path along the coast road, but Rommel hoped to cut off some of the British forces withdrawing from Mersa Matruh and deflected the Afrika Korps towards El Quseir.[28] On the evening of the 29th the Afrika Korps did

---

[27] An entry in the War Diary of 90th Light expresses disappointment after the fall of Matruh, when the division was ordered by Rommel in person to advance immediately on El Daba, and so was unable "to have a swim in the sea, and to sleep its fill after the heavy fighting for Mersa Matruh and all the hardships of the preceding days."

[28] A point in the desert about seventeen miles south of El Daba.

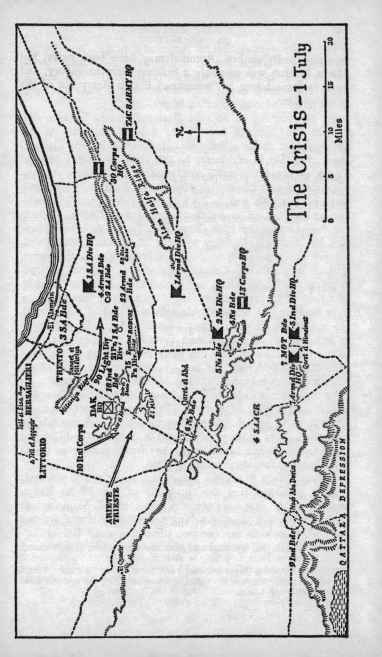

The Crisis — 1 July

Miles
0 5 10 15 20

in fact brush against the 1st Armored Division, now hurrying back to Alamein, but no serious battle developed (probably because both sides were so exhausted). This march across very rough desert imposed additional wear and tear on the tanks and used up valuable gasoline.

On the morning of 30 June Rommel formed his plan for piercing the Alamein Line.[29] He decided that the Afrika Korps should make a feint in the direction of the Qattara Depression, but should move on the night 30 June/1 July to a position about ten miles southwest of El Alamein station. We believed that the British 10th Corps, with the 50th Division and the 10th Indian Brigade, was holding the Alamein Box and a position to the southwest of it at Deir el Abyad. We thought that the 13th Corps with the 1st Armored Division, the 2nd N.Z. Division, and the 5th Indian Division was holding the southern sector of the line, between the Qaret el Abd Box and the Qattara Depression. Rommel decided to repeat the tactics which had served him so well at Matruh; under cover of the darkness the Afrika Korps was to penetrate between the boxes at Alamein and Deir el Abyad and get in rear of the 13th Corps. Ninetieth Light Division was to swing south of the Alamein Box and cut the coast road to the east of it—exactly the same orders as at Mersa Matruh. If we could once get our troops in rear of the British, Rommel was convinced that their defense would collapse.

In view of our experiences at Matruh I think that this plan offered a real hope of victory. The German forces were too weak for any heavy fighting, but they were still capable of maneuver. It is quite possible that if Rommel had got his divisions across the British rear, they would have been stampeded once more into a headlong flight.

Unfortunately Rommel's theory was never put to the test. I have remarked that the thrustline of the Afrika Korps was drawn to pass between the boxes of El Alamein and Deir el Abyad. The Afrika Korps was late—its night move from El Quseir to the concentration area near Tell el Aqqaqir was delayed by broken ground—and when it advanced

---

[29] Strictly speaking there was no such thing as an "Alamein Line," although the gap between the Qattara Depression and the sea was filled by a number of boxes.

on the morning of 1 July the corps found that there was no box at Deir el Abyad, but that the enemy was holding a box three miles farther east at Deir el Shein.[30] It might have been possible for the Afrika Korps to bypass the Deir el Shein Box and continue its move into the rear of the 13th Corps, but in that case another enemy position—actually held by the 1st S.A. Brigade north of Ruweisat Ridge—would have had to be eliminated. General Nehring decided to attack Deir el Shein, and when Rommel came up later that morning he approved of this decision.

On the afternoon of 1 July the Afrika Korps broke into the Deir el Shein Box, and after very severe fighting destroyed the 18th Indian Brigade. But we lost eighteen tanks out of fifty-five, and the fighting edge of the Afrika Korps was finally blunted. Ninetieth Light advanced during the afternoon, and attempted to bypass the El Alamein box; it ran into a crescent of fire from the 1st, 2nd, and 3rd S.A. Brigades and their supporting artillery, and was thrown into confusion not far removed from panic. Rommel himself went to 90th Light to try and urge the division forward but the volume of fire was so heavy that even he was pinned down.

Looking at the battle in retrospect it seems that our prospects of victory were hopelessly prejudiced on 1 July. Our one chance was to outmaneuver the enemy, but we had actually been drawn into a battle of attrition. First Armored Division was given an extra day to reorganize, and when the Afrika Korps advanced on 2 July it found the British armor strongly posted on Ruweisat Ridge, and quite capable of beating off such attacks as we could muster. The South African positions were strong, and 90th Light never had a chance of breaking through them. The Desert Air Force commanded the battlefield.

On 3 July Rommel abandoned the hope of getting in rear of the 13th Corps, and sought to use the Afrika Korps, 90th

[30] Held by the 18th Indian Brigade, not the 10th Indian Brigade. The Alamein box was held by the 3rd S.A. Brigade, with the 1st and 2nd S.A. Brigades holding positions outside the box and to the east of Deir el Shein. First Armored Division was not with the 13th Corps in the south, but was in rear of the 30th Corps (not the 10th Corps), and was on the east of Ruweisat Ridge.

Light, and Littorio for a concentrated thrust round the Alamein Box. We suffered a sharp reverse that morning when the New Zealanders came out of their box at Qaret el Abd, attacked Ariete Division, and captured all their artillery. Nevertheless, Rommel ordered the main attack to go in on the afternoon of 3 July, and under cover of a heavy bombardment the Afrika Korps made a determined attempt to advance. Some ground was gained on Ruweisat Ridge, but with only twenty-six tanks it was impossible to break through. When darkness fell Rommel ordered the panzer divisions to dig in where they stood; everyone realized that the offensive which opened on 26 May, and which had achieved such spectacular victories, had at last come to an end.

That night Rommel signalled to Kesselring that he had been forced to suspend his attack "for the time being." This check was all the more disappointing because our air reconnaissance reported that the British fleet had left Alexandria, and that there was much traffic en route from Egypt to Palestine; moreover, leaders of the Egyptian Liberation Movement arrived by air and made contact with Rommel. We had just failed.

9: *Farewell to Africa*

Deadlock at Alamein

ON THE MORNING of 4 July 1942 the position of Panzerarmee Afrika was perilous. The Afrika Korps had thirty-
six tanks in running order and a few hundred infantry in the
last stages of exhaustion. The artillery was very strong, for
we had a large number of captured British batteries, but our
German guns had almost run out of ammunition. (15th Panzer had two rounds per gun.) Fortunately 1,500 rounds of
25-pounder ammunition were found in Deir el Shein, and
the Italians had some reserve stocks.

There is no doubt, however, that we could not have resisted a determined attack by Eighth Army. We now know
that on 4 July Auchinleck gave orders for such an attack, but
as happened so frequently in the desert he could not stir his
corps commanders into action. Fifth N.Z. Brigade skir-
mished with the Brescia Division on the El Mireir depression, and a slight advance by British tanks on the Ruweisat
Ridge threatened to cut 15th Panzer in two. But there was no
punch or drive behind the British thrusts and a few shells
from an 88 usually sufficed to deter their tanks from any
serious assault. We survived 4 July with no real damage except to our nerves.

On 5 July our position was little better; the New
Zealanders showed some activity on the southern flank, but
their 4th Infantry Brigade was caught on the move by a
heavy and rather lucky dive-bombing attack, which by elim-

163

inating the headquarters seems to have saved us from a
thrust at El Mireir. On Ruweisat Ridge 15th Panzer had
about fifteen tanks to oppose the 1st Armored Division with
a hundred, but no attack developed. The inactivity of the
British on 5 July is particularly reprehensible, for Auchinleck was urging his subordinates to give us a knockout blow,
and a completely fresh formation— the 24th Australian Brigade—had arrived on Ruweisat Ridge.

On 6 July Rommel continued to regroup his forces and
strengthen his front; stocks of mines arrived and some reinforcements reached 90th Light and the panzer divisions. The
number of tanks in the Afrika Korps rose to forty-four, and
we began to build up a mobile reserve. The great opportunity of the British had passed; it was still possible for Auchinleck to defeat us but every day increased his difficulties.

On the morning of 9 July Rommel learned that the British
had abandoned the Qaret el Abd Box, and he at once
ordered 21st Panzer and Littorio to occupy it, and brought up
90th Light for an advance on their southern flank. We were
rather puzzled that the British should have given up such a
commanding position, and even now I find it surprising that
Auchinleck should have adopted this course. It is true that by
doing so he drew some of our forces to the south, and thus
increased his chances of success in the attack he was about
to launch at Tell el Eisa, but the yielding of a well-fortified
position like Qaret el Abd was a high price to pay.

In the early hours of 10 July the enemy opened a heavy
bombardment on Sabratha Division which was covering the
western face of the El Alamein Box, and he followed this up
with a violent attack by the 9th Australian Division along the
coast road and in the direction of Tell el Eisa. Panzerarmee
headquarters was on the coast, only a few miles behind the
front, and early that morning I was startled to see hundreds
of Italians rushing past the headquarters in the final stages of
panic and rout. Rommel had spent the night in the Qaret el
Abd Box, far to the south, and it was for me to decide what
to do. When a headquarters is threatened the first instinct is
to move and safeguard its irreplaceable equipment and documents. It was clear to me, however, that Sabratha was finished
—their artillery was already "in the bag"—and something

must be done immediately to close the road to the west. I called on the staff and personnel of headquarters to form a rough battle line, which I strengthened with our antiaircraft guns and some infantry reinforcements which happened to arrive; we succeeded in holding the Australians, who had captured the mounds of Tell el Eisa, and were seeking to thrust up the coast road. Unfortunately Lieutenant Seebohm, the brilliant head of our Wireless Intercept Section, was killed in the fighting, and most of his unit wiped out.[1]

During 10 July the main body of Infantry Regiment 382 came up; they were part of Infantry Division 164, our first substantial reinforcements from Europe. The British had launched their attack one day too late, for without these reinforcements the northern flank of the Panzerarmee could have been broken through. At noon Rommel came up from the south with his *Kampfstaffel* and a hastily organized battle group from 15th Panzer. He attempted to cut off the Australian salient at Tell el Eisa by an attack from the south, but the artillery fire from Alamein Fortress was too strong.

On 11 July the Australians renewed their attacks south of the coast road; they inflicted severe casualties on Trieste Division, and were only halted by the concentrated fire of our army artillery. The most significant feature of the new battle was that the Italian troops were no longer able to hold their positions.

On 12 July the Australians suspended their attacks, and it appeared that they were consolidating the ground gained. Rommel brought up 21st Panzer Division to the northern sector; he decided to make a direct attack on the Alamein Box on 13 July, capture that vital position, and cut off the Australians at Tell el Eisa.[2] This would have been a real victory, which might even have opened the way to the Nile.

---

[1] In his memoirs, Rommel says: "It was primarily the Panzer Army's staff, led at the time by Lieut. Col. von Mellenthin, whom we had to thank for bringing the British attack to a halt." *The Rommel Papers,* 253.

[2] Twenty-sixth Australian Brigade was in the Tell el Eisa salient. Twentieth and 24th Australian Brigades were in reserve to the east of the Alamein Box, which was held by the 3rd S.A. Brigade.

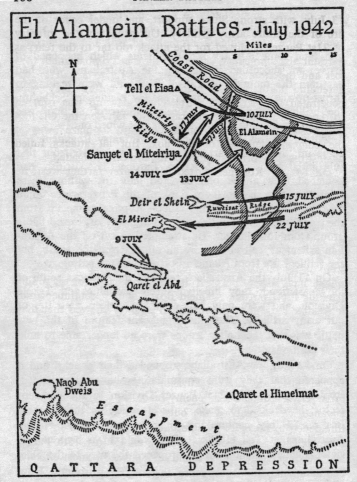

El Alamein Battles - July 1942

Miles

Coast Road

Tell el Eisa

Miteiriya

Ridge

17 JULY

10 JULY

El Alamein

21 JULY

Sanyet el Miteiriya

14 JULY   13 JULY

Deir el Shein

Ruweisat   Ridge   15 JULY

El Mireir   22 JULY

9 JULY

Qaret el Abd

Naqb Abu
Dweis

▲ Qaret el Himeimat

E s c a r p m e n t

Q A T T A R A   D E P R E S S I O N

As Rommel himself says, "the attack was to be supported by
every gun and every airplane we could muster."[3]

Twenty-first Panzer attacked the Alamein Box at noon on

[3] *The Rommel Papers,* 254.

13 July, with strong Stuka support, and under cover of the fire of the entire army artillery. Unfortunately the infantry of 21st Panzer deployed for the attack too far to the rear; as a result the immediate effect of the air bombardment was lost and the attacking troops were brought to a halt by the defending artillery and machine guns before they even penetrated the perimeter wire. The Luftwaffe was ordered to renew its attacks—concentrating this time on the enemy's gun positions—and tanks moved forward to blaze away at the concrete defenses of the box. But all attacks failed against the stubborn resistance of the 3rd S.A. Brigade.[4]

On 14 July Rommel shifted 21st Panzer farther west; he ordered the division to attack again, but to direct its thrust at the Australian positions to the southeast of Tell el Eisa, and break through to the sea. Late that evening 21st Panzer attacked with the setting sun at their backs, and under cover of heavy bombardment. But again the attacking infantry moved too late so that the paralyzing effects of the bombing were lost. Nevertheless we reached the coastal railway and might have done more, if it had not been for a galling flanking fire from the Alamein Box. Fighting continued until long after dark and the Australian infantry showed that they were the same redoubtable opponents we had met in the first siege of Tobruk.

Rommel contemplated a renewal of the attack on 15 July, but that night the 2nd N.Z. Division and the 5th Indian Brigade attacked Brescia Division on Ruweisat Ridge and broke clean through. The enemy made a deep and menacing advance, which reached the outskirts of Deir el Shein, and threatened to break our whole line. But they failed to follow up their success, and on the evening of 15 July 15th Panzer and Reconnaissance Units 3 and 33 launched a most effective counterattack, and took more than 1,200 prisoners. How-

---

[4] We believed at the time that the Alamein Box had been taken over by the 9th Australian Division—a statement repeated by Rommel in his memoirs. But the credit for this important defensive success belongs to the 3rd S.A. Brigade, and particularly to the 1st Royal Durban Light Infantry, which was manning the sector attacked, and to the 1st S.A. Field Regiment which supported them.

ever, the Italians had lost 2,000 prisoners, and the New Zealanders captured several very precious 88-mm's.[5] Moreover, the enemy retained an important foothold on Ruweisat Ridge.

On 16 July the Australians renewed their attacks from the Tell el Eisa salient; they overwhelmed the remnants of Sabratha Division but were checked by Infantry Regiment 382 and the concentrated fire of all available artillery. In the early hours of 17 July the Australians attacked again with strong tank support in the direction of Miteiriya Ridge. They pierced the front of Trieste and Trento divisions, and were only checked by German units brought from the central sector. Strong counterattacks, with Luftwaffe support, were launched during the afternoon; the Australians were forced back and lost several hundred prisoners.

The battle had developed into a struggle of attrition, and in spite of the heavy losses inflicted on Eighth Army, the Panzerarmee was passing through a dangerous crisis. We had only been able to save the front by throwing in the last reserves; the Italian units seemed to be falling to pieces and the whole burden of the battle was borne by the sorely tried German divisions. We were forced to introduce German units into the Italian divisional sectors to give them the required stiffening, and we sought by every means to improve our minefields and defenses. British authorities have criticized Auchinleck for his persistent attacks in July, 1942, but he was several times on the verge of a decisive success.

Between 18 and 21 July Eighth Army confined itself to patrol activity and harassing fire, and we utilized the breathing space to strengthen our front. Kesselring and Cavallero visited us on 17 July, and Rommel pointed out that we were

---

[5] Major General Howard Kippenberger, then commanding the 5th N.Z. Brigade, has described this action as "a bitterly disappointing battle," and ascribes the reverse in the evening to lack of co-ordination between infantry and armor. (First Armored Division was supposed to support the New Zealanders.) He says significantly that, "at this time there was throughout Eighth Army, not only in New Zealand Division, a most intense distrust, almost hatred, of our armor." See *Infantry Brigadier* (New York, Oxford University Press, 1949), 180.

near breaking point, and could not maintain our positions unless something was done about the supply question.[6]

Auchinleck was getting ready for a final attack; he proposed to renew his thrust on Ruweisat Ridge in conjunction with attacks by the 9th Australian Division from Tell el Eisa and the 1st S.A. Division towards Miteiriya Ridge. On the night of 21/22 July the 161st Indian Brigade and the 6th N.Z. Brigade attacked on Ruweisat Ridge and towards El Mireir. This attack made rapid headway, and the New Zealanders reached the El Mireir depression on the morning of 22 July after hard fighting. British tanks were supposed to support the 6th N.Z. Brigade but did not arrive in time; the 15th Panzer Division counterattacked, and took several hundred prisoners. The British 23rd Armored Brigade, which had just arrived from England, then went forward in what has been described as "a real Balaclava charge." They came under terrific antitank fire, ran onto a minefield, and were overwhelmed by a counterattack of 21st Panzer. A battalion of the 161st Indian Brigade succeeded in breaking into Deir el Shein but was wiped out in a counterattack. Thus their offensive in the center was a disaster for the British; owing to a complete lack of co-ordination and control they lost well over a hundred tanks and 1,400 prisoners.

On the northern sector the Australians and South Africans gained some ground, but failed to achieve any important breakthrough. Although our losses were heavy, particularly among the German infantry, the battle of 22 July was very favorable to us and encouraged the hope that we could hang on at Alamein.

During 23–26 July there was another lull on the front, but on the night 26/27 July the Australians made a violent attack from Tell el Eisa and captured Sanyet el Miteiriya. The plan was for the South Africans to lift mines south of this point and open a gap for the British 69th Infantry Brigade and the 1st Armored Division. Sixty-ninth Brigade advanced far into our positions, but fortunately for us the commander

---

[6] In fairness to Kesselring, this was exactly the situation which he had envisaged, when he opposed Rommel's decision to invade Egypt after taking Tobruk.

of the 1st Armored Division[7] declared that the minefield
gaps made by the South Africans were unsatisfactory and
refused to let his armor pass through until the gaps had been
improved. As a result the 69th Infantry Brigade was left
without support, and suffered crushing losses in a counterattack by a battle group of the Afrika Korps, supported by
Infantry Regiment 200. The Australians were also counterattacked and driven back to their original positions with
severe casualties.

Fighting now died down on the Alamein front; both sides
were exhausted and neither could hope for a decision without substantial reinforcements. The Panzerarmee had failed
to reach the Nile, but on 15, 22, and 27 July we had won
important defensive victories, and the balance of losses was
highly favorable to us.

The Battle of Alam Halfa

In August, 1942, the German-Italian Panzerarmee stood at
the crossroads; a decision had to be made one way or the
other. As Rommel aptly remarks, "the great summer campaign had ended in a dangerous lull."[8] Our presence at
Alamein was producing a tremendous reaction by the Anglo-
American war machine; convoy after convoy was sighted in
the Red Sea and the Gulf of Suez, and it was clear that our
enemies were gaining a decisive lead in the race to build up
supplies. Moreover these convoys were only the forerunners
of an immense flow of troops and war material to the
Middle East, and by mid-September Eighth Army would be
able to attack in overwhelming force.

Our own supply position was causing grave anxiety; we
were now paying the penalty for the failure to capture Malta, and the island was staging a remarkable recovery. A disquieting feature was the increase in range and striking power
of long-range R.A.F. bombers, which attacked shipping in
the Cyrenaican ports and interfered with the coastal traffic
towards Bardia and Mersa Matruh. Tobruk was heavily
bombed on 8 August with permanent damage to the installa-

---

[7] At this time Brigadier Fisher. General Lumsden had been wounded.
[8] *The Rommel Papers*, 262.

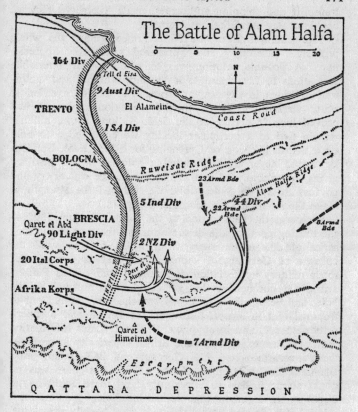

The Battle of Alam Halfa

tions; Benghazi and even Tobruk were very far from the front and the long haul between the supply ports and Alamein imposed an unbearable strain on our road transport. Because of a shortage of locomotives we were only able to use the military railway between Tobruk and El Daba to a limited degree, and here also British bombers found attractive targets. Fortunately we had captured gigantic supply dumps in Cyrenaica and Egypt, but these could no longer provide us with gasoline and ammunition. All these factors, combined with the incompetence or ill-will of the Italian transport and shipping authorities, made it obvious that we could not stay indefinitely at Alamein.

The general staff of the Panzerarmee studied the whole problem carefully and prepared detailed appreciations. A possible solution was to withdraw all nonmobile formations to Libya and to leave only armored and motorized divisions in the forward area. The British excelled at static warfare, while in mobile operations Rommel had proved himself master of the field. So long as we did not remain tied to a particular locality we could hope to hold up a British invasion of Cyrenaica for a long time. But Hitler would never have accepted a solution which involved giving up ground, and so the only alternative was to try and go forward to the Nile, while we still had the strength to make the attempt. (See footnote, page 178.)

Such was the background of the Battle of Alam Halfa—the turning point of the desert war, and the first of the long series of defeats on every front which foreshadowed the collapse of Germany. I should stress that as a matter of sober military appreciation, the general staff of the Panzerarmee did not believe that we could break through to the Nile, and before the attack was launched we pointed out to Rommel that in armored strength the British had a superiority of 3 : 1, and in air power of 5 : 1. Later information shows that we exaggerated the British superiority in armor—the Panzerarmee had 229 German and 243 Italian tanks against a British strength of about 700—but there was no doubt about British air superiority, and there could be no disputing our argument that we had insufficient gasoline for a major battle. In gun power the odds were heavily against us; and the Eighth Army front now was protected by elaborate minefields. This meant that we could not hope to defeat the British by attacking them in their fortifications, and shortage of gasoline would be a fatal handicap in any attempt to outflank and outmaneuver Eighth Army.[9]

---

[9] Cf. Chester Wilmot, *The Struggle for Europe* (London, Collins, 1952), 191. I am surprised that such an eminent military critic as Wilmot should state that "Rommel's most significant defeat occurred at Alam Halfa, seven weeks before the main battle of Alamein and at a time when Montgomery's forces were inferior in firepower and

Rommel was impressed by the arguments of his General Staff and thought seriously of giving up the offensive. But in the end he accepted Kesselring's assurance that he could fly in 90,000 gallons of gasoline a day, and we relied on a large tanker due in Tobruk at the end of August. Kesselring did in fact fulfill his promise but most of the gasoline was consumed on the long journey to the front, while the sinking of the precious tanker by a submarine off Tobruk harbor on 31 August put an end to any hope of a victorious battle. We were compelled to launch our attack on the night of 30/31 August to take advantage of the full moon. Any further delay would have meant a postponement of three weeks, which in the circumstances was out of the question.

During August we heard of important changes of command on the British side. General Alexander had replaced Auchinleck and General Montgomery had taken over command of Eighth Army. There can be no question that the fighting efficiency of the British improved vastly under the new leadership, and for the first time Eighth Army had a commander who really made his will felt throughout the whole force. Auchinleck was an excellent strategist, with many of the qualities of a great commander, but he seems to have failed in tactical detail, or perhaps in ability to make his subordinates do what he wanted. He saved Eighth Army in *Crusader* and saved it again at the beginning of July; however, his offensives later in the month were costly, unsuccessful, and from the tactical point of view extremely muddled. I am unable to say how far this was the fault of Auchinleck, or that of his corps commanders, Ramsden and Gott. But in the light of the July battles, I think Churchill acted wisely in making a change.[10]

---

armor." The Eighth Army was skilfully handled at Alam Halfa, but broadly speaking the battle is only another illustration of Napoleon's maxim that "God fights on the side of the big battalions."

[10] It is true that Churchill had wanted to put Gott in command of Eighth Army, but he was shot down and killed before he could take up the appointment. Gott was a great personality and leader, but later information throws grave doubts on his tactical skill.

Montgomery is undoubtedly a great tactician—circumspect and thorough in making his plans, utterly ruthless in carrying them out. He brought a new spirit to Eighth Army, and illustrated once again the vital importance of personal leadership in war.

Since we could not pierce the Eighth Army front, we had to seek a way round the flank, and Rommel adopted a plan broadly similar to that of Gazala. The Italian infantry, stiffened by the 164th Infantry Division and other German units, were to hold the front from the sea to a point ten miles south of Ruweisat Ridge; the striking force, consisting of the 90th Light Division (on the inner arc of the circle), the Italian Armored Corps, and the Afrika Korps, was to swing round the British left flank and advance on the Alam Halfa Ridge. This was a key position, well in rear of Eighth Army, and its capture would decide the fate of the battle. In case of success 21st Panzer was to advance on Alexandria, and 15th Panzer and 90th Light towards Cairo.[11]

The advance began on the night 30/31 August; Westphal had now returned from sick leave and resumed his duties as Ia. Rommel took Westphal with his tactical headquarters; I remained at main headquarters near Sidi Abd el Rahman, and therefore can speak only with indirect knowledge of the course of the battle.

To turn the Eighth Army front south of Qaret el Abd it was necessary to pierce a thick minebelt, which the British had laid almost as far as the Qattara Depression. Right from the start the offensive got into difficulties, for the minefields were far more elaborate than we imagined, and the British covering forces inflicted heavy losses on the mine-lifting parties. This threw our whole timetable out of gear, and gave Montgomery ample time to group his forces. The R.A.F. attacked the minefield gaps; General Nehring, the commander of the Afrika Korps, was wounded in an air

[11] In *The Rommel Papers*, 272–75, Rommel says nothing about Alam Halfa Ridge when explaining his plan, and talks rather vaguely of a thrust to the east and a subsequent advance to the coast. But the whole plan hinged on the capture of Alam Halfa, and this was fully understood before the offensive began.

attack and General von Bismarck, the brilliant commander of 21st Panzer, was killed by a mortar bomb. The dawn of 31 August found the Afrika Korps still entangled in the minefields, when Rommel had hoped that it would be sweeping north towards Alam Halfa ridge.

Rommel was half-minded to call off the attack but decided to continue when the Afrika Korps, under Bayerlein's resolute leadership, got through the minefields and made a substantial advance to the east. A heavy sandstorm blew up during the day, and although this added to the difficulties of the march it did give considerable protection from the British bombers. En route to Alam Halfa the Afrika Korps ran into very soft sand, which caused further delay and much expenditure of gasoline. In his book *Operation Victory*, General de Guingand relates how a false "going-map" was planted on us in No Man's Land by the British Intelligence; I can confirm that this map was accepted as authentic and served its purpose in leading the Afrika Korps astray.[12]

It was not until the evening of 31 August that the Afrika Korps could launch an attack on Alam Halfa. The ridge was defended by the 44th Infantry Division and the 22nd Armored Brigade, whose heavy Grant tanks had been dug-in, and were strongly supported by artillery. The Afrika Korps made a determined attack, supported by Stukas, and with the new Mark IV Special tanks in the van. Their high-velocity 75-mm guns inflicted considerable losses on the British tanks, but the defense was too strong and the attack failed.

The supply traffic through the minefields was exposed to effective attacks by the 7th Armored Division from the south and east, and on the night 31 August/1 September the leaguers of the Afrika Korps were subjected to heavy bombing attacks. On the morning of 1 September Rommel's shortage of gasoline was such that he had to limit the attack on Alam Halfa to the 15th Panzer Division. It was clear that a frontal attack offered little hope of success, and

[12] *Editor's note.* Further research shows that the practical effect of this map on German movements was slight. It should be borne in mind that part of the credit for the British victory at Alam Halfa belongs to General Horrocks, who had recently taken over the 13th Corps on the southern flank.

in other circumstances Rommel would certainly have swung
to the east and sought to maneuver the British out of the
position. However, lack of gasoline prevented any attempt
at maneuver.

Montgomery concentrated the 10th Armored Division at
Alam Halfa and had nearly four hundred tanks in this vital
area. The attack of 15th Panzer failed, the British artillery
battered the Afrika Korps unceasingly, and nonstop bombing inflicted most serious losses. Gasoline stocks were almost
exhausted, and an armored division without gasoline is little
better than a heap of scrap iron. It was no longer a question
of capturing Alam Halfa and breaking through to the coast;
the whole existence of the Afrika Korps was in jeopardy.
Throughout 1 September the panzers lay immobile, unable
to advance or retire, and under constant bombardment from
guns and aircraft.

On the morning of 2 September Rommel decided to retreat, but shortage of gasoline prevented any large-scale
withdrawal during the day, and the Afrika Korps had to remain where it was under ceaseless bombing and shellfire.
The circumstances were extremely propitious for a British
counterattack, but Montgomery made no move, apart from
the harassing operations of the 7th Armored Division north
and west of Qaret el Himeimat.

On 3 September Rommel's striking force was in full retreat to the east; we left behind fifty tanks, fifty field and
antitank guns, and about four hundred derelict vehicles.
That night the N.Z. Division attacked southwards towards
Deir el Munassib, but the attack was held after bitter fighting. By 6 September the battle was over; the one redeeming
feature was that we retained our grip on important British
minefields on the southern flank.

Eighth Army had every reason to be satisfied with this
victory, which destroyed our last hope of reaching the Nile,
and revealed a great improvement in British tactical methods. Montgomery's condust of the battle can be assessed as
a very able if cautious performance, in the best traditions of
British generalship, and strongly reminiscent of some of
Wellington's victories. There is no doubt that he deliberately

forfeited an excellent opportunity of cutting off and destroying the Afrika Korps, when it lay immobile on 1 and 2
September. Montgomery defends himself by referring to the
strategic situation and the need to build up for a major offensive, and he remarks: "The standard of training of the
Eighth Army formations was such that I was not prepared
to loose them headlong into the enemy."[13] No doubt these
are cogent arguments, but one feels that Rommel's reputation, and his well-known brilliance in counterattack had
much to do with Montgomery's caution.

The Desert War

For months I had been suffering from a severe attack of
amoebic dysentery. At the beginning of September I was no
longer indispensable on Rommel's staff, and our medical
officer strongly advised that I be flown back to Germany.
Westphal, for whom I had deputized as Ia since June, 1942,
had now returned, and there was a new Ic, Major Zolling,
who had been holding the post for a couple of months.

Nevertheless I found it hard to say good-bye to North
Africa and all my comrades, with whom I had been so closely linked during the hard and varying battles in the desert,
the more so since I realized that the situation of the German-Italian Panzerarmee had become hopeless after our final effort at the end of August.

On 9 September, when I reported "off duty" to Rommel,
he handed me an appreciation for the O.K.H. (High Command Army), which I was to give personally to the chief of
the General Staff. This appreciation pointed out the catastrophic supply situation of the Panzerarmee and asked urgently for help. The document ended as follows:

If the absolutely essential supplies cannot reach the Panzerarmee, the latter will not be in a position to resist the
united forces of the U.S.A. and the British Empire, i.e. of
two world powers. Despite its bravery the Panzerarmee will
sooner or later suffer the fate of the Halfaya garrison.

[13] Bernard L. Montgomery, *El Alamein to the River Sangro* (London,
Hutchinson, 1948).

Indeed at this stage the only course was to maintain a mobile system of defense and withdraw the main body of our forces to Libya. The refusal to consider such a policy doomed the Panzerarmee Afrika, just as the same attitude sealed the fate of Paulus' Sixth Army at Stalingrad.[14]

It is idle to speculate on what might have happened if Rommel had been present in Africa when Montgomery's attack was launched in October. Rommel was on sick leave; he flew back at once but arrived to find the position badly compromised and the reserves partially committed. Given Montgomery's great superiority in force, and his ruthless determination to win whatever the cost, I cannot see how defeat could have been avoided.

In conclusion I would like to make a few remarks about the nature of the desert war.

Firstly, as regards our Italian allies, I have no sympathy with those who talk contemptuously about the Italian soldier, without pausing to consider the disadvantages under which he labored. The armament of the Italian Army was far below modern requirements; the tanks were too light and very unreliable from a mechanical point of view. Most of the Italian guns did not have a range of over five miles, while British batteries had an effective range of five to fifteen miles. The Italian wireless sets were quite unsuited to mobile warfare and could not function on the move. The rations were inadequate, there were no field kitchens, and there was a most serious dicrimination between officers and men. The training and efficiency of the junior officers were on a very low level, and they had no close contact with their men. Senior commanders and staff officers were fairly well-trained, and proved reasonably capable.

During the North African campaign Italian troops gave many proofs of dash and courage; this applies particularly to those who came from the old cavalry regiments, and to air force units. But although they could be induced to advance with great dash, they lacked the coolness and phlegm

[14] General Warlimont, Keitel's deputy at O.K.W., visited us in July and stressed the importance of our remaining at Alamein, in view of Kleist's impending invasion of Persia from the Caucasus.

required in critical situations, and generally speaking the fighting qualities of Italian formations could not be compared with those of Eighth Army.

The divisions of Eighth Army, whether British, Indian, New Zealand, South African, or Australian, were of entirely different metal; they were tough troops and their fighting morale was high. The Long Range Desert Group was particularly good. During my service in Africa I had ample opportunity of observing the unshakeable equanimity of the British, under all conditions of war.

I do not propose to discuss British generalship; their commanders committed many grave blunders and suffered some needless and sanguinary disasters. Even the best of their generals were not as dashing or versatile as Rommel, and I don't think the British ever solved the problem of mobile warfare in open desert. In general the British method of making war is slow, rigid, and methodical; they trust to their sea power and the vast resources of their empire and dominions. It is highly probable that the senior British Air Force officers are more original and enterprising than those of the army, and I may remark in passing that their Mediterranean fleet produced some brilliant officers.

The fighting in North Africa was hard on both sides, but it was fair. Prisoners of war were decently treated, and a feeling of mutual respect developed among the combatants. This feeling forms a bond between veterans of the desert war regardless of the side on which they fought, and I have come across many instances of this when talking to former adversaries in the Union of South Africa.

One of the finest examples of the chivalrous spirit developed by the campaigns in the Western Desert, was shown in Winston Churchill's speech in the House of Commons on 27 January 1942, when he said of Rommel: "We have a very daring and skilful opponent against us, and, may I say across the havoc of war, a great general." He adds in his memoirs:

My reference to Rommel passed off quite well at the moment. Later on I heard that some people had been offended.

They could not feel that any virtue should be recognized in an enemy leader. This churlishness is a well-known streak in human nature, but contrary to the spirit in which a war is won, or a lasting peace established.[15]

[15] Winston S. Churchill, *The Hinge of Fate* (London, Cassell, 1951), 59.

They could not feel for any virtue should be rewarded in any other sense. This righteousness is well-known as it is human nature but contrary to the world in which we live one living peace assembled.

PART THREE

Russia

10: *Introduction to Russia*

Interlude

DURING OCTOBER AND part of November, 1942, I was in hospital at Garmisch in the Bavarian Alps, where I was endeavoring to get rid of the amoebic dysentery I had contracted in Africa. This is surely the most objectionable desert disease; it may easily become fatal, because these little amoebae have an unkind inclination to make a home in the liver of their victims and feed on it; if they do the end is usually near, unless an energetic war is waged on them. Luckily the German Tropical Institute had some excellent ways of combating these repulsive little fellows. A radical cure and my "convalescence" in the Russian winter of 1942–43 (with liberal and healthy doses of vodka) soon got me right again, and in no time I was up and doing.

I had been almost fifteen months in the North African desert, and the weeks I spent in the Bavarian Alps were like Paradise. Even the Royal Air Force left us alone down there, and soon we forgot all about the "German Glance"—on and near the African front one always had to be on the lookout for hostile aircraft and ready to jump for cover; this staring into the sky was called by the soldiers *Der deutsche Blick*, a parody on the *Deutsche Gruss* (the German salute).

During the quiet weeks in hospital I had long discussions with men who had gone through the ghastly winter months of 1941–42 in Russia. The German armies were surprised by this exceptional winter. The High Command had counted on a victorious conclusion to the war with Russia in the late autumn, so no special arrangements had been made to protect the troops against the hardships of a Russian winter, let alone a winter so unusual as that of 1941–42. I also spoke to an officer who had been wounded in the Caucasus a few weeks previously. The German offensive against the oilfields had seemed to be going well, but had then got stuck in the mountains. The wireless brought news about the bitter fighting near Stalingrad, but there, too, no progress was being made.

Stalingrad, El Alamein; those two names showed the immense gain of territory made by the German armies in three years of fighting. A few weeks before I had watched Rommel studying maps which showed where he proposed to cross the Nile and the Suez Canal. Decisive operations were being planned for the conquest of the Middle East—von Kleist's armies were closing in on the Caucasus, from where they were to advance into Persia. Now we were held at Alamein; our last attack had failed completely at the beginning of September. A cool appreciation of the North African situation revealed the growing strength and power of the British Eighth Army, a development which meant that sooner or later we would lose North Africa. Listening to the wireless my thoughts were always with my comrades in the desert whom I had been compelled to leave behind a few weeks before, and I followed Montgomery's offensive with a heavy heart. On 3 November he broke through our lines at El Alamein and on 8 November American and British forces landed in Morocco and Algeria. Catastrophe loomed on the horizon; the German-Italian Forces in North Africa were doomed.

Then in late November came the crushing news that the Russian armies north and south of Stalingrad had broken through the German-Rumanian lines. This meant that the German Sixth Army was encircled in the Stalingrad area, that the great offensive of 1942 had broken down, and our whole front in South Russia was in the gravest peril.

Armored Warfare in the East

In the chapters which follow I shall be dealing with some of
the most tragic events in the history of German arms—grim
and bloody battles of attrition, desperate counterattacks,
lengthy and heartbreaking retreats. These operations deserve
very careful study, for apart from their historical interest
they reveal the formidable qualities of the Russian soldier,
and the strength and weakness of his military machine. But
before discussing the somber and gloomy battles of 1943–
45, I think it would be as well if I gave some account of
German armored forces in the attack, during the days when
our offensive power was still mighty and relatively unim-
paired.

I shall say little of the battles of 1941—these have been
very fully described in General Guderian's *Panzer Leader*.
Broadly speaking our offensives of 1941 illustrate the wis-
dom of Jomini's comment, apropos of Napoleon's invasion,
that "Russia is a country which it is easy to get into, but
very difficult to get out of." In the first weeks of the invasion the German *blitzkrieg* looked as though it would carry
everything before it. At the outset the Red Air Force—tech-
nically very inferior—was overwhelmed by the Luftwaffe,
and the panzer divisions drove far and deep into Russian
territory. It will always be a question whether a different
strategy on Hitler's part would have enabled us to force a
decision in the critical year of 1941. The drive on Moscow,
favored by Guderian, and temporarily abandoned in August
in favor of the conquest of Ukraine, might have yielded decisive results if it had been ruthlessly pursued as the dominating *Schwerpunkt* of the invasion. Russia might have been
paralyzed by a thrust at the heart of Stalin's power, for the
conditions of 1941 were very different from those of 1812.
Moscow was no longer a barbaric metropolis in the middle
of a primitive and amorphous state, but was the nexus of
Stalin's administrative machine, a great industrial area, and
—perhaps most important—the center of the railway system
of European Russia.

It should not be overlooked, however, that although the

Attack by German South Wing
Summer 1942

Direction of German Thrusts ⟹   German Defensive Flank ⟹

Russian Front ·-·-·-·-■■■   Thrusts of
Russian Armoured Reserves ⟶

German forces were greatly superior in quality, and enjoyed
overwhelming air support, yet they suffered from grave disadvantages. The most serious hindrance to our invasion was
the primitive nature of the Russian road system, and on this
point Liddell Hart makes some very pertinent comments:

If the Soviet régime had given her [Russia] a road system comparable to that of western countries, she would probably have been overrun in quick time. The German mechanized forces were baulked by the badness of her roads.

But this conclusion has a converse. The Germans lost the chance of victory because they had based their mobility on wheels instead of tracks. On these mud-roads the wheeled transport was bogged when the tanks could move on.

Panzer forces with *tracked* transport might have overrun Russia's vital centers long before the autumn, despite the bad roads.[1]

A second factor was the very high quality of the Russian tanks. In 1941 we had nothing comparable with the T34, with its 50-mm maximum armor, 76-mm high-velocity gun, and relatively high speed with splendid cross-country performance. These tanks were not thrown into the battle in large numbers until our spearheads were approaching Moscow; they then played a great part in saving the Russian capital. Guderian describes how his 24th Panzer Corps was violently attacked to the northeast of Orel on 11 October 1941, and remarks significantly: "Numerous Russian T34's went into action and inflicted heavy losses on the German tanks. Up to this time we had enjoyed tank superiority, but from now on the situation was reversed."[2] As a result of Guderian's representations, measures were taken to speed up the production of our Mark III Special and Mark IV Special, and also to strengthen the existing armor of our Mark III and IV tanks.[3]

Coming to our summer offensive of 1942, I propose to describe the German breakthrough to the line of the Don,

---

[1] *The Other Side of the Hill,* 174.

[2] *Panzer Leader,* 237.

[3] After the French campaign, Hitler had seen the need for improving the firepower of our tanks and had directed that the 37-mm on the Mark III should be replaced by a long high-velocity 50-mm gun (50-mm L60). Guderian describes in *Panzer Leader,* 138, how Hitler's instructions were modified by the Army Ordnance Office, which replaced the 37-mm with the short low-velocity 50-mm L42, without seeking the Führer's authority. Guderian says that Hitler "became extremely angry and he never forgave the responsible officers of the Ordnance Office for this high-handed act." Hitler's irritation is excusable, for this disobedience went far to lose us the war.

because it illustrates very clearly the principles which governed our conduct of armored warfare, and the reasons why we achieved such spectacular tactical successes. The German offensive in South Russia in June and July, 1942, illustrates once again the vital importance of maneuver in warfare, and gives point to Guderian's expression: "The engine of the tank is no less a weapon than its gun."

During this advance our panzers were supported by a dominant air force, but in the eastern theater of war this was of less significance than in France or Africa. In the western campaigns of 1940 and 1944–45 air power had a great effect on the armored battle, but on the vast plains of Russia, tank armies were the main instrument of victory. Air support could only be secured locally and for restricted periods and never attained the degree of efficiency achieved in the western theater by the Germans in 1940 and by the Anglo-Americans in 1944–45.

I do not wish to suggest for a moment that air support is not highly desirable in Russia, but merely that the enormous fronts of 1941–42 and the relative weakness of the air forces engaged, limited the effects of air power. In fact, the Russian campaigns show that the more tank forces can be supported and supplied by air, the more extended will be the mobility of their armored units and the better their chances of success.

The sketch map on page 186 shows the front in South Russia in mid-June 1942, and the direction of the German thrusts. During the summer of 1942 our southern armies were allotted the task of smashing Marshal Timoshenko's army group and cleaning out the Don-bend between Rostov and Voronezh, thus, preparing a jumping board for a later advance on Stalingrad and towards the oilfields of the Caucasus. Operational planning set down the move on Stalingrad and the Caucasus for a later period, perhaps not before 1943.

The *Schwerpunkt* of the operation was initially with Army Group Weichs, which comprised three armies including the Fourth Panzer Army. Army Group Weichs was told to break through the Russian front in the Kursk sector. Then Fourth Panzer Army with two armored corps was to thrust through the gap and make for the Don at Voronezh. From there the Fourth Panzer Army was to swing to the right, and, incorporating the armor of Sixth Army on its flank, was to sweep southwards along the Don. It was hoped that many Russian divisions would be trapped in the great bend of the river between Rostov and Voronezh.[4]

Infantry armies were to attack simultaneously and protect the flanks and rear of the armor, particularly the northern flank which would be exposed and highly vulnerable. Army Group Weichs was to advance across ideal tank country— open rolling plains on which our panzers could maneuver with complete freedom.

Marshal Timoshenko's army group had been weakened in an abortive offensive south of Kharkov in May; moreover, the Russian High Command believed that we would attack in the Moscow area and disposed its strategic reserves accordingly. The German attack between Kursk and Kharkov was launched on 28 June, and came as a stunning surprise. A complete breakthrough was achieved, and Fourth Panzer Army thundered through the gap and headed for the Don.

General Hoth, the commander of Fourth Panzer Army, had orders to reach the Don River at Voronezh and then make a right turn to the south. He fulfilled this object within ten days, covering 120 miles, and fighting continuous actions and battles on the way. It is beyond the scope of this study to describe these operations in detail, so I will confine myself to pointing out the main factors in Hoth's success. They can be summed up as follows:

1) The order given to the armor by the High Command, i.e. by Army Group Weichs and Army Group South, was clear cut, and was never changed, amended or otherwise altered. The Russian reserves, moved up in all haste, were first overrun by the German armor, and were then dealt with by infantry divisions following up. The gravest risks were readily accepted. There was never any need for General Hoth to deviate from his true objective—the Don bank at Voronezh.

[4] For this important operation Fourth Panzer Army had eight hundred tanks and assault guns, a powerful force but by no means an overwhelming one.

2) The Luftwaffe supported the moving armor only, and no other formations were given air support.

3) Air reconnaissance flights and wings were put under direct command of Fourth Panzer Army; this enabled divisions and corps to get timely warning of the arrival of Russian armored reserves in the battle area. In the tank battle of Goroditnie—midway between Kursk and Voronezh—the leading Russian tank formations ran head on into the antitank guns of the Panzer Corps and were then wiped out by German tanks attacking them in flank and rear. As our commanders were able to look in good time at "the other side of the hill," they could set traps for the approaching Russians, and smash their counterattacks one after the other. Like the French in 1940, the Russian Command lost its head and threw in reserves piecemeal. This played into the hands of Fourth Panzer Army.

4) All senior officers, including corps commanders handling several panzer divisions, travelled in the forefront of the advance. Even General Hoth was more often with the leading tank units than with his staff, although army headquarters was always uncomfortably close to the front. The divisional commanders drove with the foremost tanks and were accompanied by armored signal links with whose help they directed the complicated movements of their troops. They got a first-hand impression of the progress of the battle and were able to take instant advantage of every opportunity. Many of the officers in Fourth Panzer Army had served in the cavalry, and retained much of the dash and élan associated with the *arme blanche*.

During the advance of Fourth Panzer Army to the Don, the infantry of the German Second Army drew an ever-thicker curtain between Voronezh and Orel, a curtain the Russian armor tried in vain to penetrate. On reaching Voronezh the panzer divisions executed their swing to the south. This "right-turn" coincided with particularly violent attacks against Second Army, and there was a strong temptation to hold back the armor to support the infantry. One Russian armored corps after another came up and hurled itself against the northern flank, which was still weak and inadequately protected. But the road to the south lay open, and the German army groups refused to be diverted from their aim. Army Group Weichs and Army Group South

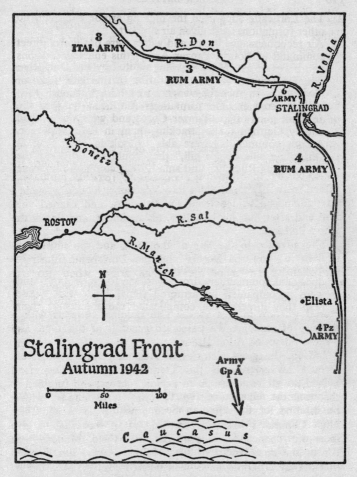

Stalingrad Front
Autumn 1942

0 50 100
Miles

brushed aside the misgivings of Second Army, and strict orders were given for all available tanks to attack southwards. Thanks to the will-power and resolution of Field Marshal von Weichs, and his colleague Field Marshal List, a spectacular victory was won. Timoshenko's armies were rolled up from north to south, and Hoth's panzers raced along the flat bare plains between the Donetz and the Don. The heat and dust were trying to the troops but nothing stopped the advance; Rostov fell on 23 July and our High Command claimed 240,000 prisoners.

The depth of the battlefield was limited by the Don River, which prevented the troops hurling themselves into unlimited space. In fact the vanguard of Fourth Panzer Army actually crossed the Don and entered Voronezh on 3 July, quite contrary to the original plan. After all, it is not easy for the High Command to restrain the daredevil, quick thinking, and resolute leader riding against the enemy in the foremost tank. In this case, a squadron commander, intoxicated by the impetus of headlong pursuit, hurled his fifteen to twenty tanks right into Voronezh, having wrenched an undamaged bridge from the Russians, and carried with him and after him his battalion, his regiment, and finally the whole division.

The advance to the line of the Don, and the subsequent exploitation towards Rostov and the Don bend, illustrates the offensive power of the German armor when properly controlled and directed. The tactical superiority of our panzer divisions was fully demonstrated, but the conduct of armored warfare in vast spaces also requires generals with a mastery of strategy. We possessed generals of this type, and we also possessed Adolf Hitler.

Indeed, the great victories of June and July, 1942, were thrown away because the German Supreme Command lacked the strategic insight to exploit success, and fumbled at the moment when decisive victories were almost within reach. The Russians had suffered crushing losses and their High Command was badly rattled, but it was vital to give them no chance to recover balance. Field Marshal von Kleist, the commander of First Panzer Army, has asserted that Stalingrad could have been taken in July, 1942, and he told Liddell Hart:

The 4th Panzer Army was advancing . . . on my left. It could have taken Stalingrad without a fight at the end of July, but was diverted south to help me in crossing the Don. I did not need its aid, and it merely congested the roads I was using.

When it turned north again, a fortnight later, the Russians had gathered just sufficient forces at Stalingrad to check it.[5]

There followed one of the greatest misfortunes in German military history—the splitting of our effort between Stalingrad and the Caucasus. It was von Kleist's opinion that he could have attained his object and reached the vital oilfields of the Caucasus if his forces had not been drawn away piecemeal to assist our Sixth Army at Stalingrad. When Stalingrad was not taken in the first rush, it would have been better to mask it, for by concentrating his offensive on a great city and resorting to siege warfare, Hitler was playing into the hands of the Russian Command. In street warfare the Germans forfeited all their advantages in mobile tactics, while the inadequately trained but supremely dogged Russian infantry were able to exact a heavy toll.

In the autumn of 1942 Hitler committed the oldest and simplest mistake in warfare—neglect of the principle of concentration. The diversion of effort between the Caucasus and Stalingrad ruined our whole campaign.

Encirclement at Stalingrad

There is very little authentic material available on the Battle of Stalingrad—Plivier's book[6] contains some grim and vivid pen-pictures but it is essentially a work of fiction, written without direct knowledge of the events it purports to portray. Very fortunately I have had the assistance and advice of a senior officer who was with the Stalingrad army until a few days before the final surrender. This is Colonel H. R. Dingler of the German General Staff; he served as Ia of the 3rd Motorized Division and has put his detailed account of the operations at my disposal.

Dingler says that on reaching Stalingrad the German attackers had reached the end of their power. Their offensive strength was inadequate to complete the victory, nor could they replace the losses they had suffered. These facts were

[5] *The Other Side of the Hill*, 214.
[6] Theodor Plivier, *Stalingrad: The Death of an Army* (London, Athenaeum, 1952).

sufficient not only to justify a withdrawal but to compel a retreat. However, the German Supreme Command refused to accept the idea of retreat, disregarding the lessons taught by history and the experience of previous wars. The result of this attitude was Stalingrad and the utter destruction of an army.

In this connection Dingler quotes Clausewitz:

The condition in which an attacking force may find itself on attaining its objectives may be such that even a victory may compel a withdrawal, because the attacker may not have enough offensive power left to enable the troops to exploit their victory or because he is unable to replace casualties.

This dictum seems to recall Napoleon's comment on the Battle of Borodino in 1812: "Had I pressed my victory home, I would have had no troops for further victories." Such a state of affairs can easily occur in operations against Russia, with her vast spaces, unyielding climate, and immense resources.

Dingler relates that on 21 August 1942, the 16th Panzer Division and the 3rd Motorized Division of the 14th Panzer Corps advanced from the Don bridgehead at Peskowatka towards the Volga north of Stalingrad. Fourteenth Panzer Corps was given the task of covering the northern flank of the main German forces advancing between the Volga and the Don on Stalingrad; the distance between the two rivers was approximately forty-five miles. Sixteenth Panzer Division was to take up a position facing north, with its right wing on the western bank of the Volga. Third Motorized Division was to join the left wing of the 16th Panzer Division; the line between the 3rd Motorized Division and the Don River was to be occupied by infantry divisions.

The terrain between Don and Volga is steppe country with desert characteristics. The altitude varies between 225 and 500 feet above sea level. The German advance was hampered by numerous Balkas (dry river beds with steep and precipitous banks mostly running in a north–south direction). The resistance offered by the Russians between the Don and the Volga was comparatively slight. Centers of resistance were usually left alone by the mobile troops, and were dealt with later by the infantry who followed behind. Fourteenth Panzer Corps did not find it very difficult to take up its allotted north-facing defensive positions. But in the sector of the 3rd Motorized Division there was one hill and one Balka which did not surrender and were to give great trouble for a number of weeks.

Dingler points out that the initial resistance of the Russians on the hill was not taken very seriously, and it was confidently expected that it would fall as soon as the whole division came up. He says: "Had we known that this very hill would cause us so much trouble and many losses during the months to follow, we would have pressed home our attack more energetically." Dingler draws the following conclusion:

This incident taught us an important lesson. When we were unsuccessful in throwing the Russian out of his position, or in breaking through or surrounding him, while we were still carried forward by the momentum of our forward move, further attempts usually brought us heavy losses or demanded much stronger forces to subdue resistance. The Russians are masters at digging in and erecting field fortifications. They are infallible at discovering positions which are essential for future operations, such as this hill, where they could sit and look far into our rear.

The Balka held by the Russians was in the rear of the 3rd Motorized Division; it was long, narrow, and very deep, and held out for week after week. Dingler's account of the operation reveals the tenacity of the Russian soldier when fighting on the defensive:

All our attempts to get the better of the Balka held by the enemy had so far been in vain. We tried Stuka attacks and artillery shoots. We had assault troops attacking it; they achieved nothing, but suffered heavy losses. The Russians had dug themselves in too well. We thought that about four hundred men was a more or less correct estimate of the enemy's strength. In normal circumstances a force of that size should have surrendered after a fortnight. After all, the Russians were completely cut off from the outside world. Nor was there any chance of supply by air, as at that time we had undoubtedly air superiority. Now and then at night small single-seater open aircraft tried their luck and dropped an insignificant quantity of supplies to the encircled Russians. One must not forget that Russians are not like normal soldiers where supplies are concerned. On many occasions we found out how little they needed.

This Balka was a thorn in our side, but we could not count on reducing it by starving the garrison. Something had to be done.

Having exhausted all the wiles and arts which our training as staff officers had taught us, we thought it would be a good thing to allow the real fighting man a chance. Therefore we called in our lieutenants. Three of them were instructed to go into the matter and think up something useful. After three days they reported back and submitted their plan. They suggested subdividing the Balka into several sectors and putting tanks and antitank guns opposite the holes of the Russians on the slopes below. Then our assault troops were to work themselves down to these holes and smoke them out.

Everything went according to plan—the Russians didn't even wait to be fetched personally from their holes but followed the invitation of a few hand grenades and other explosives. We were very surprised when we counted our prisoners and found that instead of four hundred men, we had captured about *a thousand*. For nearly four weeks these thousand men had subsisted on grass and leaves and on a minimum of water which they dug up by sinking a deep hole into the ground. What is more, they not only had lived on so little, but put up a stiff fight to the very end.

Meanwhile the main German assault was proceeding against the City of Stalingrad. Russian resistance was very strong and determined and the attacking troops were compelled to fight their way forward street by street, block by block, and house by house. The losses suffered were fearful and the fighting strength of the troops dwindled alarmingly.

Stalingrad is situated on the western bank of the Volga, which is more than two miles broad at this point, and the city extends from north to south for over twenty miles. The core of the city consists of modern factories, while on the outskirts there are, or rather were, the small wooden dwellings of the population. The precipitous bank of the river offers excellent possibilities for the defender, and small nests of resistance held out here until Stalingrad was again in Russian hands. The factory buildings also had great defensive value and our efforts to liquidate these positions caused us very disproportionate losses. By Hitler's personal order five engineer battalions were flown to Stalingrad, but their strength ebbed away after a few days. Tactically these nests of resistance did not influence the general situation in the Stalingrad area at all, but Hitler thought that the mopping-up of the city was a matter of political prestige. Thus many of the best German formations were sacrificed and irreparable losses were suffered.

During this fighting the 14th Panzer Corps was settling down in defensive positions on the northern flank of the Stalingrad sector. The terrain was flat and open rising gently to the north, and as far as the 3rd Motorized Division was concerned, it was very difficult to find positions not overlooked by the Russians—they still held the dominating hill mentioned above. Divisional headquarters dug trenches in a very shallow Balka, and Dingler says, "There we sat for two months and many an anxious moment was spent there." He adds: "Our shallow Balka had only one advantage; no senior officer ever risked visiting us."

Early in September the Russians began to attack the 14th Panzer Corps to ease the position of the defenders of Stalingrad. These attacks were invariably supported by strong armored forces; day after day more than a hundred tanks with the typical Russian massed infantry hurled themselves against the panzer corps. The attacks conformed to the accepted Russian principle—once "Ivan" makes up his mind to launch an attack and gain certain objectives, he throws in masses of troops and continues to do so until he has secured his objectives or exhausted his reserves. Consideration for casualties plays no part whatever, and does not influence Russian determination at all. The attacks against the northern sector continued until late in October, and Dingler makes the following comments on them:

I do not say too much when I state that during these attacks our position seemed hopeless on more than one occasion. The reinforcements in men and material we received from home

were utterly insufficient. Those men who had no previous
battle experience were quite useless in this hard fighting. The
losses they suffered from the first day in the fighting line were
staggering. We could not "acclimatize" these people gradually to battle conditions by attaching them to quiet sectors,
because there were no such sectors at that time. Nor was it
possible to withdraw veterans from the front to give these raw
recruits thorough training.

The Russian artillery fire was very heavy indeed. Not only
did the Russians shell our forward lines, but their long-range
guns fired far into our rear. It may be worthwhile to make
a few remarks on our experiences during those anxious weeks.
Our artillery then became one of the most important factors
in the defense system. As casualties increased and the strength
of our infantry decreased, the main burden of repulsing
Russian attacks had to be borne by the guns. Without our
artillery, so well-trained and efficient, it would have been
impossible to hold out as long as we did against massed
attacks, persistently repeated. In principle we only used concentrated artillery fire, and we tried to shoot up the Russian
assembly areas before they had time to develop their attacks.
It was interesting to note that Russians are very sensitive to
artillery fire, if to nothing else.

We learned not to use positions on forward slopes, as they
could not be protected against attacks by armor. It must not
be forgotten that our main antitank defense lay in our armor,
and we concentrated all tanks in hollows immediately behind
the main line of resistance. From these positions they were
able to knock out the Russian tanks as soon as they reached
the crest of the height above. At the same time the panzers
were able to protect our infantry on the reverse slope from
being overrun by Russian armor.

That our tactics were quite effective is shown by the fact
that we counted more than two hundred Russian tanks
knocked out during this two months fighting on our divisional
front.

The commander of the 14th Panzer Corps, General von
Wietersheim, realized that the situation was deteriorating
rapidly, as his corps became weaker day by day, whereas the
Russian attacks grew fiercer and were carried out with an
unheard-of sacrifice of men and material, and a complete
disregard of the most bloody carnage. The moment would

soon come when he would no longer be able to protect the northern flank of the forces attacking in the Stalingrad area. General von Wietersheim reported along these lines, and submitted that the formations operating in the Stalingrad venture be withdrawn to the west bank of the River Don, if no reinforcements could be made available. Had his proposal been accepted, there would have been no Stalingrad catastrophe. But it was not accepted, nor were reinforcements sent forward; the only result of von Wietersheim's report was that he was relieved of his post because he held opinions which those above him regarded as too pessimistic.[7] During October the Russian attacks against the 14th Panzer Corps diminished in strength; the enemy was regrouping his forces and getting ready for a big counteroffensive.

Divisional and even corps staffs in the Stalingrad area knew precious little about the general situation, as Hitler's orders allowed nobody to know more than was absolutely necessary for carrying out his immediate task. Consequently, mad rumors circulated among the rank and file. But quite apart from rumors, the strategic situation was serious enough. Six miles south of Stalingrad the Russians still held a strong bridgehead at Beketonskaya, and they also retained bridgeheads on the western bank of the Don. It became known that Hungarian, Italian, and Rumanian armies had occupied positions on the Don from Voronezh southwards; this certainly did not serve to encourage the German troops —the fighting value of our allies was never overestimated, nor was their poor equipment calculated to enhance their reputation. Nobody could understand why Rumanian formations had given up part of the huge Don bend, allegedly to save troops for other purposes, but actually yielding an area which it would have been easy to defend, and thus handing over a most valuable bridgehead to the Russians.

In November a new panzer corps, consisting of a German and a Rumanian armored division, moved into the Don bend. This was the 48th Panzer Corps, and at the end of November I was appointed its chief of staff. But meanwhile

---

[7] He was replaced by General Hube.

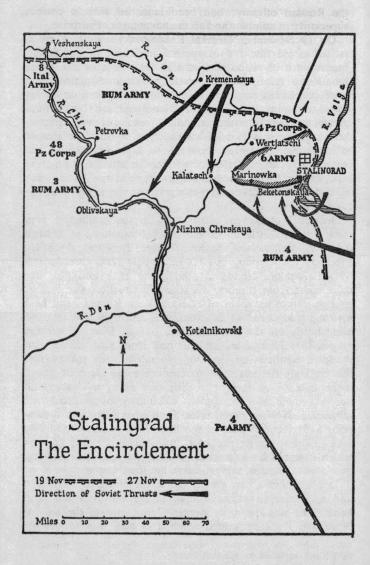

Stalingrad
The Encirclement

19 Nov === 27 Nov ====
Direction of Soviet Thrusts ⟵

Miles 0 10 20 30 40 50 60 70

the Russian offensive had been launched with a crushing superiority in numbers and all the advantages of surprise.

On 19 November General Rokossovsky's Tank Army attacked in overwhelming strength from its bridgehead at Kremenskaya in the Don bend; the thrust was launched in conjunction with an attack from the Beketonskaya bridgehead south of Stalingrad. Both blows fell on Rumanians—their Third Army was holding the Don bend, and their Fourth Army was south of Stalingrad. I pass in silence over the scenes of panic and confusion produced by this new Russian offensive;[8] the two thrusts made rapid headway, and converged towards Kalatsch on the River Don.

Colonel Dingler thus describes how the news of these developments was received in the 3rd Motorized Division:

On 20 November things began to happen around Stalingrad. Sixteenth Panzer Division, our neighbor on the right, received orders to leave their present positions at once and move to the western bank of the Don by way of Kalatsch. Something very serious must have happened.

On 21 November we heard from our supply troops who were stationed on the east bank of the Don and south of Kalatsch, that Russian tanks were approaching the town from the south. Other supply units stationed in the area west of the Don informed us by wireless that Russians were approaching Kalatsch from the north. It was clear that the *encirclement* of Stalingrad would soon be a reality. We realized how difficult it would be to break that ring with the forces at our disposal—their weakness was only too apparent.

If the Russians decided to advance with powerful forces in

[8] In his book *Stuka Pilot* (Dublin, Euphorion, 1952), 63, Hans Rudel says of the breakthrough in the Don bend on 19 November: "One morning after the receipt of an urgent report our wing takes off in the direction of the bridgehead at Kletskaja. The weather is bad, low lying clouds, a light fall of snow; the temperature probably 20 degrees below zero; we fly low. What troops are those coming towards us? We have not gone more than half way. Masses in brown uniforms— are they Russians? No, Rumanians. Some of them are even throwing away their rifles in order to be able to run the faster; a shocking sight, we are prepared for the worst. We fly the length of the column heading north, we have now reached our allies' artillery emplacements. The guns are abandoned not destroyed. The ammunition lies beside them. We have passed some distance beyond them before we sight the first Soviet troops."

the area west of the Don their line of encirclement would be a very hard nut to crack. In spite of all these worries everybody remained calm in our sector. There was not the slightest suspicion of panic—after all, most of us had gone through the experience of an encirclement or two. It couldn't be very much worse this time, and everything would turn out all right in the long run.

All remained quiet on the northern front. On 24 November it became clear beyond any doubt that we had been encircled by strong Russian forces. In his large-scale offensive, the enemy coming from the north had broken through the Don bend and, having been stopped for a short time on the southern edge of the bend, had appeared in Kalatsch with a huge tank force. It was most regrettable that, making use of the moment of surprise and of the general confusion prevailing on the German side, he had succeeded in taking possession of the bridge across the Don before it could be demolished.

Simultaneously Russian forces, debouching from their bridgehead at Beketonskaya, had advanced through the steppe from the south without encountering any serious resistance, as there were no German fighting troops in that sector, only supply units.

Our formations fighting on the west bank of the Don were pressed eastwards and, crossing the river on still undamaged bridges near Wertjatschi, joined the beleaguered German forces round Stalingrad. The headquarters of Sixth Army on the Don bank found itself in the direct line of advance of the Russian armor, and had to withdraw for the time being to the Chir sector west of the Don. However, a few days later army headquarters moved by air into the Stalingrad area, and established itself near Gumrak.

Sixth Army now had to reorganize its dispositions. Fourteenth Panzer Corps had to fold back its left wing, which until then had been in position on the Don; the 3rd Motorized Division received orders to push towards Kalatsch and the Don. But the enemy was far too strong and the division was halted west of Marinowka.

At the end of November Colonel General Paulus, commander in chief of Sixth Army, decided to launch an attack in a westerly direction to break the line of encirclement, and join up with the Germans and Rumanians fighting west of the Don. But Hitler sent the order: "Hold out. Relief will come from outside."

Paulus believed this promise and believed it too long.

11: *"And Quiet Flows the Don"*

The High Command

WHEN I RETURNED from Africa in September, I had reported to Colonel General Halder, chief of the Army General Staff, and had given him Rommel's letter stressing the gravity of the position at Alamein. Halder had received me with his accustomed courtesy and asked various questions in his academic and rather professorial manner. The interview took place at the Führer's headquarters at Rastenburg in East Prussia, and although Halder was concerned at the situation in the desert, I had no doubt that his thoughts, and indeed the attention of the whole O.K.W.,[1] were concentrated on the campaign in Russia.

We now know that in September, 1942, Halder had bitter arguments with Hitler on the advisability of continuing the offensive at Stalingrad, and drew his attention to the dangers of exposing a long flank, manned by inferior troops, to the full weight of the Russian counteroffensive. Halder foresaw the catastrophe which was impending between the Volga and the Don, but his insistence merely led to his removal, and his replacement on 25 September by General Zeitzler. Hitler is said to have remarked: "I dismissed General Halder because he could not understand the spirit of my plans."

In November I was discharged from hospital and after a

---

[1] Oberkommando Wehrmacht or Supreme Headquarters. I also reported at army headquarters (O.K.H.).

short convalescence, I understood that I was to get an "easy assignment" somewhere on the Channel coast. But it was not to be; I received orders to report to General Zeitzler in East Prussia, and on 27 November I stood in the same quiet room where I had spoken to General Halder some weeks before. Zeitzler's manner was different from that of his predecessor; he was sharp and abrupt, but was clearly a very competent staff officer with a mastery of detail.[2] He informed me of my appointment as chief of staff of the 48th Panzer Corps, and gave me his appreciation of the situation around Stalingrad. It was my impression that Zeitzler did not think it would be possible to relieve Sixth Army, and that Paulus' only chance was to break out. We now know that he gave this advice to Hitler, but it was summarily rejected by the Führer, who accepted Göring's assurance that he could supply Sixth Army by air.[3]

On leaving Zeitzler I sought more detailed information in the Operations Room. On 19 November the Russians had broken out of the Kremenskaya bridgehead with three armored corps, two cavalry corps, and twenty-one rifle divisions; they had pierced the Rumanian positions and made a breach twenty miles wide. Forty-eighth Panzer Corps, in reserve behind the Rumanian Third Army, had counterattacked with the 13th Panzer Division and the Rumanian tanks under its command, but had been hurled back by the Russian masses. The corps commander, General Heim, and his chief of staff, Colonel Friebe, had been relieved of their posts for alleged inability to take a decision. A few days later I heard from Colonel von Oppeln of the 13th Panzer Division that the advance of his panzer regiment was indeed delayed, because the lighting flexes of his tanks had been eaten through—by mice. However, rightly or wrongly,

---

[2] Zeitzler's rise had been very rapid. At the beginning of the war he was only a regimental commander; he was chief of staff to von Kleist's Panzer Army in France in 1940, and Russia in 1941. In 1942 he was appointed chief of staff to von Rundstedt in France.

[3] At a conference on 12 December 1942 Hitler insisted on the impossibility of a retreat from Stalingrad as this would involve sacrificing "the whole meaning of the campaign." See *Hitler Directs his War,* ed. by Felix Gilbert (New York, Oxford University Press, 1950).

corps headquarters was held responsible for the delay—hence my appointment.

The Russian advance from the Beketonskaya bridgehead on the Volga had been made by two armored corps and nine rifle divisions, which had joined hands with their comrades at Kalatsch on 22 November, thus closing the ring round Sixth Army. Between the Volga and the Don six Russian armored brigades and twenty rifle divisions were exerting strong pressure on the northern flank of Sixth Army.

The large situation map in the Operations Room was not pleasant to look at. I tried to find the location of my 48th Panzer Corps, but there were so many arrows showing breakthroughs and encirclements that this was far from easy. In fact on 27 November the 48th Panzer Corps was itself encircled in a so-called "small cauldron" to the northwest of Kalatsch.

Such were the impressions at the Führer's headquarters on 27 November; on the morning of the 28th I set off by air for Rostov, where I was to report to the newly-formed headquarters of Army Group Don. There seemed to be no end to the flight of the good old Ju.52 from East Prussia; we flew over battered Warsaw, then across the roadless Pripet Marshes, and the snow-covered plains of the Ukraine. We came down for a brief halt at Poltava, with its ominous memories of the invasion of Charles XII, and arrived at Rostov late in the afternoon. Covering 1,500 miles, I gained a good impression of the endless spaces of Russia, and the immense distances involved.

That evening I reported to Field Marshal von Manstein, and his chief of staff, General Wöhler. Manstein had aged since he had visited our division in Poland in 1940, but his reputation had grown with the years, and his exploits in the initial advance into Russia, and subsequently in the conquest of the Crimea, had raised his fame higher than that of any commander on the Eastern Front. As an expert on siege warfare he had been sent to the Leningrad sector to plan the capture of the old Russian capital, whence he had been hastily summoned to restore the situation on the Don and open a way to Stalingrad. Manstein, who has been aptly de-

scribed as "an emotional man who seeks protection under
an icy exterior,"[4] passed me on to his Ia, Colonel Busse.

From Busse I obtained new information, to supplement
what I had learned in the Operations Room at O.K.W. According to him, Sixth Army with twenty divisions was encircled by approximately sixty Russian divisions. The Rumanian Fourth Army between Elista and Stalingrad had
been crushed by the Russian advance from the Volga and
could no longer be regarded as a fighting force. But there
was a thin screen of elements of Fourth Panzer Army under
Colonel General Hoth, on a line extending from Elista to
Kotelnikovski. This screen had the task of covering the rearward communications of Army Group A under Field Marshal von Kleist. The latter army group was fighting in the
Caucasus and its rearward communications ran through
Rostov. The first reinforcements for Fourth Panzer Army
were already en route from the Caucasus front.

It appeared that the main body of the enemy east of the
Don was still facing Sixth Army. This had made it possible
for Luftwaffe formations and rear-services personnel to build
up defensive positions west of the Don bend, though they
were but thinly manned. The Rumanian Third Army had
been rushing back to the west, but thanks to the energetic
steps of Colonel Wenck, who was attached to the Rumanians
as their chief of staff, the retreat was halted and some line
of resistance was established in the Oblivskaya area as far
north as Veshenskaya on the Don. (See the map on page
200.) There the Rumanians joined hands with the east wing
of the Italian 8th Army which had yet to be attacked (a
pleasure to come!). Forty-eighth Panzer Corps with its 13th
Panzer Division, not to speak of its one half of a Rumanian
armored division, had fought its way out of encirclement and
had withdrawn; the corps had taken up positions on the
River Chir, west of Petrovka.

Army Group Don was assembling forces on both sides of
Kotelnikovski. These reinforcements came mainly from the
Caucasus front; they were to strengthen Hoth's Fourth Pan-

[4] R. T. Paget, *Manstein: His Campaigns and His Trial* (London,
Collins, 1951), 2.

zer Army and enable him to relieve Stalingrad. When the
situation allowed, the 48th Panzer Corps was to move south
of the Don and support Fourth Panzer Army in its fateful
counterattack.

At dawn on 29 November I flew to the battle headquarters of the 48th Panzer Corps. My aircraft was a Storch, and
the pilot and I watched out carefully, lest we land on the
wrong side of the front. Flying at tree-top height I obtained a truthful impression of "Mother Russia." The terrain on both sides of the Don is one vast endless steppe,
broken occasionally by deep valleys, in which villages are
tucked away. The landscape recalled the North African
desert, but with snow instead of sand. As we came down on
the small frontline airfield, I realized that I had entered a
new and very grim phase of my military career.

With the 48th Panzer Corps

On my arrival at headquarters of the 48th Panzer Corps I
found a situation which gave no cause for rejoicing. After
the unsuccessful counterattack, the corps commander and
his chief of staff had been relieved of their posts; their dismissal was so summary that they were not even given time
to hand over to their successors. It goes without saying that
this is not the way in which things should be done. But it
was Hitler's way. The only man I could turn to in this
turbulent situation was the Ia, Major von Ohlen, a member of
the General Staff and an old friend of mine. He and I had
been together at many steeplechases—back in happier days.

To obtain a realistic picture of the situation, I proceeded
to the tank regiment of the 13th Panzer Division, which was
about to launch a counterattack to regain ground lost during
the previous night. This counterattack was successful and
two captured villages were retaken, the Russians literally
fleeing in panic. The success was due to perfect co-operation
of artillery, panzergrenadiers, and tanks. In this action, as in
so many others I was to see in the future, the absolute
superiority of German armored troops over Russian was
glaringly apparent. But the German armored units were like
isolated rocks in a vast ocean with the Russian masses rush-

ing past to their right, to their left, and far behind. I also went to see the Rumanian formations under our command. During my inspection it became painfully clear that they could not possibly stand up against an offensive as formidable as the present one. The Rumanian artillery had no modern gun to compare with the German and, unfortunately, the Russian artillery. Their signals equipment was insufficient to achieve the rapid and flexible fire concentrations indispensable in defensive warfare. Their antitank equipment was deplorably inadequate, and their tanks were obsolete models bought from France. Again my thoughts turned back to North Africa and to our Italian formations there. Poorly trained troops of that kind, with old-fashioned weapons, are bound to fail in a crisis.

On 30 November General Cramer took over the temporary command of the 48th Panzer Corps. Cramer at a later date was captured by the British when he was in command of the Afrika Korps in Tunisia; he was an old veteran of the desert and had fought with distinction at Sidi Rezegh. But it was no time to indulge in reminiscences; the situation at the front was critical enough and demanded immediate action. Although the Rumanian Third Army, of which the 48th Panzer Corps was the most efficient formation, had succeeded in forming a line along the River Chir, yet I for one had grave doubts whether it would hold against a resolute attack. Reserves were very weak and the line had only been established by the desperate expedient of drawing men from the supply services and forming new units out of stragglers. At this time we were still holding a small bridgehead on the left bank of the Don at Nizhna Chirskaya, only twenty-five miles from the nearest troops of Sixth Army at Marinowka. But the Russians were well aware of the need to force us back westwards, and early in December their Fifth Tank Army launched heavy attacks and crossed the Chir at various points.

When these attacks developed the headquarters of the 48th Panzer Corps had left Petrovka, and had moved on 4 December to Nizhna Chirskaya, where the Chir flows into the Don. (The 13th Panzer Division and the Rumanian tanks were left behind to sustain the defense of the Ruma-

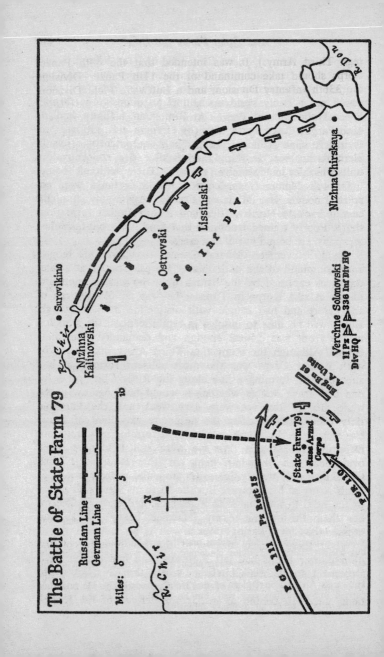

The Battle of State Farm 79

Russian Line
German Line

Miles: 0   5   10

N

R. Chir

R. Don

Surovikino

Nizhna Kalinovski

Ostrovski

Lissinski

Nizhna Chirskaya

36 Inf Div

Verchne Solmovski

11 Pz Div HQ   336 Inf Div HQ

State Farm 79
I Russ Armd Corps

Bng Bn 61
AA Units

PzGB 111

Pz Regt 15

PzGB 110

nian Third Army.) It was intended that the 48th Panzer Corps should take command of the 11th Panzer Division, the 336th Infantry Division, and a Luftwaffe Field Division, which on 4 December were still moving up to the front.[5] When Hoth's Fourth Panzer Army moved on Stalingrad, the 48th Panzer Corps was to cross the Don and join hands with their left flank. Colonel Adam, a member of the staff of Sixth Army, was at Nizhna Chirskaya, with some scratch units which he had assembled there.

On 4 December General von Knobelsdorff, the newly appointed commander of the 48th Panzer Corps, arrived at our headquarters; it was my privilege to serve as his chief of staff during the almost uninterrupted defensive and offensive fighting on the Chir, on the Donetz, and subsequently around Kharkov and Kursk. He was a man of remarkable attainments, flexible and broad-minded, and highly esteemed by all members of his staff. Almost at once the new commander found himself involved in a dangerous crisis.

The Battles on the Chir River

On 6 December the 336th Infantry Division took up positions on the Chir between Nizhna Chirskaya and Surovikino, and that day General Balck, the commander of 11th Panzer, arrived at Nizhna Chirskaya to reconnoiter the sector where his division was to cross the Don to co-operate with Hoth's Fourth Panzer Army. But we were not destined to play any part in the attempt to relieve Stalingrad—on 7 December the Russian 1st Armored Corps forced its way over the Chir on the left flank of the 336th Division and swept forward to the settlement of Sowchos 79, far in rear

---

[5] These troops differed greatly in quality. Eleventh Panzer and the 336th Infantry were excellent divisions but the Luftwaffe Field Division was less satisfactory. These divisions were a creation of Göring who aspired to command ground troops as well as the Luftwaffe. His divisions were given excellent human material and the best of equipment, but their training was quite inadequate. They were commanded by air force men who knew nothing about land fighting. The Ia of this particular Luftwaffe division was a charming fellow, whom I had known as Air Liaison Officer of the 3rd Corps in 1939. He had then carried out his duties very well, but he had no idea of the responsibilities of the Ia of an ordinary infantry division.

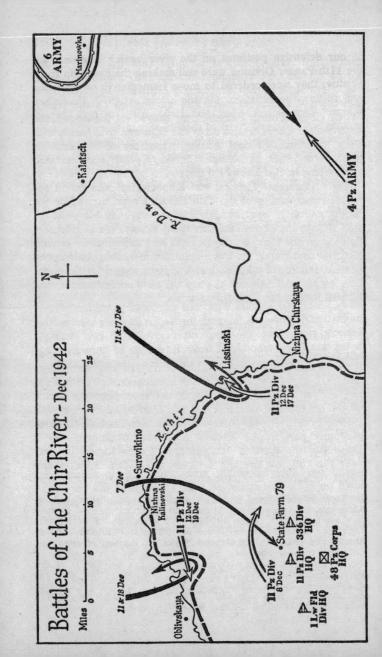

Battles of the Chir River – Dec 1942

of our defensive positions on the river bank.[6] The units of the 11th Panzer Division were still making their way up from Rostov; they were ordered to move immediately on Sowchos and restore the situation. On the afternoon of 7 December Panzer Regiment 15 engaged large Russian tank forces around Sowchos, and checked their further advance.

It was obvious that we could not allow the Russians to remain at Sowchos, and General Balck was ordered to throw them out. As a first step he set up his battle headquarters alongside that of the 336th Division at Verchne Solonovski; this made for the closest co-operation between the two divisions.

Three hundred thirty-sixth Division wanted Balck to make a frontal attack on Sowchos, so as to relieve their critical position with a minimum of delay. Balck protested that the terrain was unsuitable for armor and that in any case a frontal attack would merely push the enemy back, and not lead to his destruction. He decided to make his main effort along the heights west and north of Sowchos, where tanks could move easily, and throw his panzers across the Russian rear. (See the map on page 210.) The decisive thrust was to be made by Panzer Regiment 15 supported by Panzer Grenadier Regiment 111, while Panzer Grenadier Regiment 110 was to deliver a holding attack from the southwest. Balck stationed his antiaircraft guns and engineer battalion to the south of Sowchos to prevent the Russians bursting out in that direction. The artillery of the 336th Division was to co-operate on the northeastern flank.

On the night 7/8 December the 11th Panzer Division regrouped in accordance with Balck's orders, and the units moved into their assembly areas. When they attacked at dawn on 8 December they hit the Russians at the very moment when they were about to advance against the rear of the 336th Division, in the confident belief that the Germans were at their mercy. Panzer Regiment 15 bumped a long column of Russian motorized infantry coming from the

---

[6] I am indebted to General Balck for his detailed personal account of the operations of the 11th Panzer Division. Incidentally the word "Sowchos" literally means "collective or state farm," and occurs frequently on maps of Russia.

north and took them completely by surprise; lorry after
lorry went up in flames as the panzers charged through the
column throwing the Russians into the wildest panic. The
column was destroyed, and Balck's panzer regiment then advanced into the rear of the Russian armor at Sowchos, with
panzergrenadiers and artillery in close support. The Russians
fought bravely, but their tanks were caught in a circle of fire
from which they vainly attempted to escape. When the short
winter day drew to a close the Russian 1st Armored Corps
had been completely bowled over, and fifty-three of its tanks
were knocked out.

Between 9 and 13 December Balck was continually engaged in clearing up Russian bridgeheads across the Chir.
The Luftwaffe Field Division took over a sector on the left
flank of the 336th Division and these two infantry formations did their best to hold the line of the river along the
48th Panzer Corps front, which extended for forty miles between Oblivskaya and Nizhna Chirskaya. But the Russians
were very persistent and 11th Panzer was repeatedly called
upon to restore the front.

The evening of 11 December brought this message to
Balck: "Enemy broken through at Lissinski and at Nizhna
Kalinovski, the one breakthrough 22 km. as the crow flies
away from the other." The commander of 11th Panzer decided to beat the enemy at Lissinski first; after a night
march the panzer regiment arrived near Lissinski at dawn on
12 December and liquidated the Russian force which had
broken through. This decision was dictated by Balck's appreciation that the front of the 336th Division was the pivot
and the shield for the operations of 11th Panzer, and that this
front had to hold at all costs. Three hundred thirty-sixth
Division was fully aware of the importance of its task; the
division faced every new crisis with nerves of steel and endeavored to master each with its own resources, so as to
leave Balck free to counterattack with his whole force when
the intervention of tanks was absolutely essential. Not once
did General Lucht, the commander of the 336th Division,
lose his nerve or claim the assistance of detachments of the
11th Panzer Division, even in moments of the utmost danger. This attitude would have been impossible without the

close co-operation produced by the proximity of the two divisional headquarters. Moreover, every evening the corps commander met Balck, and the situation was thoroughly discussed.

After destroying the Russians at Lissinski on 12 December, 11th Panzer marched northwest, and that very afternoon, having covered a distance of fifteen miles, the division cut into the Russian bridgehead at Nizhna Kalinovski and compressed it considerably.

At dawn on 13 December, when the division was about to launch its final attack on Kalinovski, it was hit on the right flank by a strong Russian attack which produced a temporary crisis. One battalion was surrounded. Eleventh Panzer discontinued its assault on the bridgehead and turned against the attacker, the encircled battalion was freed, and the battle ended with an indubitable German defensive success. Unfortunately it was not possible to liquidate the Russian bridgehead at Nizhna Kalinovski, and this produced serious consequences later on. Eleventh Panzer had been moving by night and fighting by day for eight days and was desperately in need of rest.

On 10 December, Fourth Panzer Army launched its attack —impatiently awaited by Sixth Army—to relieve Stalingrad. During this period Colonel General von Richthofen, who was responsible for supplying the encircled army by air, visited our battle headquarters. According to his appreciation the supply position at Stalingrad had looked anything but rosy as early as the beginning of December—of the 500 tons regarded as the bearable daily minimum for Sixth Army, no more than 100 tons a day were being flown into the ring. The number of available transport planes of the Ju.52 type was totally insufficient for the magnitude of the task, and bomb-carrying planes of the He.3 type were pressed into service to ease the situation. They could carry 1½ tons and their absence was keenly felt at the front, where they were badly needed to support the ground troops.

However, Hoth's attempt to cut a way through to Stalingrad was now in full swing, and in spite of the critical situation on the Chir, the 48th Panzer Corps was called upon to play its part. Unfortunately our bridgehead across the Don

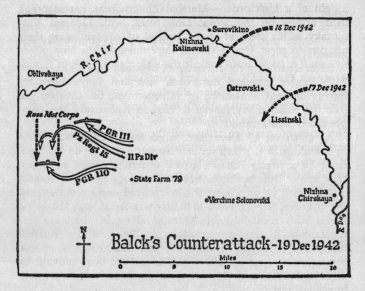

Balck's Counterattack-19 Dec 1942

at Nizhna Chirskaya had been lost under the impact of continuous Russian attacks, and it was necessary to regain it before we could fulfil our role and join hands with Fourth Panzer Army. All was quiet along the Chir front on 14 December and on the 15th the 11th Panzer Division withdrew from its positions covering the Russian bridgehead at Kalinovski, and moved to Nizhna Chirskaya to force a passage over the half-frozen Don and link up with Hoth's relieving force. The sector facing the Kalinovski bridgehead was taken over by *Alarmeinheiten*,[7] drawn from the Luftwaffe Field Division.

By 16 December Hoth's advance guard had reached the banks of the Aksay river less than forty miles from the nearest troops of Sixth Army, and we arranged for the 11th Panzer Division to fight its way across the Don on the 17th and advance southeast to support Hoth's left flank. (I shall deal in detail with Hoth's operations in the next chapter.) At this juncture the Russian Command showed strategic

[7] Units earmarked for action in case of an alert.

insight of a high order—Marshal Zhukov was commanding
their armies on the Volga–Don front, with General Vassilevsky as his chief of staff.[8] Instead of concentrating their
reserves to meet Hoth's thrust, they unleashed a new offensive on a massive scale against the unfortunate Italian Eighth
Army on the middle Don, and extended their attacks to include the sector of *Armee Abteilung Hollidt*[9] (which had
replaced the Rumanian Third Army on our left flank) and
the positions of the 48th Panzer Corps on the River Chir.
The crisis on our own front and the collapse of the Italians
not only forced the cancellation of 11th Panzer's attack
across the Don, but compelled von Manstein to draw heavily
on Hoth's Fourth Panzer Army in order to build up a new
front to cover Rostov. This decided the fate of Sixth Army
at Stalingrad.

On 16 December the situation was far from clear on the
front of the 48th Panzer Corps. The Fifth Russian Tank
Army had discontinued its attacks along the line of the Chir,
and it seemed possible that it might have crossed the Don to
oppose Hoth. No air reconnaissance was possible as the
Luftwaffe had been grounded for several days because of unfavorable weather. But on the 17th doubts were set at rest;
just as 11th Panzer was about to make its assault across the
Don, a violent Russian attack broke through the positions of
the 336th Division, about six miles north of Nizhna Chirskaya. There was nothing for it but to commit 11th Panzer,
which drove the Russians back to the river bank. On the
18th 11th Panzer continued its attack with a view to elimi-
nating this Russian foothold across the Chir, and would certainly have succeeded if a report had not come in of another
Russian offensive from the Nizhna Kalinovski bridgehead,
twelve miles to the northwest. A motorized corps had
broken through on a wide front, and the resistance of the
Alarmeinheiten had dissolved. General von Knobelsdorff felt
compelled to move 11th Panzer to close the breach, although

---

[8] Vassilevsky was later promoted Marshal, and in April 1943 was
appointed chief of the Soviet General Staff. In 1949 he was appointed
commander in chief of the Soviet Armed Forces.

[9] Literally, Army Detachment Hollidt.

Balck protested that he would prefer to eliminate the enemy on the front of the 336th Division before doing so.

General Balck decided to set off immediately, march through the night, and fall on the enemy at dawn, at the very moment when the Russians would be preparing to move. For this purpose Panzer Grenadier Regiment 110 was to take up a frontal blocking position, Panzer Regiment 15 was to attack the enemy's eastern flank, and Panzer Grenadier Regiment 111 was to follow in the right rear to protect the flank and be handy as a reserve. (See sketch map on page 216.)

By 0500 on 19 December all preliminary moves had been carried out. At first light the advance elements of Panzer Regiment 15 saw strong Russian tank units fully deployed and moving southwards. As the approach route of the panzer regiment had concealed its advance, the twenty-five tanks remaining to the regiment followed the Russian armor and in a few minutes had knocked out forty-two Russian tanks, before the latter realized that the tanks moving behind them as a second wave were German and not their own. The dominating Height 148.8 was captured. On the other side of this height another line of tanks was seen moving in a similar way to the first one. Once again the German tanks brilliantly led by Captain Lestmann, attacked the Russians from behind and destroyed them before they had time to realize what was happening. (Literally a case of being kicked in the pants!) Thus twenty-five German tanks destroyed sixty-five Russian tanks in the shortest possible time and without any loss to themselves. This broke the back of the Russian attack. Their remaining troops fled before the panzers without offering any serious resistance.

On the evening of the 19th the Russian 3rd Mechanized Brigade made a diversionary attack on the left flank of 11th Panzer and overran 1st Battalion of P.G.R.110.[10] But Panzer Regiment 15 soon restored the position.

On 20 December the 11th Panzer Division resumed its advance with a view to finally hurling the enemy across the Chir. The advance was going well, but towards evening a

[10] P.G.R. will be used in the text to abbreviate Panzer Grenadier Regiment, and P.G.D. to abbreviate Panzer Grenadier Division.

Members of the War Academy being entertained at a state dinner at the Reichs Chancellery in Berlin, 1937. Captain von Mellenthin is third from Hitler's left.

General Walther von Brauchitsch, Lieutenant General Kaempf, and Lieutenant General Franz Ritter Halder, study a campaign map shortly after the invasion of Poland took place. *Army Signal Corps Photo.*

German armored equipment rolls through the streets of Vilna, Poland. A defeated people quickly became accustomed to seeing the invading German tanks and panzer troops. *Army Signal Corps Photo.*

Tank group Koppenburg advancing near Belfort, France, in June, 1940. *Army Signal Corps Photo.*

A German tank division moves into battle during the last days of fighting before the fall of France in 1940. The tanks were widely dispersed so as not to present a concentrated target. *Wide World Photo.*

On the occasion of his birthday in 1943, Adolf Hitler visited a German armament factory turning out panzer equipment. *Army Signal Corps Photo.*

Field Marshal Erwin Rommel studying area maps during the Tunisian campaign. *Army Signal Corps Photo.*

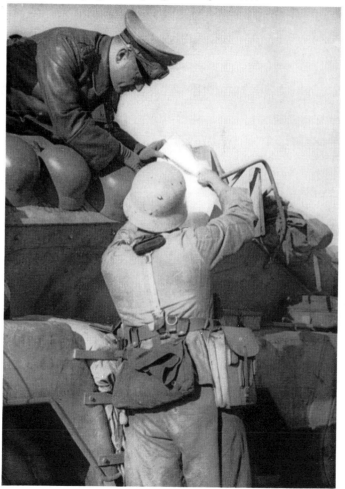

An example of German armor used in North Africa. A 150-mm heavy infantry gun was mounted on a self-propelled carriage converted from a Mark III. *Army Signal Corps Photo.*

German tank column advances to Mersa Brega in North Africa, which fell before this German armored strength. *Wide World Photo.*

At El Adem in November, 1941, Major von Mellenthin and Colonel Siegfried Westphal study *Crusader* battle maps.

Field Marshal Rommel makes a point during a field conference with Colonel Menny in North Africa. *Army Signal Corps Photo*.

General Cruewell, commander of the Afrika Corps at El Agheila, January, 1942.

Fleeing Russians crowded the highways as the Germans swept into Russia in the summer of 1941. *Wide World Photo.*

German troops and tanks attack houses believed to be camouflaged nests of Russian resistance. *Wide World Photo.*

A German armored regiment moves into battle position near Ssolonenkoje in the Ukraine. *Army Signal Corps Photo.*

German soldiers observe the city of Novgorod from an armored reconnoitering car. Novgorod, in northern Russia on the way to Leningrad, was captured by the Germans in August, 1941. *Wide World Photo.*

German tank crew observes a burning Russian village in the distance. Early autumn snows had already fallen in October on the Eastern Front. *Wide World Photo.*

German armored vehicles sank axle-deep in mud along the Eastern Front, Russia's poor roads were a definite hazard to the advance of German armor. *Wide World Photo.*

Weary German soldiers followed by tanks, advance on the Kuban front in Russia. The soldiers here are wearing camouflaged uniforms. *Wide World Photo.*

A German panzer unit moves toward the front, seeking contact with the Russian mechanized strength in the Belgorod area. *Wide World Photo.*

German tanks and half-tracks advancing on Soviet positions and fortifications in an unsuccessful counterthrust in the Orel-Belgorod sectors. *Wide World Photo*.

The "storm gun" was part of the German armored strength along the Eastern Front. *Wide World Photo*.

Colonel General Herman Hoth, General Walter Nehring, Colonel von Mellenthin, and General von Knobelsdorff in field conferences during the Battle of Kursk, July, 1943.

General Herman Balck, Major Briegleb, and Colonel von Mellenthin spent Christmas, 1943, at Zhitomir on the Eastern Front.

Brigadier General Russwurm, inspector of all German Army Signal Troops (shown here with Field Marshal Paul von Kleist), dealt with some of the serious military problems facing the German Army on the Western Front late in 1944. *Army Signal Corps Photo.*

General Balck, Field Marshal von Rundstedt, and General von Knobelsdorff held field conferences to discuss the defensive strategy of Army Group G, November, 1944.

Lieutenant Hans von Rundstedt with his father General Field Marshal Gerd von Rundstedt, who served as Commander in Chief West of the German Army until relieved of the command early in 1945. *Army Signal Corps Photo.*

General Herman Balck, commander of Army Group G in the West until dismissed by Hitler in 1944. When the war ended in 1945, Balck was commander of the Sixth Army in Hungary.

heavy Russian counterattack hit the division on its right flank, and broke into the rear of P.G.R. 111. This crisis was removed by the panzer regiment, and ten Russian tanks were knocked out.

In view of this strong Russian attack General Balck decided to stand on the defensive on the 21st and gave orders for the regiments to regroup under cover of darkness. At 0200 hours that morning both the panzergrenadier regiments reported that their lines had been broken through; the night was brightly lit up by a full moon and Russian tanks and infantry had broken into our units at the moment when they were busy regrouping. Panzer Regiment 15 launched an immediate counterattack and soon better reports came in from the panzergrenadiers. Balck sent Motorcycle Battalion 61 to attack the Russians at the junction of P.G.R.'s 110 and 111, where the main Russian onslaught seemed to be directed. By daylight it was clear that the 11th Panzer Division had gained a great defensive success—hundreds of fallen Russians lay in front of our lines. But German losses were also grave.

On 22 December all was quiet on the front of the 48th Panzer Corps; in fact our great defensive battle on the line of the Chir had come to an end. But the debacle on the sector of the Italian Eighth Army had opened a hideous gap on our left flank, through which the Russian First Guard Army was pouring. On 22 December our corps headquarters was ordered to leave the Chir front and move with 11th Panzer Division to Tatsinskaya, ninety miles to the west—unless we moved fast nothing could save Rostov.

Before concluding this account of the battles on the Chir, I must pay tribute to General Balck, a born leader of armor. Throughout the fighting his panzer division had acted as the "fire brigade," moving behind the two infantry divisions to quell one dangerous conflagration after another. When the infantry found it impossible to deal with the larger Russian bridgeheads, Balck came tearing down on the enemy with the whole weight of his armor in accordance with the old maxim: No stinting, but stunning. (*Nicht kleckern, sondern klotzen.*) His brilliant achievements were the fruit of exemplary co-operation with the two infantry di-

visions and the headquarters of the 48th Panzer Corps.
Balck never left a single tank in direct support of the infantry, as this was regarded as of no avail and a waste of
much-needed armor. Mobile tactics of this kind retrieved
dangerous situations on numerous occasions and inflicted
huge losses on the enemy. During this period more than
seven hundred tanks were knocked out in the sector of the
48th Panzer Corps. I, the newcomer, saw and understood that
the Russian masses of men and material could be successfully fought, if they were faced by men with steady nerves
and by concentrated armor and artillery.

The following are Balck's own comments on these operations.

Eleventh Panzer Division was responsible for decisive deeds
of heroism on the Chir river. If the defense had broken down
in this sector, and if the Russians had been allowed to advance
to Rostov, the fate of Army Group Caucasus would have
been sealed. Its line of withdrawal would have been cut and
it would have been drawn into the maelstrom of Stalingrad.
Thus the situation made it imperative for the 11th Panzer
Division to give of its very best.

We were fortunate that after the hard fighting in previous
campaigns all commanders whose nerves could not stand the
test had been replaced by proven men. There was no commander left who was not absolutely reliable.

For weeks on end the division moved by night, and before
dawn was at the very spot where the enemy was weakest,
waiting to attack him an hour before he was ready to move.
Such tactics called for unheard-of efforts, but saved lives, as
the attack proper cost very few casualties, thanks to the Russians having been taken completely by surprise. The axiom
of the Division was, "night-marches are lifesavers." It is true,
however, that the question of when the men of 11th Panzer
got any sleep was never clearly answered.

Orders were exclusively verbal. The divisional commander
made his decision for the next day during the evening, and
he gave the necessary orders verbally to his regimental commanders on the battlefield; then he returned to his main
headquarters and discussed his intentions with the chief of
staff of the 48th Panzer Corps. If approval was obtained the
regiments were sent the wireless message: "no changes," and
all the moves were carried out according to plan. If there

were fundamental changes, the divisional commander visited all his regiments during the night and gave the necessary orders, again verbally. Divisional operations were conducted from the forward position on the battlefield. The divisional commander had his place with the group which was to make the main effort; he visited the regiments several times a day. The divisional headquarters was somewhat farther back and did not change its location during operations. There information was collected and collated, supplies were handled, and reinforcements sent on their way. Communications between the divisional commander and his staff were maintained by R/T; there were few opportunities to make use of the telephone.

Three hundred thirty-sixth Division, which was commanded by Lieut. General Lucht with exemplary calm and efficiency, was handicapped by serious deficiencies in equipment. Many a crisis would not have arisen, had the division possessed a larger number of antitank guns. In this field our organization did not come up to requirements.

On both sides newly established and poorly equipped formations were thrown into the fray. On the German side there were the Luftwaffen field divisions. After a few days they were gone—finished—in spite of good mechanical equipment. Their training left everything to be desired, and they had no experienced leaders. They were a creation of Hermann Göring, a creation which had no sound military foundation— the rank and file paid with their lives for this absurdity.

On the Russian side the tank crews, particularly in the Motorized Corps, had hardly any training. This shortcoming was one of the essential reasons for the German victory on 19 December.

Not much has been said in this narrative about the artillery, which during such highly mobile and fluctuating warfare was not called upon to play a major role. But at night, artillery was often used to shoot up hostile bivouac areas with concentric fire. Not much is known of the effect of these tactics, but as the Russians were compelled by the icy winter cold to seek protection in villages it may be assumed that corresponding results were achieved.

The fighting on the Chir river was made easier by the methods adopted by the command of the Russian Fifth Tank Army. They sent their various corps into battle without co-ordinating the timing of their attacks, and without the co-operation of the numerous infantry divisions. Thus the 11th

Panzer Division was enabled to smash one corps after the other, until the hitting power of the Fifth Tank Army had been weakened to such an extent that it was possible for the division to withdraw and start the game all over again with another Russian Tank Army.

First Impressions of Russian Tactics

I propose to conclude this chapter by giving my first impressions of Russian tactics as they emerged during the fighting on the Chir. These impressions were later confirmed on many occasions.

Practically every Russian attack was preceded by large-scale infiltrations, by an "oozing through" of small units and individual men. In this kind of warfare the Russians have not yet found their masters. However much the outlying areas were kept under observation, the Russian was suddenly there, in the very midst of our own positions, and nobody had seen him come, nor did anybody know whence he had come. In the least likely places, where the going was incredibly difficult, there he was, dug in and all, and in considerable strength. True, it was not difficult for individual men to seep through, considering that our lines were but thinly manned and strong-points few and far between. An average divisional sector was usually more than twelve miles broad. But the amazing fact was that in spite of everybody being alert and wide awake during the whole night, the next morning entire Russian units were sure to be found far behind our front line, complete with equipment and ammunition, and well dug in. These infiltrations were carried out with incredible skill, almost noiselessly, and without a shot being fired. Such infiltration tactics were employed by the Russians in hundreds of cases, bringing them considerable successes. There is only one remedy against them: strongly manned lines, well organized in depth and continuously patrolled by men wide awake and alert, and—most important of all—sufficient local reserves ready at a moment's notice to go into action and throw the intruders out.

Another characteristically Russian principle is the forming of bridgeheads everywhere and at any time, to serve as bases for later advances. Bridgeheads in the hands of the Russians are a grave danger indeed. It is quite wrong not to worry about bridgeheads, and to postpone their elimination. Russian bridgeheads, however small and harmless they may appear, are bound to grow into formidable danger-points in a very brief time and soon become insuperable strong-points. A Russian bridgehead, occupied by a company in the evening, is sure to be occupied by at least a regiment the following morning and during the night will become a formidable fortress, well-equipped with heavy weapons and everything necessary to make it almost impregnable. No artillery fire, however violent and well concentrated, will wipe out a Russian bridgehead which has grown overnight. Nothing less than a well-planned attack will avail. This Russian principle of "bridgeheads everywhere" constitutes a most serious danger and cannot be overrated. There is again only one sure remedy which must become a principle: If a bridgehead is forming, or an advanced position is being established by the Russians, attack, attack at once, attack strongly. Hesitation will always be fatal. A delay of an hour may mean frustration, a delay of a few hours does mean frustration, a delay of a day may mean a major catastrophe. Even if there is no more than one infantry platoon and one single tank available, attack! Attack when the Russians are still above ground, when they can still be seen and tackled, when they have had no time as yet to organize their defense, when there are no heavy weapons available. A few hours later will be too late. Delay means disaster: resolute energetic and immediate action means success.

Russian tactics are a queer mixture; in spite of their brilliance at infiltration and their exceptional mastery of field fortification, yet the rigidity of Russian attacks was almost proverbial. (Although in some cases Russian armored formations down to their lowest units were a conspicuous exception.) The foolish repetition of attacks on the same spot, the rigidity of Russian artillery fire, and the selection of the terrain for the attack, betrayed a total lack of imagination and mental mobility. Our Wireless Intercept Service heard many a time the frantic question: "What are we to do now?" Only a few commanders of lower formations showed independent judgment when faced with unforeseen situations. On many occasions a successful attack, a breakthrough, or an accomplished encirclement was not exploited, simply because nobody saw it.

But there was an exception to this general clumsiness: The rapid and frequent exchange of units in the front line. Once a division was badly mauled, it disappeared overnight and re-appeared fresh and strong at some other place a few days afterwards.

That is why fighting with Russians resembles the classic contest between Hercules and the Hydra.

12: *Disaster at Stalingrad*

The Ordeal of Sixth Army

WHILE GREAT ARMORED battles were raging on both banks of the Don, the condition of Paulus' Sixth Army was growing increasingly desperate. An enormous prize was at stake between the Volga and the Don, and the Russians were fully aware of it. Hitler's veto on any break-out attempt appears incredibly rash when one considers the forces involved. For this was no ordinary army invested at Stalingrad; Sixth Army represented the spearhead of the Wehrmacht, in what was intended to be the decisive campaign of the war. The following forces were locked up in the Stalingrad ring:

Headquarters and the entire command organization of Sixth Army.

Headquarters of five army corps: 4, 8, 11, 14 Panzer, and 51.

Thirteen infantry divisions: 44, 71, 76, 79, 94, 100 Jaeger, 113, 295, 305, 371, 376, 389, and 397.

Three panzer divisions: 14, 16, and 24.

Three motorized divisions: 3, 29, and 60.

One antiaircraft division: 9.

A total of twenty German divisions.

In addition there were the remnants of two Rumanian divisions (1st Cavalry and the 20th Infantry) together with a

Croat regiment, service troops, and members of the Organization Todt.

According to information provided by the quartermaster general's branch, 270,000 men found themselves encircled on 24 November 1942. The destruction of these divisions was bound to alter the whole balance of power on the Eastern front.

Such was the army which Reichsmarshal Göring had rashly undertaken to supply by air, in the midst of a Russian winter, and while violent battles were raging along a front of a thousand miles. Droves of Ju.52 transport planes appeared over Stalingrad, like black omens of defeat, and when the inevitable capitulation came two months later, some 500 of these aircraft had fallen victims to the weather or the new high-speed Russian fighters. In spite of these sacrifices—so ruinous to the Luftwaffe at such a critical stage of the air war —the quantity of supplies received fell far below the minimum required to maintain Paulus' unfortunate army. I have mentioned the forebodings of Colonel General von Richthofen when he visited headquarters of the 48th Panzer Corps early in December; he certainly did not share the optimistic appreciation of his commander in chief. As a matter of sober fact the delivery of the minimum five hundred tons of supplies required the services of 250 Ju.52's a day, and to ensure the daily quota a thousand machines of that type were needed, in order to cope with casualties, repairs and rest for the crews. The number of aircraft never approached that figure and only on a single day were as many as three hundred tons flown in, while the daily average was about one hundred tons.

The effect of this failure on Sixth Army is thus described by my friend, Colonel Dingler:

Night after night we sat in our holes listening to the droning of the aircraft engines and trying to guess how many German machines were coming over and what supplies they would bring us. The supply position was very poor from the beginning, but none of us thought that hunger would become a permanent thing.

We were short of all sorts of supplies. We were short of bread and, worse, of artillery ammunition, and worst of all, of gasoline. Gasoline meant everything to us. As long as we had gasoline our supply—little as it was—was assured. As long as we had gasoline we were able to keep *warm*. As there was no wood to be found anywhere in the steppe, firewood had to be fetched from the city of Stalingrad by lorry. As we had so little gasoline, trips to the city to fetch firewood had to be limited to the bare minimum. For this reason we felt very cold in our holes.

Until Christmas, 1942, the daily bread ration issued to every man was 100 grammes. After Christmas the ration was reduced to 50 grammes per head. Later on only those in the forward line received 50 grammes per day. No bread was issued to men in regimental headquarters and upwards. The others were given watery soup which we tried to improve by making use of bones obtained from horses we dug up. As a Christmas treat the army allowed the slaughtering of four thousand of the available horses. My division, being a motorized formation, had no horses and was therefore particularly hard hit, as the horseflesh we received was strictly rationed. The infantry units were better off as they were able to do some "illegal" slaughtering.

During the first period of encirclement the Russians left Sixth Army alone, as they had quite enough on their hands elsewhere. The troops did what they could to improve their positions against inevitable attack, but in spite of the large numbers of men locked up in the ring, the strength of the fighting units was already ominously low. For example, the 3rd Motorized Division in the "nose of Marinowka" had two rifle regiments, each of three battalions—an impressive establishment until one considers that each battalion had only eighty men. This meant that the division had only 500 infantry to hold a front of ten miles. The artillery regiment of thirty-six guns was intact, but the panzer battalion had only twenty-five tanks out of an establishment of sixty. The reserve consisted of the engineer battalion of 150 men.

Of course the lack of gasoline had a very serious effect on tank operations. As I have explained in dealing with the battles on the Chir, the ability to maneuver armor is of vital importance in repulsing Russian attacks, but in view of the gasoline shortage the units of Sixth Army had to think twice before moving even a single tank. The result was that most

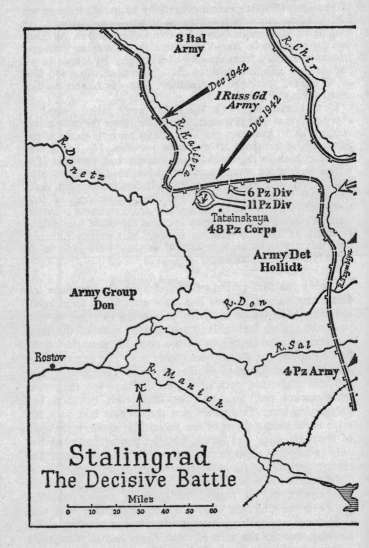

8 Ital
Army

R. Chir

Dec 1942

1 Russ Gd
Army

Dec 1942

R. Kalitva

R. Donetz

6 Pz Div

11 Pz Div

Tatsinskaya

48 Pz Corps

R. Tzymlya

Army Det
Hollidt

Army Group
Don

R. Don

R. Sal

Rostov

R. Manich

4 Pz Army

N

Stalingrad
The Decisive Battle

Miles

0   10   20   30   40   50   60

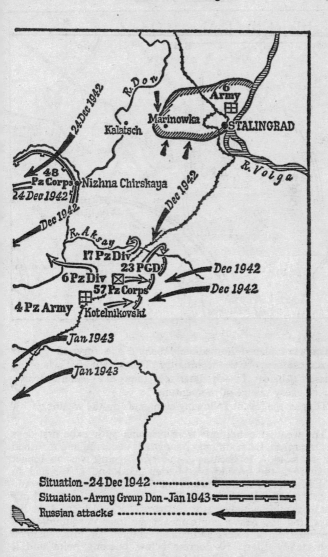

R. Don

6 Army

Marinowka •STALINGRAD

Kalatsch

R. Volga

24 Dec 1942

48 Pz Corps — Nizhna Chirskaya

24 Dec 1942

Dec 1942

Dec 1942

R. Aksay

17 Pz Div

23 PGD

6 Pz Div

Dec 1942

57 Pz Corps

Dec 1942

4 Pz Army

Kotelnikovski

Jan 1943

Jan 1943

Situation - 24 Dec 1942 ....

Situation - Army Group Don - Jan 1943

Russian attacks ....

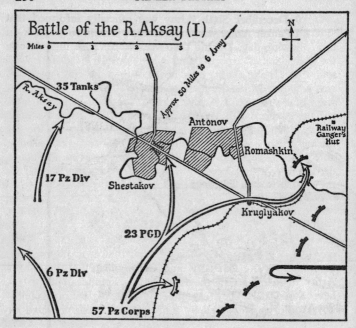

Battle of the R. Aksay (I)

tanks were placed immediately behind the forward line to give close support to the infantry. This meant that when the Russians broke in—as later on they did—counterthrusts lacked every vestige of momentum.

Dingler makes the following comments on the weather:

The weather conditions were bearable during the first days of December. Later on heavy snowfalls occurred and it turned bitterly cold. Life became a misery. Digging was no longer possible as the ground was frozen hard and if we had to abandon our lines this meant that in the new lines we would have no dugouts or trenches. The heavy snow diminished our small gasoline supplies still further. The lorries stuck in the snow and the heavy going meant a larger consumption of gasoline. It grew colder and colder. The temperature remained at a steady 20 or 30 degrees below freezing point and it became increasingly difficult for aircraft to fly in.

On 9 December Sixth Army was officially informed that Fourth Panzer Army would commence its relieving attack on the following day. During that week hopes rose high among the beleaguered troops, and when on 16 December the sound of distant gunfire was heard within the ring, everyone was convinced that the hour of liberation was at hand. Plans were made for Sixth Army to cut through the Russian lines and join hands with Hoth's spearheads, but General Paulus decided that they could not be put into effect until the relieving force was within twenty miles. Shortage of gasoline and general weakness limited the striking power of Paulus' divisions, and they could only wait with anxious hearts for the outcome of the battle to the south.

The Relieving Attack

During the first days of December, three panzer divisions, one infantry division, and three Luftwaffen field divisions, all coming from the Caucasus and Orel, joined Fourth Panzer Army to take part in the forthcoming counterattack to relieve Stalingrad. They assembled in the region of Kotelnikovski and were covered by a protective screen, provided by the remnants of the Rumanian Fourth Army and a few German battle groups.

This was the area where the Russians had pressed back the German lines to a distance of more than sixty miles from Stalingrad, whereas on the Chir at Nizhna Chirskaya, the 48th Panzer Corps was only twenty-five miles away. The problem was carefully examined by Field Marshal von Manstein, a master of strategy, faced with an immense responsibility. He decided that a crossing of the Don would be a hazardous and difficult operation, and that the Kotelnikovski area southeast of the Don offered the best spring-board from which to launch the offensive.

It was here on 10 December 1942 that Colonel General Hoth, commander of Fourth Panzer Army and an officer with a great and deserved reputation, launched the attack which had been long awaited by those in the cauldron of Stalingrad. As I have explained, the break-out of Sixth Army was not to be attempted until Hoth was within twenty miles of

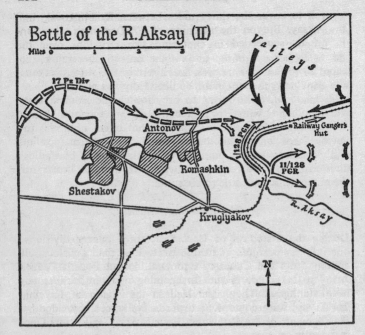

their outer defenses. Forty-eighth Panzer Corps was to cross the Don in support of Hoth when he reached the banks of the Aksay River. Given the conditions prevailing in December, 1942, I do not think that a better plan could have been devised. It is arguable, however, that Paulus was unduly pessimistic, and plans should have been made for Sixth Army to strike at an earlier stage.

Fifty-seventh Panzer Corps delivered the main assault of Fourth Panzer Army. Twenty-third P.G.D. was on the right, the 17th Panzer Division on the left, and the 6th Panzer Division in reserve. From the outset Hoth met with furious opposition from large forces of Russian tanks and infantry, under General Vatutin, one of their ablest commanders.[1] So fierce and determined was the Russian resistance that it took

[1] Later promoted marshal. He captured Kiev in November 1943, and died there four months afterwards.

a week to cover the thirty miles between Kotelnikovski and the Aksay. But on the morning of 17 December, the 23rd P. G. D. succeeded in capturing two crossings over the Aksay by a *coup de main*. Thus the last formidable obstacle separating the two armies was overcome and the actual distance between them had shrunk to forty-five miles.

But as I have shown in the previous chapter, this was the very moment chosen by Marshal Zhukov to unleash a new offensive on the grand scale against the Italian Eighth Army on the middle Don, combined with heavy attacks on the 48th Panzer Corps along the Chir. Numerous Russian armored and infantry formations crashed through the Italian front and opened a gap sixty miles wide, through which they poured southwards towards Rostov. Manstein was a commander of iron nerve, and if it had been possible to leave Fourth Panzer Army intact he would have done so. But it was not possible; the loss of Rostov would have been fatal to the 48th Panzer Corps, to Hoth's Army, and to Field Marshal von Kleist's Army Group in the Caucasus. Indeed it may be that Zhukov, with fine strategic insight, deliberately withheld his attack on the Italians until he was sure that Hoth was fully committed towards Stalingrad; by adopting this course he may well have hoped to trap all our southern armies.[2]

With a heavy heart Manstein was compelled to detach the 6th Panzer Division from Hoth's Army and send it northwest by forced marches to try and stem the Russian flood. This was the best division at Hoth's disposal, it was still intact, and if it had remained under his command it is possible that he would have broken through to Paulus. Moreover, the eastern flank of Fourth Panzer Army was exposed to continuous attack by Russian columns emerging from the steppe,

[2] It is not generally realized that Zhukov received much of his early training in Germany. Together with other Russian officers, and by arrangement with the Reichswehr, he attended courses at German military schools in the 1920's. For a time he was attached to the cavalry regiment in which Colonel Dingler was serving as a subaltern; Dingler has vivid recollections of the uproarious behavior of Zhukov and his companions, and the vast quantities of liquor which they were accustomed to consume after dinner. But in the military sphere it is clear that Zhukov's time was not wasted.

and Hoth's infantry divisions—mainly composed of inferior
Luftwaffe troops—were tied down in protecting the line of
communications between the Aksay River and Kotelnikovski.

In spite of this intolerable weakening of the 57th Panzer
Corps, the attack was continued, stubbornly and persistently,
and with the desire burning in every man's heart to bring
help to the men in Stalingrad, for whom they were the only
remaining hope of salvation. The following account is based
on the narrative of a General Staff officer who took part in
these tragic battles. His narrative seems to me particularly
valuable, because although it confirms that on the whole
Russian commanders of medium and lower formations are
slow and cumbersome in their methods, yet it shows that
there are some commanders, particularly in the armored
units, capable of making rapid and bold decisions.

The two panzer divisions remaining to Fourth Army had
together no more than thirty-five tanks; most of the tanks
originally available had been lost owing to atrocious going
conditions and the uninterrupted heavy fighting. These
thirty-five tanks were all placed under command of the 17th
Panzer Division, in order to avoid splitting up this little
force.

The terrain, although cut by numerous narrow valleys,
offers no obstacle to the eye for many miles, as there are
hardly any ground elevations in the steppe; nor is there any
cover. At that time of year the ground was slippery with ice
and very smooth; the Aksay is twenty-five yards wide and
its valley deeply cut. There was but little snow, and it was
very cold, the thermometer registering a temperature far below freezing point.

On this somber stage a drama was played out whose
historical importance it is difficult to exaggerate; it is not
fanciful to regard the struggle on the banks of this little
unknown river as marking a crisis in the fortunes of the
Third Reich, the end of Hitler's hopes of empire, and a
vital link in the chain of events leading inevitably to the fall
of Germany.

On the morning of 17 December, P.G.R. 128 of the 23rd
P.G.D. was holding positions on the north bank of the
Aksay between Kruglyakov, on the main railway line to

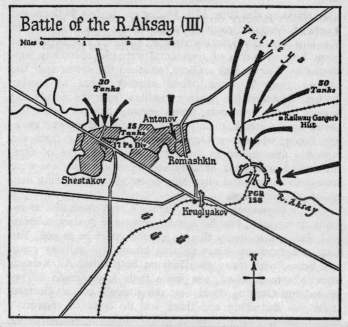

Stalingrad, and Shestakov, where there was a road bridge across the river. (Both the rail and road bridges had been captured intact.) Seventeenth Panzer Division with all thirty-five tanks had concentrated at Klymovka on the left flank. (See maps I and II.) That day Russian infantry supported by tanks kept attacking the German bridgehead at Kruglyakov, and fifteen Russian tanks were thrown into the battle near Shestakov, held by the engineer battalion of the 23rd P.G.D. The attacks were beaten off with heavy loss, and the Russian 87th Rifle Division and the 13th Armored Brigade were identified.

On the night 17/18 December P.G.R. 128 made a successful attack on the right flank and enlarged the bridgehead along the railway as far as "the little house of the railway ganger." In view of this success General Hoth felt justified in making preparations to continue the advance towards Stalingrad.

At 0800 on the 19th, 17th Panzer on the left flank moved across to Antonov; reconnaissance reports indicated that the Russians were considerably stronger than the day before. At noon Russian forces of regimental strength, effectively supported by aircraft and artillery, attacked the sector near the railway ganger's house, while another force of similar strength attacked the panzergrenadiers from the deeply cut valleys to the northwest. Some seventy Russian tanks followed up the attack, mainly in the area of the railway ganger's house, whereupon German armor advancing from the Antonov area joined in the battle. Under the fire of German antiaircraft guns, artillery and tanks, the Russians were unable to deploy, and after nine hours of fierce fighting they called off their attack.

On 20 December the 57th Panzer Corps attempted to resume its advance, but the Russian resistance was so stubborn and their fire so heavy that no ground could be gained. The next two days saw bitter fighting around the railway ganger's house, with many casualties on both sides. All Russian attacks were repulsed, but while their losses could be replaced the German could not; the strength of the German units was dwindling and there was no hope of reinforcements. On the 23rd, German armor thrusting eastwards up the railway bumped into eighty Russian tanks, and finally threw them back after four hours' intense fighting.[3]

On Christmas Eve the Russians attacked in great force along the whole line. The ganger's house was lost and P.G.R. 128 was driven back to the railway bridge; on the left flank the composite panzer regiment suffered such heavy casualties that it had to be withdrawn across the Aksay to the village of Romashkin. After dark twenty Russian tanks attacked Shestakov while other tanks on the river bank shelled Romashkin; the night was lit up with the flashes of a great artillery duel, but finally the Russians seemed to have had enough and withdrew. This was deceptive; at dawn thirty Russian tanks rushed down on Shestakov at top speed and crushed the resistance of the engineer battalion. Supported

---

[3] It is certainly arguable that at this stage Paulus should have attacked in order to tie down the Russians on his front and prevent their concentrating overwhelming forces against the 57th Panzer Corps.

by fire from the direction of Antonov, Russian tanks tried to cross the bridge; one got over but the bridge collapsed under the weight of the second. (Some days before a German tank had left the bridge and had fallen into the river beside it.)

It was clear that the Russians were not content with crushing the German bridgehead; they sensed an opportunity to cross the river and destroy the German troops whose weakness had become apparent during the incessant fighting. Nevertheless, throughout that heartbreaking Christmas day, all Russian attempts to gain a foothold on the south bank of the Aksay were beaten off. Eighty-eight-mm guns proved their worth in dealing with the Russian armor, and the railway bridge was held against massed infantry assaults, strongly supported by bombers and artillery.

On the night 25/26 December Russian infantry, covered by close-range tank fire, stormed across the wreckage of the Shestakov bridge; receiving reinforcements in a continuous stream they entered Romashkin. The remnants of P.G.R. 128 were destroyed in a night battle for the railway bridge at Kruglyakov, and the bridge was finally lost when fifty tanks attacked it early on the 26th.

During the morning the Russians improvised a bridge across the two tanks, German and Russian, which had fallen into the river at Shestakov. This proved capable of bearing armor, and their tanks poured across. German resistance finally broke down, and the remnants of the 57th Panzer Corps withdrew to the south.

The characteristic features of this dramatic battle were mobility, quick reaction, and utter perseverance on both sides. Tanks were the main weapon used and both sides realized that the main task of the armor was to destroy the opposing tanks.

The Russians did not stop their attacks when darkness fell, and they exploited every success immediately and without hesitation. Some of the Russian attacks were made by tanks moving in at top speed; indeed, speed, momentum, and concentration were the causes of their success. The main effort of the attacking Russian armor was speedily switched from one point to another as the situation demanded. Whether these results were due to the influence of General Vatutin I do not know, but the tactical conduct of the battle by the Russians was on a high level.

Of the heroism of the men of the 57th Panzer Corps in this vain attempt to rescue their comrades at Stalingrad, it is unnecessary to say more. By 26 December the corps was almost nonexistent; it had literally died on its feet.

The End of the Sixth Army

Sixth Army was doomed; nothing could save Paulus now. Even if by some miracle a break-out order had been wrung from Hitler, even if the exhausted and starving troops had cut through the Russian ring, the means did not exist to get them back across the icy steppe to Rostov. The army would have perished on the march, as surely as Napoleon's veterans between Moscow and the Berezina.

Hitler took the Stalingrad area under his personal command; it was designated as a "War Theatre under the Supreme Command." He assumed direct responsibility for everything regarding Stalingrad. Without having been there, he gave the most detailed instructions, and controlled and commanded the Stalingrad garrison from his headquarters in East Prussia, 1,300 miles away!

The Russian offensive on the Don had captured the two airfields at Morovskaya and Tatsinskaya which were the nearest points from where supplies could be flown to Stalingrad. From these airfields it had been possible to maintain three flights a day, which meant a quasi-regular supply for Sixth Army. Now the front line had receded hundreds of miles. From the available airfields it took two to three hours to reach Stalingrad, which meant that supplies could only be flown in once a day. The deterioration in weather conditions made the supply position still more hopeless.

One of the most difficult problems was the care of the wounded, and in this connection the garrison was short of every necessity. Until then there had been some means of bringing the wounded to the Pitomnik airfield from where they could be flown out. But in view of the shortage of gasoline and vehicles this was no longer feasible. The num-

ber of wounded and of those suffering from frostbite grew
so rapidly that it was quite impossible to evacuate even the
most serious cases. Most of the aircraft, which arrived in
ever-decreasing numbers, preferred to drop their cargo, as
landing had become very difficult indeed. There were some
nights when not a single aircraft touched down.

Colonel Dingler says:

I must emphasize the fact that the aircraft crews did a job
which can be called superhuman. It is certainly not the crews
who should be blamed for the inefficient way in which our
supply problem was handled.

Although everyone realized how difficult and desperate our
situation was, there was never a hint of panic. The morale of
the soldiers was above praise; camaraderie and preparedness
to help each other were not the exception but the rule.

At about this time we began to discuss what to do if the
worst were to happen. We talked about captivity. We talked
about the question of committing suicide. We discussed the
question of defending what we held to the last bullet but one.
Of course there were as many opinions as people and it must
be emphasized that there was no compulsion from above in
any direction. These things were left to be decided by the
individual himself.

On 8 January white flags fluttered at the outposts—a
Russian *parlementaire* presented terms of surrender. Signed
by Colonel General Rokossovsky[4] and Marshal of Artillery
Voronov the terms offered "honorable surrender, sufficient
rations, care for the wounded, officers to keep their weapons, repatriation after the war to Germany or any other
country." The fundamental condition was that all equipment
had to be handed over undamaged. The terms were broad-
cast to the troops by innumerable pamphlets dropped by
aircraft.

Dingler says:

The Russian offer was refused. It was refused unanimously
by the rank and file because they did not have much faith in
Russian promises. We all knew "Ivan" too well; one never

---

[4] Rokossovsky is a Pole by birth, and a former officer of the Tsarist
Army. He is now C. in C. of the army of satellite Poland.

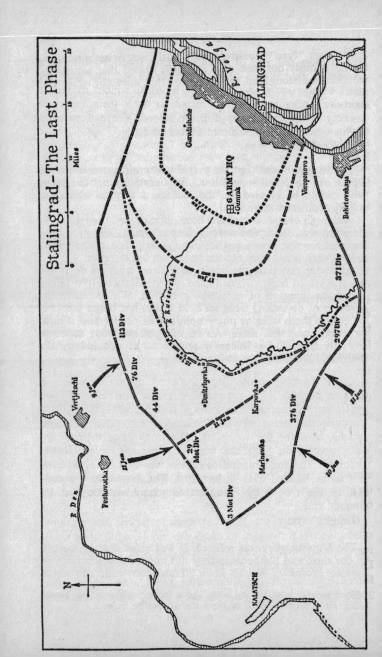

Stalingrad–The Last Phase

knew what "Ivan" would do next, promises or no promises. Subconsciously our men may still have hoped that somebody would come along and get us out of this tight corner in the nick of time, which after all would be better than a doubtful captivity in Siberia.

The men in command of our beleaguered army had yet another reason for refusing to surrender. They had received information that our forces in the Caucasus were about to withdraw. We at Stalingrad were surrounded by three Russian armies which would be free for other operations if we capitulated. But if we held out, our army in the Caucasus would probably be able to carry out the planned withdrawal in an orderly fashion.

On 10 January the Russians started their offensive against Stalingrad with everything they had. The main onslaughts were directed against the southern and western sectors. While no breakthrough was made on the southern sector, the "nose of Marinowka," held by the 3rd Motorized Division, had to be abandoned and the troops were forced to withdraw to a new "line," marked as such on staff maps but in reality nonexistent. There were no trenches and no positions for the riflemen; the decimated troops, overtired, exhausted, and with frostbitten limbs, simply lay in the snow. Heavy weapons and tanks had to be abandoned as there was no gasoline to move them, and it was evident from the start that this so-called "position" could not be held for any length of time.

Some soldiers, who had fallen into Russian hands, were returned to the German lines after they had been given bread and bacon. They were supposed to incite the troops to surrender. But the trick did not work and these men took up their positions at the side of their comrades without a word of complaint.

On 11 January the Russians again attacked the western salient, and had the luck to catch our troops while they were regrouping. Twenty-ninth Motorized Division and the 376th Division were virtually destroyed, and the German line was forced back across the Russoschka valley. (See map, page 240.) The new line ran across deep snow, without trenches or dugouts; Sixth Army headquarters designated this as "the final position."

On 16 January the Russians resumed their attacks to the west and south, and pushed forward remorselessly towards Gumrak, the last airfield remaining to the beleaguered garrison. Whenever the Russians met determined resistance they stopped, and attacked somewhere else. By 19 January the ring round Sixth Army had grown very tight, and Paulus held a conference with his corps commanders. It was seriously proposed that on 22 January all troops in the "fortress" should rise as one man, and break out in small groups in an endeavor to reach the German lines on the Don. As Dingler comments, "this was a plan which despair alone could suggest," and it was quietly forgotten.

During this period various senior commanders and staff officers received orders to fly out of the Stalingrad ring. Among these was Colonel Dingler, whose shattered 3rd Motorized Division was then holding a small sector near the water tower of Voroponovo. Together with General Hube, the commander of the 14th Panzer Corps, he was to leave Stalingrad and try to improve the supply position of those in the ring. It was with a heavy heart that he left his men behind, and he did not do so before discussing the order with his divisional commander and other officers, who saw a ray of hope in this mission. The one and only transport vehicle left to the Division—a motorcycle combination—brought him to the Gumrak landing ground; the road was covered with dead soldiers, burnt-out tanks, abandoned guns, indeed, all the debris of an army in the last stages of dissolution. The airfield presented a similar picture of destruction—a snowy desert littered with aircraft and vehicles. Everywhere lay the corpses of German soldiers; too exhausted to move on, they had just died in the snow.

Discipline on the landing ground was good, and nobody was allowed to board a plane without a written permit signed by the chief of staff of the army. The wounded were given priority, although by this time only those who could walk or crawl were able to reach the airfield. During the night 19/20 January only four aircraft touched down at

Gumrak. The landing ground was under continuous artillery fire, as the Russians were not more than two miles away.

Dingler's aircraft took off on a moonlit night with light snow falling; he remarks that it was a miracle that Gumrak held out for three more days. On 23 January it fell to the Russians; the last human contact with the outer world was broken and from then on supplies had to be dropped.

In this manner Sixth Army dragged out a nominal existence for another week. On 30 January the Russians overran the southern pocket of Stalingrad, and captured Paulus and his headquarters. The northern pocket fell two days later, and on 3 February the German Supreme Command announced the news as follows:

The battle for Stalingrad has ended. Faithful to its oath to fight to the last breath, the Sixth Army under the exemplary leadership of Feld Marshal Paulus has been overcome by the enemy's superior force and by adverse circumstances.

The official communiqué was far from reflecting the true opinions of Hitler. Evidence produced since the war shows that the capture of Paulus infuriated him; he had expected his newly-promoted field marshal to commit suicide. Hitler told his staff:

What hurts me most, personally, is that I still promoted him to field marshal. I wanted to give him this final satisfaction . . . a man like that besmirches the heroism of so many others at the last moment. He could have freed himself from all sorrow and ascended into eternity and national immortality, but he prefers to go to Moscow.[5]

The Russians claimed 90,000 prisoners; 40,000 men had been flown out, therefore 140,000 soldiers must have lost their lives. The German Army had suffered an irreparable defeat.

[5] *Hitler Directs his War*, 21–22.

13: Manstein's Great Achievement

Retreat to the Donetz

IT WILL BE recalled that on 22 December the headquarters of the 48th Panzer Corps and the 11th Panzer Division were ordered to leave the line of the Chir and move with all speed to Tatsinskaya, some ninety miles to the west. This step was forced upon Manstein by the Italian collapse on the middle Don; the Russian First Guard Army was pouring through the gap and by Christmas its spearheads were barely eighty miles from Rostov. (See map on pages 228–29.)

Our orders were to take command of the 6th and 11th Panzer Divisions and restore the front to the north and west of Tatsinskaya, where a Guards Armored Corps was driving towards the Donetz. I hurried to Tatsinskaya with the Operations Section of the Corps and set up our battle headquarters there. On Christmas Eve the Russians overran a large airfield to the west of the town, which was being used to supply the Stalingrad garrison. Terrible atrocities were committed there, and when the airfield was retaken we found the corpses of many of our comrades, with eyes gouged out and ears and noses cut off.[1]

Sixth Panzer Division was ordered to attack north of Tatsinskaya and close the gap in the front, thus cutting off

---

[1] See also Rudel, *Stuka Pilot*, 70. In *Manstein*, 187, R. T. Paget remarks that, "The Slavs, particularly when drunk, appear to have a taste for fantastic mutilations."

the retreat of the Guards Corps, which had broken through. Eleventh Panzer was told to deal with these gentlemen and wipe them out. The perfectly flat snow-covered steppe was ideal for armored movement, and the two panzer divisions carried out their task with magnificent dash and *élan,* recalling the spirit of the old cavalry regiments. The Guards Corps was encircled by 11th Panzer and sent out frantic messages for help—most of them in clear. The appeals were all in vain; General Balck and his troops did a thorough job and the whole force was destroyed or captured.

As a result of this victory the immediate danger to Rostov from the northeast was warded off, but new perils menaced us on other sectors of the immense front. Because of the withdrawal of 11th Panzer, the positions on the Chir could no longer be held, and resistance collapsed during the last days of December. Army Detachment Hollidt formed an improvised line along the Tzymbiya river, thirty miles west of the Chir, and three Russian armies hurled themselves against it. To the south of the Don the relics of Hoth's Fourth Panzer Army were driven out of Kotelnikovski and back to the line of the Sal. The Russian advance in this direction menaced Rostov from the south, and in any case seemed certain to cut the line of withdrawal of Field Marshal von Kleist's Army Group, now trying to extricate itself from the Caucasus, nearly four hundred miles to the southeast.

Manstein was faced with strategic problems of a magnitude and complexity seldom paralleled in history. He handled the situation with masterly coolness and judgment, shrewdly assessing the risks, and moving his slender reserves from point to point as the situation demanded. To find another example of defensive strategy of this caliber we must go back to Lee's campaign in Virginia in the summer of 1864.

The position of the Caucasus armies remained critical during January. Seventeenth Army withdrew into the Kuban bridgehead, while First Panzer Army was directed on Rostov. At the same time the 48th Panzer Corps and Army Detachment Hollidt were brought back to the line of the Donetz, to the southeast of Voroshilovgrad. Forty-eighth

Panzer Corps was allotted the 6th and 7th Panzer Divisions, and the 302nd Infantry Division, which had just arrived from France, after receiving its baptism of fire at Dieppe a few months before. With these troops we successfully contained violent Russian attacks along the Donetz during the second half of January.

Eleventh Panzer Division was detached from the 48th Panzer Corps and sent south of the Don to assist Fourth Panzer Army in protecting the Caucasus "bottleneck." While in this area it fought an interesting action which is worth describing in detail.

The Action at Manutchskaya

During January Fourth Panzer Army was driven from its positions on the banks of the Sal and back to the line of the River Manich which runs southeast from Rostov. The Russians[2] swept down the river as far as its point of junction with the Don, barely twenty miles from Rostov. Not only that, they forced a crossing of the Manich at Manutchskaya, and occupied this village, which lies on the western bank of the river. They then pushed boldly towards Rostov and across the line of withdrawal of First Panzer Army.

It was vital to restore the situation, and on 22 January Manstein brought the 11th Panzer Division across to the south bank of the Don to support the counterattack of Fourth Panzer Army. The following account is based on General Balck's personal report.

On 23 January, 11th Panzer, in conjunction with the 16th Infantry Division, struck the advancing Russians and rolled them back to their bridgehead at Manutchskaya. On the 24th they attacked the village but were beaten off. It was essential to capture the place with its big road bridge across the Manich, for unless it could be taken a repetition of the attack on Rostov would be possible at any time. On 25 January, the 11th Panzer Division was ordered to eliminate the bridgehead at all costs; the division was urgently required on the right wing of Fourth Panzer Army where another crisis had arisen.

[2] Commanded by General Yeremenko.

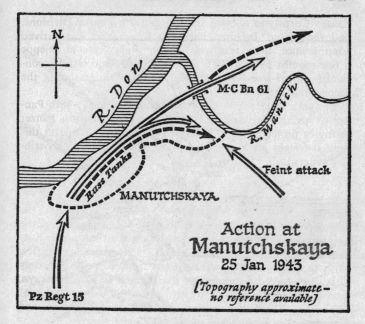

N

R. DON

M·C Bn 61

R. Manich

Feint attack

Russ Tanks

MANUTCHSKAYA

Action at
Manutchskaya
25 Jan 1943

*[Topography approximate—
no reference available]*

Pz Regt 15

The locality was strongly fortified and numerous tanks had been dug in between the houses to serve as bunkers; they were difficult to discover and to counter. The first attack had failed under their unopposed fire, although our losses were light as the troops had now developed a very fine sense of danger, and pulled back in time.

For the second attack it was important to lure the Russian tanks—most of them entrenched in the southern part of the village—from their lair. To achieve this, the fire of the entire artillery was concentrated on the northeastern sector of the village, and a feint attack was mounted at this point by armored cars and "half-tracks" under cover of a smoke screen. Then suddenly the fire of the divisional artillery was directed on the southern part of the village and concentrated in a single mighty blow on the point where we intended to break in; the rate of fire was increased to maximum inten-

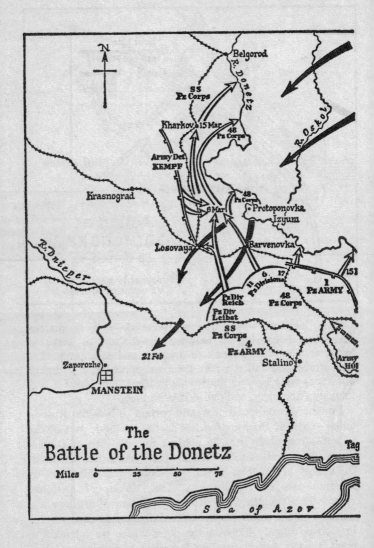

N

Belgorod

R. Donetz

R. Oskol

SS
Pz Corps

Kharkov 15 Mar 48
Pz Corps

Army Det
KEMPF

Krasnograd

48
Pz Corps

Protoponovka

Izyum

5 Mar

R. Dnieper

Losovaya

Barvenovka

15?
1
Pz ARMY

6 17
Pz Divisions

II

Pz Div
Reich

48
Pz Corps

Pz Div
Leibst

SS
Pz Corps

4
Pz ARMY

Stalino

21 Feb

Army
Hol

Zaporozhe

MANSTEIN

The
Battle of the Donetz

Miles   0   25   50   75

Tag

Sea of Azov

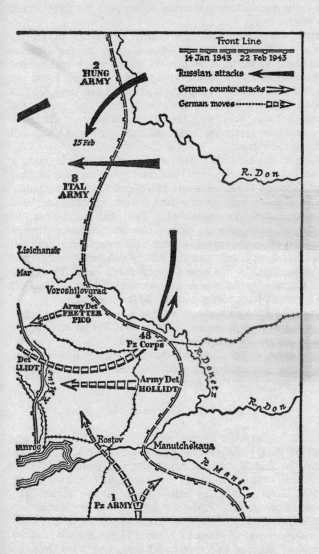

Front Line
14 Jan 1943   22 Feb 1943
Russian attacks
German counter-attacks
German moves

2 HUNG ARMY

15 Feb

8 ITAL ARMY

R. Don

Lisichansk

Mar

Voroshilovgrad

Army Det FRETTER PICO

48 Pz Corps

R. Donetz

Det LLIDT

Army Det HOLLIDT

R. Don

R. Mius

anrog

Rostov

Manutchskaya

R. Manich

1 Pz ARMY

sity. Only one battery continued to support the feint attack with smoke shell.

While the shells were still falling, the tanks of Panzer Regiment 15 charged the village and rolled up the defenses from south to north. The Russian tanks which had moved to the northern part of the village were attacked from the rear and destroyed by our panzers after a fierce struggle. The Russian infantry took to their heels and fled across the Manich without destroying the bridge; Motorcycle Battalion 61 was sent to intercept them, while the tank battle was still raging in the village.

At first the divisional staff conducted the battle from a hill south of Manutchskaya, but later on joined the leading tanks. German losses were one killed and fourteen wounded; on the Russian side twenty tanks were knocked out and 500–600 killed or wounded. This battle showed in the clearest way how an action can be conducted with a minimum of losses, provided the attacking forces are well co-ordinated, and can turn the enemy's dispositions to their own advantage. In this case General Balck decided to break in at the very point where our previous attack had failed; thus his feint attack completely fooled the Russians.

From the Russian point of view it would have been better not to dig in their tanks in the front line, but to concentrate them in reserve for a mobile counterattack.

This well-planned attack by the 11th Panzer Division was of decisive importance in smashing the Russian offensive against Rostov from the south.

Manstein's Counterstroke

On 15 January the Russian High Command let loose another of their tremendous offensives, directed this time against the 2nd Hungarian Army south of Voronezh. These operations were co-ordinated by Marshal Vassilevsky, and Marshal Vatutin had also been brought to this sector. The Hungarian troops were of better quality than the Rumanians or Italians, but they could not withstand the flood. The Russian columns poured through a gap 175 miles wide, and by the end of January had captured Kursk, and were over the

Donetz to the southeast of Kharkov. In spite of the successful withdrawal of the Caucasus armies, another Stalingrad loomed up for Manstein. The direction of the Russian prongs pointed ominously towards the Dnieper crossing at Zaporozhe, the main supply center for Army Group Don. (See map on pages 248–49.)

Manstein was not unduly worried and felt that he could cope with the situation, provided he could get permission to maneuver and yield ground where necessary. But this was precisely the point on which Hitler would never compromise; he always thought of defensive warfare in terms of the Western Front of 1914–18, with its rigid defense and the contesting of every yard of ground. His convictions on the point had been strengthened by the success of his strategy in the Russian winter of 1941–42; in December, 1941, he had refused requests for large-scale withdrawals and events had proved him right. Manstein had now got First and Fourth Panzer Armies on to the northern bank of the Don; with this striking force he felt confident of smashing the Russian offensive if he was given a free hand to withdraw from the line of the Donetz, evacuate Rostov, and take up a much shorter front along the Mius river—the original starting point of the 1942 offensive. Hitler refused point-blank, but the situation was too critical for trifling and Manstein demanded an interview. On 6 February Hitler came to see Manstein at his headquarters near Zaporozhe, and tense and prolonged discussions took place.

Perhaps the surrender of Paulus six days before had put the Führer in a more receptive frame of mind; anyhow, he yielded to Manstein's representations. The greatest obstacle to victory had now been overcome, and Manstein could frame his plans with an easy mind.

During the first half of February everything seemed to go well for the Russians. Army Detachment (*Armee Abteilung*) Hollidt gave up its positions on the lower Donetz, and withdrew through Rostov and Taganrog to the entrenchments along the Mius. On 10 February the 48th Panzer Corps, which had repulsed all attacks, fell back from the line of the Donetz; the corps assembled for new operations to the north of Stalino, in the heart of the Dombas industrial area. On 16 February Army Detachment Kempf was compelled to evacuate Kharkov, as its northern wing was being enveloped from the direction of Belgorod. A gap opened between Army Detachment Kempf and the left flank of Army Detachment Fretter Pico at Izyum on the Donetz. The Russians exploited the situation and pushed southwards from Barvenovka and southwestwards through Losovaya. On 21 February Russian tanks reached the Dnieper and came within sight of Manstein's headquarters at Zaporozhe.

Manstein was perfectly calm; indeed he watched the Russian maneuver with satisfaction. On 17 February Hitler had visited him again to demand the immediate recapture of Kharkov, and Manstein had explained that the farther the Russian masses advanced to the west and southwest, the more effective would be his counterstroke. He was drawing the Russians into a most dangerous pocket, because Army Detachment Kempf was standing firm at Krasnograd, thanks to the arrival of reinforcements, including P.G.D. "Gross Deutschland."

On 21 February Army Detachment Hollidt and First Panzer Army were holding a strong front along the line of the Mius and to the northeast of Stalino. To the northwest of that town, Fourth Panzer Army stood ready to counterattack; the 48th Panzer Corps was on the right with the 6th, 11th and 17th Panzer Divisions and the S.S. Panzer Corps was on the left, with Panzer Division "Leibstandarte" and Panzer Division "Das Reich."[3]

On 22 February these five panzer divisions started their drive in a northwesterly direction. The move was a concentric one and carried out under strictly co-ordinated control. Forty-eighth Panzer Corps moved towards Barvenovka and its rapid advance came as a complete surprise to the Russians. In a few days the 17th Panzer Division on the right flank gained the Izyum-Protoponovka sector on the Donetz river, while the S.S. Panzer Corps took Losovaya and established contact with Army Detachment Kempf, which had joined in the attack from the west.

[3] The S.S. panzer divisions and P.G.D. "Gross Deutschland" each had a battalion of the new Tiger tanks.

The terrain was almost completely open, slightly undulating, and cut here and there by narrow brooks which were then completely frozen. It resembled the area west of Stalingrad, and indeed was very much like the North African desert. Russian columns streaming back to the north were visible at a distance of eight to twelve miles and were taken under effective artillery fire at that range. Some Russian formations succeeded in escaping the trap, but the First Guard Army and Armored Group Popov suffered very heavy losses in men and equipment. By 6 March several large Russian armored formations and one cavalry corps were completely cut off by Fourth Panzer Army and Army Detachment Kempf; 615 tanks were destroyed and more than 1,000 guns captured. Forty-eighth Panzer Corps pressed forward to the east of Kharkov, and by the middle of March the line of the Donetz was firmly held and the front again faced east. The S.S. Panzer Corps continued its victorious advance and on 15 March the German War Flag again floated over the great square of Kharkov.

In the sector of First Panzer Army between Lisichansk and Izyum the Russians were also defeated and thrown back across the Donetz. Thus in a few weeks Manstein had been able to carry out a successful withdrawal, to launch a counterattack on a large scale, to eliminate the threat of encirclement, to inflict very heavy losses on a victorious enemy and to reestablish the southern front from Tagarog to Belgorod as a straight defensive line. In numbers of divisions the ratio of strength was 8 to 1 in favor of the Russians, and these operations showed once again what German troops were able to do when led by experts in accordance with accepted tactical principles, instead of being hampered with "holding at all costs" as the battlecry.

Having regard to the problems which faced Manstein between December, 1942, and February, 1943, it may be questioned whether any achievement of generalship in World War II can approach the successful extrication of the Caucasus armies and the subsequent riposte to Kharkov. The German military writer, Ritter von Schramm, spoke of "a miracle of the Donetz," but there was no miracle; victory was gained by masterly judgment and calculation.

The following points were evident in the counterstroke of
Fourth Panzer Army in February and March:

1) High level commanders did not restrict the moves of
   armored formations, but gave them "long range tasks."
2) Armored formations had no worries about their flanks,
   because the High Command had a moderate infantry
   force available to take care of flanks.
3) All commanders of armored formations, including panzer
   corps, conducted operations not from the rear, but from
   the front.
4) The attack came as a surprise regarding time and place.

It is interesting to see how the Russians reacted to this
surprise attack. The Russian soldier is temperamentally
unstable; he is carried on by the herd instinct and is therefore not able to endure a sudden change from a triumphant
advance to an enforced and precipitate withdrawal. During
the counterattack we witnessed scenes of almost unparalleled
panic among the Russians, to the astonishment of those who
had experienced the stubborn, almost fanatical resistance the
Russians put up in well-planned and efficiently organized defenses. It is true that the Russian can be superb in defense
and reckless in mass attacks, but when faced by surprise
and unforeseen situations he is an easy prey to panic. Field
Marshal von Manstein proved in this operation that Russian
mass attacks should be met by maneuver and not by rigid
defense. The weakness of the Russian lies in his inability to
face surprise; there he is most vulnerable. Manstein realized
his weakness. He also realized that his own strength lay in
the superior training of his junior commanders and their
capacity for independent action and leadership. Thus he
could afford to let his divisions withdraw for hundreds of
miles, and then stage a smashing counterattack with the
same divisions, which inflicted heavy blows on their startled
and bewildered opponents.

Political Problems

The Kharkov counterattack was followed by three months
of comparative calm, and I took advantage of this leisure

to study the Russo-Communist problem at first hand. When I had the chance I visited factories in Stalino and Kharkov and learned as much as I could about the conditions of life of the urban and rural population. This activity had its lighter side, and I joined in many a gay and frolicsome Ukrainian peasant dance.

I deem myself lucky not to have had too intimate an acquaintance with the partisans, who rarely operated in the immediate vicinity of the front. Nor were the open plains of the Ukraine suitable for partisan operations, whereas the densely wooded areas of central and northern Russia were ideal for the purpose. As regards partisans, we soldiers adopted a principle which in my opinion is recognized by every army, namely, that no means are too hard if they serve their purpose in protecting the troops against partisans, guerilas, or *franctireurs*.[4] The rules and conventions of warfare have been carefully built up since the seventeenth century; they cannot be applied to partisan activity, and a heavy responsibility rests with those governments who deliberately organize and support this terrible form of war. In the Soviet Union the partisan forces had been thoroughly trained and organized in peacetime. They depended for their success, however, on the sympathy of the local population, which they certainly did not get in the Ukraine.

During the spring of 1943 I saw with my own eyes that German soldiers were welcomed as friends by Ukrainians and White Russians. Churches were reopened. The peasants who had been degraded to kolkhoz workers were hoping to get their farms back. The population was relieved to to have got rid of the Secret Police and to be free of the constant fear of being sent to forced-labor camps in Siberia. Interrogation of thousands of prisoners of war and long discussions with many of them convinced me that the average Russian is distrustful of the Communist Party; many are filled with bitter hatred, particularly against party officials. There were thousands of Ukrainians and White Russians, who even after the numerous and disastrous setbacks the

---

[4] See for example General Eisenhower's draconian "Ordinance No. 1 of Military Government," directed against potential partisan activity in Western Germany.

German armies suffered during the winter of 1942–43, took up arms to free Russia from the yoke of Communism.

It was interesting, though by no means encouraging, to see how the German political leaders dealt with this situation. The armed forces did not receive any political directives for the conduct of the war in Russia. Hitler liberated the Russians from their Communist commissars and gave them Reichs commissars instead; in particular the Ukrainians were saddled with the ill-famed Gauleiter Koch. The Russians hoped for a Russian government to oppose Stalin and his clique, but nothing was done to fulfil their hopes. The kolkhoz's remained in being; they were rebaptized and given the name of "communal property." No Russian army was established, for had he done so, Hitler would have been compelled to make certain promises contrary to his political plans. Some local Cossack and Ukrainian divisions were allowed—grudgingly. In a condescending way the Russian was given permission to be a "Hiwi,"[5] but this did not put our political leaders under any obligation. Instead of being sent to Siberia, thousands of Russian men and women were sent to Germany and called *Ostarbeiter* (workers from the east). They were virtually slaves.

Such was the "liberation" of the Russian people, many of whom had welcomed the German soldiers as friends and benefactors.

Soviet propaganda was not slow to take advantage of the incredible psychological mistakes made by Hitler and his Reichs commissars. In a most skilful way Stalin played on the Russian's innate love for "Little Mother Russia," and his propaganda machine soon succeeded in presenting the war as a struggle for the "Fatherland." The traditions of the former Tsarist army were all revived. Soon we had to face Guards divisions and Guards brigades. Officers proudly displayed their shining epaulettes, which veteran Communists had branded as symbols of reaction. Terms were even made with the Church.

German policy was one of the chief reasons for the intensified partisan warfare, and the German soldier had to

---

[5] *Hilfswilliger*—a person rendering voluntary assistance.

suffer for it. Numerous enthusiastic and patriotic Russians were driven into the ranks of the partisans, disappointed by the ruthless treatment meted out to them by the German political administration. Finally in September, 1944, when no German soldier was left on Russian soil, General Vlassov[6] was allowed to build up a Russian army—but then it was too late.

The German political leaders missed the chance given them by fate to smash Russian communism with the help of the Russian soldier.

[6] Vlassov, a very capable commander, distinguished himself in the defense of Moscow in November, 1941, and was captured in Manstein's counterattack in February, 1943. Together with his principal associates he was executed by the Russians after the war.

It has been estimated that some 400,000 Russian prisoners were incorporated into the *Wehrmacht*.

14: The Battle of Kursk

"It Must Not Fail"

AT THE END of March, 1943, the thaw started on the Eastern front; "Marshal Winter" gave way to the still more masterful "Marshal Mud," and active operations came automatically to an end. All panzer divisions and some infantry divisions were withdrawn from the front line, and the armor in the Kharkov area was concentrated under the 48th Panzer Corps. We assumed command of the 3rd, 6th and 11th Panzer Divisions, together with P.G.D. "Gross Deutschland." Advantage was taken of the lull to institute a thorough training program, and exercise the units on peacetime lines.

Training began on troop and platoon level and was progressively extended up to divisional exercises; maneuvers were held under active service conditions and shoots with live ammunition were regularly carried out. I personally set out to make myself proficient in handling the Tiger tank; I learned to drive this massive vehicle and fire its 88-mm gun. With this powerful gun and very strong armor the Tiger was the most successful and effective tank in the world until the end of the war; it had already shown what it could do in the counterattack on Kharkov. The Russian Stalin tank of 1944 was a very formidable opponent, but I do not consider it the equal of the Tiger.

On 31 March we were visited by the famous General Guderian; he had been disgraced after the failure to capture Moscow in 1941, but his brilliant gifts could no longer be neglected, and Hitler had recalled him as "Inspector-General of Armored Troops." Guderian particularly wanted to discuss the experiences of the Tiger battalion of the "Gross Deutschland" Division in the recent offensive, and Count Strachwitz, the very dashing commander of their panzer regiment, was able to give him many interesting details regarding the performance and limitations of the new tank. As a result of his visit Guderian ordered a speed-up in the production of Tigers and Panthers.[1]

All our thoughts were concerned with the next campaign, which was bound to be affected by the strategic situation as a whole. By the spring of 1943 the military position of Germany had worsened immeasurably. In Russia the moral comfort of Manstein's latest victory could not obscure the fact that the whole balance of power had changed, and that we were faced by a ruthless enemy, possessed of immense and seemingly inexhaustible resources. The hope of forcing a decision in Russia had faded forever in the autumn and winter of 1942; the best we could hope for was a stalemate, and even for this our prospects were clouded by disasters in other theaters of war. The U-boat campaign was being mastered, Tunisia was tending rapidly towards another Stalingrad, and Anglo-American strategic bombing was imposing a grave strain on the population and industries of the Reich. Japan had shot her bolt, and Italy was desperate.

Strong German forces were now tied permanently to Italy and Western Europe to meet potential or actual invasion, and in particular a high proportion of our fighter aircraft had been drawn away from Russia to cope with increased bombing in the West. The Red Air Force was growing into a formidable power; the help given by the Anglo-Americans was bearing fruit and Russian planes in increasing numbers swarmed over the battlefront. Fortunately their efficiency in no way corresponded with their numbers and we could

---

[1] The Panther was regarded as the *dernier cri* in armor. Like the Tiger it mounted an 88-mm gun but had lighter armor and was more mobile. (Later models mounted a 75-mm.) At this time there were two types of Tiger—the "Henschel" Tiger and the "Porsche" Tiger. The latter model, named after the designer, had no machine gun—a grave error which rendered them incapable of close-range fighting.

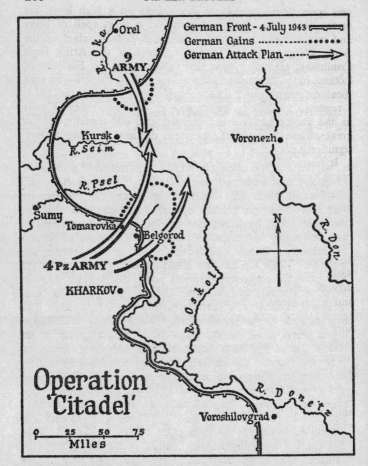

still gain air superiority over limited sectors and for limited periods. But it was clear that one of our great advantages had been whittled away.

In the circumstances the German Supreme Command was faced with a grave dilemma. Should we stand purely on the defensive in the East, or should we launch a limited attack in an endeavor to cripple Russia's offensive power? I was soon drawn into these discussions on a high level, for at the beginning of April I went on a short spell of leave and was ordered to report to General Zeitzler, chief of the Army General Staff. The headquarters of the Army High Command (O.K.H.) was then situated in the Fortress of Lötzen, in the Masurian Lakes region of East Prussia—an area recalling memories of Hindenburg's great victories of 1914. I reported to Zeitzler on the role of the 48th Panzer Corps in the recent battles, and learned that he contemplated a great offensive in which we were destined to play a very significant part.

It is true that in view of the losses suffered in preceding years there could be no question of seeking a decision. Zeitzler's object was a limited one; he wished to bite out the great Russian bulge which enclosed Kursk and projected for seventy-five miles into our front. A successful attack in this area would destroy a number of Soviet divisions and weaken the offensive power of the Red Army to a very considerable degree. As part of Fourth Panzer Army, the 48th Panzer Corps was to be the spearhead of the main drive from the south. I welcomed the idea, for our hardened and experienced panzer divisions had suffered little in the recent thrust on Kharkov, and were fit and ready for another battle as soon as the state of the ground would permit us to move. Moreover, at this stage the Russian defenses around Kursk were by no means adequate to resist a determined attack.

Zeitzler then said that Hitler wanted to make the results still more decisive and wished to postpone the offensive until the arrival of a Panther brigade. I listened to this with misgiving, and reported that according to the latest intelligence appreciations the Russians were still smarting under our recent blows, and the losses incurred in the rapid and costly withdrawal from Kharkov had not been made good. A delay of one or two months would make our task far more formidable.

Such was my introduction to the fateful Battle of Kursk —the last great German offensive in the East.

Zeitzler outlined the plan for Operation *Citadel*, as the new attack was to be called. All our available armor was

to be concentrated in two great pincers—Colonel General
Model with his Ninth Army was to attack from the north,
and Colonel General Hoth with Fourth Panzer Army from
the south. In the initial assault Hoth was to have eight
panzer divisions and Model five; several infantry divisions
were to join in the attack and to obtain them the neighboring fronts were to be thinned out beyond the limits of
prudence. From the strategic aspect *Citadel* was to be a veritable "death-ride," for virtually the whole of the operational
reserve was to be flung into this supreme offensive.

Because so much was at stake, hesitations and doubts
were bound to arise. When the attack was originally proposed, Field Marshal von Manstein was strongly in favor
and believed that if we struck soon a notable victory could
be won.[2] But Hitler kept postponing D day, partly in order
to assemble stronger forces and partly because he had the
gravest doubts about our prospects of success. Early in May
he held a conference at Munich and sought the views of
the senior commanders. Field Marshal von Kluge, the commander of Army Group Center, was strongly in favor;
Manstein was now dubious, and Model produced air photographs which showed that the Russians were constructing
very strong positions at the shoulders of the salient and
had withdrawn their mobile forces from the area west of
Kursk. This showed that they were aware of the impending
attack and were making adequate preparations to deal with
it.

Colonel General Guderian spoke out and declared that
an offensive at Kursk was "pointless";[3] heavy tank casualties
were bound to be incurred and would ruin his plans for
reorganizing the armor. He warned that the Panthers, on
which "the chief of the Army General Staff was relying so
heavily, were still suffering from many teething troubles in-
herent in all new equipment." But General Zeitzler was still

[2] Manstein had pointed out, however, that there was much to be
gained by adopting a strategy of maneuver. He suggested withdrawing
his right wing to the Dnieper, and then counterattacking from the
area of Kharkov. Such a conception had no appeal for Hitler.

[3] *Panzer Leader*, 307.

confident of victory, and, perplexed by the conflict among the experts, Hitler put off the decision until a later date.

At this conference on *Citadel*, Hitler made the significant and perfectly accurate comment, that "it must not fail." On 10 May Guderian saw him again and begged him to give up the idea; Hitler replied, "You're quite right. Whenever I think of this attack my stomach turns over."[4] Yet under the pressure of Keitel and Zeitzler he ultimately gave way and consented to an operation of grandiose proportions. The attack from the south was to be made by ten panzer, one panzergrenadier, and seven infantry divisions; the northern thrust would be delivered by seven panzer, two panzergrenadier, and nine infantry divisions.[5] It was to be the greatest armored onslaught in the history of war.

The Preliminaries

For two months the shadow of *Citadel* hung over the Eastern Front and affected all our thoughts and planning. It was disquieting to reflect that after all our training, our profound study of the art of war, and the bitter experiences of the past year, the German General Staff should be dabbling with a dangerous gamble in which we were to stake our last reserves. As the weeks slipped by it became abundantly clear that this was an operation in which we had little to gain and probably a great deal to lose. Hitler kept postponing D day; the ostensible reason was that the Panthers were not ready, but it appears from Guderian's memoirs that the Führer distrusted the whole conception of *Citadel*—on this occasion his intuition did not play him false.

It is an accepted fact that plans and preparations for an operation of such magnitude cannot be kept secret for any length of time. The Russians reacted to our plans exactly as was to be expected. They fortified likely sectors, built several lines of resistance, and converted important tactical points into miniature fortresses. The area was studded with

---

[4] *Panzer Leader,* 309.
[5] These totals include reserves not committed in the initial assault.

minefields, and very strong armored and infantry reserves were assembled at the base of the salient. If *Citadel* had been launched in April or May, it might have yielded a valuable harvest, but by June the conditions were totally different. The Russians were aware of what was coming, and had converted the Kursk front into another Verdun. Even if we should hack our way through the minefields and bite off the salient, little would be gained. The losses were certain to be enormous, and it was unlikely that many Russian divisions would be caught in the sack. As for wearing down the Russian reserves and thus forestalling their summer offensive, it was far more likely that our own reserves would be destroyed. One is reminded of the comment of General Messimy prior to Nivelle's offensive in April, 1917: "Guns yes, prisoners yes, territory yes, but all at an outrageous cost and without strategic results."

The German Supreme Command was committing exactly the same error as in the previous year. Then we attacked the city of Stalingrad, now we were to attack the fortress of Kursk. In both cases the German Army threw away all its advantages in mobile tactics, and met the Russians on ground of their own choosing. Yet the campaigns of 1941 and 1942 had proved that our panzers were virtually invincible if they were allowed to maneuver freely across the great plains of Russia. Instead of seeking to create conditions in which maneuver would be possible—by strategic withdrawals or surprise attacks in quiet sectors—the German Supreme Command could think of nothing better than to fling our magnificent panzer divisions against Kursk, which had now become the strongest fortress in the world.

By the middle of June Field Marshal von Manstein, and indeed all his senior commanders, saw that it was folly to go on with *Citadel,* Manstein urged most strongly that the offensive should be abandoned, but he was overruled. D day was finally fixed for 4 July—Independence Day for the United States, the beginning of the end for Germany.

Broadly speaking the plan was very simple—Fourth Panzer Army from the south, and Ninth Army from the north were to advance towards each other and meet east of Kursk. The main thrust of Fourth Panzer Army was to be delivered on both sides of Tomarovka, with the 48th Panzer Corps on the left and the S.S. Panzer Corps on the right. The S.S. Corps had been given three panzer divisions ("Leibstandarte," "Totenkopf," and "Das Reich"); Army Detachment Kempf, with one panzer corps and two infantry corps under command, was to advance from Belgorod in a northeasterly direction, thus acting as flank cover for the main drive. In the 48th Panzer Corps we had the 3rd and 11th Panzer Divisions, and P.G.D. "Gross Deutschland."

"Gross Deutschland" was a very strong division with a special organization. It mustered about 180 tanks, of which 80 were part of a "Panther Detachment" commanded by Lieutenant Colonel von Lauchert, and the remainder were in the panzer regiment. The division also had two motorized infantry regiments, one a grenadier regiment, the other a rifle regiment.[6] There was an artillery regiment with four detachments,[7] an assault gun detachment, an antitank detachment, an engineer battalion and the normal signals and administrative units. For the first and last time during the Russian campaign the divisions enjoyed a few weeks' rest before the attack, and were up to full strength in personnel and equipment. Eleventh and 3rd Panzer Divisions each had an armored regiment with 80 tanks and full strength artillery. Forty-eighth Panzer Corps thus had some 60 assault guns, and more than 300 tanks, a striking power it was never to see again.

The terrain, over which the advance was to take place, was a far-flung plain, broken by numerous valleys, small copses, irregularly laid out villages, and some rivers and brooks; of these the Pena ran with a swift current between steep banks. The ground rose slightly to the north, thus favoring the defender. Roads consisted of tracks through the sand and became impassable for all motor transport during rain. Large cornfields covered the landscape and made visibility difficult. All in all, it was not good "tank country," but it was by no means "tank proof." There had been

---

[6] There was little difference in the establishment of these units. The panzergrenadiers had a somewhat higher proportion of heavy weapons.

[7] The German artillery *Abteilung* or detachment was somewhat larger than the British battery—twelve or sometimes sixteen guns.

sufficient time to make thorough preparations for the attack.

For weeks the infantry had been in the positions from which the attack was to be launched. From there they had reconnoitered all the details of the Russian defenses and noted the peculiarities of the terrain. Officers in command of the attacking troops, down to company commanders, spent days in these positions, in order to acquaint themselves with the ground and the enemy. No precautions were omitted; none of the panzer men wore their black uniforms lest they give the show away. The fire plan, and co-operation between artillery and infantry, were carefully worked out. Air photos were available for every square yard of the Kursk salient. But though these photographs showed the depth and size of the Russian positions, they did not reveal details or give any indication of the strength of their forces, for the Russians are masters in the art of camouflage. Inevitably their strength was considerably underestimated.[8]

The most conscientious steps were taken to ensure the closest co-operation between air and ground forces: indeed, no attack could have been better prepared than this one. No movement whatever was allowed by day. To assemble so large a number of tanks and motorized troops was a difficult matter, the more so as few suitable roads were available. For nights on end the staff officers responsible for the movements of troops and munitions stood by the roadside and at road crossings to ensure that everything would go off without a hitch. Rain and cloudbursts did not allow the timetable to be adhered to in all respects, but the assembly was completed in time, and suffered no interference whatsoever from the Russians.

Contrary to the normal practice, we were not to attack at dawn, but in the middle of the afternoon. On 4 July the weather was hot and sultry and there was a feeling of tension along the battlefront. The morale of the attacking troops was of the highest; they were prepared to endure any losses and carry out every task given them. Unhappily they had been set the wrong tasks.

[8] The Russian armies on the Kursk front were commanded by Marshals Rokossovsky and Vatutin.

The Assault

The Battle of Kursk began at 1500 hours on 4 July with an attack on the forward Russian lines, preceded by a short but sharp artillery preparation and air bombardment. On the front of the 48th Panzer Corps, these lines ran some three miles south of the villages of Luchanino, Alexejewka, and Sawidowka. Grenadiers and riflemen supported by assault guns and engineers penetrated the Russian forward line that evening. During the night the tanks were moved up and P.G.D. "Gross Deutschland" was ordered to advance the next morning between Ssyrzew and Luchanino (Sketch 1). Third and 11th Panzer Divisions were to attack on the flanks of "Gross Deutschland." But as bad luck would have it, a violent cloudburst that night transformed the ground along the banks of the stream between Ssyrzew and Sawidowka into a morass. This proved of the greatest advantage to the Russian second line to the north of the stream and immensely increased its already considerable defensive strength.

On the second day of the attack we met our first setback, and in spite of every effort the troops were unable to penetrate the Russian line. "Gross Deutschland," assembling in dense formation and with the swamp on its immediate front, was heavily shelled by Russian artillery. The engineers were unable to make suitable crossings, and many tanks fell victims to the Red Air Force—during this battle Russian aircraft operated with remarkable dash in spite of German air superiority. Even in the area taken by the German troops on the first day Russians appeared from nowhere, and the reconnaissance units of "Gross Deutschland" had to deal with them. Nor was it possible to cross the stream and swamp on the night 5/6 July. On the left flank the attacks of the 3rd Panzer Division against Sawidowka were as unsuccessful as those of "Gross Deutschland" against Alexejewka and Luchanino. The entire area had been infested with mines; and the Russian defense along the whole line was supported by tanks operating with all the advantage of high ground. Our assault troops suffered considerable

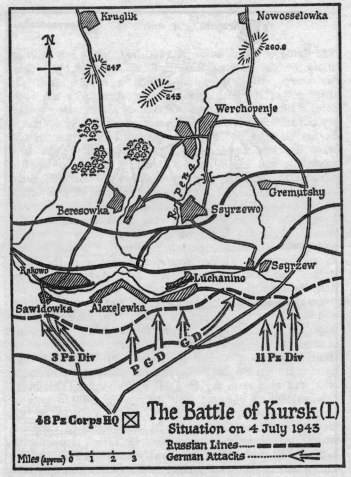

Kruglik

Nowosselowka

N

247

260.8

243

Werchopenje

R. Pena

Gremutshy

Beresowka

Ssyrzewo

Rakowo

Ssyrzew

Luchanino

Sawidowka   Alexejewka

3 Pz Div

P G D

G D

11 Pz Div

48 Pz Corps HQ

The Battle of Kursk (I)
Situation on 4 July 1943
Russian Lines ....
German Attacks ....

Miles (approx)   0   1   2   3

casualties, and the 3rd Panzer Division had to beat off counterattacks. In spite of several massive bombing attacks by the Luftwaffe against battery positions, the Russian defensive fire did not decrease to any extent.

On 7 July, the fourth day of *Citadel*, we at last achieved some success. "Gross Deutschland" was able to break

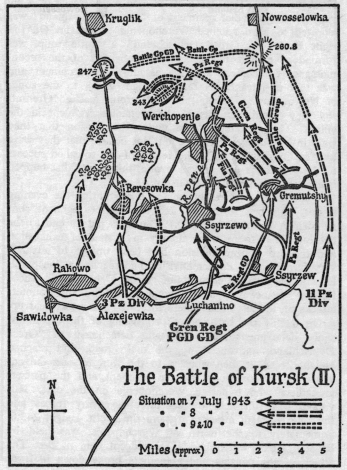

The Battle of Kursk (II)

Situation on 7 July 1943

Miles (approx) 0 1 2 3 4 5

through on both sides of Ssyrzew, and the Russians withdrew to Gremutshy and Ssyrzewo. The fleeing masses were
caught by German artillery fire and suffered very heavy
casualties; our tanks gained momentum and wheeled to the
northwest. But at Ssyrzewo that afternoon they were halted
by strong defensive fire, and Russian armor counterattacked.

However, on the right wing we seemed within reach of a big victory; the grenadier regiment of "Gross Deutschland" was reported to have reached Werchopenje (Map II). On the right flank of "Gross Deutschland" a battle-group was formed to exploit this success; it consisted of the reconnaissance detachment and the assault-gun detachment and was told to advance as far as Height 260.8 to the south of Nowosselowka. When this battle-group reached Gremutshy they found elements of the grenadier regiment in the village. The grenadiers were under the illusion that they were in Nowosselowka and could not believe that they were only in Gremutshy. Thus the report of the so-called success of the grenadiers was proved wrong; things like that happen in every war and particularly in Russia.

A hill north of Gremutshy was taken during the evening against stubborn resistance; and the panzer regiment shot Russian tanks off Height 230.1. Darkness put an end to the fighting. The troops were already in a state of exhaustion and the 3rd Panzer Division had been unable to advance very far. Eleventh Panzer Division had reached a line parallel with the forward elements of "Gross Deutschland" whose further advance was badly hampered by fire and counterattacks on the left flank, where the 3rd Panzer was held up.

On 8 July the battle-group, consisting of the reconnaissance detachment and assault-gun detachment of "Gross Deutschland," advanced up the main road, and reached Height 260.8; it then wheeled to the west to ease the advance of the divisional panzer regiment and the panzergrenadiers who bypassed Werchopenje on the east. This village was still held by considerable enemy forces and the rifle regiment attacked it from the south. Height 243.0, immediately to the north of Werchopenje, was held by Russian tanks, which had a magnificent field of fire. The attack of the panzers and grenadiers broke down in front of this hill; the Russian tanks seemed to be everywhere and singled out the spearhead of "Gross Deutschland," allowing it no rest.

That afternoon the battle-group on the right of "Gross Deutschland" repulsed seven attacks by Russian armor and knocked out twenty-one T34s. Forty-eight Panzer Corps ordered the *Schwerpunkt* of "Gross Deutschland" to wheel westward and bring some help to the 3rd Panzer Division where the threat to the left flank remained as grave as ever. Neither Height 243.0 nor the western outskirts of Werchopenje were taken on that day—it could no longer be doubted that the back of the German attack had been broken and its momentum had gone.

However, on 9 July the 3rd Panzer Division was at last able to advance to the left of the Rakowo-Kruglik road and to prepare for an outflanking attack against Beresowka. During the night 9/10 July the tanks of 3rd Panzer entered Beresowka from the west, but the division's attack to the north was again checked in front of a small forest to the north of the village.

Eleventh Panzer Division was unable to advance very far, while the S.S. Panzer Corps operating on our eastern flank had to ward off strong armored counterattacks all along the line; like ourselves it had gained but little ground.

The slow progress of the southern pincer was disappointing, but we had in fact done much better than our comrades on the northern flank of the salient. General Guderian says of his visit to Ninth Army:

. . . the ninety Porsche Tigers, which were operating with Model's army, were incapable of close-range fighting since they lacked sufficient ammunition for their guns, and this defect was aggravated by the fact that they possessed no machine gun. Once they had broken into the enemy's infantry zone they literally had to go quail-shooting with cannons. They did not manage to neutralize, let alone destroy, the enemy rifles and machine guns, so that the infantry was unable to follow up behind them. By the time they reached the Russian artillery they were on their own. Despite showing extreme bravery and suffering unheard-of casualties, the infantry of Weidling's division did not manage to exploit the tanks' success. Model's attack bogged down after some six miles.[9]

After a week of hard and almost uninterrupted fighting "Gross Deutschland" was showing signs of exhaustion and

[9] *Panzer Leader*, 311.

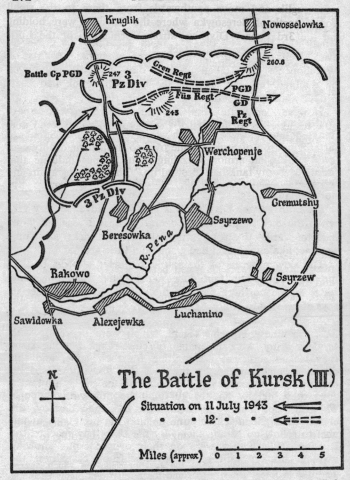

Kruglik

Nowosselowka

Battle Gp PGD

247 3 Pz Div

Gren Regt

260.8

Füs Regt

PGD GD Pz Regt

243

Werchopenje

Gremutshy

3 Pz Div

Ssyrzewo

Beresowka

R. Pena

Rakowo

Ssyrzew

Sawidowka

Alexejewka

Luchanino

N

The Battle of Kursk (III)

Situation on 11 July 1943

• • • 12 • • •

Miles (approx) 0 1 2 3 4 5

its ranks had been thinned out considerably. On 10 July this division was ordered to wheel to the south and south-west and clean up the enemy on the left flank. The panzer regiment, the reconnaissance detachment and the grenadier regiment were to advance towards Height 243.0 and to the north thereof; they were then to seize 247.0 to the south of Kruglik and move southwards from there to the small forest north of Beresowka where the Russians were holding up the 3rd Panzer Division; strong formations of the Luftwaffe were to support this attack.

The air bombardment was extraordinarily effective and the War Diary of the reconnaissance detachment describes it as follows:

With admiration we watch the Stukas attacking the Russian tanks uninterruptedly and with wonderful precision. Squadron after squadron of Stukas come over to drop their deadly eggs on the Russian armor. Dazzling white flames indicate that another enemy tank has "brewed up." This happens again and again.[10]

Supported by the splendid efforts of the Luftwaffe, "Gross Deutschland" made a highly successful advance; heights 243.0 and 247.0 were taken, and Russian infantry and armor fled before the panzers and sought refuge in the wood north of Beresowka. Trapped between "Gross Deutschland" and the 3rd Panzer, it seemed as if the enemy on the left flank had at last been liquidated, and the advance to the north could now be resumed. On 11 July the 48th Panzer Corps issued orders for the units of "Gross Deutschland" to be relieved by the 3rd Panzer Division during the night; "Gross Deutschland" was to assemble astride the road south of Height 260.8, and to stand by for an advance to the north. In view of the breakdown of Model's attack, a successful advance in this quarter offered the only hope of victory.

On the night 11/12 July the units of "Gross Deutschland" were relieved by the 3rd Panzer Division according to plan,

[10] The Battle of Kursk was the first occasion on which aircraft operated in force against armor and the results were highly encouraging. The famous Stuka pilot, Hans Rudel, experimented with cannon-firing Stukas, and says: "In the first attack four tanks explode under the hammer blows of my cannon; by the evening the total rises to twelve . . . the evil spell is broken, and in this aircraft we possess a weapon which can speedily be employed everywhere and is capable of dealing successfully with the formidable numbers of Soviet tanks." *See* Rudel, *Stuka Pilot*, 86.

but the panzergrenadiers moved off with a sense of uneasiness. The last stages of the relief were carried out under heavy enemy shelling, and the men of "Gross Deutschland" left their trenches to the accompaniment of the battle noises of a Russian counterattack. Their fears—alas—came true, for that very night the 3rd Panzer Division was thrown out of its forward positions.

On the morning of 12 July "Gross Deutschland" was assembled and concentrated astride the road south of Nowosselowka, waiting to launch the decisive advance to the north at first light on the 13th (Map III). The twelfth of July was their first day without fighting; this breathing space was used to replenish ammunition and fuel and to carry out such repairs as could be effected in the forward area. Reconnaissance to the north reported that Nowasselowka only seemed to be occupied by insignificant forces. Heavy firing was heard to the west, and the news from the 3rd Panzer Division was not encouraging.

On 13 July patrolling to the north was intensified, but the expected order to advance did not come through—instead unpleasant reports were received from neighboring formations. Strong Russian counterattacks had been launched against the S.S. Panzer Corps and the 11th Panzer Division; it was true that the number of Russian tanks knocked out on the whole front was enormous, but new tanks took the place of the casualties; faithful to their principle the Russians kept on throwing in fresh troops, and their reserves seemed inexhaustible. On the afternoon of 13 July, the corps commander, General von Knobelsdorff, appeared at the battle heaudqarters of "Gross Deutschland" and gave orders which left no hope for any advance to the north: in fact the division was again to attack westwards. This attack, to be carried out on the 14th, was practically identical with those of 10 and 11 July: the object was to reach the Rakowo–Kruglik road. Indeed the situation on the left flank had deteriorated to such a degree that an attack northwards was no longer possible. On 12 and 13 July the 3rd Panzer Division had lost Beresowka, had been driven off the Rakowo–Kruglik road and had been compelled to give up Height 247.0 under stubborn on-

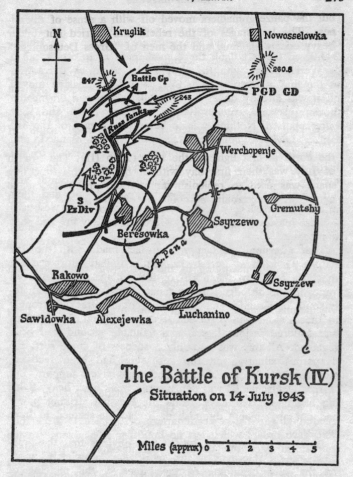

Kruglik

Nowosselowka

N

260.8

247 Battle Gp

243

PGD GD

Russ tanks

Werchopenje

3 Pz Div

Gremutshy

Ssyrzewo

Beresowka

R. Pena

Rakowo

Ssyrzew

Sawidowka Alexejewka Luchanino

The Battle of Kursk (IV)
Situation on 14 July 1943

Miles (approx) 0 1 2 3 4 5

slaughts by Russian armor. The enemy was being reinforced, and the 3rd Panzer Division was now too weak to
stem the Russian advance from the west.

At 0600 hours on 14 July "Gross Deutschland" advanced
westwards for the second time. A battle-group was formed
on the right wing consisting of the reconnaissance detach-

ment, the assault-gun detachment, a rifle company, and a tank company, to advance to Height 247.0 In the center the panzer regiment and riflemen were to advance on Height 243.0, on the left flank the grenadiers were to attack north of Werchopenje, with the little forest north of Beresowka as the final objective (Map IV). When the division moved off it was already under heavy artillery fire, and during the morning several counterattacks from the north and west were repulsed. Nothing was to be seen or heard of the 3rd Panzer Division, but the attack went in as planned, and Height 243.0 was retaken. Slow progress was made by the battle-group on the right which became involved in fierce fighting against Russian counterthrusts. On the center and left numerous Russian tanks were knocked out, and their infantry suffered very heavy losses and piled back westward —these masses were caught by German artillery fire and shot to pieces.

That afternoon contact was at last made with the 3rd Panzer Division at Beresowka, and a united effort secured the little forest to the north of that village. But it proved impossible to dislodge Russian tanks from the hill immediately south of Kruglik, and the enemy counterattacked strongly in that area. When night fell it appeared that the Russians had suffered serious losses, and valuable ground had been regained. All this was certainly a success of some sort; the dangerous situation on the left wing had been rectified, and the 3rd Panzer Division had been given support. But "Gross Deutschland" was dangerously weak after heavy fighting lasting for ten days, while the Russian striking power had not appreciably diminished. In fact, it seemed to have increased.

By the evening of 14 July it was obvious that the time-table of the German attack had been completely upset. At the very beginning of the offensive, the piercing of the forward Russian lines, deeply and heavily mined as they were, had proved much more difficult than we anticipated. The terrific Russian counterattacks, with masses of men and material ruthlessly thrown in, were also an unpleasant surprise. German casualties had not been light, while our tank losses were staggering. The Panthers did not come up to expectations; they were easily set ablaze, the oil and gasoline feeding systems were inadequately protected, and the crews were insufficiently trained. Of the eighty Panthers avaiable when battle was joined only a few were left on 14 July. The S.S. Panzer Corps was no better off, while on the northern flank Ninth Army had never penetrated more than seven miles into the Russian lines and was now at a complete standstill. Fourth Panzer Army had indeed reached a depth of twelve miles, but there were another sixty miles to cover before we could join hands with Model.

On 13 July, Field Marhals von Manstein and Kluge were summoned to East Prussia, and Hitler informed them that *Citadel* must be called off immediately as the Allies had landed in Sicily; troops must be transferred from the Eastern Front to deal with the invasion. Manstein had not committed all his forces and was in favor of continuing the offensive as a battle of attrition; by smashing up Russian armored reserves in the Kursk salient we might forestall major offensives in other sectors. This situation should have been foreseen before *Citadel* was launched; we were now in the position of a man who has seized a wolf by the ears and dare not let him go. However, Hitler declared that the attack must stop forthwith.

The Russian High Command had conducted the Battle of Kursk with great skill, yielding ground adroitly and taking the sting out of our offensive with an intricate system of minefields and antitank defenses. Not satisfied with counterattacking in the salient, the Russians delivered heavy blows between Orel and Bryansk and made a serious penetration. With Hitler's decision to go on to the defensive, the situation on the Eastern Front became very critical. Fourth Panzer Army was informed that the S. S. Panzer Corps would be withdrawn immediately for operations in Italy, while the 48th Panzer Corps was told to release "Gross Deutschland" and send it to the assistance of Field Marshal von Kluge's Army Group Center. In the circumstances it was impossible to hold our gains in the Kursk salient, and by 23 July Fourth Panzer Army had been pushed back to its start line.

Citadel had been a complete and most regrettable failure.

It is true that Russian losses were much heavier than German; indeed tactically the fighting had been indecisive. Fourth Panzer Army took thirty-two thousand prisoners, and captured or destroyed more than two thousand tanks and nearly two thousand guns. But our panzer divisions—in such splendid shape at the beginning of the battle—had been bled white, and with Anglo-American assistance the Russians could afford losses on this colossal scale.[11]

With the failure of our supreme effort, the strategic initiative passed to the Russians.

Armored Tactics during Citadel

The light and medium tanks used during the first three years of the war had done a splendid job during that period. However, as Russian antitank weapons had become more effective and Russian tanks bigger and stronger, the earlier models were now obsolete. Heavy and super-heavy tanks had come to the forefront, and armored tactics had to be changed accordingly. Panzer leaders were in the best position to watch these developments, as they had to adapt their tactics to the new weapons.

German antitank tactics of 1941 were no longer effective, for they did not provide for the massive Russian attacks with great numbers of tanks. It soon became apparent that a single antitank gun, or a cluster of them operating independently, was quickly discovered and knocked out. For this reason a new method was developed, which the German panzer troops called the *Pakfront*. Groups of guns up to a total of ten were put under the command of one man, who was responsible for concentrating their fire on a single target. Groups of antitank guns were thus welded into one unit, the groups were organized in depth and strewn all over the defended area. The idea was to draw the attacking armor into a web of enfilade fire. Fire discipline was of the first importance, and to open fire too early was the gravest mistake that could be made.

[11] Marshal Koniev afterwards described the Battle of Kursk as "the swan-song of the German armored force."

The Russians copied these tactics and soon became past masters of them, as we learned to our cost in *Citadel*. It was a Russian speciality to fortify these *Pakfronts* with minefields or antitank ditches, and to scatter mines haphazard among the minebelts. The rapidity with which mines were laid by the Russians was truly remarkable. Two or three days and nights were quite sufficient for the Russians to lay more than thirty thousand mines and it was no rare thing to have to lift forty thousand mines a day in the sector of a German corps. During the Kursk offensive, and after penetrating to a depth of twelve miles, we still found ourselves in the midst of minefields and opposed by *Pakfronts*. In this connection mention should be made again of the masterly camouflage work of the Russians. Neither minefields nor *Pakfronts* could be detected until the first tank blew up, or the first Russian antitank gun opened fire.

The question of how it was possible for the German armor to fight its way through these Russian antitank defenses is difficult to answer; the method chosen depended upon local conditions and on the forces available for the operation. The detailed preparations for *Citadel* and the exemplary co-ordination between ground and air forces were of course largely responsible for such success as was achieved. During *Citadel* the German armor moved and fought in wedge formation, the *Panzerkeil*, which up to then had proved very effective indeed; the spearhead of the wedge was formed by the heaviest tanks, and the Tigers proved their worth against the Russian antitank fronts organized in depth. The Tiger's 88-mm gun was superior to anything the Russians had, but as I have mentioned, the Panthers were still in their infancy and were a failure. Our Mark IV's were not good enough to effect a breakthrough against a deep antitank front, and the capture of so many Russian positions was due to the perfect co-operation of all heavy weapons.

Citadel and other operations proved that the fire of the antitank front can be neutralized by the concentric and expertly conducted fire of the attacking armor. To put this theory into practice called for changes in armored formations and tactics. The tank-wedge was replaced by the

Panzerglocke (tank bell). This *Panzerglocke*, with super-
heavy tanks in the center, medium tanks to the right and
left rear in a widening arch, light tanks behind the center
and held ready for pursuit, was the best formation to bring
to bear against a wide fire front. The Panzer commander,
together with observers for all the heavy weapons, travelled
in the *Glocke* immediately behind the leading medium
tanks. He had to be in wireless communication with the
commander of the fighter-bombers, and other aircraft supporting the ground-troops. Engineers in armored vehicles
traveled just behind the forward tanks of the *Glocke,* ready
to clear gaps through minefields. An attack along these
lines was generally successful if the attacking formations
practised close co-operation of all weapons.

Night attacks provided another means of breaking
through deep antitank fronts, although a night attack was
always regarded with some trepidation. The terrain had to
be suitable for armor, and the weather had to be favorable;
moonlit nights were preferred. The ground had to be reconnoitered during daylight by the officers concerned. As we
had no suitable compasses for the tanks, a road clearly
visible at night or a sand track were used to indicate
direction. Even in night attacks the *Panzerglocke* proved its
usefulness; the advance was made in closer formation and
with shorter distances between tanks. Darkness seriously
hampered the defending guns, and a well-prepared night
attack usually went off without appreciable losses. Well-
trained officers and experienced tank drivers were indispensable.

The success of attacks by armor against antitank fronts
seems to depend on the following conditions:[12]

1) Every opportunity must be taken for reconnaissance in
   the air and on the ground.
2) The armored formation carrying out the attack must be
   made as strong as possible by super-heavy tanks, brought
   to bear in the *Schwerpunkt.*

[12] These remarks apply to the conditions prevailing in 1943. In
general they are still applicable, but there have been slight changes in
detail. For example, the latest tanks need not stop to fire.

3) Fire concentrations by tank guns must be rapid and effective; the armor must keep moving and tanks should only stop to fire their guns.

4) Observers for all heavy weapons supporting the attack must travel with the armor. Wireless communication between the tank leader and the air is most essential.

5) Engineers in armored vehicles must follow the armor.

6) Light tanks must be at hand to exploit success.

7) Fuel and ammunition supply for the armor must be assured during the battle by armored supply carriers. Much experience is needed to carry out this difficult operation.

8) Tanks should be supplied with smoke gear to blind enemy antitank weapons, and with colored-smoke grenades for unit commanders to indicate direction.

9) For night attacks tanks should be supplied with direction-finding equipment.

Russian Reactions to Bombardment

Experience shows that the Russian soldier has an almost incredible ability to stand up to the heaviest artillery fire and air-bombardment, while the Russian Command remains unmoved by the bloodiest losses caused by shelling and bombs, and ruthlessly adheres to its preconceived plans. Russian lack of reaction to even the heaviest shelling was proved though not explained during Operation *Citadel*. The question is worth considering, and the following factors may influence their attitude.

The stoicism of the majority of Russian soldiers and their mental sluggishness make them quite insensible to losses. The Russian soldier values his own life no more than those of his comrades. To step on walls of dead, composed of the bodies of his former friends and companions, makes not the slightest impression on him and does not upset his equanimity at all; without so much as twinkling an eyelid he stolidly continues the attack or stays put in the position he has been told to defend. Life is not precious to him. He is immune to the most incredible hardships, and does not even appear to notice them; he seems equally indifferent to bombs and shells.

Naturally there are Russian soldiers of a more tender

physical and psychological structure, but they have been trained to execute orders to the letter and without hesitation. There is an iron discipline in the Russian army; punishment meted out by officers and political commissars is of a draconian character and unquestioned obedience to orders has become a feature of their military system.

In my experience idealistic motives and enthusiasm for the Communist regime were not apparent during the last war. However, it must be expected that in future the Russian soldier will execute the most senseless and silly orders, moved by idealism and devotion to the "cause."

Russian indifference to bombardment is not new; it was apparent during World War I and Caulaincourt comments on it in his description of the Battle of Borodino in 1812.[13] He describes how the Russians "stood firm under the fire of a devastating bombardment," and says that, "the enemy, smashed by the guns, and pressed simultaneously on all points, massed their troops and held firm despite the ravages made in their ranks by the guns." He quotes Napoleon as saying that, "it was quite inexplicable to him that redoubts and positions so audaciously captured and so doggedly defended should yield us so few prisoners," and he gives the Emperor's comment, "these Russians let themselves be killed like automatons; they are not taken alive. This does not help us at all."

Regarding Russian officers in command it is as well to know that:

a) in almost every situation and every case they strictly and rigidly adhere to orders or to previous decisions. They disregard changes in the situation, the reaction of the enemy, and losses of their own troops. Naturally this attitude has serious drawbacks, but it brings certain compensatior.s.

b) they have at their disposal almost inexhaustible resources

---

[13] *Memoirs of General de Caulaincourt* (London, Cassell, 1934), 196–201. Russian casualties in the single day's fighting at Borodino amounted to nearly 50,000 men. Five hundred eighty-seven French guns fired 120,000 rounds, and the casualties of the Grande Armée were over 35,000. Even by the standards of World War II, Borodino was not a light ordeal.

of human material to replace casualties. The Russian Command can afford high losses and ignores them.

In planning an operation it will be wise to take into account the reaction or lack of reaction of Russian troops and their command; tactical timing, assessments of success, and the quantity of weapons to be used will depend very much on this factor. It must be pointed out, however, that there were cases when battle-hardened Russian formations panicked or showed nervousness under light shelling. But such cases were few and far between, and to count on them would be criminal. It will be much better to overestimate Russian toughness; softness is the exception and nobody can ever depend on the lucky case when Russians will prove soft.

15: *Back to the Dnieper*

The Russian Summer Offensive

MILITARY CRITICS HAVE commented on the sudden collapse of Germany in 1918 and have concluded that this was a natural reaction to the failure of Ludendorff's great offensive. Reference has been made to "the loss of morale an army suffers when it knows it has expended its last ounce of energy, and expended it in vain."

Similarly in 1943 the flower of the Germany Army had fallen in the Battle of Kursk, where our troops attacked with a desperate determination to conquer or die. They had gone into the battle with a spirit no less determined than that of the storm troops of 1918, and it might be thought that a weakening of morale would follow our withdrawal from the ill-fated salient of Kursk. Actually nothing of the sort occurred; our ranks had been woefully thinned, but the fierce resolution of the fighting troops remained unshaken. This is not the place for a detailed discussion of this question, but it is obvious that the character of our adversary had much to do with the unyielding spirit of the troops. The Churchill-Roosevelt demand for "Unconditional Surrender" gave us no hope from the West, while the men fighting on the Russian Front were well aware of the horrible fate which would befall eastern Germany if the Red hordes broke into our country. So whatever the strategic consequences of the Battle of Kursk—and they were

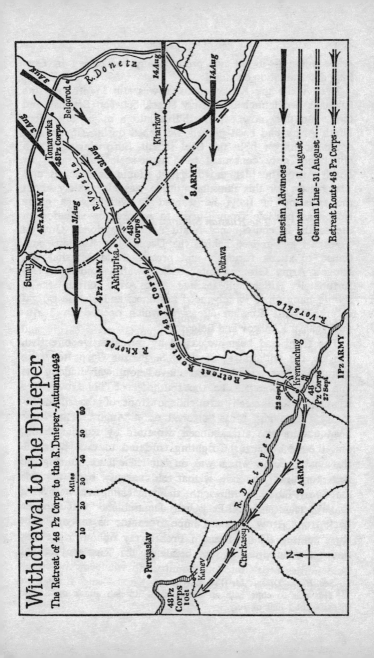

Withdrawal to the Dnieper

The Retreat of 48 Pz Corps to the R. Dnieper-Autumn 1943

Russian Advances ········

German Line – 1 August ──────

German Line – 31 August ──·──·──

Retreat Route 48 Pz Corps ⇒⇒⇒⇒

R. Donetz

3 Aug

5 Aug

5 Aug

Belgorod

Tomarovka

48 Pz Corps

14 Aug

14 Aug

Kharkov

4 Pz ARMY

R. Vorskla

8 ARMY

11 Aug

Sumy

4 Pz ARMY

Akhtyrka

48 Pz Corps

48 Corps

Poltava

R. Khotol

R. Vorskla

Retreat Route

48 Pz Corps

Kremenchug

22 Sept

48 Pz Corps

27 Sept

1 Pz ARMY

Miles

0   10   20   30   40   50   60

Pereyaslav

Kanev

48 Pz Corps

10 Oct

Cherkassy

R. Dnieper

8 ARMY

N

grave enough—it did not produce any weakening in German determination or morale.

Even while the Kursk offensive was still in progress the Russians had launched a heavy attack between Bryansk and Orel, and they now expanded this into a major operation. Ninth Army had been gravely weakened during *Citadel* and could no longer hold the Orel salient. Surprisingly enough Hitler not only consented to a large-scale withdrawal by Ninth Army, but demanded that it should be speeded up.[1] The reason for this unusual attitude was his anxiety about the situation in Italy; he wanted to withdraw as many troops as possible from Russia to restore the situation in the south. In consequence Ninth Army abandoned Orel on 5 August and retired behind the Desna. The Russians continued to attack furiously and pressed Field Marshal von Kluge's Army Group Center back towards Smolensk. Unfortunately Hitler still insisted that Army Group South should hang on to its advanced positions, and oppose a rigid defense to the Russian offensive, which opened on 3 August against Kharkov and Belgorod.

The front had been weakened by our abortive offensive, and by the withdrawal of the S.S. Panzer Corps to Italy; moreover, reserves had been moved southwards along the line of the Donetz.[2] To the southeast of Tomarovka the Russians broke clean through the front of the 52nd Infantry Corps and took Belgorod on 4 August. The corps headquarters was attacked and dispersed by Russian tanks, and the 48th Panzer Corps was ordered to take over the threatened sector, which was on our right flank. During the next fortnight our line was forced steadily back towards the Sumy–Kharkov railway; the Soviet offensive was on a massive scale and P.G.D. "Gross Deutschland" was brought back from Army Group Center to enable us to cope with these masses. The German Eighth Army on our right was under terrific pressure, but although the Russians crossed

---

[1] See *Hitler Directs his War*, 61–70.

[2] This was to cope with an unsuccessful Russian attack on Stalino in the second half of July.

the Donetz and reached the suburbs of Kharkov on 14 August, the city held out for another week.

During this phase an operation took place which illustrated once again our superiority in maneuver. On 20 August a Russian armored corps and infantry division broke through the Eighth Army front on the right of "Gross Deutschland," then holding a sector around Akhtyrka. The division was ordered to take immediate action to restore the situation. An assault group was formed under command of Colonel von Natzmer, Ia of "Gross Deutschland," and consisted of the following units:

One panzer detachment with about twenty tanks.
One company of the reconnaissance unit.
One battalion of infantry on armored vehicles.
One troop of artillery with self-propelled gunes.

This group was childishly small in comparison with the Russian forces to be pushed back, but accomplished its task within twelve hours. Success was due primarily to surprise and the skillful handling of the few available tanks. The Russians had thought that the 48th Panzer Corps was tied down on the Akhtyrka front and the appearance of our tanks and their attack on the Russian flank came as a complete surprise. Initial resistance was negligible and at first there was no serious opposition. Leaving behind masses of equipment of every description the Russians withdrew in panic, abandoning their gains almost without fighting. Interrogation of prisoners showed that the enemy had overrated the size of the German units and thought them many times stronger than they actually were.

The Russian reaction was certainly exceptional, but tends to prove how isolated they feel when attacked in flank, particularly when such attacks come as a surprise and are carried out by armor. During World War II such incidents occurred on many occasions, and we learned that skillful use of a few tanks, or well-executed tank raids, often brought much greater results than very heavy artillery fire

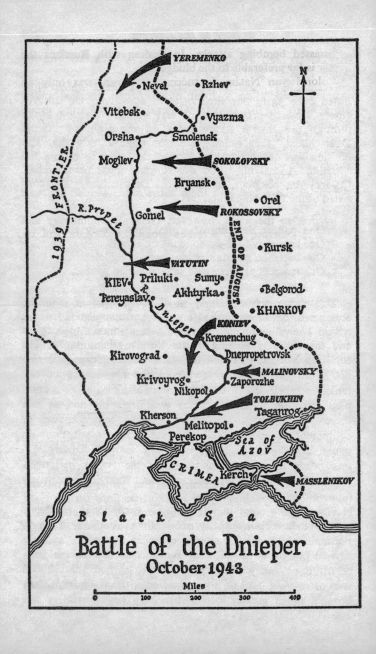

Battle of the Dnieper
October 1943

or massed bombing attacks. In dealing with Russians the rapier is far preferable to the bludgeon.

Colonel von Natzmer's success, however, was only an isolated incident on a front of over one hundred miles, from Sumy to the Donetz; General Koniev's army group continued to attack strongly, and on 22 August Kharkov was lost.[3] Nevertheless, we succeeded in halting his main drive towards Poltava, and late in August the Russian assaults on the front of Eighth Army and Fourth Panzer Army died away. We took advantage of the lull to extricate the panzer divisions and give them some much needed rest and replenishment.

Farther to the south, however, Generals Malinovsky and Tolbukhin pierced the defenses along the Donetz and on the Mius river; at the end of August our 29 Corps was encircled in Taganrog and had great difficulty in breaking out. On 3 September von Manstein flew to Hitler's headquarters to warn him that Army Group South was facing catastrophe and to demand a change in the conduct of operations. The interview was a stormy one, and led to no result. The situation at the front became increasingly critical, for early in September the Russians captured Stalino and smashed their way into the Donetz industrial area. Moreover, Koniev resumed his offensive on the sector of Fourth Panzer Army. Forty-eighth Panzer Corps was the target of strong attacks, and the Russians broke through our left flank, while they also severely handled the northern wing of Eighth Army on our right.

Not until then, when Army Group South was in imminent danger of breaking up into isolated groups, did the supreme commander of the Wehmacht give permission for a withdrawal behind the Dnieper.[4] But Hitler had refused to permit the construction of any fortifications on the river bank, on the ground that if his generals knew there was a reserve line they would at once fall back there. Thus it

---

[3] Koniev was one of the most successful of the Russian commanders. He was promoted marshal in March, 1944, and in 1946 was appointed commander in chief of Soviet land forces.

[4] Permission was given on 8 September when Hitler visited Manstein at Zaporozhe.

was very doubtful whether we would be able to stop the Russians on the Dnieper, and to make matters worse there were only five crossings available. The situation could only be mastered if the Russians advance was delayed.

As is well known the Russians make very limited use of supply columns, and their troops live mainly on the country. Their method is not new; it is essentially similar to that of the Mongols of Genghiz Khan, or the armies of Napoleon. The only means of slowing down armies of this kind is to totally destroy everything that can be used to feed and house them. In the autumn of 1943 the German Army deliberately adopted this policy, and R.T. Paget remarks very appropriately:

Some five years later, lawyers were to argue for hours as to the legality of the demolitions and requisitions carried out by the Germans during their retreat, but I am afraid that no law that conflicts with an army's capacity to survive is ever likely to be effective.[5]

We certainly did not relish the idea of destroying all food supplies and putting a zone of scorched earth between us and the pursuing Russians. But the existence of an entire army group was at stake, and if we had not adopted such measures, many thousands of troops would never have succeeded in reaching the Dnieper and establishing an effective defense line under cover of the river. There is no doubt in my mind that Army Group South would have been overwhelmed and lost for future operations. In any case the hardships we inflicted on the civil population of the Ukraine were trivial in comparison with those of the hundreds of thousands of civilians who were killed or maimed in Allied raids on German cities. Field Marshal von Manstein's conviction in 1949 for carrying out the scorched earth policy of the Supreme Command is therefore a glaring example of the age-old principle of *Vae victis*.

During September Fourth Panzer Army retired westward through Priluki towards Kiev, while First Panzer Army fell back into the great bend of the Dnieper at Dnepropetrovsk.

[5] *Manstein*, 63.

These withdrawals were fairly methodical and were covered by raging fires which destroyed the crops over wide areas. Forty-eighth Panzer Corps, now under Eighth Army, was less fortunate; we were harried all the time by Russian mobile columns and had great difficulty in getting into the bridgehead at Kremenchug, where we hung on for a few days to protect the crossing of the Dnieper by Eighth Army.

At the end of September Fourth Panzer Army formed a thin front on both sides of Kiev, and Eighth Army and First Panzer Army were stretched out along the river as far as Zaporozhe. Manstein was still holding Melitopol and covering the approaches to the Crimea. Father north the Russians were keeping up a terrific offensive against Army Group Center; Bryansk fell on 17 September, and Smolensk on the 23rd. Von Kluge still held a bridgehead at Gomel, but in general the German armies had been forced back to the Dnieper along the greater part of its 1,400-mile course. We were holding the last great natural obstacle before the Dniester, the Carpathians, and the outer defenses of the Reich.

Problems of Withdrawal

Of all operations of war, a withdrawal under heavy enemy pressure is probably the most difficult and perilous. Indeed it is recorded of the great Moltke, that when he was being praised for his generalship in the Franco-Prussian War, and was told by an admirer that his reputation would rank with such great captains as Napoleon, Frederick, or Turenne, he answered, "No, for I have never conducted a retreat."

During World War II the German Supreme Command could never decide on a withdrawal while the going was good. It made up its mind either too late or when a retreat had been forced upon our armies and was already in full swing. The consequences of this stubbornness were usually disastrous for the commanders and the troops. In this section I propose to consider some of the problems which faced us when conducting withdrawals on the Eastern Front.

A classic example of a retreat, smoothly and efficiently conducted, occurred in March, 1943, when Hitler was persuaded to evacuate the dangerous salient of Vyaz'ma–Rzhev on the front of Army Group Center. This operation was known by the code name of *Buffalo* and is worth describing in detail; indeed it may serve as a model for staff officers who want to learn the intricate art of withdrawal.

First of all thorough preparations were made. Roads, bridges, tracks, and river crossings were systematically improved, assembly areas for troops were chosen and camouflaged, elaborate calculations were made to determine what equipment and material could be moved, and what transport would be required. All telephone lines were removed—a vital precaution—and command posts and battle headquarters were established in rear before the movement began. Demolitions, road blocks, and minefields were designed to fit in with the plan for delaying actions on specific lines of resistance.

The gravest problem was the evacuation of civilians, for in *Buffalo* the entire population, old and young, healthy and sick, peasant and townsfolk, all insisted on coming along, so great was their dread of the soldiers and commissars of their own country. Of course, a mass migration of this sort had not been foreseen by the German military authorities, and to cope with it a special organization had to be improvised. The main thing was to canalize the movement, but to direct it off the main lines of withdrawal of auxiliary tracks and routes. Engineers and construction detachments were sent to build bridges and roads to enable these masses to keep going in orderly fashion. Supply and ration centers were organized; medical and veterinary aid posts were not forgotten. The most important point was traffic control, for these wandering masses had to be very carefully handled. As long as they were near the front line, their moves took place by night. If day moves were inevitable, the refugees were taught to avoid bunching together and to move in dispersed order as a protection against Russian aircraft, which attacked anything that moved, civil or military alike.

The vast spaces and huge forests helped to bring this

mass migration to a successful conclusion. No serious losses were suffered and military operations were not greatly hindered. But it was touch and go. In modern war long-range planning and detailed preparations have to be made to help the civil population in their flight, otherwise the movements of troops will be brought to a complete standstill.

The gravity of this question was illustrated in May, 1940, when the French government ordered the evacuation of the whole of northeastern France. A mass movement of unprecedented dimensions was set afoot. In spite of the dense road net available, which could have carried the traffic if properly organized, the panicky masses jammed all the main roads and thoroughfares and threw the supply columns of the French Army and the movement of their reserves into the wildest disorder.

Apart from the problem of traffic control, the Red Air Force makes a point of attacking refugees. It is almost impossible to open a route for military traffic when bombs have done their horrible work and filled the roads with debris and whirling, shrieking, screaming crowds of terror-stricken civilians.[6] It must be accepted as a foregone conclusion that any population will flee before the advance of a Russian Army. It is impossible to stop them. Thus in modern war there is no such thing as a purely military withdrawal; the civil population has to be included in any plans for a retreat.

Turning now to military factors, it is essential to keep secret the intention to withdraw, and to conceal the retreat as long as possible after it has started. The withdrawal of reserves does not present many problems as it is comparatively easy for them to move by night and occupy rearward positions. The real difficulty starts when the forward troops are drawn out of the line. They must get out immediately after dark, without making any noise, and their "first bound" should be as far back as possible. On no account should they form columns of more than battalion strength

---

[6] The Russians have another method of dealing with refugees—in eastern Germany they drove heavy tanks backwards and forwards through the columns.

and each company must move as a separate unit. Reconnaissance aircraft equipped with parachute flares may discover them, and as soon as a flare is dropped all movement must stop. Every man must stand still as if frozen to the ground, and there should be no running for cover. By daybreak all troops should be in their new positions.

The enemy must be denied the use of airfields or landing strips at all costs; at the same time they must remain operational for one's own aircraft up to the very last moment and then be thoroughly blown up. This applies not so much to the buildings, as to the tarmac and the landing and taking-off strips. There are usually enough heavy bombs (1,000 lb. and heavier) available for the demolition parties to do a thorough job. Preparations take time, especially the burying of the bombs, and in the last hours aircraft have to take the risk of landing and taking off on fully mined runways. When the last plane has left, up go the bombs and all that should remain is a landscape of bomb craters, reminiscent of photographs of the moon.

Of course it frequently happened that we were unable to carry out a systematic withdrawal, for not much planning is possible when troops have to break contact after a lost battle. Thus in September, 1943, the 48th Panzer Corps found itself in a position of the gravest peril; there was no longer a coherent front and Russian mobile units were already operating far in our rear. We had to get back to the Dnieper as quickly as possible, and grave risks and heavy sacrifices had to be readily accepted. There was no stopping by day; the position was too serious for us to worry about the Red Air Force and those who fell behind or were smashed up by Russian aircraft had to be left to themselves.

A withdrawal of this kind, harassed by the enemy and carried out in the greatest hurry, does not absolve commanders from their duty to maintain order and discipline. This depends partly on the example and leadership of the officers, and partly on their ability to keep their heads and improvise some sort of plan. Even in a hurried withdrawal there is much that can be done.

Engineers must guard and keep intact all bridges and prepare their demolition; construction units have to be handy to repair roads and tracks; recovery parties with tractors must be placed along the routes to keep vehicles and guns on the move or to pull total casualties off the road. Antiaircraft guns have to be stationed at crossroads and important bridges and defiles.

Fighter protection, if available, should be provided to cover the main arteries of the withdrawal. Traffic control points should be numerous, and are indispensable at road crossings, at bridges and in narrow lanes. There must be a number of officers, including high-ranking ones, in charge of control points. This is important, as the military police N.C.O. is unable to wield enough authority in withdrawals of this kind.

But there may be times when it is no longer possible to continue to take along all weapons, vehicles, and equipment, and when one has to be content to save the men and their personal weapons. So as to avoid chaos the responsible commanders must issue clear orders, stating which units are to destroy their heavy weapons and vehicles. It is in circumstances such as these that thorough staff training proves its value.

During our retirements in the East we were frequently harassed by guerillas, although this applied more to the troops on the central and northern fronts. But very fortunately the Red Air Force lacked the flexibility, and the high quality ground organization, required to bring new airfields and landing grounds into rapid operation. Thus we frequently "got away" with tightly packed convoys, travelling bumper to bumper, and presenting superb targets from the air. Bad roads, heavy rain, and thick mud or snow sometimes made movement very difficult.

In general, however, the wide spaces of Russia favor well-organized withdrawals. Indeed if the troops are properly disciplined and trained, a strategic retreat is an excellent means of catching the enemy off balance and regaining the initiative.

Defense of the Dnieper

On 27 September the 48th Panzer Corps had abandoned the bridgehead at Kremenchug, and stood safely on the southern bank of the Dnieper. The river itself was a comforting obstacle, about four hundred yards wide at this point, and with the bank considerably higher on our side of the stream. However, thick reeds extending some distance into the water made it relatively easy for the Russians to hide boats and camouflage their prepaations. Moreover, it has been most wisely said that, "few indeed are the instances in history of a river line athwart the advance of a superior army proving an effective defense."[7]

Indeed on 27 September we learned that the Russians had already gained a foothold across the Dnieper near Pereyaslav, south of Kiev. We were ordered to liquidate the bridgehead at once and for this purpose the 7th Panzer Division and the 20th P.G.D. were put under our command. Moving rapidly up the Dnieper towards the danger point we caught the Russians advancing southwards, and our panzers went straight into action without waiting to deploy. The Russian columns were thrown into great disorder and were driven back into a bend of the river. There they hung on and could not be dislodged.

The next fortnight passed quietly on our front; the scorched earth tactics were bearing fruit and the Russians were still unable to mount an offensive on a large scale in this sector. Forty-eighth Panzer Corps was under command of Eighth Army, which held a front of over two hundred miles from Kremenchug to south of Kiev. This army was commanded by General Wöhler with the highly capable General Speidel as his chief of staff. The only Russian bridgehead on the front of Eighth Army was the one which the 48th Panzer Corps was containing to the south of Pereyaslav. There was no doubt that the Russians would attack again in this quarter, and reconnaissance and intelligence reports showed that a constant stream of reinforcements

[7] Winston Churchill, *The World Crisis* (London, Butterworth, 1931), 318.

was moving into the bridgehead. They had thrown several bridges across the Dnieper, and such was their skill at field engineering that they actually built bridges below water level on which troops or animals could wade across.

On the German side feverish preparations were made to meet the coming attack. Seventh Panzer Division was withdrawn from our command, but we still had the 20th P.G.D. while 19th Panzer and the 1st Infantry Division were moved up. Under the supervision of the artillery commander of the 48th Panzer Corps, the guns of all divisions were co-ordinated in such a way that fire could be concentrated in a single massive blow against any threatened point or hostile assembly area.

The antiaircraft guns had a very important part to play in the general fire-plan. We adopted the principle that anti-tank work was the task of all weapons, and of every individual man. Antitank ditches, roadblocks, cross country obstacles of every conceivable kind, minefields and minebelts were all devised to canalize the expected torrent of Russian tanks and direct them into prearranged channels. All obstacles were covered by fire—a simple tactical precaution but one too frequently neglected.

That the attack was imminent was clear from the aggressive reconnaissance thrusts carried out by considerable Russians forces; trenches were dug as far forward as possible to enable their infantry to rush our advance positions, and numerous deserters infiltrated into our lines. Night air reconnaissance reported large movements of motorized columns in the direction of the bridgehead, and air photographs showed a great number of new artillery positions. The best and most reliable source of intelligence was our Wireless Intercept Service, but soundlight ranging detachments of our artillery observer units brought valuable information during the last phase on the eve of the attack, when the Russian gunners started their range-finding shoots.[8]

At 0630 on 16 October the Russians launched their at-

___

[8] The Russian artillery was very formidable in quantity but somewhat primitive in its methods. Accurate survey and "silent registration" had little place in their system.

tacks against the positions of the 48th Panzer Corps; I happened to be in one of the forward observation posts of the 19th Panzer Division, and had to stay there for fully two hours. The artillery bombardment was really quite impressive. No movement was possible, for 290 guns of all calibers were pounding a thousand yards of front and during those two hours the Russians expended their normal ammunition allowance for one-and-a-half days. The bombardment reached as far back as divisional battle headquarters, and the two divisions holding the corps front were shelled with such intensity that it was impossible to gauge the *Schwerpunkt*. Some Russians guns fired over open sights from uncovered gun emplacements. After two hours' bombardment our trench system looked like a freshly ploughed field, and, in spite of being carefully dug in, many of our heavy weapons and antitank guns had been knocked out.

Suddenly Russian infantry in solid serried ranks attacked behind a barrage on a narrow front, with tanks in support, and one wave following the other. Numerous low-flying planes attacked those strong-points which were still firing. A Russian infantry attack is an awe-inspiring spectacle; the long grey waves come pounding on, uttering fierce cries, and the defending troops require nerves of steel. In dealing with such attacks fire-discipline is of vital importance.

The Russian onslaught made some headway but during the afternoon the armored assault troops, whom we were keeping in reserve, were able to wipe out those Russians who had penetrated the defense system. We only lost a mile or so of ground.

On subsequent days the Russian breakthrough attempts were repeated in undiminished strength. Divisions decimated by our fire were withdrawn, and fresh formations were thrown into the battle. Again wave after wave attacked, and wave after wave was thrown back after suffering appalling losses. But the Russians did not desist from their inflexible and rigid methods of attack. On our side artillery and armor bore the main burden of the fighting. Our fire plans were flexible, allowing for concentrations where they were most needed, and designed to break up the Russian columns before they could advance to the attack. Wherever a deep penetration occurred it was quickly patched up, and a few hours later counterattacks by our tanks were delivered against the flanks of the bulge. This battle continued for more than a week and the defensive strength of the 48th Panzer Corps began to dwindle. Eighth Army moved up its last reserve—the 3rd Panzer Division—to the danger point.

At this time General von Knobelsdorff was away on leave and General von Choltitz was acting commander of the 48th Panzer Corps. Day after day he spent most of his time in the foremost lines and personally conducted the battle in any sector where the situation was most dangerous. One fateful evening he talked to me about the way things were going, and expressed his anxiety at the terrific pressure on our front. Then he had a vision. He saw how the Soviet masses would close in on us like giant ocean waves. All the dams built to stem their onrush would be shattered and the Russians would go on and on and eventually submerge Germany. He wanted to go and see Hitler himself and tell him the facts about this unequal struggle and of the untenable situation at the front. He declared he would resign and by his resignation give the danger signal which would compel Hitler to make new decisions.

I did my best to convince the General by quoting sober figures, to show that even the flood of Russian manpower was bound to run dry. I pointed to the incredibly high losses the Russians had suffered at the hands of his corps, which had fought with unrivalled bravery and courage, and I told him that one day even the Russian attacks would peter out. My arguments made little impression and he remained unmoved in his decision. He did not believe that our front would hold on the following day. He wanted to spare his troops this horrible ordeal; they were growing weaker and weaker and there was no hope of getting replacements or reinforcements. The next morning he drove away from corps headquarters, still determined to put his views before Hitler.

Two days after General von Choltitz had left, the Russian attacks on the front of the 48th Panzer Corps broke down. It seemed that the General had been unduly pessimistic, but during the winter of 1945, when the Soviet hordes broke over my country, I often thought of this memorable conversation.[9]

[9] *Editor's note.* Somewhat surprisingly General von Choltitz survived this episode, and his career suffered only a temporary setback. In 1944 he commanded the 84th Corps in Normandy and vainly attempted to resist the American advance west of St. Lo. On 15 July he reported to Seventh Army: "The whole battle is one tremendous bloodbath such as I have never seen in eleven years of war." (Wilmot, *The Struggle for Europe*, 388.) Appointed military governor of Paris, he surrendered the city on 25 August.

16: *The Kiev Salient*

Victory at Zhitomir

THE GREAT RUSSIAN offensive along the line of the Dnieper was now in full swing. Forty-eighth Panzer Corps had brilliantly repulsed the attacks south of Pereyaslav, but on our flanks matters did not go so well. By mid-October General Koniev had gained three bridgeheads east of Kremenchug, and he then struck heavily towards the important industrial center of Krivoyrog, as famous for its iron ore as Nikopol for its manganese. Dnepropetrovsk fell on 25 October, and it looked as though we would soon lose the Dnieper bend. Indeed it would have been fortunate if we had done so at this stage. By insisting that the retention of Nikopol and Krivoyrog was essential to German industry, Hitler forced Army Group South to adopt dispositions which were nonsensical from the strategic point of view.

To the south of Zaporozhe General Tolbukhin captured Melitopol, and thrust past the Perekop Isthmus towards the mouth of the Dnieper. Manstein wanted to evacuate the great bend of the river, but Hitler insisted that he should counterattack to save Nikopol and Krivoyrog. Manstein did so on 2 November and tactically the operation was a notable success; Koniev's columns were caught in flank and flung back towards the Dnieper. But three hundred miles to the northwest, Marshal Vatutin's Army Group crossed the river in great force on both sides of Kiev; on 3 November he broke out of his bridgeheads with thirty infantry divisions, twenty-four armored brigades, and ten motorized brigades. The German defense was swamped and on 6 November a Special Order of the Day from Marshal Stalin proclaimed the capture of Kiev.

The Russians vigorously exploited their success. On 7 November their spearheads reached Fastov, forty miles southwest of Kiev, on the 11th they were at Radomyshl, fifty-five miles west of the Dnieper, and by the 13th their tanks stood on the outskirts of the important town of Zhitomir. A broad and deep wedge threatened to separate Army Group South from Army Group Center, and immediate countermeasures had become essential. (See map on page 306.)

On 6 November Manstein decided to concentrate all available panzer divisions in the area Fastov-Zhitomir, with a view to thrusting towards Kiev, and battle headquarters of the 48th Panzer Corps was ordered to move to the area south of Fastov without delay. On 7 November I set up the headquarters at Belaya Tserkov, approximately fifteen miles south of Fastov; we were now under command of Fourth Panzer Army. It was our intention to build up a defensive line through Fastov to cover the concentration of the panzer divisions, but the Russians gave us no time. Fastov, which was garrisoned by two *Landesschuetzen* battalions[1] and an improvised battalion made up of men returning from leave, was lost on the evening of the 7th.

Unfortunately the 25th Panzer Division was prematurely involved in the fighting at Fastov. This division had an unfortunate history; it was formed in Norway and since August, 1943, had been training in France. It was far from fit for operations, but against the advice of General Guderian, the inspector general of panzer troops, the division was sent off to the Ukraine, and rushed into battle. To make matters worse, Army Group South had arranged for the wheeled elements of the division to detrain in the Berdichev area, while the tracked units went to Kirovograd, 125 miles to the southeast. In view of the critical situation west of Kiev, Army Group South arranged for the wheeled ele-

---

[1] Composed of elderly men of second-grade value.

ments to move straight from their trains towards the battle area. On the evening of 6 November Fourth Panzer Army ordered the division to advance with the utmost speed towards Fastov, and hold it "at all costs" in conjunction with a regiment of the S.S. Panzer Division "Das Reich." The divisional Panzer Regiment could not possibly arrive for several days.

Orders and dispositions such as these would have imposed a grave strain on a highly experienced division and staff, and their effect on such raw troops was disastrous. At noon on 7 November the advance guard of P.G.R. 146 ran into T.34 tanks south of Fastov and was thrown into a panic. Unused to any fighting the troops streamed back in great disorder, and although they were rallied by the personal efforts of General von Schell, the divisional commander, yet they had great difficulty in escaping from the Russians, who destroyed most of their transport. On the afternoon of 8 November von Schell arrived at our headquarters at Belaya Tserkov, and his division passed under our command.

On 9 November their Panzer Regiment arrived from Kirovograd, together with the Ia, Major Count Pückler, an old friend and comrade of mine from the 7th Cavalry Regiment. Twenty-fifth Panzer Division was now ordered to make every effort to stop the Russians advancing farther to the southwest and south. Thanks to the splendid leadership of General von Schell, the division advanced as far as the eastern outskirts of Fastov, where it was held up by very superior Russian forces. This fighting gained us a breathing space to gather armor for a deliberate counterattack, but unfortunately 25th Panzer lost so heavily in men and material that we were unable to use the division for weeks to come in any offensive operation. The experience of the 25th Panzer Division proved once again that while veteran troops can outmaneuver the Russians, yet untrained units have little chance against them.

Meanwhile the German Supreme Command was taking stock of the situation around Kiev, and was hurrying up reinforcements from Italy and the West. The strategic background is sketched very clearly by General Guderian:

Hitler decided to counter-attack. In accordance with his usual bad habit this attack was to be launched with inadequate forces. After discussing the matter with the Chief of the Army General Staff I took advantage of a conference on tank questions, held on November 9th, 1943, to propose to Hitler that he give up the idea of numerous small-scale counter-attacks and that he concentrate all our panzer divisions available south of Kiev for the proposed operation through Berdichev towards Kiev. In this connexion I proposed that the panzer division which was taking part in Schörner's defence of the Nikopol bridgehead be withdrawn, together with the panzer divisions of Kleist's army group which was holding the Dnieper in the Kherson area. I used my favourite old expression, *Klotzen, nicht kleckern* [roughly: 'boot 'em don't spatter 'em']. Hitler paid attention to what I said, but did not make his arrangements accordingly.[2]

During the week 8-15 November the 48th Panzer Corps assembled strong forces to the south of the Kiev salient and to my great joy General Balck was appointed corps commander just before our counterattack was launched. He was one of our most brilliant leaders of armor; indeed, if Manstein was Germany's greatest strategist during World War II, I think Balck has strong claims to be regarded as our finest field commander. He had a superb grasp of tactics and great qualities of leadership, and he demonstrated his powers at every level—as the commander of a rifle regiment in France in 1940, of a panzer regiment in Greece in 1941, and of a panzer division in Russia in 1942–43. Later he was to win new laurels as an army and army group commander in Poland, France and Hungary.

When Balck was in command of the 11th Panzer Division during the fighting on the Chir river, it was my privilege as chief of staff of the 48th Panzer Corps to work with him—a fruitful and most pleasant task. From now on I was happy to serve him in the 48th Panzer Corps, in Fourth Panzer Army, and later on in Army Group G on the Western Front. Between him and myself there was that ideal co-operation, based on unlimited mutual faith—a state of things which could not be improved upon between a commander and his chief of staff. Together we worked out appreciations, and together we arrived at similar conclusions—we both hailed from the cavalry and had the same views on armored warfare. Balck always arrived at a definite decision, and it did not matter whose opinion had won the day. Balck never interfered in the details of staff work; for such work his chief of staff was required to take sole responsibility. I was particularly grateful to General Balck, who was renowned throughout the army for his great personal courage, for allowing his chief of staff to visit the front every second or third day, and thus enabling me to keep alive the intimate contact which should exist between the General Staff and the fighting troops.[3]

For the counterattack on the Kiev salient the 48th Panzer Corps was given no fewer than six panzer divisions, and one infantry division. I was proud to know that we were regarded as the *corps d'élite,* and that our headquarters was entrusted with any operation of particular difficulty or significance. Our Order of Battle was made up as follows:

1 Panzer Division.
7 Panzer Division.
S.S. Panzer Division "Leibstandarte Adolf Hitler."
19 Panzer Division—not available before 18 November.
25 Panzer Division—weakened by losses.
S.S. Panzer Division "Das Reich"—equivalent in
    strength to a weak battle group.
68 Infantry Division.

Our plan was to use this powerful force to advance from Fastov directly towards Kiev, thus cutting in towards the base of the huge salient, hamstringing any further Russian advance to the west, and perhaps trapping and destroying very considerable forces. Unfortunately Colonel General Rauss, the commander of Fourth Panzer Army, regarded this

---

[3] Balck was born in 1893, and came from an old military family. (His father wrote a well-known text book on tactics, which was translated into English and used for instruction in the United States.) He served through World War I, and in the course of his career has been wounded six times. He now lives in Stuttgart.

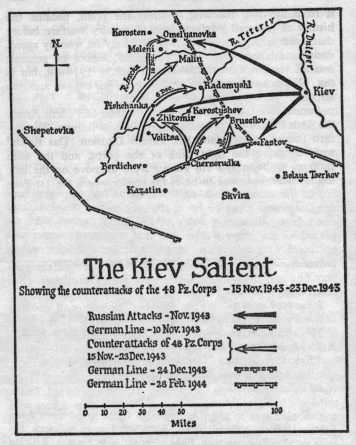

The Kiev Salient
Showing the counterattacks of the 48 Pz. Corps — 15 Nov. 1943 – 23 Dec. 1943

Russian Attacks – Nov. 1943
German Line – 10 Nov. 1943
Counterattacks of 48 Pz. Corps
15 Nov. – 23 Dec. 1943
German Line – 24 Dec. 1943
German Line – 28 Feb. 1944

0   10   20   30   40   50   100
                        Miles

plan as too ambitious, and felt that it was essential to recapture Zhitomir, and wipe out the Russian forces there before turning towards Kiev. Our idea of a lightning thrust far
into the rear of the Russian masses was discarded in favor of
an operation which was essentially orthodox in character.
Rauss was a fine soldier, but the events of the next few
weeks showed that in spite of great tactical successes, it was
impossible to crush the huge Kiev bridgehead by pushing at

it frontally from the west. I stress the point, because the history of armored warfare—and of cavalry warfare before that—shows that the great prizes can only be won by speed, daring, and maneuver. The "play safe" school of generals was all very well on the Western Front in 1914–18, but is out of place in this age of the gasoline engine and the airplane.[4]

Forced to modify our plan on the orders of Fourth Army, the 48th Panzer Corps made dispositions as follows. Twenty-fifth Panzer Division and S.S. Panzer Division "Das Reich" were to guard the right flank of the corps, and the 68th Infantry Division and 7th Panzer were to move on the left. The *Schwerpunkt* was to be in the center where the 1st Panzer Division and Panzer Division "Leibstandarte," both veteran formations and well up to strength, were to thrust from Chernorudka towards the railway Kiev–Zhitomir. On 15 November their advance began; they hit the Russians on the left flank and took them completely by surprise. On 17 November 1st Panzer and "Leibstandarte" reached the railway line and flung the Russians back to the northeast. (See map on page 308.)

Bound by our orders, we now had to swing off towards Zhitomir. "Leibstandarte" was left in position facing east, while the 1st Panzer Division advanced on Zhitomir, in conjunction with 7th Panzer and the 68th Infantry Division (both of these formations were rather tired, but they were brilliantly led and their morale was superb). On the night 17/18 November the 1st and 7th Panzer Divisions entered Zhitomir—a typical old Russian town, with swelling domes and ancient churches.

Meanwhile the Russian Command had pulled itself together, and concentrated large forces around Brussilov. On 17 and 18 November the Russians counterattacked violently at

---

[4] Glaring cases of the "play safe" attitude abound in World War II. I shall mention only one classic example.

In 1941 Hitler pulled back Reinhardt's Panzer Group, which had swept towards Leningrad, far in advance of the infantry of Army Group North. Hitler turned them away from a city which was weakly defended and taken completely by surprise, and so prevented a rapid link-up with the Finns, which would have brought the campaign in the north to a rapid conclusion.

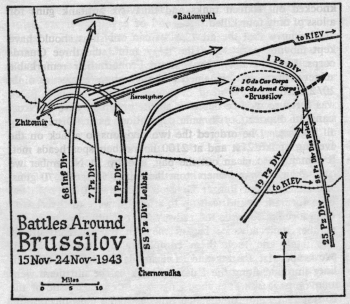

Battles Around
Brussilov
15 Nov–24 Nov–1943

Miles
0   5   10

Karostyshev and Brussilov with the 1st Guards Cavalry
Corps and the 5th and 8th Guards Armored Corps. They
met with no success, and General Balck decided to destroy
this Russian Tank Army in a pincer attack. The newly
arrived 19th Panzer Division was to attack from the south,
"Leibstandarte" was to attack Brussilov from the west, 1st
Panzer was to thrust along the Zhitomir–Kiev road, and the
7th Panzer Division was to bypass Radomyshl and form a
protective front to the north. Although the preparations
were made with great energy, the attack could not be
launched before 20 November.

The frontal attack of "Leibstandarte" on Brussilov failed;
it was the first time in the war that this famous division had
launched an attack and failed to gain its objective. But on
the flanks all went well. Seventh Panzer carried out its role
perfectly, 1st Panzer thrust deeply across the Russian rear,
and the 19th Panzer Division, although still very tired from
previous battles, smashed through on the right flank and

knocked out sixteen tanks and thirty-six antitank guns for a loss of only four killed.

Obviously the 1st and 19th Panzer Divisions should have kept moving, and closed the ring around the three Guards corps. Unfortunately they did not exploit their remarkable achievements, and remained where they were on the night 20/21 November instead of continuing the advance. Balck was furious when he heard of the delay which gave the Russians an opportunity to build up a new front. Disregarding all arguments, he ordered the two divisions to attack on the evening of the 21st and at 2100 hours their spearheads met. It remained to clean out the bag, and by 24 November we had taken many prisoners, together with 153 tanks, 70 guns, and 250 antitank guns. The bodies of three thousand dead Russians littered the ground.

The success was by no means complete, for in a most skilful way the Russians extricated a considerable part of their forces from the trap. It was practically impossible to prevent even large units from sneaking through the German lines during the long and dark winter nights, and there were many gaps in our encircling ring. It was characteristic of the Russian mentality that first of all the staffs, the officers, and certain specialists were taken out of the ring, while the bulk of the men were left to their fate. In the whole Brussilov area no staffs were captured nor was the dead body of a senior officer ever found. Thus the Russians saved the cadres for new formations. They were sent to the rear, where they received fresh troops and equipment, of which the Red Army seemed to possess an inexhaustible supply.

Our victory was gained in the nick of time. On 26 November the cold weather broke, and mud and slush stopped practically every movement.[5] Thus our proposed attack on Kiev had to be cancelled. Losses increased, as in this horrible mud nobody wanted to throw himself on the ground to avoid presenting a good target to the enemy.

Our tactical achievement at Brussilov was impressive, but we failed to gain the smashing victory, on which we had a right to count. Too much time was lost through the detour

[5] A characteristic of the winter in South Russia is that periods of bitter cold alternate with fairly warm days.

to Zhitomir; the Russians were given a respite, and the
mistake was irreparable.[6]

Victory at Radomyshl

After our victory on 24 November the situation was as
follows: The Russians had built up a new and strong front
east of Brussilov, which we could not possibly assault as
long as the mud conditions lasted; moreover the Russians
were concentrating strong reserves in that sector. On the
other hand the forces we had driven from Zhitomir had
taken up new positions not far north of the Zhitomir–
Radomyshl road, and were well placed to attack our left
flank should we attempt to thrust directly from Brussilov
towards Kiev. The headquarters of the Russian Sixtieth
Army was identified in this area.

Army Group South decided to eliminate this threat. On
30 November the 48th Panzer Corps received orders to
make a surprise attack on the right flank of the Russians on
the Zhitomir–Radomyshl front, and to roll up and destroy
their whole line from west to east. The operation looked
simple on paper but was rather difficult in practice. The
situation on the Zhitomir–Radomyshl sector was clear
enough—it was covered by the German 13th Corps consisting of more or less tired infantry and security divisions. But
the position to the north and west of Zhitomir was very
obscure.

Nobody knew where the Russian right flank rested. It
was quite possible that there was no gap and that the front
merely bent northwards in a continuous line, and it was
equally possible that the gap was covered by guerillas. Air
reconnaissance produced no information, and we decided
not to send out ground recce forces, as their activity would
have told the Russians that something was afoot. To increase
the difficulties it appeared that all bridges in the area between Korosten and Zhitomir had been destroyed.

Forty-eighth Panzer Corps decided that the troops should

---

[6] Fourth Panzer Army only gave a grudging permission for the
attack on Brussilov, and did not believe that it would succeed.

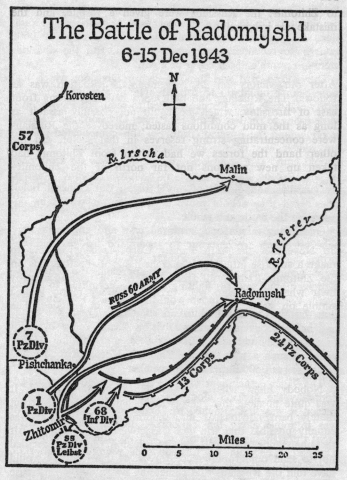

The Battle of Radomyshl
6-15 Dec 1943

N

Korosten

57 Corps

R. Irscha

Malin

R. Teterev

RUSS 60 ARMY

Radomyshl

7 PzDiv

Pishchanka

24 Pz Corps

13 Corps

1 PzDiv

68 Inf Div

Zhitomir

SS Pz Div Leibst

Miles

0   5   10   15   20   25

remain in their present areas before advancing as a surprise
move; the 68th Infantry Division was then to thrust from
Zhitomir directly against the Russian right wing; to the left
of the infantry, Panzer Division "Leibstandarte" was to attack the enemy's flank, and to the left of "Leibstandarte,"
the 1st Panzer Division was to swing across their rear. Thir-

teenth Corps was to join in the attack with its main effort on the left. On D day the spearheads of both panzer divisions were to cross the Zhitomir–Korosten road at 0600 hours. No reconnaissance was permitted, and the divisions were to assemble under cover of night.

Our trump card was the 7th Panzer Division, which had now been brought up to full strength in men and material. Forty-eighth Panzer Corps intended to send 7th Panzer on a wide swing to the left of the 1st Panzer Division, and to move it far behind the Russian front. For this complicated plan to succeed it was of the utmost importance that the thrust should come as a complete surprise. This was far from easy as the division had to move over difficult ground, infested by guerillas and devoid of any bridges. But General Balck considered that a bold move by 7th Panzer would be decisive for the battle as a whole.

On D day minus one, armored cars and engineers were sent northwest to Zhitomir to repair the bridges and improve the roads which 7th Panzer would have to use. They were given strict orders not to approach the Zhitomir–Korosten road and no fighting unit was permitted to follow them. We hoped this move would not attract Russian attention, but it was essential to do something about the roads and bridges. Seventh Panzer Division was to move by night in a single bound along these routes, and to time its advance in such a way that the Zhitomir–Korosten road could be crossed at 0600 hours on 6 December.

The Tiger detachment of 7th Panzer was too heavy to accompany the division along its line of march and for this reason it was first attached to "Leibstandarte"; on D day it was to move along the Zhitomir–Korosten road and drive right through enemy territory to join up with the 7th Panzer Division. The role of this division required great skill, adaptability, and energy. However, it was commanded by General Hasso von Manteuffel, an officer who possessed these qualities in abundance, and also had the personal dash and courage required to inspire his men in this very difficult and dangerous task.

Light frost and a moon were predicted for the night of the attack. All orders were given verbally and were discussed in detail at the battle headquarters of the various divisions. For security reasons divisional commanders and staff officers were not called together for an order group; had this been done the Russians would probably have heard about the meeting and drawn conclusions accordingly. On the evening before the attack we moved the battle H.Q. of 48th Panzer Corps to Pishchanka, immediately behind the forward line.

At 0600 hours on 6 December the spearheads of all three panzer divisions crossed the Zhitomir–Korosten road. Contrary to what we expected, there was a strongly manned position running along the road, although it was still in course of construction. The Russians were taken completely by surprise as they had seen absolutely nothing of our outflanking maneuver. On this line they offered brave but uncoordinated resistance which was speedily broken down, particularly on the front of the 7th Panzer Division. From then onwards the thrust went on smoothly and penetrated far into hostile territory. At no time was there any crisis.

In those days we were really good at intercepting Russian wireless traffic; enemy messages were promptly deciphered and passed to Corps in time to act on them. We were kept well informed of Russian reactions to our movements, and the measures they proposed to take, and we modified our own plans accordingly.[7] At first the Russians underestimated the importance of the German thrust. Later a few antitank guns were thrown into the fray. Then slowly the Russian Command got worried. Wireless calls became frantic. "Report at once where the enemy comes from. Your message is unbelievable." Reply: "Ask the Devil's grandmother; how should I know where the enemy comes from?" (Whenever the Devil and his near relations are mentioned in Russian signals one can assume that a crack-up is at hand.) Towards noon the Russian Sixtieth Army went off

---

[7] The Red Army of World War II was vastly different from the Imperial Russian Army of 1914–17, but in two important respects the Russians have not changed. They are still addicted to mass attacks, and they still show an extraordinary indifference to wireless security. Ludendorff's dispositions at Tannenberg were based on intercepted signals, and Hindenburg speaks of "their incomprehensible lack of caution."

the air, and soon afterwards our tanks overran the army headquarters.

By evening the Russian front had been rolled up for a length of twenty miles. The attack was brilliantly supported by the aircraft of General Seidemann, who had established his H.Q. in close vicinity to that of the 48th Panzer Corps.[8] The Air Liaison Officer from the 8th Fliegerkorps travelled in an armored car with our leading tanks and kept in direct wireless contact with the air squadrons.

The advance continued without a halt. During the night 7/8 December "Leibstandarte" thrust deeply through the Russian lines. Unfortunately the success could not be exploited, as the tanks ran out of gasoline and "Leibstandarte" was kept busy the whole day rescuing immobile tanks. First Panzer Division broke down all resistance and pushed through as far as the Teterev river. Fighting stubbornly the 7th Panzer Division smashed the Malin bridgehead on the banks of the Irscha and on 9 December the area between the two rivers was mopped up. Seventh Panzer eliminated the bridgehead south of Malin while the divisions of the 13th Corps took up positions in rear of our armor.

The results so far achieved were satisfactory. The Russian Sixtieth Army had been completely disrupted, and it was clear from their huge ammunition dumps and the intricate roadnet they had developed that we had forestalled an offensive of gigantic dimensions.

At the battle H.Q. of the 48th Panzer Corps we realized that no more could be done for the present, and we suggested to Fourth Panzer Army that the armor should be withdrawn and regrouped for another blow. We proposed to outflank the Russians at Malin by swinging westwards through Korosten.

Before a new role could be accepted the 48th Panzer Corps was required to cover the 13th Corps, while it settled down in the new positions. Balck decided to solve this task offensively. There was still a fair-sized Russian bridgehead in the Radomyshl area, to the west of the Teterev river,

---

[8] Seidemann had been *Fliegerfuehrer Afrika* in 1942, and was responsible for the air support of Rommel's Panzerarmee. His close and cordial co-operation with the army became a byword.

and this was eliminated in an attack by the 1st Panzer Division and "Leibstandarte," both well co-ordinated and firmly controlled by corps headquarters. Three-and-a-half Russian divisions were encircled and then destroyed on the following day, and we also inflicted heavy punishment on troops who attempted to relieve their comrades inside the circle. The booty included 36 tanks and 204 antitank guns.

On 14 December a thrust was made in the opposite direction, and we wiped out another Russian bridgehead to the north of Radomyshl. Then the panzers were withdrawn into reserve, and the infantry of the 13th Corps took over the new front along the rivers Teterev and Irscha. The Russians were certainly flabbergasted by these ghost-like thrusts, which seemed to come from nowhere, and their wireless traffic provided abundant evidence of their bewilderment and anxiety. By 15 December we had stabilized the front, and the 48th Panzer Corps stood ready for another battle.

The Meleni Pocket

Meanwhile the 57th Corps had captured Korosten and was pushing eastwards. There was reason to believe that the Russians intended to cut in between the 13th and 57th Corps, and we were given orders to forestall them. Balck decided on another of those enveloping attacks, which had proved fatal to so many Russian divisions and corps, and which he could execute with such consummate skill. As a preliminary the 7th Panzer Division was ordered to cross the Irscha to the north of Malin, and form a strong bridgehead there. This done, Balck planned to move the 1st Panzer Division and Panzer Division "Leibstandarte" in two night marches to the area south of Korosten. From there he proposed to launch the two divisions in a surprise attack towards the area north of Meleni, in conjunction with a thrust by 7th Panzer from the bridgehead at Malin. By this means the powerful Russian forces assembling near Meleni might be caught in a trap. (See map on page 316.)

The troop movements and concentrations of 1st Panzer and "Leibstandarte" were carried out in the strictest secrecy. No reconnaissance was permitted; we had the highest

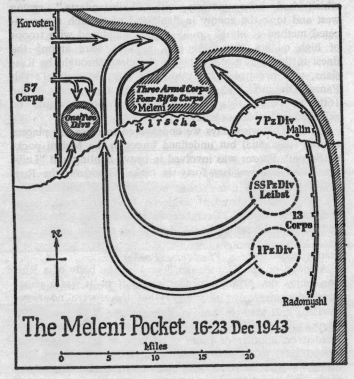

Korosten

57 Corps

One/Two Divs

Three Armd Corps
Four Rifle Corps
Meleni

Rtscha

7 Pz Div
Malin

SS Pz Div
Leibst

13 Corps

1 Pz Div

Radomyshl

N

The Meleni Pocket 16-23 Dec 1943

Miles

0   5   10   15   20

confidence in the skill of these two divisions, and hoped to make a surprise breakthrough of the Russian front to the west of Meleni. The attack was planned for 0900 on the 16th, and the divisions got into position with only a very slight delay.

The attack was launched under cover of a very heavy bombardment. Thirty batteries and a mortar brigade put down concentrated fire on the front of "Leibstandarte," and the division then moved forward with the tanks of 1st Panzer under its command. As soon as "Leibstandarte" had made reasonable headway, the artillery and mortars switched their fire to the sector of 1st Panzer. The panzer-grenadiers of this division assaulted the Russians in front, and their tanks, which had been moving with "Leibstandarte," swung west and took the enemy in flank and rear. Such a complicated method of attack could only be employed with troops of high quality, but these two divisions were among the finest in the Wehrmacht. They broke clean through the Russians, and penetrated far into their rear. Manteuffel's 7th Panzer Division also got on well, and by the evening of the 16th we hoped that a miniature Tannenberg would be achieved in the Meleni area.

On the following days we endeavored to close the pincers around substantial but undefined forces in the Meleni pocket. Seventh Panzer was involved in heavy fighting and "Leibstandarte" knocked out forty-six tanks. Gradually the Russian resistance stiffened and on 21 December their forces in the pocket launched counterattacks on a scale which took our breath away. Fighting furiously against superior forces within and without the ring, our heroic troops mastered every crisis, but the Russians were in much greater strength than we expected.

At noon on the 21st a map, found on the body of a Russian major, was brought to our headquarters. It was a sensational document, for it showed that there were no fewer than three armored corps and four rifle corps in the pocket we were attempting to encircle. The Russian Command had in fact been concentrating their forces for a massive offensive from Meleni towards Zhitomir, and our own attack with three panzer divisions must have seemed to them an instance of classical audacity.

At 1500 that afternoon we heard that a large number of Russian senior officers had met at a conference. This fact, and the situation on our front, indicated that the enemy was changing his plan; it was probable that he would now relinquish his proposed attack on Zhitomir, and concentrate on annihilating the 48th Panzer Corps. For this reason we decided to go on to the defensive, and abandon this attempt to encircle forces so greatly superior to our own. But "Leibstandarte" was ordered to try and capture Meleni and join hands with 7th Panzer to the south of the pocket.

On 22 December "Leibstandarte" gained no ground, but 1st Panzer repulsed the attacks of two armored corps, and knocked out sixty-eight tanks. On 23 December we pulled back our enveloping wings, and fighting entirely on the defensive, we warded off every attempt to cut off our divisions. Forty-eighth Panzer Corps had the satisfaction of knowing that it had forestalled and thoroughly disrupted another great offensive, which would probably have overwhelmed the 13th Corps.

Our withdrawal had begun just in time. Fifty miles to the south the Russians attacked again at Brussilov—our old battlefield of 22/24 November—and the 24th Panzer Corps was completely bowled over. Fourth Panzer Army had no reserves, and issued an urgent SOS, calling on our corps to pull out of the Meleni sector and hurry southwards with our three panzer divisions to restore the broken front. By this time we had established ourselves as the "fire-brigade" of Army Group South, and were well used to being rushed from crisis to crisis.

Thus ended the offensive battles of the 48th Panzer Corps in the Kiev salient. From the tactical aspect the conduct of operations was the most brilliant in my experience. General Balck handled his corps with masterly skill; he showed a complete understanding of the classic principles of maneuver and surprise, and he displayed a resourcefulness, a flexibility, and an insight into tactical problems, strongly reminiscent of the methods of the great captains of history.

For his own reputation Balck had done much, but for the German armies in the Ukraine he had done more. It is true that the main task—the capture of Kiev—proved beyond our strength. Yet the Russians regarded our first attack at Brussilov as the most dangerous of all, and if Balck had been allowed to carry out the original plan, it is possible that we would have retaken the Holy City of the Dnieper. In that case we would have cut off very large Russian forces, and the situation on the southern front would have been radically changed.

But we had inflicted terrific losses on the Russians; on the front of Fourth Panzer Army, of which we were the spearhead, more than 700 tanks and 668 guns were captured during this period. Of the three Russian groups which flooded across the Dnieper in November, the first at Brussilov had been smashed as an organized force, the second in the Zhitomir–Radomyshl area had been utterly destroyed, and the third east of Korosten had been so badly mauled that it was no longer capable of offensive operations.

It is true that Russian reinforcements kept pouring through Kiev, and with their help the broken armies were reformed. But the quality of the new levies left much to be desired. Fifty per cent of the prisoners whom we captured in December were lads between fifteen and eighteen years old, and some were mere children of thirteen. Moreover the other half was largely composed of Asiatics, dragged from the deepest recesses of the Soviet empire, or of old men more suited to the fireside than the battlefield. There were no really strong, young people.

There is no doubt that at this stage of the war the Russians collared for their ordinary infantry divisions anyone, regardless of training, age, or health—and sometimes of sex —and pushed them ruthlessly into battle. The fitter men were held back for their Guards corps and assault divisions. When a force was cut off they strove at all costs to preserve the officers and N.C.O.'s to serve as cadres for the future. Nevertheless, in this grim month of December, 1943, the German soldiers in the Ukraine felt a flicker of hope, for it was clear that the limits of Soviet manpower were being reached; the Russians could not continue to suffer these huge losses indefinitely and "the bottom of the barrel" was already visible.

This is a very important question, for it shows what might have been done on the Eastern Front if the German Supreme Command had been controlled by a Manstein instead of a Hitler. After the failure of our offensives of 1941– 42—and it is far from certain that they would have failed if our strategy had been on a higher level—the war with Russia was by no means lost. The critical month was October, 1942, when Sixth Army could easily have been extricated from the Stalingrad salient. A cautious and circumspect policy—combining strategic withdrawals with tactical offensives —would have played havoc with the Russian masses, while conserving our own manpower and material. The Russian principle of pressing attacks regardless of loss could have been turned against them with terrible effect. I think we could certainly have achieved a strategic stalemate in the East, and it is by no means impossible that the collapse of 1917 would have been repeated.[9]

Even after the Stalingrad disaster, there would still have been some hope if Hitler had not consented to the fatal attack on Kursk. He should have been content to "let the monster destroy himself by his own exertions."

[9] In his *Meine Kriegserinnerungen* (Berlin, E. S. Mittler, 1938), Erich Ludendorff says of Brussilov's attacks in October, 1916: "I felt that even Russia's manpower could not endure losses on such a frightful scale." Revolution came six months later.

17: The Withdrawal from the Ukraine

Ukrainian Christmas

ON CHRISTMAS EVE, 1943, the situation of Army Group South had again become very critical. We knew that the 24th Panzer Corps had been heavily defeated and that the Russians were pouring through the gap at Brussilov; they were reported to be heading for Zhitomir, and the 48th Panzer Corps was called upon to stop them. On Christmas Day our corps staff arrived at Zhitomir, which was packed with supply columns and administrative troops, including the rear services of the 13th and 24th Corps. We made our way through the crowded streets with difficulty, and established the headquarters to the south of the town. The panzer divisions of the 24th Corps (the 8th, 19th and S.S. "Das Reich") were placed under our command, but no one had the slightest idea where they were, or what their losses had been. We assumed that they would be found somewhere in the forests to the east of Zhitomir; at all events it was now our responsibility to extricate these unfortunate divisions and re-establish a fighting front.

Our problems were complicated by the frightful congestion in Zhitomir where the situation contained all the elements of panic and rout. Apart from supply troops Fourth Panzer Army had sent an artillery division into the town, with the result that more than twenty thousand men and thousands of vehicles were crammed together in the streets. In-

321

deed the place had become a veritable rat trap, and to make matters worse the absence of good roads compelled our three panzer divisions coming from the north (the 1st, 7th, and S.S. "Leibstandarte") to pass through Zhitomir.

With great difficulty and only after General Balck had taken drastic steps, the 1st Panzer Division infiltrated through the town and moved eastward to gain contact with the remnants of the 24th Corps. Eventually 1st Panzer reported that it had broken through to S.S. "Das Reich" and the headquarters of the 8th Panzer Division, but that 19th Panzer and part of the 8th Panzer Division were cut off to the south by strong Russian forces. After some delay our corps headquarters got into wireless contact with 19th Panzer, and ordered it to break through to the area south of Zhitomir where S.S. "Leibstandarte" would try and meet them. Unfortunately Zhitomir was now jammed beyond imagination, and "Leibstandarte" moved through, bit by bit, and at a snail's pace.

I shall never forget that extraordinary Christmas Day. A signal came through from 19th Panzer: "Am attacked by 30 enemy tanks. No gasoline. Help, help help"—then silence. General Balck absolutely refused to send "Leibstandarte" into action in dribs and drabs, even if this meant the total loss of the 19th Panzer Division. Eventually, after nearly six hours of anxious waiting, a signaller handed me a most welcome message from 19th Panzer: "We are withdrawing to the west in tolerable order."

On 26 December 19th Panzer and part of the 8th Panzer Division made contact with "Leibstandarte" in the Volitsa area. Their withdrawal was brilliantly conducted by General Kaellner and Colonel von Radowitz; they had lost hardly any equipment and had knocked out many tanks. They had done what the Russians used to do—left the road and found a way through the forests.

Intelligence reported that the Russians were advancing in great strength, and thrusting straight for Zhitomir. On 27 December we expected very strong attacks, and awaited them with much anxiety. But the Russian columns did not appear. Whether they had been made cautious by the bold thrust of 1st Panzer, whether they had too many formations moving on the same road, or whether their forces had been thrown into confusion in trying to envelop ours, I cannot say, but the fact remains that they did not attack and this greatly eased our situation.

The first part of our task was now accomplished—we had extricated the divisions of the 24th Panzer Corps and had formed a new front to the east of Zhitomir. Fourth Panzer Army decided to take advantage of this, and to move the 48th Panzer Corps farther south to cover the sector Kazatin –Berdichev. (See map on page 329.) There was every reason to fear a Russian thrust in this quarter, for a victory here would enable them to get across the main railway communications of the divisions in the Dnieper bend. The Russians had already taken Kazatin, and we were ordered to concentrate rapidly for a counterattack.

On 27 December S.S. "Leibstandarte" took over the area east of Berdichev, and on the 28th 1st Panzer passed through them with orders to recapture Kazatin. (Seventh Panzer was still en route from the north.) Forty-eighth Panzer Corps mustered between 100 and 150 tanks with which to cope with the 500 Russian tanks in this area.

Heavy fighting developed on 29 December. "Leibstandarte" had to hold a sector of twenty miles, and was attacked by 140 tanks. Meanwhile 1st Panzer gained some ground, but met fierce resistance from very superior forces. Sixty-eight tanks were knocked out on the front of "Leibstandarte," but the divisional front was pierced at several places, forty tanks penetrating far into the rear of the division. To meet this threat Balck decided to shorten his front and to withdraw his two divisions to a new line on both sides of Berdichev. On the morning of 30 December our position was very critical. The ground was slippery with ice and gravely hampered the retreat of the 1st Panzer Division, and "Leibstandarte" had to hack its way through strong Russian columns. Moreover, the advance of 7th Panzer was delayed. But we knocked out thirty-two tanks during the day, and by noon had established a coherent front.

On 31 December the Russians came on in force and

launched violent attacks which cost them sixty-seven tanks. Once again we got the impression that the spearheads of the Red Army were no longer followed by heavy infantry masses. The numerous prisoners were mostly lads of sixteen and some young boys of thirteen were found amongst them. This slaughter of children sickened even hardened veterans of the Eastern Front—our men spoke of another "Massacre of the Innocents."

One of the Russian tank commanders captured by "Leibstandarte" had been a factory worker in the Urals. He said that on 17 November a proclamation by Stalin was read out, saying that anyone who could drive a tank must now go to the front. Off he went, and within a month found himself in battle, without having had any training at all. The conclusion that Russian manpower was melting away was naturally accepted, and strengthened our determination to "stick it out."

The calm and able leadership of Colonel General Rauss, the commander of Fourth Panzer Army, had succeeded in overcoming a most dangerous crisis. It is true that the Russians captured Zhitomir on 31 December, and on 3 January had the satisfaction of crossing the 1939 frontier of Poland. But in fact their offensive power had been worn down, the German front in the Western Ukraine was still relatively intact, and the fighting spirit of our troops remained unbroken.

After the defensive victory at Berdichev a few weeks of comparative peace could be expected. I was still not quite rid of amoebic dysentery—my legacy from the African campaign—and General Balck told me that this was a good opportunity to get some home leave and go back to the hospital at Garmisch for a complete cure. Then I could return fit and well for the terrific battles which we all expected in 1944.

Problems of Defensive Warfare

On the whole, the defensive battles in the Western Ukraine were successful because there was no rigid defense line, but an elastic one, which was allowed to bend but not to break. For this reason the enemy was never able to wipe out German formations. The junior commanders took advantage of every opportunity to counterattack, with a view to destroying as many Russians as possible.

On the other hand, a rigid defense system, like that of the 24th Corps east of Brussilov, usually broke to pieces in a very short time. Such dispositions must be blamed on local commanders. Armor employed en masse and in surprise attacks pierced almost any front, as in the vast spaces of Russia every defensive line was more or less a screen. The secret of a successful defense depended on the dispositions of the reserves, and the weight and vigor of counterattacks.

Our difficulties were aggravated by faults in the German War Establishments. We did not possess antitank divisions (i.e. divisions consisting mainly of antitank artillery) although such formations have a very important place in modern war. At the beginning of a battle divisions of this type should be kept in reserve, and should only be committed when a serious breakthrough is threatened. After they have stabilized the front, the armored divisions can be thrown into a counterattack. Our lack of antitank divisions was the cause of many misfortunes, and it would have been very easy to form them. Forty-eighth Panzer Corps strongly advocated this course, but our representations were turned down on the ground that the required equipment was not available. This excuse does not hold water, as the 48th Panzer Corps alone captured between five and six hundred Russian antitank guns in December, 1943. These would have been ample to equip a division; the Russian antitank artillery was of high quality, and it was easy to adapt their guns to German ammunition.

Although we had no antitank divisions, an artillery division was very much in evidence during the fighting at Zhitomir. It comprised several artillery regiments, an assault gun unit, and a battalion of heavy cannons. The division was a complete misfit, and did nothing but block the roads and lose its guns. There was some idea in high quarters that it could be used as an armored division, but it proved a failure

in attack or defense, and was quite incapable of holding
Zhitomir. If its regiments had been used purely as artillery,
the division could have done useful work under corps control.

One of the great problems of defensive warfare is the
organization of rear areas and lines of communication. I
have mentioned the deplorable traffic congestion in the vital
road junction of Zhitomir—the same thing happened at Berdichev and many other towns. The difficulty was that the
rear services of all front-line formations congregated at the
road junctions. During a Russian offensive these places became centers for people who were not keen to fight, and of
masses of vehicles impossible to disentangle. If the Russians
broke through, hundreds and thousands of vehicles were lost
and had to be burnt; moreover, important movements of
armor were drowned in this quagmire of men and vehicles.
The root of the trouble was that life in the towns was easy
and soft, and that the open country was dominated by
guerillas. It was perhaps the most effective, but least recognized, consequence of guerilla warfare, that all rear services
crammed together in traffic centers.

The lesson of Zhitomir was afterwards applied by the
48th Panzer Corps in other towns; we simply declared such
road junctions out of bounds to all troops and ruthlessly
enforced this order. The rear services were spread out and
accommodated in villages, a practice which automatically put an end to guerilla warfare. Moreover, Russian
air attacks on these traffic centers became relatively ineffec-
tive. The rear services had certainly to put up with a number
of inconveniences so far unknown to them; in particular
they had to find more guards and perform security duties.
As a result the 48th Panzer Corps was inundated with a
flood of applications for accommodation in larger towns.
They were all carefully substantiated by a number of good
reasons, and declared that otherwise the troops could not be
regularly and efficiently supplied. However, General Balck
remained adamant, and it should be emphasized that our
policy produced no disadvantages—on the contrary, supply
and administration went much more smoothly than before.

"No Withdrawal"

On 27 December 1943 a very important conference was held at Hitler's headquarters.[1] The subject under discussion was a memorandum which Manstein had submitted, advocating a limited withdrawal from the great bend of the Dnieper and the evacuation of Nikopol. Manstein's proposals would have secured a shortening of the front by 125 miles, but Hitler refused to consider them. He based his objection on the ground that any extensive withdrawal in the Dnieper bend would enable the Russians to concentrate against the Crimea, and that the loss of the Crimea would have a "catastrophic" effect on relations with Rumania and Turkey. There was certainly some truth in this, but in war it is often necessary to choose the lesser of two evils. In vain did Zeitzler point out that, "the Crimea will be lost in the near future anyway."

Hitler rightly said that the Russians "must lose their breath some time," but what he could not see was that the best way to wear them down was to adopt an elastic strategy, and in no circumstances to permit the German armies to be caught in dangerous salients. But it was impossible to argue with the man; when pressed by Zeitzler he fell back on vague generalizations: "Just wait and see. We've lived through a couple of those cases when everyone said that things were beyond repair. Later it always turned out that things could be brought under control after all."[2] Such was the sort of leadership which the German Army was compelled to accept, when the situation demanded ice-cold judgment and a complete mastery of strategy.

In this conference on 27 December, one can trace the root of all disasters which befell the German armies in the Ukraine in the next three months. Just at the time when Russian manpower was strained to the limit, Hitler persisted in holding a front which was strategically indefensible. As I

---

[1] *Hitler Directs his War*, 87–98.
[2] In the conference of 28 December Hitler went further and said: "I am worrying myself sick for having given permission for retreats in the past."

was on leave until the middle of April, I will not describe these battles in detail. Nor are they of particular significance to students of strategy; they merely illustrate that war is a science and that its principles cannot be defied with impunity.

In mid-January the Red Army resumed the offensive. The front of the 48th Panzer Corps held firm, and the Russians made little progress in the Western Ukraine. Farther to the east they gained important successes, and Nikopol fell on 8 February. By this time our Eighth Army was holding a most perilous salient, which enclosed Korsun and extended as far as the Dnieper. Hitler insisted on its retention, and the result was a miniature Stalingrad. Marshal Vatutin's "First Ukrainian Front" and Marshal Koniev's "Second Ukrainian Front" broke through on both sides of Korsun, and trapped over fifty thousand troops in the pocket. With great difficulty Manstein succeeded in extricating about thirty-five thousand men, but the losses were heavy, particularly in artillery. Most of the guns had to be abandoned in the mud.

Vatutin fell ill and his command was taken over by Marshal Zhukov. In March this army group opened a new offensive; there were two main thrusts, the first was directed towards southern Poland, but after capturing Rovno and Lutsk it was held between Lemberg and Tarnopol. The second thrust was the more dangerous, and smashed its way towards the headwaters of the Dniester and the foothills of the Carpathians. Meanwhile Koniev's "Second Ukrainian Front" reached the Bug and pushed towards the southwest to join hands with Zhukov's spearheads. (See map on page 329.)

Forty-eighth Panzer Corps was still holding firm to the south of Berdichev, and was now threatened with envelopment on both flanks. The corps was permitted to withdraw towards Tarnopol—a task which required plenty of nerve and very great skill. General Balck says in his report that "the main point was to inspire faith, to remain cool, calm and steadfast, and to avoid creating the impression that this was a 'hand-to-mouth' operation."

During this very risky march across the front of Zhukov's advancing armies, the 48th Panzer Corps adopted the principle of moving by night and fighting by day. General Balck

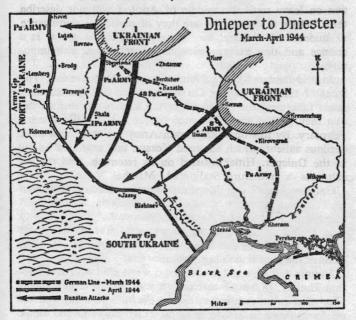

paid particular attention to the location of his corps head-quarters, for during a retreat it is vital to maintain control. Balck did not hesitate to place the headquarters far behind the front so that it could stay put in the same place for several days, before making another long step to the rear. As a result of these measures there was never a moment when the divisions were not in wireless contact with their corps.

As every Russian attack was aimed at large towns (possibly with a view to attracting Stalin's notice in a Special Order of the Day) these places were avoided like the plague. Many disasters were caused in the Russian campaign by locating higher headquarters in large towns, or by putting them too near the front for reasons of misplaced bravado. In consequence headquarters were frequently "sucked" into the battle, and command and control completely broke

down. Balck avoided this error, and took care to site his
H.Q. away from the main roads.

During a withdrawal the 48th Panzer Corps was always
careful to issue warning orders at an early stage, to give the
divisions plenty of time to make their arrangements. The
troops appreciated thoughtfulness of this kind, as is shown
by the following incident. On one occasion S.S. Panzer Division "Leibstandarte" returned to the command of the 48th
Panzer Corps after an absence of six weeks. When it received the usual warning orders from Corps explaining
exactly what was to be done during the next forty-eight
hours, "Leibstandarte" signalled back: "Hurrah, we hear our
Master's Voice."

Forty-eighth Panzer Corps succeeded in concentrating west
of Tarnopol, where it assisted in establishing a firm front.
Meanwhile First Panzer Army had been entrapped by Zhukov
in a pocket at Skala to the southeast of Tarnopol. At the
beginning of March this army was on the right flank of Army
Group South, and holding positions near Kirovograd. When
Zhukov's offensive got under way, First Panzer Army was
moved west by forced marches to try and stem the Russian
flood, but found itself encircled at Skala. The army was cut
off for weeks and had to be supplied by air; however, its determined resistance tied down strong Soviet forces, and as a
result Zhukov's dangerous thrust into northern Rumania lost
momentum and was brought to a halt. On 9 April First
Panzer Army succeeded in breaking out to the west and
reaching the main German front in Galicia. It was a brilliant
feat of arms, for the army saved all its heavy equipment.

The encirclement of First Panzer Army at Skala brought
about the final crisis between Hitler and Field Marshal von
Manstein. Hitler at first refused permission for the army to
break out, and on 25 March von Manstein flew to East Prussia
in a mood of desperation. After heated arguments he offered to resign, and finally got permission to make plans to
extricate First Panzer Army. He flew back to his headquarters, but within a week was removed from his command.

On 10 April the Russians captured Odessa, and Field Marshal von Kleist's Army Group A retired across the Dniester
into Rumania. Worse was to follow, for on 11 April General

Tolbukhin opened a terrific assault on the Perekop Isthmus; his columns broke through and swept into the Crimea. The remnant of the German and Rumanian divisions in the peninsula were driven into Sevastopol with a loss of thirty thousand prisoners, and the fortress itself fell on 9 May. Yet another army had been sacrificed to the strategy of "holding at all costs."

If Army Group South and Army Group A were not annihilated in the first months of 1944 the credit must go to the German commanders and troops, who refused to panic and fought their way out of the most critical situations. Nevertheless the effects of the campaign were most serious. General Guderian says: "The severe casualties suffered during the heavy winter fighting had utterly confounded the O.K.H."[3] He points out that these losses played havoc with the program for building up forces in the West to meet the Anglo-American invasion, now certain to come in the first half of 1944.

The spring thaw brought operations on the Eastern Front to a close, but we had every reason for viewing the future with anxiety. The sands were running out; the war of two fronts, dreaded by German strategists since the days of von Schlieffen, was about to assume its final and fatal form.

[3] *Panzer Leader*, 323.

18: The Defense of Poland

Prelude

IN THE SPRING and early summer of 1944 the German Army was making ready to meet unprecedented assaults from the east and the west. General Foy says in his memoirs that Napoleon's soldiers marched to Waterloo "without fear and without hope," and this sentiment aptly expresses the feelings of most German officers during the first months of 1944. The rank and file were more optimistic, for tactically the German Army was still superior to any of our adversaries, and the confidence of the men in their officers and weapons remained unshaken. There was talk of wonderful new inventions which would annihilate our enemies; moreover, Hitler's prestige was still a very potent factor. His spectacular rise to power, and the extraordinary triumphs between 1933 and 1941, inspired a hope that somehow or other this fantastic man would contrive to extricate Germany from her agony. But when one considered the overwhelming air power of the Anglo-Americans, the unlimited resources on which they could draw, and the vast and unbroken might of the Soviet Union, serious students of war realized that the struggle could have only one conclusion.

Our only real hope was a cleavage between the Soviet Union and the Anglo-Americans, for it was perfectly obvious that the annihilation of Germany would destroy the balance of power in Europe. In his way, however, Roosevelt was as single-minded as Hitler, and was prepared to go to extraordinary lengths in order to placate Stalin. The political consequences of his policy lie beyond the scope of this book, but the military aid he extended to Russia had an effect on operations on the Eastern Front which even now is insufficiently appreciated.

In 1941 and even in 1942 the flow of Anglo-American supplies to Russia was relatively small and cannot be said to have had a material effect on events. In 1943, however, great quantities of arms and equipment were poured into Russia, and in the last twelve months of the war the flow of war material became a veritable flood. According to a statement issued by the United States government in October, 1945, the following items were dispatched to the Soviet Union:

        13,300 aircraft
         6,800 tanks
       312,000 tons of explosives
       406,000 motor trucks (including 50,000 jeeps)
         1,500 locomotives
         9,800 freight cars
       540,000 tons of rails
     1,050,000 miles of telephone cable

(in addition to great quantities of food, tires, clothing, steel, gasoline, and high-grade machine tools).

About half these supplies were delivered in the last year of the war. Moveover, British and Canadian aid should not be forgotten. It included 5,480 tanks, 3,282 aircraft, and 103,500 tons of rubber.

From the Russian point of view the most important items were the aircraft and motor vehicles. These greatly increased the striking power of the Red Army, and enabled the Russians to speed up the whole tempo of their operations. The dramatic advance from the Dnieper to the Vistula in June and July, 1944, and the subsequent rapid breakthroughs in Hungary and Poland, can be attributed directly to Anglo-American aid. Thus did Roosevelt ensure that Stalin would make himself master of Central Europe.

In the middle of April, 1944, I reported to General Balck

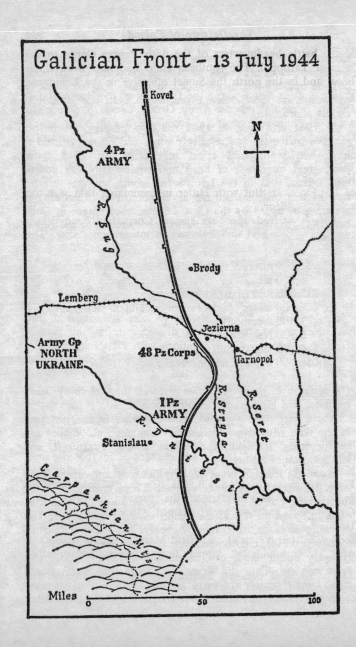

Galician Front – 13 July 1944

N

Kovel

4 Pz ARMY

R. Bug

Brody

Lemberg

Jezierna

Army Gp NORTH UKRAINE

48 Pz Corps

Tarnopol

1 Pz ARMY

R. Strypa

R. Seret

Stanislau

R. Dniester

Carpathian Mts.

Miles

0   50   100

at the battle headquarters of the 48th Panzer Corps to the west of Tarnopol. The southern front had now been stabilized, and in the north the Soviet offensive in the Leningrad area had been halted along the frontiers of the Baltic States. Despite persistent attacks Army Group Center had retained a considerable part of White Russia, including Vitebsk and the important railway junction of Orsha.[1] The Eastern Front was still too long for an effective defense, and we would have gained much by evacuating Estonia and White Russia and withdrawing to the line Riga–Lemberg–mouth of the Dniester. But with Hitler in command, that was too much to hope for.

When I arrived, the 48th Panzer Corps had been drawn out of the line and was engaged in intensive training. The whole front was quiet; the spring thaw discouraged large-scale movements and moreover the wastage in the winter of 1943–44 had been too much even for the Russian masses. We were now under First Panzer Army, and had the 1st and 8th Panzer Divisions under command.

General Balck did his utmost to take advantage of the lull and bring the two panzer divisions up to the highest standard of efficiency. Our relations with First Panzer Army were very cordial; Colonel General Rauss was the army commander and his chief of staff, Major General Wagener, was an old friend of mine. In peacetime he had served in a Silesian cavalry regiment, stationed near to my own; he was a very keen horseman and we had frequently hunted together. He told me what had happened to First Panzer Army when it was caught in the Skala pocket in March, and we thoroughly discussed the recent operations in the Ukraine. Naturally we were both very concerned at the removal of Field Marshal von Manstein, the one man whose strategic genius might have frustrated the Russian masses. Army Group South had now been renamed Army Group Northern Ukraine (rather inappropriately as we no longer had any footing in that country) and Field Marshal Model had taken over. He was an alert, dapper, fiery little man, never sepa-

---

[1] The repulse of successive Russian offensives in this area was due mainly to the brilliant leadership of Colonel General Heinrici, the commander of Fourth Army.

Central Front Offensive June–July 1944

Miles 0 100 200 300 400

rated from his monocle, and although a soldier of great driving power and energy, yet he could hardly be regarded as an adequate substitute for Manstein. In particular Model was too prone to interfere in matters of detail and to tell his corps and army commanders exactly where they should dispose their troops. General Balck found this very irritating.[2]

[2] There is no truth in the story that Model was a man of humble origin, and that he had close connections with the Nazi Party. He was a product of the German General Staff, brave, efficient and hardworking, although somewhat unorthodox in his methods.

For more than two months nothing happened on the Eastern Front, although the wireless brought us plenty of exciting news from other theaters of war. We heard of the great battles in Italy, the terrific bombing attacks by day and night against Germany and France, the fall of Rome, and finally the landing in Normandy. To those who had studied the problem of the Anglo-American invasion it was perfectly obvious that the first few days—probably the first twenty-four hours—would be decisive. I knew that my old commander, Field Marshal Rommel, would see matters in that light and would make a supreme effort to throw our enemies into the sea before they could consolidate any bridgeheads. By 14 June it was clear that he had not succeeded—I did not know then how his plan for concentrating the panzer divisions close to the coast had been frustrated—and from now on our inadequate forces in the West were committed to a long and bloody struggle of attrition, which could only end in disaster and collapse.[3]

Meanwhile our Russian friends seemed to be engaged in large-scale reorganization, though it became increasingly evident that their own offensive was about to burst on an enormous front from the Baltic to the Carpathians. In mid-June the 48th Panzer Corps moved back into line and took over the vital sector immediately south of the Lemberg–Tarnopol railway. The area had been the scene of tremendous battles in 1914 and 1916, and there was every reason to believe that it was about to sustain its reputation.

Koniev Breaks Through

The front of the 48th Panzer Corps ran along the river Strypa and enclosed some marshes between the Seret and the headwaters of the Bug (see map on page 334). First and 8th Panzer Divisions had passed under command of the 3rd Pan-

[3] The key to a successful defense of Normandy lay in the disposition of the ten panzer and panzergrenadier divisions in France. Since Rommel and Hitler were both agreed that Normandy would be the scene of the invasion, the way in which our panzer divisions were disposed can only be regarded as nonsensical. It was a case of too many cooks spoiling the broth—Rommel, Rundstedt, Geyr von Schweppenburg, O.K.W., and, last but not least, Adolf Hitler.

zer Corps, and we were given eight infantry divisions, an artillery division, and some independent units. No precise information was available about Russian intentions. Wireless intercept and interrogation of prisoners produced most contradictory reports. At one moment an attack was believed to be imminent, and at another it seemed improbable. The picture kept changing from day to day. Only second-rate Russian formations were identified in the front line, but this meant nothing, as it was their habit to concentrate assault troops at the last moment.

To the 48th Panzer Corps it appeared dangerous to allow the enemy to retain the ground west of the line of lakes on the Seret River. The sector between Jezierna and Brody was covered by dense forests, which would enable the Russians to conceal their preparations and deployment. We suggested that the Russians should be attacked and driven back to the line of the Seret, but the proposal was turned down. Instead we were ordered to make a reconnaissance in force, with two battalions supported by tanks and artillery. The operation was duly carried out, and merely demonstrated that it would be quite easy to reach the Seret and forestall the Russian offensive. But we were forbidden to do more.

Meanwhile something very unpleasant was happening on the Central Front. On 22 June the Red Army commemorated the third anniversary of our invasion by launching an offensive with four army groups (146 infantry divisions and 43 tank brigades) on a front of three hundred miles extending in a great semicircle from Mozyr on the Pripet to Polotsk on the Dwina. Field Marshal Busch, the commander of Army Group Center, had seen what was coming and had requested permission to step back to the line of the River Berezina, and throw the elaborate Russian preparations out of gear. Hitler of course imposed his veto, and the unfortunate Army Group Center, stretched out on far too wide a front, simply broke to pieces before the onslaught.[4] Vitebsk fell on 26 June, Orsha on the 27th,

---

[4] By a strange oversight Chester Wilmot says nothing about this battle in *The Struggle for Europe*. It was, however, one of the greatest events of the war, and as a military operation was on a far grander scale than the invasion of Normandy.

Mogilev on the 28th, and Bobruisk on the 29th. Large German pockets were isolated, and our losses in prisoners soon swelled to over 80,000 men. On 1 July the Russians forced the passage of the Berezina, and on 3 July their spearheads entered Minsk, the capital of White Russia. Marshal Rotmistrov's tanks then swept across the plains of northern Poland; General Guderian says, "They poured forwards and it seemed as though nothing could ever stop them."[5] Twenty-five German divisions simply disappeared.

By 13 July the Russians had taken Vilna and Pinsk, and had reached the outskirts of Kovno and Grodno. They were within a hundred miles of the German frontier, and there was "a very real danger" of their "breaking through into East Prussia as a result of their victory and of our absence of reserves."[6] This was the moment chosen by Marshal Koniev to launch a new offensive in Galicia.

During the first part of July the 48th Panzer Corps was preparing for the blow, but our problem was complicated by the uncompromising attitude of Field Marshal Model. Army Group Northern Ukraine laid down the following principle: "Forward lines are to be held at all costs, artillery and armor are to be disposed in rear along a defensive line showing no gaps; if the enemy breaks through he must meet with obstacles everywhere."

General Balck had very different ideas, for in his view the forward line should consist merely of outposts, and the main defense line should be located far in rear and out of effective artillery range. To put the bulk of the infantry in the forward positions would be to expose them to the full weight of the Russian artillery. The orders of Army Group Northern Ukraine required that the forward lines should be fully manned all night, and that the bulk of the troops should retire to the main position at dawn. Such orders were bound

---

Between 1 June and 31 August 1944 the German armies in the West suffered 293,802 casualties. During the same period our losses on the Russian front totalled 916,860 men (American Official History, *The Lorraine Campaign*, 31).

[5] *Panzer Leader*, 336.

[6] *Ibid.*, 338.

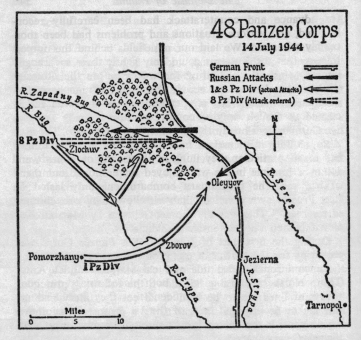

to exhaust the troops before the battle had even begun.
Moreover, Balck thought it wrong to deploy the artillery
and antitank weapons in a long unbroken line, for this would
prevent our using concentrated fire. We proposed to organize
the artillery in groups, and to locate detachments of assault
and antitank guns as mobile reserves. The essential point,
however, was that we should hold a line of outposts, eche-
lonned in depth, and that the main defensive position should
be three to four miles in rear, and very well camouflaged.

All this led to heated arguments with Army Group
Northern Ukraine, but gradually we succeeded in bringing
them round to our point of view. When the attack began we
had succeeded in disposing our infantry in the way we
wanted, but the regrouping of the artillery and antitank
guns was still incomplete. Third Panzer Corps, with the 1st
and 8th Panzer Divisions, was acting as our reserve. Its routes

for advance and counterattack had been carefully reconnoitered, and various situations and problems had been thoroughly rehearsed. We laid our minefields behind the outpost line, so that the Russians could only get at them by actually launching an attack. During the weeks before the offensive the Russians endeavored several times to gain possession of dominating heights, but all penetrations were driven off by counterattacks, strongly supported by artillery.

At 0820 on 14 July the great onslaught began. The Red Army employed masses of material on a scale never known before; in particular they flung in thousands of aircraft and for the first time in the war enjoyed unquestioned command of the air. The preliminary bombardment only lasted an hour but was very violent; it was followed by concentrated attacks in two sectors. By 0930 it was clear that two of our infantry divisions had been hit very heavily and would be incapable of mastering the situation on their own, so we asked for the 1st and 8th Panzer Divisions to counterattack.

General Balck faced this new crisis with complete calm. The two panzer divisions were both placed under our command, and we were very confident that they would restore the broken front. The move of the 1st Panzer Division was executed with perfect smoothness; on 15 July it counterattacked at Oleyyov and after some hard fighting brought the Russians to a halt. Things went very differently with the 8th Panzer Division. The breakthrough had occurred at the expected point, and the division had only to obey orders and move through the forest on a route previously arranged (see map, page 340). But unfortunately the divisional commander decided to depart from his instructions, and to save time he moved along the great road Zlochuv–Jezierna. General Balck had specifically forbidden any troop movements along this main road, and the result justified his worst fears. Eighth Panzer was caught on the move by Russian aircraft and suffered devastating losses. Long columns of tanks and lorries went up in flames, and all hope of a counterattack disappeared. A Galician S.S. Division was holding a reserve position in the forest, but its resistance was feeble. The Russians made a deep penetration into the left wing of the 48th Panzer Corps.

Meanwhile the 13th Corps on our left flank had fared very badly; the Russians succeeded in enveloping the corps and completely encircled it. Fortunately on 15 and 16 July the 48th Panzer Corps managed to restore a defensive front, and so we could do something to help our comrades. On 17 July the 13th Corps was trying to cut its way through in the sector northeast of Lemberg, and we decided to form an assault group to join hands with them. For this purpose General Balck told me to take command of the 8th Panzer Division.

On the evening of 17 July I tried to make wireless contact with the 13th Corps in order to arrange for them to attack southwards on the 18th, while the 8th Panzer Division struck north, but communications failed. I assembled the regimental commanders and explained my plan; in particular I stressed the moral significance of the attack on which depended the salvation of forty thousand of our encircled comrades. Our task was anything but easy; strong Russian armored units had pierced the front south of Brody and a barrage of infantry and antitank guns had been placed between the 13th Corps and the 48th Panzer Corps.

In order that there should be no confusion over command I placed the infantry units holding our front line under command of the panzer regiment for the duration of the night. At dawn on the 18th I went to the battle H.Q. of the panzer regiment accompanied by my artillery commander, and on the way I found to my astonishment that our infantry—due to attack in half an hour's time—were withdrawing southwards. When I tackled the commander of the panzer regiment, he confessed that he had ordered this withdrawal, as he wished to regroup before launching the attack. I immediately relieved him of his command, but once again the disobedience of this division had done irreparable harm. Valuable time was lost, and, what is more, the Russians observed our movements. With incredible speed they laid new minefields, and concentrated their tanks and artillery. In the circumstances I had no choice except to cancel the attack. Our only hope was to surprise the Russians with a concentric, rapid, and well-camouflaged armored attack; I knew from bitter experience that if they were given time to organize a defense, our chances of success would be nil.

Two days later the bulk of the 13th Corps, led by Generals Lasch and Lange, succeeded in fighting their way through to our lines. Thousands of men formed up in the night in a solid mass and to the accompaniment of thunderous "hurrahs" threw themselves at the enemy. The impact of a great block of desperate men, determined to do or die, smashed through the Russian line, and thus a great many of the troops were saved. But all guns and heavy weapons had to be abandoned, and a huge gap was opened in the front. Marshal Koniev's tanks poured through and the whole German position in southern Galicia became untenable.

On 27 July Lemberg fell, and by 1 August Koniev's columns had captured Lublin and had reached the Vistula on a wide front south of Warsaw. Fourth Panzer Army was driven over the Vistula, and First Panzer Army, with the 48th Panzer Corps, was forced back to the Carpathian Mountains. There was no telling where the disaster would end, and at this stage General Balck was ordered to take over command of Fourth Panzer Army. I followed him as chief of staff a fortnight later.

The Baranov Bridgehead

At the beginning of August, 1944, the German Reich seemed to be in imminent danger of a total collapse. In Normandy the Americans had broken through at Avranches, and Patton's Third Army was about to set out on its tremendous sweep into Brittany and Anjou. In Italy the Allies had reached the line of the Arno, and Florence was about to fall. In Germany the bomb explosion at Hitler's headquarters on 20 July was to be followed by a murderous blood-bath, seriously affecting the command of our armed forces. Finally there was the catastrophe in the East, where our whole battlefront threatened to dissolve.

On 31 August Hitler said at a conference: "I really think one can't imagine a worse crisis than the one we had in the East this year. When Field Marshal Model came, the Army

Group Center was nothing but a hole."[7] Towards the end of July Marshal Bagramyan, commanding the First Baltic Front, broke through our line south of the Dvina and reached the Gulf of Riga; the effect of this thrust was to cut off Army Group North. On 2 August the Polish Underground Army rose in revolt and seized the greater part of Warsaw. To complete the picture, Marshal Koniev's Army Group had reached the Vistula on a broad front and was threatening to drive a wedge between First and Fourth Panzer Armies.

Such was the situation when Balck and I reached Fourth Panzer Army, then trying to form a front in the great bend of the Vistula, near its confluence with the San. Strong Russian forces had crossed the Vistula at Baranov and were threatening to roll up the front from south to north. Our 56th Corps was holding a front from Solec to the river Pilica; in this sector the Russians had already established two bridgeheads at Koshenice and near Ivangorod.[8] From Solec the front of our 42nd Corps ran westwards towards Ostrowiec. There was a gap on the right flank of this corps, and the 3rd Panzer Corps was moving up to fill it (see map, page 345). To the south of the Vistula Seventeenth Army was detraining in the Cracow area to cover the gap between First and Fourth Panzer Armies; meanwhile the advance of the Russians across the San west of Przemysl was being delayed by the 24th Panzer Division.[9]

The situation at Baranov was particularly critical between 5 and 9 August. Forty-second Corps was under terrific pressure from large Russian tank forces, but fortunately it

---

[7] *Hitler Directs his War*, 106. Model had been put in command of Army Group Center in July, while still retaining command of Army Group Northern Ukraine. Colonel General Harpe acted as his deputy in the latter command. On 21 July Guderian replaced Zeitzler as chief of the General Staff.

[8] Deblin according to the Poles. In October, 1914, there was violent fighting here, when the armies of the Grand Duke Nicholas sought to establish bridgeheads west of the Vistula.

[9] This division carried out its task brilliantly. It formed battle groups, which operated on a wide front, and repeatedly attacked the Russian masses. By adopting "hit and run" tactics and exploiting mobility to the utmost, the 24th Division gained time for Seventeenth Army to form a new front between the Carpathians and the Vistula.

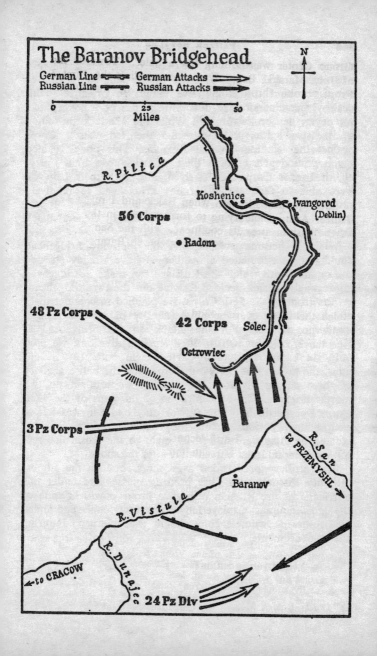

The Baranov Bridgehead

German Line
Russian Line
German Attacks
Russian Attacks

N

0   25   50
         Miles

R. Pilica

Koshenice

Ivangorod
(Deblin)

56 Corps

• Radom

48 Pz Corps

42 Corps

Solec

Ostrowiec

3 Pz Corps

R. San
to PRZEMYSHL

• Baranov

R. Vistula

R. Dunajec

to CRACOW

24 Pz Div

was an *élite* formation with very able commanders. Defense
was organized in depth, and the supply and administrative
services behind the front were taught to organize "tank
destroyer commandos" to deal with parties of Russian tanks
whenever they broke through. While the 42nd Corps fought
a defensive battle, Balck directed the 3rd Panzer Corps
against the left rear of the Russians. This attack gained
much ground and brought their offensive to a halt. Forty-
eighth Panzer Corps now arrived, and with their help we
were able to reduce the Baranov bridgehead to relatively
small proportions. In *Panzer Leader* Guderian says: "It was
thanks to the inexhaustible energy and skill of General Balck
that a major disaster was finally avoided."[10]

When it became evident that the Baranov bridgehead
could not be eliminated altogether—I have already stressed
the rapidity with which the Russians can make a bridgehead
impregnable—Balck decided to wipe out the two bridgeheads
on the front of the 56th Corps. He planned to conduct these
attacks with an overwhelming quantity of material and a
minimum of men. For the attack on the bridgehead at
Koshenice, held by two to three Russian divisions, we used
only six battalions, but supported them with 120 assault
guns, the artillery of the 42nd Corps, and the entire artillery
of three panzer divisions. In addition we brought up two
mortar brigades. The concentration of the guns of the 42nd
Corps was particularly daring, for only one gun was left in
each battery position facing the Russians on the Baranov
front. The guns were moved by night to the Koshenice sector and were returned immediately after the shoot.

The artillery preparation was short, but of the utmost
intensity. Assault guns were used en masse, and under this
hurricane of fire Russian resistance broke down, in spite of
the great courage displayed by some individuals and units.
The following wireless conversation was intercepted during
the bombardment:

> A. "Hold your position!"
> B. "I am finished."

[10] *Panzer Leader*, 374.

A. "Reinforcements are moving up."

B. "To hell with your reinforcement. I am cut off. Your reinforcements won't find me here anymore."

A. "For the last time I forbid you to speak openly over the wireless. I would prefer you to shoot your own people than allow the enemy to shoot them."

B. "Tovaric No. 54; perhaps you will grasp the situation when I tell you that I have nobody left I can shoot, apart from my wireless operator."

Meanwhile the general situation in Poland had improved considerably. The uprising in Warsaw had looked very threatening, but tension eased when the Russians failed to push through to link up with the insurgent Poles. The German Ninth Army, which was fighting in this sector, formed the impression that the Russians had outrun their supplies of gasoline and ammunition and were too weak to break our line. However this may be, the Red Army did nothing to help the Poles and their resistance was systematically overcome.[11] In the Baltic provinces the situation had also improved. Guderian, the new chief of staff, persuaded Hitler to order the evacuation of Estonia and Latvia, and on 16 September a German attack from Courland broke through to Riga, and enabled Army Group North to join hands again with Army Group Center. In this fighting my old friend, Colonel Count Strachwitz, particularly distinguished himself.

Unfortunately the situation in Rumania took a disastrous turn. Marshal Antonescu was a sincere friend of Germany, and also showed a shrewd grasp of the military situation. He proposed that Moldavia and Bessarabia should be evacuated, and a strong front should be formed along the Carpathians and then across to Galati and the mouth of the Danube. Some such course was now essential, as German reserves had been moved northwards to restore the situation in Poland. There were also ugly rumors of treachery in Rumania,

---

[11] The Russian refusal to allow the Anglo-Americans to use their airfields for supplying the Poles certainly puts the worst possible interpretation on their actions. But as Guderian aptly says, "This is a matter for the former Allies to sort out among themselves."

which made it desirable to concentrate the German troops in Wallachia. Nothing was done, and when the Red Army attacked on 20 August the Rumanian divisions went over to the Russians and turned their guns against the retreating Germans.[12] Our former allies seized the crossings over the Danube and the Prut, so that sixteen German divisions were completely destroyed. Our position in the Balkans went to pieces; Bulgaria and Rumania were occupied by the Russians, and in September they invaded Hungary.

The front of Fourth Panzer Army on the Vistula was now firmly held, but General Balck and I were not destined to remain long in a relatively quiet sector. The Normandy campaign had ended in the frightful disasters of Mortain and Falaise, Paris fell on 25 August, and the spearheads of Patton's Third Army were already probing eastwards towards the frontiers of the Reich. In September General Balck received a summons to report at Hitler's headquarters; he was to be appointed to the command of Army Group G in the West, and I was to accompany him as chief of staff. So at last I said farewell to the Russian front, and set out for yet another theater of war.

[12] There is a parallel here with the conduct of the Saxon Corps in the crisis of the Battle of Leipzeig.

19: The Red Army

IN THIS CHAPTER I propose to sum up my impressions of the Red Army. Naturally, as time passes, the value of the experience gained by German troops when fighting the Russians will decline, and new assessments of their military capacity will be required. Nevertheless, the character and qualities of the Russian soldier, and his typical methods of fighting, are unlikely to change materially. The experiences of World War II provide the essential foundation on which to build up a serious appreciation of Russia's military power.

Psychology of the Russian Soldier

No one belonging to the cultural circle of the West is ever likely to fathom the character and soul of these Asiatics, born and bred on the other side of the European frontiers.[1] Yet the Russian character must contain the key to an understanding of their soldierly qualities, their achievements, and their way of fighting. The human heart, and the psychology of the individual fighting man, have always been the ruling factors in warfare, transcending the importance of numbers and equipment. This old maxim held good during World War II, and I think it will always do so.

[1] I am of course aware that the Slavs migrated into Russia from the west, and were originally a European people. But the Mongol invasion of 1241, and the two centuries of domination which followed, gave an Asiatic twist to the Russian outlook and character, a development accentuated by the policy of the Tsars.

There is no way of telling what the Russian will do next; he will tumble from one extreme to the other. With experience it is quite easy to foretell what a soldier from any other country will do, but never with a Russian. His qualities are as unusual and many-sided as those of his vast and rambling country. He is patient and enduring beyond imagination, incredibly brave and courageous—yet at times he can be a contemptible coward. There were occasions when Russian units, which had driven back German attacks with ferocious courage, suddenly fled in panic before a small assault group. Battalions lost their nerve when the first shot was fired, and yet the same battalions fought with fanatical stubbornness on the following day. The Russian is quite unpredictable; today he does not care whether his flanks are threatened or not, tomorrow he trembles at the idea of having his flanks exposed. He disregards accepted tactical principles but sticks to the letter of his field manuals. Perhaps the key to this attitude lies in the fact that the Russian is not a conscious soldier, thinking on independent lines, but is the victim of moods which a Westerner cannot analyze. He is essentially a primitive being, innately courageous, and dominated by certain emotions and instincts. His individuality is easily swallowed up in the mass, while his powers of endurance are derived from long centuries of suffering and privation. Thanks to the innate strength of these qualities the Russian is superior in many ways to the more conscious soldier of the West, who can only make good his deficiencies by superior mental and moral training.

A feature of the Russian soldier is his utter contempt for life or death, so incomprehensible to a Westerner. The Russian is completely unmoved when he steps over the dead bodies of hundreds of his comrades; with the same unconcern he buried his dead compatriots, and with no less indifference he faces his own death. For him life holds no special value; it is something easy to throw away.

With the same indifference the Russian soldier endures cold and heat, and the pangs of hunger and thirst. Unheard-of hardships make no impression on his soul. He lacks any true religious or moral balance, and his moods alternate between bestial cruelty and genuine kindness. As part of a mob he is full of hatred and utterly cruel, but when alone he can be friendly and generous. These characteristics apply to the Asiatic Russian, the Mongol, the Turkoman, and the Uzbek, as well as to the Slavs west of the Urals.

The Russian soldier is fond of "Little Mother Russia," and for this reason he fights for the Communist regime, although generally speaking he is not a political zealot. I have remarked that interrogation of prisoners often disclosed a profound distrust and sometimes an unquenchable hatred towards the Communist Party and its officials. But the fact remains that the Party and its organs are all-powerful in the Red Army. The political commissars rule with cunning, craft, and violence, and their narrow-meshed net encompasses the entire army in its toils. The commissars are almost exclusively city men and derive from the working class; they are courageous to the point of recklessness; they are also very intelligent, and know no scruples. Although they have no bond of sympathy with the troops, they have given the Russian Army what it lacked during World War I—an iron and absolutely unshakeable discipline. This ruthless military discipline—which I am convinced no other army would endure—has transformed a mob into a fighting instrument of terrific hitting power. Discipline is the trump card of Communism, the motive power of the army, and was the decisive factor in Stalin's extraordinary political and military successes.

The Russian soldier is independent of seasons or environment; he is a good soldier everywhere and under any conditions; he is also a reliable tool in the hands of his leaders who can unhesitatingly subject him to sufferings far beyond the conception of the European mind. This has important implications in an age of atomic warfare. One of the main points in Russia's favor would be her capacity to endure ruin and slaughter on the largest scale, and to make unprecedented demands on her population and fighting troops.

The ration problem is of secondary importance to the Russian Command, for their soldiers are virtually independent of army food supplies. The field kitchen, almost holy in the eyes of other troops, is a welcome surprise to the Russian soldier if it turns up, but he can do without it for days and weeks. He is quite content with a handful of millet or rice and for the rest he takes what nature offers him. This nearness to nature is also responsible for his ability to become part of the soil; one may say that he allows himself to be sucked up by the soil. The Russian soldier is a past master of camouflage, of digging and shovelling, and of building earthworks. In an incredibly short time he literally disappears into the ground, digging himself in and making instinctive use of the terrain to such a degree that his positions are almost impossible to locate. The Russian soldier properly dug in, hugging Mother Earth, and well camouflaged, is an enemy doubly dangerous. Even after long and careful scanning it is often impossible to detect his positions. One is well advised to exercise extreme caution, even when the terrain is reputedly free of enemy.

The industrialization of the Soviet Union, carried through with ruthless force, has provided the Red Army with a large number of highly skilled technicians. The Russians have rapidly mastered the handling of new weapons, and surprisingly enough have shown a considerable aptitude for technical warfare. Carefully selected technicians are distributed among the rank and file, and instruct them in the use of the most complicated weapons and equipment. They have achieved notable success, especially in the signals service. The longer the war lasted, the better did the Russians master their sets, and the more skilful they became in interception, jamming, and deception.[2]

To some extent the good military qualities of the Russians are offset by dullness, mental rigidity, and a natural tendency towards indolence. But during the war they were improving all the time, and the higher commanders and staffs learned much from the Germans and from their own experience. They became adaptable, energetic, and ready to take decisions. Certainly in men like Zhukov, Koniev, Vatutin, and Vassilevsky Russia possessed army and army group com-

[2] Scrutiny of lend-lease figures shows that the Russians induced the Americans to give them vast quantities of signals equipment. Two hundred forty-five thousand telephones and 768,000 miles of telephone wire were supplied up to 30 April 1944, and these figures increased considerably by the end of the war.

manders of a very high order. The junior officers, and many among the middle command group, were still clumsy and unable to take decisions; because of draconian discipline they were afraid of shouldering responsibility. Purely rigid training squeezed the lower commanders into the vice of manuals and regulations, and robbed them of the initiative and originality which are vital to a good tactician. Among the rank and file the gregarious instinct is so strong that an individual fighter is always submerged in the "crowd." Russian soldiers and junior commanders realized instinctively that if left on their own they were lost, and in this herd instinct one can trace the roots of panic as well as deeds of extraordinary heroism and self-sacrifice.

But in spite of these shortcomings there is no doubt that on the whole the Russian makes an excellent soldier, and when handled by capable commanders he is a very dangerous enemy. It would be a serious mistake to underestimate him, even though somehow he does not quite fit into the picture of a modern war fought by modern soldiers. The strength of the Western soldier lies in his personal qualities, his moral and mental training, his initiative and his high standard of intelligence. To a veteran of World War II it is hardly conceivable that a Russian private soldier should be capable of independent action. But the Russian is so full of contradictions that it would be a mistake not to reckon even on this quality, which may well be lying dormant. The skillful and persistent methods of Communism have produced astonishing changes in Russia since 1917; there is no doubt that the Russian is becoming more conscious of himself, and his standard of education is steadily improving. It is quite possible that a long period of peacetime training will develop his personal initiative.

Such a renaissance would certainly be furthered by the military authorities as far as they can. The Russian High Command knows its job better than the high command of any other army; it is well aware of the weaknesses in the Red Army and will do all it can to eliminate them. There are indications that their training methods now aim at developing independent tactical action by the individual soldier, and at encouraging junior officers to take bold decisions. To the Communist regime there is of course a real peril in the development of individual action and critical thought, and such a tendency would hardly accord with their ruthless and unquestioning discipline. But given a long period of peace the Red Army may well work out some sort of compromise.

Russian Tactics

The Russian form of fighting—particularly in the attack— is characterized by the employment of masses of men and material, often thrown in unintelligently and without variations, but even so frequently effective. Russians have always been renowned for their contempt for death; the Communist regime has exploited this quality and Russian mass attacks are now more effective than ever before. An attack delivered twice will be repeated a third and a fourth time irrespective of losses, and the third or fourth attack will come in with the same stolid coolness as the first or second. Such ruthless methods represent the most inhuman and at the same time the most expensive way of fighting.

Right up to the end of the war the Russians did not bother to loosen up their attacking waves and sent them forward almost shoulder to shoulder. The herd instinct and the inability of lower commanders to act for themselves always resulted in densely packed attacks. Thanks to superiority in numbers, many great and important successes were achieved by this method. However, experience shows that it is quite possible to smash these massed attacks if they are faced by adequate weapons handled by trained men under determined commanders.

The Russians attacked with divisions, very strong numerically and on very narrow sectors. In no time the terrain in front of the defenders was teeming with Russians; they appeared to spring from the soil, it seemed impossible to stem the oncoming tide, and huge gaps made by our fire were closed automatically. The waves came on and on until the supply of men was exhausted, then perhaps the waves rolled back. But in many cases they did not roll back, but swept forward with an impetus impossible to contain. The repulse of this sort of attack is not merely a question of material; it is more particularly a matter of nerves. Only veteran soldiers were able to overcome the fear which is bound to grip everyone; only the soldier who is conscious of his duty and ability, only he who has learned to act on his own, will be able to withstand the terrible strain of a Russian massed attack. Sometimes the Russians supplied vodka to their storm battalions, and the night before the attack we could hear them roaring like devils.

After 1941 the Russians added masses of tanks to masses of men. Such onslaughts were of course far more difficult to stop, and nervous strain was proportionally increased.

Although the Russians are perhaps not masters of improvisation, they certainly understand the art of having new formations ready at any time to take the place of those smashed or decimated in battle. They replaced their exhausted units with surprising speed and in doing so displayed a ruthlessness only too typical of the Russian mentality. There were cases when Russian military leaders conscripted the male inhabitants of a whole town or an entire district; they pulled them in regardless of age, nationality, or occupation. They sent these people into battle after a few days' training or with no training at all; they were committed without uniforms, and sometimes without weapons. They learned what they could on the field of battle, where they picked up the weapons of their fallen comrades. Russian officers knew well that the military value of such people was very slight, but they helped to fill gaps, and so fulfilled their purpose.

I have already discussed the Russian genius for infiltration, a form of warfare in which they have no equals. I have also stressed their passion for bridgeheads, or indeed for any advanced position. I must emphasize that it is a fatal attitude to acquiesce in Russian bridgeheads "for the time being." The bridgehead will continue to receive new troops, new tanks, new guns, until it finally boils over.

The Russians favor troop movements by night, and carry them out with very great skill; however, they do not favor night attacks on a large scale. They seem to realize that their junior commanders are insufficiently trained for such operations. Nevertheless they sometimes make night attacks for limited objectives, either to recover lost ground or to facilitate a daylight attack.

When fighting Russians it is necessary to get accustomed to a new sort of warfare. Fighting must be primitive and ruthless, rapid, and versatile. One must never allow oneself to be bluffed; one must be alert for surprises as anything may happen. It is not enough to fight according to well-proven tactical principles, for one can never be sure what Russian reactions will be. It is impossible to say what effect encirclement, surprise, deception, and so on will have on Russians. In many situations the Russians relied on instinct rather than tactical principles, and it must be admitted that their instinct frequently served them better than the teaching of many academies could have done. At first their measures might seem incomprehensible, but they often turned out to be fully justified.

There was one tactical error which the Russians never eradicated in spite of bitter lessons; I mean their almost religious belief in the importance of high ground. They made for any height and fought for it with the utmost stubbornness, quite regardless of its tactical importance. It frequently happens that the occupation of high ground is not tactically desirable, but the Russians never understood this and suffered accordingly.

Characteristics of Various Arms

My remarks so far apply mainly to the Russian infantry, which during World War II fully maintained the great traditions of Suworov and Skobeleff. In spite of tremendous technical changes in warfare the Russian infantryman is still one of the most important military factors in the world; he is so formidable because he is so close to nature. Natural obstacles simply do not exist for him; he is at home in the densest forest, in swamps and marshes as much as the roadless steppe. He crosses broad rivers by the most primitive means; he can make roads anywhere. In a few days he will lay miles of corduroy road across impenetrable marshland; in winter, columns ten men abreast and a hundred deep will be sent into forests deeply covered in snow; in half an hour these thousand men will stamp out a path, and another thousand will take their place; within a few hours a road will exist across ground deemed inaccessible by any Western standard. Unlimited numbers of men are available to haul heavy guns and weapons across any sort of terrain; moreover, Russian equipment is admirably adapted to their needs. Their motor vehicles are of the lightest pattern and are reduced to the indispensable minimum; their horses are tough and need very little care. They are not encumbered with the impedimenta which clogs the movements of all Western armies.

The Russian infantry are well armed. The Russian and his antitank weapon are inseparable; sometimes it seemed as if every infantryman carried his own antitank rifle or antitank gun. He displays great skill in siting his antitank weapons, and takes them everywhere. Moreover, the Russian antitank gun with its flat trajectory and great accuracy is a handy weapon in any sort of fight.

There is one remarkable point; the Russian infantryman is not inquisitive, and his reconnaissance is usually poor. Although a born scout, he makes little use of his ability in this respect. The reason is probably his dislike of independent action, and his inability to express the results of his reconnaissance in intelligible form.

Like the infantry the Russian artillery is also employed in mass. Infantry attacks without artillery preparation were rare, nor does Ivan care much for short bombardments in order to gain surprise. He has the guns and shells, and he likes to fire them off. For large-scale attacks the Russians normally had 200 guns on every half-mile of front.[3] If thought necessary the number was increased to 300, but never went below 150 guns. The preliminary bombardment usually lasted two hours, and their gunners had a standing order to fire off the ammunition ration for one to one and a half days during that period. Another day's ration was held ready for the first phase of the assault, and ammunition reserves were kept farther back. Under such concentrated fire the thin German lines were usually plowed upside down in a

---

[3] This number includes heavy mortars, but excludes rockets.

very short time. Heavy weapons, in particular antitank guns, were soon shot to bits, however carefully they were sited, and however well they were dug in. Then the packed masses of men and tanks rolled into the smashed lines. When mobile reserves were available the situation could be restored with comparative ease, but usually there were none. Thus the burden of the battle rested on the shoulders of the survivors in the front line.

The Russian artillary bombardments reached far behind the front, and singled out command posts and battle headquarters. Frequently there was no special concentration of fire and no definite *Schwerpunkt;* the same intensity was maintained all along the line. The rigidity of Russian fire plans was sometimes astounding. Moreover, the Russian artillery was not versatile enough to keep pace with the advancing infantry and armor. The guns followed slowly, and often remained glued to their original emplacements, so that the attacking waves, after making deep penetrations, were left for a long time without artillery support.

For this reason the German method of hanging on stubbornly to "cornerstones" on the flanks of large Russian penetrations and breakthroughs was a grave error, and often proved fatal to the defenders. These "cornerstones" were the right and left wings of a sector which had been pierced and pressed back by the Russians; the usual order was for them to hold on at all costs, so that reserves, hastily scraped together, would be able to counterattack at right angles to the breakthrough, and sever the roots of the attack. Obviously the reserves concentrating behind these "cornerstones" were exposed to the full weight of the Russian guns and were soon battered to pulp. Thus the immobility of the Russian artillery was turned to their advantage because of faulty German tactics. The flanking attacks against the Russian wedge should have started much farther back and outside artillery range. Similarly these "cornerstones" should have been pulled back instead of engaging in a costly battle. In some cases this was done successfully, in defiance of orders from "above" insisting on a rigid defense and "cornerstone" tactics. Then it was possible to stem the Russian troops and armor advancing without artillery support, and to form another front line. The Russians were forced to work out a new fire plan and find new gun positions, thus giving the defenders a respite.

The best antidote to the Russian massed artillery is counterbattery fire at an early stage and with plenty of ammunition. The deployment of such huge masses of artillery and the dumping of large quantities of ammunition took the Russians a considerable time, and in certain cases extended over several weeks. In spite of very effective camouflage, air reconnaissance and photography usually discovered the preparations and traced their development. Night after night new battery emplacements would be dug by the Russians; for a few days they would remain empty; one morning the first of them would be occupied, and finally—usually two nights before the attack was scheduled to start—the last guns would take up their positions. In the very few cases when we had enough artillery and ammunition, excellent results were achieved by systematic counterbattery fire, starting at the moment when the Russians began to deploy their guns. Attacks by bomber squadrons of the Luftwaffe also proved a very effective remedy, and sometimes the Russian artillery deployment was completely disorganized.

The offensive tactics employed by the Russian artillery improved considerably during the war, and many new features were developed. Their preliminary bombardments became veritable drum fires of destruction. In particular they developed a technique of ceasing fire on very narrow sectors, sometimes not more than a hundred yards wide, while continuing to bombard with great fury along the rest of the line. This created the impression that preliminary shelling was still in full swing, when in reality the infantry assault had already begun along these narrow corridors.

In spite of shortcomings the Russian artillery is a very formidable arm, and fully deserves the praises which Stalin showered upon it. During the war the Red Army employed a larger number of heavy guns in the field than any other belligerent.

I come now to the tank arm, which began the war with the great advantage of possessing in the T.34 a model far superior to any tank on the German side. In 1942 their heavy Klim Voroshilov tanks were not to be despised; they then produced an improved model of the T.34, and finally in 1944 the massive Stalin tank which gave our Tigers plenty of trouble. The Russian tank designers understand their job thoroughly; they cut out refinements and concentrate on essentials—gun power, armor, and cross-country performance. During the war their system of suspension was well in advance of Germany and the West.

In 1941 and 1942 Russian tank tactics were clumsy, and the armor was dissipated in small units scattered over wide fronts. Then in the summer of 1942 the Russian Command learned its lesson and began to form entire tank armies, with armored and mechanized corps. The task of the armored corps, which were not particularly strong in motorized infantry and artillery, was to assist infantry divisions in making a breakthrough. The role of the mechanized corps was to exploit the breakthrough and thrust far behind the front; for this purpose they had the same number of tanks as the armored corps, but were not given the heavy models. In addition their establishment included large numbers of motorized infantry, artillery and engineers. The rise of the Russian tank arm dates from this reorganization; by 1944 it had become the most formidable offensive weapon of the war.

At first the Russian tank armies had to pay heavily for their lack of experience, and in particular the lower and middle commands showed little understanding or aptitude for armored warfare. They lacked the daring, the tactical insight, and the ability to make quick decisions. The initial operations of the tank armies were a complete failure. In tight masses they groped around in the main German battle zone, they moved hesitantly and without any plan. They got in each other's way, they blundered against our antitank guns, or after penetrating our front they did nothing to exploit their advantage and stood inactive and idle. Those were the days when isolated German antitank guns or 88's had their heyday, and sometimes one gun would shoot up and knock out more than thirty tanks an hour. We thought that the Russians had created a tool which they would never be able to handle expertly, but even in the winter of 1942–43 there were signs of improvement.

Nineteen-hundred forty-three was still a year of apprenticeship for the Russian armor. The heavy German defeats on the Eastern Front were not due to superior Russian tactical leadership, but to grave strategic errors by the German Supreme Command, and to the vast Russian superiority in numbers and material. It was not until 1944 that these large armored and mechanized formations developed into a highly mobile and keenly edged tool, handled by daring and capable commanders. Even the junior officers became remarkably efficient; they showed determination and initiative, and proved willing to shoulder responsibility. The destruction of our Army Group Center, and the sweeping advance of Marshal Rotmistrov's tanks from the Dnieper to the Vistula marked a new stage in the history of the Red Army and one of ominous import to the West. Later we were to see the same methods in the great assault of January, 1945.[4]

The extraordinary development of the Russian tank arm deserves the very careful attention of students of war. Nobody doubts that Russia can produce a Seidlitz, a Murat, or a Rommel—several of their generals in 1941–45 were certainly on that level. But this was more than the development of a few gifted individuals. In this case an apathetic and ignorant crowd, without training or natural aptitude, was endowed with brain and nerves. In the fiery furnace of war the tank crews of the Red Army were elevated far above their original level. Such a development must have required organization and planning of the highest order; it may be repeated in other spheres—for instance in their air force or submarine fleet, whose progress is furthered by the Russian High Command by every available means.

From the days of Peter the Great to the revolution of 1917, the armies of the Tsar were massive, cumbersome, and slow. In the campaign in Finland, and during the

---

[4] To illustrate the growing versatility of the Red Army and its ability to conduct armored operations over vast distances and at a rapid tempo, I draw attention to Marshal Malinovsky's sensational advance into Manchuria in August, 1945.

operations of 1941–42, the same criticisms could be made of the Red Army. The rise of the Russian tank arm has changed all that. Today, any realistic plan for European defense must visualize that the air fleets and tank armies of the Soviet Union will throw themselves upon us with a velocity and fury far eclipsing any Blitzkrieg of World War II. Europe is threatened by a torrent of steel, controlled by men whose spiritual outlook is not far removed from that of Attila or Genghiz Khan.

Army without Baggage

It is characteristic of the Russians that even their armored divisions have far fewer vehicles than those of Western Powers. It would be wrong to attribute this to lack of productivity in the Russian motor industry, for even infantry divisions with horse-drawn transport have a low complement of animals and wagons. Moreover, the strength returns of any Russian regiment or division are much lower than those of Western armies. But in any Russian formation the strength returns of the actual fighting troops are relatively the same as in the West, for they have far fewer men in their supply columns and administrative units. Apart from the records of officers, N.C.O.'s, and specialists, the Russians do not bother to maintain any personnel branch.[5] When a unit requires replacements, it calls for so many men. Similarly the supply columns of the Red Army do not have to worry about clothing, tents, blankets and many other items regarded as essential in the West; during an advance they can afford to forget about rations, for the troops "live on the country." The chief task of the supply columns is the movement of gasoline and ammunition, and even these items are frequently packed on what a Western army calls "fighting vehicles." In a Russian motorized division, the soldier has no luggage apart from what he carries on his person. Somehow or other he squeezes on to a vehicle packed with gasoline or ammunition.

[5] This remarks applies to 1941–45.

This scarcity of vehicles has a dual effect, tactical, and psychological. Because the number of vehicles in a motorized division is much lower than in the West, the division is far more mobile; it is easier to handle, to camouflage, or to move by rail.[6] The psychological aspect is also interesting. Every Western soldier is linked somehow or other with his rearward services; they bring him the sustenance and comforts which make his hard life bearable. When a unit is "rubbed out" in battle, the survivors usually cluster around the field kitchen or baggage train to seek refuge and solace. Even the shirker or the shell-shocked usually reappears at this focus on one pretext or another. There is nothing like that for a Russian. He has only his weapons, and there are no atttractions for him in the rear. There is no field kitchen and no baggage train; his refuge is his gun, his tank, or his machine gun. If he loses them he has lost his home; if he wanders into the rear he will be rounded up sooner or later by the patrols of the M.V.D.

Thus the low Russian vehicle establishments bring them significant advantages; their High Command has a deep understanding of the mentality of the Russian soldier, and has contrived to turn his weaknesses into strength.

The Red Air Force

In June and July, 1941, the Red Air Force suffered a devastating defeat, and was struck down so hard that it seemed probable that it would never rise again. Yet this disaster was followed by a revival of unexpected dimensions, only rendered possible by the inexhaustible resources of a vast country.

The difficulties to be overcome by the Russian air arm were far more formidable than those of the ground forces. The aircraft factories were much more vulnerable and were thoroughly disorganized by the advance of the German armies. The transfer of factories to the Urals and Siberia

[6] Incidentally, the Russians showed very considerable ability at moving troops by rail. They did not have a "railway atlas," and they did not employ the elaborate calculations of Western staffs, but they moved the troops with a minimum of delay from point to point.

caused serious delays in production, and the losses of experienced air crews and ground staffs had been so heavy, that it was extremely difficult to improvise training programs for the new drafts of pilots and technicians. But the Soviet state proved itself fully capable of tackling the enormous task and in this respect the help given by the Anglo-Americans was of the greatest importance.

The Red Air Force never disappeared entirely from the sky, and even in the winter of 1941–42 it delivered some effective blows. During 1942 the Luftwaffe had air superiority but it could not control every sector of the immense front, and the Russians frequently gained local command of the air. In 1943 the tide began to turn, until in the autumn of that year 1,500 German first-line aircraft faced 14,000 Russian machines. The ratio became still more unfavorable later on.

It is true that the efficiency of the Red Air Force did not correspond with its numerical strength. The casualties among experienced personnel in the first months of the war were never made good, and the types of aircraft in mass production were decidedly inferior to our own. Senior officers seemed unable to adapt themselves to the principles of modern air warfare.

The Russians had virtually no strategic air force, and the few long-range operations they carried out did not inconvenience us at all. Reconnaissance planes occasionally flew thirty to sixty miles behind the front, but it was rare to see bombers or fighters more than twenty miles beyond our lines. This proved of tremendous advantage to the German Command, and even in the worst periods of the war the movement of troops and supplies could proceed smoothly in rear areas.

The Russian aircraft operated as a tactical air force in the battle zone, and from the summer of 1943 they swarmed over the battlefield from morning to night. Their heavily armored Stormoviks specialized in low-flying attacks and their pilots certainly showed plenty of dash and courage. Their night bombers operated singly, and their main object seemed to be to disturb our sleep. Certainly the degree of co-operation between air and ground forces kept improving all the time, and their technical inferiority gradually disappeared. Tactically they were always inferior, and their pilots were no match for our own.

Russia was the first country to experiment with airborne landings and parachute operations on a large scale, and their *Ossoviachim* trained many thousands of parachutists before the war. Yet in spite of favorable opportunities, particularly in 1944–45, they never attempted any air landings.[7] However, they did develop a very effective system for supplying and reinforcing partisans from the air.

It is difficult to forecast the role of the Red Air Force in a future war. It seems likely that ground operations will still be the main task, with antitank operations as the dominating feature. Anyhow it would be unwise to underestimate their air force. During 1941–45 it was still being built up, and the quality of the aircraft which the Chinese used in Korea shows that the Red Air Force is potentially very formidable. It is also safe to assume that more attention is being paid to the strategical branch, and that their long-range bombers will not remain idle.

Is the Red Army Invincible?

The achievements of the German soldiers in Russia clearly prove that the Russians are not invincible. In the late autumn of 1941 the German Army was definitely in sight of victory in spite of vast spaces, the mud and slush of winter, and our deficient equipment and inferior numbers. Even in the critical years of 1944–45 our soldiers never had the feeling of being inferior to the Russians—but the weak German forces were like rocks in the ocean, surrounded by endless waves of men and tanks which surged around and finally submerged them. The Russians should certainly not be underestimated, but their virtues and deficiencies should be calmly and coolly appreciated. Nothing is impossible as far as their actions are concerned, but it would be wrong to

[7] *Editor's note.* With the exception of a minor operation behind the Dnieper front in 1943. It was a complete fiasco.

regard them as invincible as long as the strength ratio is not fantastically unequal.

Experience gathered in the war shows that the Germans fought successful actions with a strength ratio of 1:5, as long as the formations involved were more or less intact and adequately equipped. Success was sometimes achieved with an even more unfavorable strength ratio, and it is unlikely that any other Western army could do better.

The Russian armed forces are at their best on the ground and were not particularly formidable on the water or in the air. In spite of postwar achievements the Red Air Force will find it difficult to attain the level of Western air power—and there can be no doubt that the Russian Navy has still very much to learn. In the war of the future Russia's main strength will again be in her ground forces and particularly in her huge numbers of tanks. We must expect far-reaching offensives, delivered with lightning rapidity, and co-ordinated with disorders fostered by Communist sympathizers in other lands. What effect atomic warfare will have on such operations it is still impossible to say, but Russia's vast spaces and the veil of secrecy which shrouds her activities make her a formidable opponent if it comes to swapping atom bombs.

No air force, however powerful, will be able to stop the Russian masses. The Western World's most crying need is for infantry, determined to do or die, and ready to stem the Russian onslaught with antitank weapons. The West also needs strong armored and mechanized formations to counterattack and hurl back the Russian invader.[8]

The Western soldier has to be carefully and systematically trained for this fateful fight. Not only tactical but physical training must be planned so the troops can meet the Russians on equal terms; we must take into consideration the peculiarities of Russian fighting methods and adapt our preparations accordingly. The essential points are personal hardiness, initiative and readiness to shoulder responsibility. Strict discipline is another fundamental for fighting against

---

[8] I stress the need for infantry although my service during the war was almost exclusively with armor.

Russians; sport, however intensively practiced, is certainly not enough to equip men for a struggle which will be unspeakably tough.

The most important factor is the moral attitude of the Western man; we require an indomitable will to protect Western civilization from the clutches of the Soviet hordes.

PART FOUR

Campaign in the West

20: Crisis in the West

Change of Command

On 20 September 1944 General Balck and I arrived at the headquarters of Army Group G, then situated at Molsheim in Alsace. It was our unpleasant duty to relieve the army group commander, General Blaskowitz, and his chief of staff, Lieutenant General Heinz von Gyldenfeldt. As we drove up to the headquarters, with the wooded crests of the Vosges rising above, I thought of my last visit to this region—the breakthrough of the Maginot Line, the fiercely contested advance on Donon, the drive to the headquarters of the French 43rd Corps, and the formal capitulation of General Lescanne and his staff. Then I had been Ia of a division at the end of a brilliant and victorious campaign, now I was chief of staff of an army group, which had barely escaped annihilation and was facing as difficult a crisis as could be imagined.

General Blaskowitz was an officer of the old school, with all the staunch virtues associated with his native province of East Prussia. He had just extricated his army group from the south of France under extremely difficult conditions, but his offense was that he had quarreled with Himmler, first in Poland and recently in Alsace. Like so many others Blaskowitz was made a scapegoat for the gross blunders of Hitler and his entourage. He later commanded our troops in Holland with high distinction, and committed suicide at Nürnberg in particularly tragic circumstances.[1]

Before taking over command Balck had reported to Hitler, and was treated to a long harangue on the military situation. According to the Führer the Anglo-American advance was bound to come to a stop on a line running from the mouth of the Scheldt along the West Wall to Metz, and from there to the Vosges. Supply difficulties would force the enemy to halt, and Hitler declared that he would take advantage of this pause to launch a counter-offensive in Belgium. He mentioned the middle of November as a likely date for this operation—in fact it was delayed about four weeks—and then went on to discuss the affairs of Army Group G. In a voice ringing with indignation Hitler severely criticized the way in which Blaskowitz had commanded his forces, and reproached him with timidity and lack of offensive spirit. In fact he seems to have thought that Blaskowitz could have taken Patton's Third Army in flank and flung it back on Reims. (The absurdity of this criticism soon became clear to us.) Finally Hitler announced his formal orders: Balck was to hold Alsace-Lorraine in all circumstances—the political situation demanded that the old Reichs provinces should be retained—he was to fight for time, and on no account must he allow a situation to develop in which forces earmarked for the Ardennes offensive would have to be sidetracked to Army Group G.

At the beginning of September Field Marshal von Rundstedt was reappointed as Commander in Chief West, with my old friend Lieutenant General Westphal as his chief of staff.[2] Field Marshal Model, the former C. in C., now took over Army Group B in Holland and Belgium; he had done well in rallying the broken remnants which had survived the blood-bath in Normandy, and he soon added to his reputation by a resolute defense of southern Holland. In late September the situation there was relieved by the victory of Arnhem.

---

[1] While awaiting trial for an alleged war-crime, he dived over the railing of a gallery and broke his neck.

[2] Westphal came from Italy where he was chief of staff to Kesselring.

Our relations with Field Marshal von Rundstedt and his headquarters were extremely cordial, a point which was to prove of the greatest importance during the next three months. I had known the field marshal in peacetime—he was a man one could honor and respect—and he shared with Manstein the reputation of being Germany's finest strategist. Westphal of course was my very close friend, and during our association in the desert we had developed a perfect understanding and co-operation. These personal contacts were useful, because "Old Rundstedt" was inclined at first to shake his head at Balck's appointment, on the ground that he had no experience against the Western Powers. Balck was a commander of very forceful personality who never hesitated to express his views; moreover, during the past year he had risen in a spectacular manner, from the command of a division to that of an army group. Rundstedt knew little about recent operations in the East (where Balck had displayed a tactical genius rarely equalled in modern history) and it was natural for the old field marshal to have some doubts about the new appointment. We soon settled down very happily, and perhaps my acquaintance with Rundstedt and Westphal had something to do with it.[3]

Situation of Army Group G

When Balck took over command on 21 September, Army Group G was disposed as follows:

First Army (General von Knobelsdorff) in the Metz–
    Château-Salins area.
Fifth Panzer Army (General Hasso von Manteuffel)
    covering the northern Vosges between Lunéville and
    Épinal.

[3] I regret that in that remarkable work, *The Struggle for Europe* (p. 538), Chester Wilmot has followed the estimate of Balck's qualities given in the American official history, *The Lorraine Campaign* (p. 230), where Balck is portrayed as a swashbuckling martinet. Apart from the comments on Balck I have no quarrel with the American history, which gives a very solid and on the whole impartial study of these operations.

Nineteenth Army (General Wiese) covering the southern Vosges and the Belfort Gap.

Knobelsdorff was my old commander of the 48th Panzer
Corps, and had taken up his new command on 6 September
after a long period on the Eastern Front. Manteuffel had
also come straight from the East, and assumed command
on 11 September; he also was very well known to us and
had played a brilliant part in the battles in the Kiev salient.
Wiese was an experienced infantry officer, who took over
Nineteenth Army in June, 1944, at a time when it was
employed on the Mediterranean coast. His retreat up the
valley of the Rhone had been conducted with considerable skill.

Balck assumed command at a moment of crisis, and to
understand the situation it is necessary to go back to the
beginning of September. At that time General Patton's Third
United States Army, after taking Paris on 25 August and
sweeping on through Reims to Verdun, had been forced
by lack of gasoline to pause on the western bank of the
Moselle. Eisenhower had decided that the bulk of available supplies should be given to the British Second Army
and the First United States Army for an advance through
Belgium, and so the fiery Patton was compelled to halt at
the moment when he seemed about to break triumphantly
into Germany.[4]

By 4 September Patton's gasoline position had improved,
and with the approval of Bradley, the army group commander, Third U.S. Army resumed the offensive. The blow
fell on the German First Army which at the end of August
had consisted of only nine battalions of infantry, two

---

[4] I do not propose to discuss the vexed question of whether Eisenhower should, or should not, have accepted Montgomery's plan for a
single thrust through Belgium to the Ruhr. In *The Struggle for Europe*,
Chester Wilmot argues the case for Montgomery's plan with great
force and cogency, but the field marshal's own chief of staff, General
de Guingand, takes exactly the opposite view in *Operation Victory*.
It should be noted that although a single thrust on the Ruhr would
have simplified the Allied supply problem, it would also have simplified
the German defense problem. Divisions assembling on the Moselle to
stop Patton could have been diverted to Belgium to stop Montgomery.

batteries, and ten tanks, but which was now strengthened by the arrival of the 3rd and 15th P.G.D.'s from Italy, and also by the very exhausted 17th S.S. P.G.D. Moreover, several battalions of police and two of the new "volksgrenadier" divisions had arrived from Germany to join First Army.[5]

The advance of the American XIIth Corps in the Pontà-Mousson sector encountered stubborn resistance, and fierce fighting developed along the Moselle between 5 and 10 September. The Americans had been thinking in terms of a rapid advance to the Rhine, but now had to modify their plans and settle down to a set-piece battle. Nevertheless by 12 September bridgeheads over the Moselle had been secured north and south of Nancy, and orders were given for a pincer attack to bite out the old capital of Lorraine. These operations were successful and Nancy fell on 15 September, but the Americans failed to exploit a fine opportunity for a rapid advance to the Saar. General Eddy, the commander of the XIIth Corps, turned down a request from the 4th U.S. Armored Division, whose commander, Major General J.S. Wood, realized that our First Army had no reserves and could not resist a bold thrust along the Marne–Rhine Canal to Sarrebourg.

On 16 September General Patton ordered the XIIth U.S. Corps to advance northeast without a moment's delay, gain the Rhine in the Darmstadt area, and form a bridgehead on the east bank. This was the order of a commander who could think on big lines, and who thoroughly understood the character of armored warfare; it could not possibly be misunderstood or misconstrued. However, the XIIth Corps postponed the advance until the 18th in order to clear up German pockets near Nancy and thus gave our First Army time to concentrate in the Château–Salins sector.

Meanwhile there was heavy fighting at Lunéville, which changed hands several times, and also south of Metz where

---

[5] *Editor's note.* The volksgrenadier divisions had a much lower establishment than the normal infantry divisions, and represented the last reserves of German manpower. They were a product of the great crisis of the summer of 1944, and were committed to battle with a minimum of training.

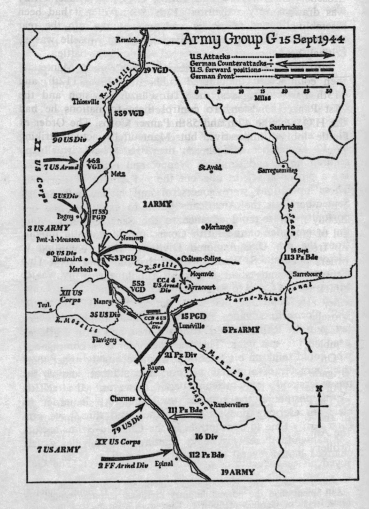

Army Group G 15 Sept 1944

U.S. Attacks ----------
German Counterattacks ----------
U.S. forward positions ----------
German front ----------

Miles
0   5   10   15   20   25   30

Remich

19 VGD

R. Moselle

Thionville

559 VGD

Saarbrucken

90 US Div

XX US Corps

7 US Armd   462 VGD   Metz

St. Avold

Sarreguemines

5 US Div

R. Saar

1 ARMY

17 SS PGD

Pagny

3 US ARMY

Pont-à-Mousson   Nomeny

Morhange

80 US Div   3 PGD

Dieulouard

Marbach   R. Seille   Château-Salins

16 Sept   113 Pz Bde

Moyenvic

XII US Corps   553 VGD   CCA 4 US Armd Div   Arracourt

Sarrebourg

Toul.   Nancy   Marne-Rhine Canal

35 US Div   CCB 4 US Armd Div   15 PGD

R. Moselle   Lunéville   5 Pz ARMY

Flavigny

21 Pz Div

R. Meurthe

Bayon   R. Mortagne

Charmes   Rambervillers

112 Pz Bde

79 US Div   111 Pz Bde

XV US Corps   16 Div

7 US ARMY   2 FF Armd Div   Epinal   19 ARMY

N

the XXth U.S. Corps gained a small bridgehead across the Moselle.[6] On 18 and 19 September our Fifth Panzer Army was drawn into the fighting around Lunéville; it had been assembling for a deliberate counterattack far into the rear of the Americans, but the situation on the Moselle was so critical that Manteuffel was ordered to join in the battle.

Fifth Panzer Army attacked on 18 September; Manteuffel then commanded the 15th P.G.D., the 111th, 112th, and 113th Panzer Brigades, the 11th Panzer Division and the 21st Panzer Division. To control these formations he had the H.Q.'s of the 47th and 58th Panzer Corps. The Order of Battle looked impressive, but Manteuffel's actual striking power was very small. Twenty-first Panzer had virtually no tanks, and was now only a second-rate infantry formation; the 11th Panzer Division was still en route from Nineteenth Army and had been shot to pieces in the withdrawal from southern France; the 15th P.G.D. had been weakened in bloody fighting; the 112th Panzer Brigade had only a handful of tanks, and the 113th Panzer Brigade was still moving up from the detraining area at Sarrebourg. According to orders issued to Blaskowitz by High Command West (but actually originating with Hitler) Fifth Panzer Army was to attack the 4th U.S. Armored Division in flank; retake Lunéville, and wipe out the American bridgeheads across the Moselle. Hitler's great error was to insist on the counterattack being delivered before all available forces were assembled.

On 18 September the 15th P.G.D. and the 11th Panzer Brigade broke into Lunéville after hard fighting, and on the 19th the 113th Panzer Brigade made a determined attack on C.C.A.[7] of the 4th Armored Division at Arracourt, north of the Marne–Rhine Canal. Our Panthers were superior to the American Sherman tanks, but the enemy had very strong artillery and antitank support, and when the fog lifted enjoyed all the benefits of overwhelming air power. The Ger-

---

[6] In this fighting, cadets of the German Officers' Training School at Metz fought with heroic courage.

[7] Combat Command A—somewhat weaker than a British armored brigade.

man attack cost nearly fifty tanks and achieved nothing.[8] (See map, page 318.)

In spite of Manteuffel's objections Blaskowitz ordered him to renew the attack on the 20th; he attempted to do so but the American forces in the Arracourt area were too strong for the 111th and 113th Panzer Brigades and forced them on the defensive.[9] There was now a real danger that the XIIth Corps would drive a wedge between First Army and Fifth Panzer Army, and that the American spearheads would soon crash through to the Rhine.

Such was the situation when General Balck and I arrived at Army Group G.

The Battles of Château–Salins

On 21 September Balck issued orders for attacks on a large scale; it was imperative to halt the XIIth Corps around Château–Salins, and in any case Hitler's directive to eliminate the American bridgeheads across the Moselle was still very much in force. First Army was warned to attack on its left flank, and Fifth Panzer Army was ordered to resume its assaults on the 4th Armored Division around Arracourt. Fifty-eighth Panzer Corps was to attack with the 111th Panzer Brigade; meanwhile the 11th Panzer Division was moving to its support from Nineteenth Army.

The morning of 22 September was shrouded in fog and so our tanks were protected against the dreaded fighter-bombers, which dominated the battlefields in the West. At first the attack of the 111th Panzer Brigade against Juvelize went well, but as soon as the sky cleared the *Fabos*[10] swarmed down on the panzers. American artillery kept up a heavy fire, and their tanks put in a vigorous counterattack. The result was that the 111th Panzer Brigade was virtually destroyed and at the end of the day was left with seven tanks and eighty men.

---

[8] Patton visited the battlefield during the day and formed the impression that a deep breakthrough towards Sarreguemines might be possible on the 20th (*The Lorraine Campaign*, 225).

[9] These brigades were under the command of the 58th Panzer Corps.

[10] German word for fighter-bombers.

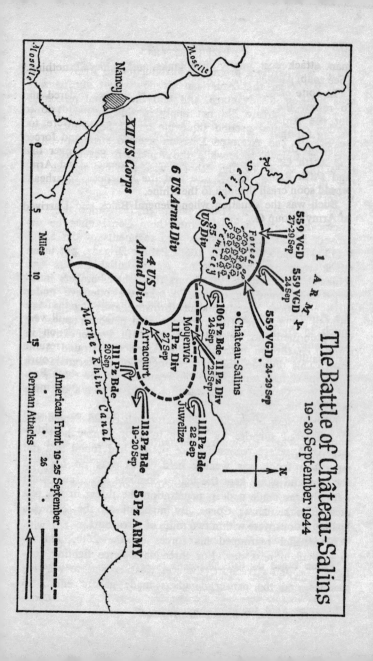

The Battle of Château-Salins
19-30 September 1944

Moselle

Nancy

XII US Corps

6 US Armd Div

4 US Armd Div

35 US Div

Forest of Gremecy

559 VGD 27-29 Sep

559 VGD 24 Sep

559 VGD 24-29 Sep

Château-Salins

106 Pz Bde 11 Pz Div 24 Sep

Moyenvic

11 Pz Div 25 Sep

11 Pz Div 27 Sep

Arracourt

111 Pz Bde 22 Sep

Juvelize

111 Pz Bde 20 Sep

113 Pz Bde 19-20 Sep

Marne-Rhine Canal

5 Pz ARMY

1 ARMY

N

Miles
0   5   10   15

American Front 19-25 September
26
German Attacks

This was hardly a promising introduction to Army Group
G; it was clear that American air power put our panzers
at a hopeless disadvantage, and that the normal principles
of armored warfare did not apply in this theater. Heavy
fighting continued around Lunéville on 22 September, and
the French 2nd Armored Division exerted strong pressure
north of Épinal. Meanwhile the American Seventh Army
from the valley of the Rhone was moving against the
left flank of our Nineteenth Army and threatening the
Belfort Gap.

On 22 September Hitler reiterated his order that the
Americans north of the Marne–Rhine Canal must be destroyed, and on 24 September two regiments of the 559th
V.G.D.[11] supported by the 106th Panzer Brigade, put in an
attack west of Château-Salins. Again initial success was
achieved, and then at 1000 hours the fighter-bombers intervened with smashing effect. To take the offensive under
these conditions merely meant throwing away troops, but
nothing could move Hitler. In spite of a personal appeal by
von Rundstedt he insisted that the 11th Panzer Division
should be thrown in against the Americans around Arracourt. This division had two regiments of panzergrenadiers
but only sixteen tanks; with the remnants of the 58th Panzer Corps, General von Manteuffel could muster about fifty
tanks for his counterattack.

Nevertheless Manteuffel did pretty well on 25 September.
He achieved surprise by putting in 11th Panzer north of
Arracourt, where reconnaissance patrols had found that the
American front was weakly held. Luck was on his side
for rain and cloud kept the fighter-bombers away, and when
11th Panzer made a deep penetration, he threw in the rest
of the 58th Panzer Corps. By nightfall on the 25th his
leading troops were within two miles of Arracourt.

Manteuffel regrouped his forces on the 26th, and attacked again next day. For three days fierce fighting continued around Arracourt; the wet weather was to our advantage and the panzergrenadiers made gallant efforts to

[11] V.G.D. denotes Volksgrenadier Division.

dislodge the 4th Armored Division, which was ably commanded by Major-General J.S. Wood. On 29 September the fighter-bombers intervened in force, and Manteuffel's attack broke down. General Balck paid a personal visit to Rundstedt's headquarters and insisted that he would need at least another three divisions with adequate supporting arms for any further attacks. The High Command had no reserves to offer, for the offensive of the First United States Army on Aachen was now in full swing. Rundstedt recognized that the striking power of Army Group G was exhausted and that in spite of Hitler's orders our counteroffensive had to come to an end. In a report on the operations General Krüger, the commander of the 58th Panzer Corps, attributed his failure to the enemy's overwhelming superiority in aircraft and artillery.

During 27–29 September the 559th V.G.D. attacked the forest of Grémecey west of Château-Salins, and pushed back the front of the American 35th Division.[12] Balck called off the attack on 29 September as a result of his interview with Rundstedt, but the American Command was gravely disturbed and on 30 September General Eddy, the commander of the XIIth Corps, agreed to a withdrawal behind the Seille. This order infuriated General Patton, who very rightly countermanded it, and told the 6th U.S. Armored Division to counterattack.[13]

Quite apart from Hitler's orders, our attacks on the XIIth Corps at Grémecey and Arracourt appeared to have some justification. When Balck took over Army Group G on 21 September it looked as though the Americans were determined to force their way through to the Saar and the Rhine, and General Patton might well have done so if he had been given a free hand. At that time the West Wall was still unmanned, and no effective defense could have been made there. From our point of view there was much to

---

[12] The 559th V.G.D. was under the 13th S.S. Corps, and formed the left wing of First Army. It would have been better if we had put these troops under Fifth Panzer Army, so that one army could have co-ordinated the fighting in the Château-Salins area.

[13] See *The Lorraine Campaign*, 252.

be said for counterattacking the spearheads of the XIIth Corps to discourage the Americans from advancing farther. Although our attacks were very costly it appeared at the time that they had achieved their purpose, and had effectively checked the American Third Army.

We now know that Patton was compelled to halt by Eisenhower's orders of 22 September. The Supreme Allied Commander had decided to accept Montgomery's proposal to make the main effort on the northern flank, clear the approaches to Antwerp, and try to capture the Ruhr before winter. Third U.S. Army received categorical orders to stand on the defensive. The rights and wrongs of this strategy do not concern me, but it certainly simplified the problems of Army Group G. We were given a few weeks' grace to rebuild our battered forces and get ready to meet the next onslaught.

Lull in October

October passed quietly enough, apart from a few limited attacks on our front south of Metz, and in the sector of Nineteenth Army on the western slopes of the Vosges. In view of the critical situation around Aachen, we had to part with the 3rd and 15th P.G.D.'s, and received only a security division in return. Offensive operations on our front were out of the question, and all efforts were concentrated on improving the defenses.

Those of us who had come from the Russian front, where the German formations were still in tolerable fighting order, were shocked at the condition of our Western armies. The losses in material had been colossal; for example, Nineteenth Army had possessed 1,480 guns, and lost 1,316 in the withdrawal from southern France. The troops under our command provided an extraordinary miscellany—we had Luftwaffe personnel, police, old men and boys, special battalions composed of men with stomach troubles or men with ear ailments. Even well-equipped units from Germany had received virtually no training and came straight from the parade-ground to the battlefield. Some panzer brigades had never even done any squadron training, which explains our enormous losses in tanks.[14]

The condition of our troops meant that an enormous amount of staff work devolved on Army Group G. We had to find places for all these men and fit them in where they could be most useful. The new panzer brigades were sent for training to the 11th and 21st Panzer Divisions—two of the finest formations in the Wehrmacht, with a long tradition of victory in Russia and Africa. Unfortunately the German Supreme Command had adopted the faulty policy of continually forming new armored units—chiefly in the Waffen-S.S.—and neglected the supply of men and equipment to the old panzer divisions.

I had a bad shock towards the end of October when von Rundstedt arrived at our headquarters and explained that he was on his way to the state funeral of Field Marshal Rommel. He said that Keitel had telephoned him to say that Rommel had died from a relapse, when convalescing from his injuries in an air attack in Normandy, and that Rundstedt was to act as Hitler's representative at the funeral. It is absolutely certain that Field Marshall von Rundstedt did not have the slightest idea of the way in which Rommel was murdered. Indeed it was not until I was behind barbed wire as a prisoner of war that I learned the gruesome truth about Rommel's death.

Those in high positions were often deliberately misled and did not always accept or condone what occurred. According to a personal order of Hitler, nobody was allowed to know more than was absolutely necessary for carrying out his particular task. Senior officers were kept in the dark, and the rank and file were whipped up to further resistance by talk of new miracle weapons, increased submarine warfare, political disputes among our enemies, and similar devices of Goebbels' propaganda machine. This book is a military study, and so I refrain from further comment on these extremely painful questions.

We anticipated that the next American thrust would come

[14] We were also given a Russian division—the 30th S.S. Grenadier —but it was in a mutinous mood and we advised that it should be disbanded. This request was refused.

through the historic "Lorraine Gateway" between Metz and the Vosges—the traditional path of invasion between Germany and France. In 1914 this area was chosen by the French General Staff as the stage for their notorious Plan 17, and between Château-Salins and Morhange Castelnau's Second Army suffered a crushing defeat at the hands of the Crown Prince Rupprecht of Bavaria. Now thirty years later we were faced with another great offensive in the same region. As in 1914, we had also to consider the Belfort Gap, where the American Seventh Army threatened to break into Alsace from the south. But we had no doubt that the main thrust would be in Lorraine, for an attack on Alsace was bound to come to a standstill on the banks of the Rhine— at least for the time being.

For this reason First Army was given priority for replacements and supplies. Eleventh Panzer Division was drawn out of the line, and placed in army reserve near St. Avold. We lost the headquarters of Fifth Panzer Army and the 47th and 58th Panzer Corps, and only received the headquarters of the 89th Corps in exchange. Broadly speaking First Army covered the "Lorraine Gateway" and Nineteenth Army was responsible for the front along the Vosges.

In our training we concentrated on night fighting, for it was obvious that attacks in daylight were futile in view of the overwhelming American air superiority. Our plans were based on the principle of elastic defense, whose value had been fully proved in the great battles in Russia. Troops packed into forward positions were doomed to destruction by artillery and air bombardment, so we issued instructions that when an attack appeared imminent the forward troops were to withdraw to a line some miles in rear. Only patrols were to remain in the forward area. In this way the enemy might be induced to "off load" his destructive fire on empty trenches, and our troops could be conserved for the main battle.

In our rear a special staff and labor service was working on the West Wall, and we ourselves constructed several defense systems in advance of these fortifications. Administrative services and the civil population were roped in to do the digging. Time was short, and the defenses were far from ready when the Americans attacked, but even so they were a tremendous help in the bitter fighting which followed. In addition thousands of mines were laid.[15]

At the beginning of November our line was far stronger than a month before, and mud and slush could be relied upon to clog the movements of the American armor. Yet there was nothing really solid, and nothing dependable about our front. Under the impact of day and night bombing the supply system worked spasmodically and ammunition was woefully short. We had hardly any assault guns, and some divisions had none at all. We had a considerable quantity of field artillery, but much of it consisted of captured guns with only a few rounds of ammunition. We had 140 tanks of all types; 100 of these were allotted to First Army.

Balck has been accused of being a "notorious optimist,"[16] but he was under no illusions about the resisting power of this Cinderella among army groups. Writing to Jodl to request reinforcements, he confessed that he had never commanded "such a mixture of badly equipped troops."

[15] The defenses of the Maginot Line were of little value to us as they faced the wrong way, but the underground shelters were useful.
[16] Wilmot, *The Struggle for Europe*, 538.

21: The Struggle in Alsace-Lorraine

Patton Attacks

ON 18 OCTOBER a very important conference was held at Brussels between Eisenhower, Bradley, and Montgomery.[1] It was agreed to make another attempt to reach the Ruhr; the main effort would be entrusted to the First and Ninth U.S. Armies, co-ordinated by General Bradley. Patton's Third Army was to attack towards the Saar "when logistics permit." On 21 October Bradley issued orders to these three armies; the First and Ninth were to launch their offensive on 5 November and Patton was to join in five days later. On 2 November Third Army was authorized to attack as soon as the weather cleared.

Patton now assured Bradley that he could get to the Saar in three days and "easily breach the West Wall." With six infantry and three armored divisions, plus two groups (i.e. brigades) or mechanized cavalry, Third Army numbered approximately a quarter of a million officers and men. Its opponents, the First German Army, had a total strength of only 86,000. Seven of the eight enemy divisions were strung out on a front of 75 miles and the only reserve was the 11th Panzer Division with 69 tanks. While the German formations were necessarily dispersed defensively, Patton, with command of the air and ample mobility on the ground, had the capacity to concentrate overwhelming force at any point he chose.

[1] Wilmot, *The Struggle for Europe*, 562–63.

Even on a basis of direct comparison he had an advantage of three to one in men, eight to one in tanks and a "tremendous superiority in the artillery arm."[2]

During late October it became very clear to me that another big offensive was impending on our front. Our advanced posts on the western bank of the Moselle were pushed back, and the American guns kept up a continuous range-finding fire. There was some sharp local fighting to the southeast of Pont-à-Mousson, and indications of a strong concentration in the Thionville sector north of Metz. We estimated that one of the American thrusts would come from Thionville and we anticipated another big push in the Château-Salins area, aimed directly at Saarbrücken; the effect of these two drives would be to "bite out" the Fortress of Metz.

Although we had no air reconnaissance, our intelligence was pretty good, and reports from agents kept us well informed of the American preparations.[3] Once again our Wireless Intercept Service proved its value, for the Americans were careless about telephone conversations and signals security. Yet the actual attack on 8 November came as a surprise to the front-line troops—the weather was most unfavorable and there was a slackening in our ground observation.

On 5 November torrential rain turned the ground into a sea of mud and converted rivulets and streams into swollen rivers. Even for tracked vehicles the going became fearfully difficult and nearly all the bridges over the Moselle were carried away. The American XXth Corps was to attack in the Metz sector, and their XIIth Corps on a thirty-mile front across the River Seille towards Saarbrücken. General Eddy, the commander of the XIIth Corps, had good reason for seeking a postponement, but Patton would not hear of it. Supported by a terrific bombardment the infantry of the XIIth Corps advanced at dawn on 8 November.

As I have mentioned, the initial attack came as a surprise

---

[2] *Ibid.,* 564.

[3] However, the American Intelligence did trick us into believing that their 14th Armored Division was at Thionville, when actually it was not even on French soil.

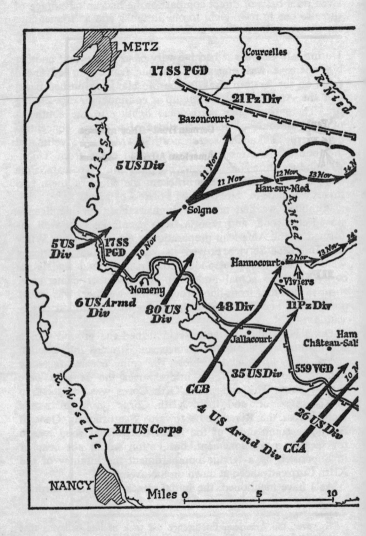

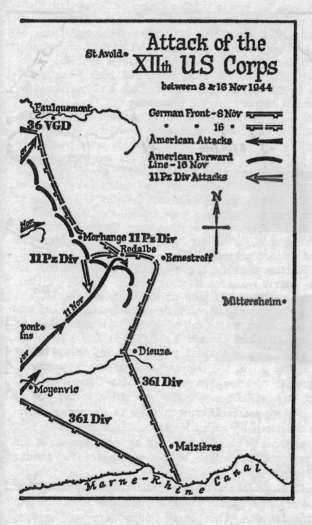

Attack of the XIIth US Corps

between 8 & 16 Nov 1944

German Front – 8 Nov
• • 16 •
American Attacks
American Forward Line – 16 Nov
11 Pz Div Attacks

N

St Avold•

Faulquemont•
36 VGD

Noz.

•Morhange 11 Pz Div
Rodalbe
11 Pz Div   •Benestroff

Mittersheim•

11 Nov

pont• ins

•Dieuze.

361 Div

•Moyenvic

361 Div

•Maizières

Marne-Rhine Canal

to our forward troops, and they failed to put into effect Balck's plan for elastic defense and a withdrawal to rearward positions. On the XIIth Corps front the Americans attacked our 48th and 559th Divisions and the right wing of the 361st Division; they were heavily hit by the bombardment and the Americans made several crossings over the Seille. General Eddy used the 26th, 35th, and 80th Infantry Divisions in the assault, and kept the 4th and 6th Armored Divisions in reserve to exploit a breakthrough.

On 9 November the American armor was flung into the battle, but the conditions were quite unsuitable. Tanks were confined to the roads and some of them were badly shot up by our 88's. In any case I think the armored divisions were committed too early, and that Eddy would have done better to wait until his infantry had eaten away more of our main defense zone. However, the 4th U.S. Armored Division was a tough and experienced formation, and in spite of the abominable weather their Combat Command B smashed through the left flank of the 48th Division and reached Hannocourt and Viviers.

On 10 November the 11th Panzer Division—our only armored reserve—counterattacked and recaptured Viviers. Rain and snow were keeping off the American aircraft, and clogging the movements of their vehicles and armor; our veteran panzer units took full advantage of this and knocked out thirty American tanks that day. On 11 and 12 November the 11th Panzer Division covered the withdrawal of the badly shaken 559th Division and took up new positions on high ground covering Morhange. Combat Command A of the 4th Armored Division came into action to the east of Château-Salins and reached Rodalbe on 11 November, where it was contained by minefields and antitank fire. Sixth U.S. Armored Division also did well, and on the afternoon of the 11th captured the bridge at Han-sur-Nied in a dashing *coup de main.*

On 12 November 11th Panzer launched a counterattack from Morhange against Combat Command A of the 4th Armored Division. The panzer troops were well used to fighting in mud and snow; on the 13th they retook Rodalbe and captured an entire American battalion. Thus we gained time to reform our front and move up reserves.

The Americans continued to attack stubbornly and with great determination. Combat Command B and the 35th Infantry Division thrust at Morhange from the west, and the 6th Armored Division endeavored to break through at Faulquemont on the direct road to Saarbrücken. We moved 21st Panzer and the 36th Division into this sector,[4] while 11th Panzer clung grimly to the high ground around Morhange. On 15 November we pulled the remnants of the 48th and 559th Divisions out of the line and combined them in one battle group.

On the morning of the 15th our troops withdrew from the battered ruins of Morhange, but for the present this was the limit of the American success. That day the XIIth U.S. Corps felt compelled to call a temporary halt; apart from the heavy losses and very difficult ground, the northern flank of the corps was exposed as a result of the efforts of the XXth U.S. Corps to envelop Metz.

The Fall of Metz

On the night 8/9 November the XXth Corps began its attack on Metz. Units of the 90th U.S. Division crossed the Moselle in assault boats to the north of Thionville and took the German defenders completely by surprise.[5] By the evening of the 9th the division had as many as eight battalions across the river, and had established a firm bridgehead. Little resistance was offered by our two divisions in this area—the 416th Infantry and the 19th Volksgrenadier; their fighting quality was low and in any case they were stretched out on far too wide a front.[6]

---

[4] Twenty-first Panzer had nineteen tanks and four panzergrenadier battalions of about sixty to seventy men each.

[5] Ninetieth U.S. Division was commanded by General Van Fleet, who was later to win distinction in Korea.

[6] The 416th Division had recently come from Denmark and was nicknamed the "Whipped Cream Division." The average age of the men was thirty-eight, and none had ever been in battle. There were no assault guns, and their artillery consisted of obsolete fortress pieces and captured Russian 122-mm's.

At Army Group G we were extremely concerned at the rapid growth of the Thionville bridgehead; First Army was now without reserves and we had to ask Rundstedt for a panzer division. But the Commander in Chief West could not authorize such a step on his own responsibility, and the question was referred to Hitler.[7] Negotiations with O.K.W. lasted more than a day but eventually the 25th P.G.D. was given to us. This formation then lay east of Treves and had to be replenished; as there was no gasoline it could not go into action until the 12th. The delay was most unfortunate, for the strong current of the Moselle and accurate German artillery fire prevented the 90th U.S. Division from completing a bridge over the river until the evening of the 11th, and for three days the American infantry were without tanks or heavy antitank guns. Nevertheless they resisted stubbornly, beat off counterattacks by our infantry (we did not have a single tank to bring against them) and on the afternoon of the 11th took Forts Metrich and Königsmacher by storm.

At dawn on 12 November the 25th P.G.D. counterattacked with ten tanks and two panzergrenadier battalions, and was doing well when it ran into a force of American tanks and infantry which had crossed the Moselle the previous night. Meanwhile American artillery on the western bank of the river kept up a violent fire, and our counterattack failed with heavy loss. Hard fighting continued on the afternoon of the 12th and throughout 13 November, and some villages changed hands several times.

On the afternoon of 14 November the 10th U.S. Armored Division crossed the Moselle; their Combat Command B thrust towards Merzig on the River Saar, while Combat Command A attacked in the direction of Bouzonville in an endeavor to cut the roads and railways leading to Metz. The city was directly threatened by the 95th U.S. Division attacking west of the Moselle, and by the 5th U.S. Division, which was approaching from the south and meeting strong

---

[7] It was at this stage of the war that Rundstedt made the comment that the only troops he was allowed to move were the sentries outside the door of his headquarters.

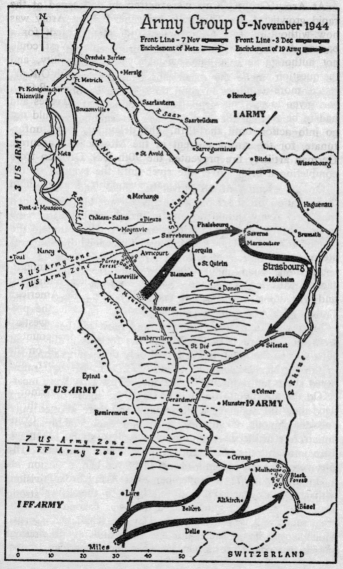

Army Group G—November 1944

Front Line - 7 Nov ▬▬▶
Front Line -3 Dec ▬▬▶
Encirclement of Metz ▬▬▶
Encirclement of 19 Army ▬▬▶

N

Orscholz Barrier

Merzig

Ft Metrich

Ft Königsmacher
Thionville

Bouzonville

Homburg

Saarlautern

R. Saar

Saarbrücken

I ARMY

Metz

R. Nied

St Avold

Sarreguemines

Bitche

Wissenbourg

3 US ARMY

R. Seille

Morhange

Saar Canal

Haguenau

Pont-à-Mousson

Château-Salins

Dieuze

Sarrebourg

Phalsbourg

Saverne

Brumath

Moyenvic

Marmoutier

Toul

Nancy

Avricourt

Lorquin

St Quirin

Strasbourg

3 US Army Zone

7 US Army Zone

Parroy
Forest

Lunéville

Blamont

Molsheim

R. Meurthe

Donon

Baccarat

R. Moselle

Rambervillers

St Dié

Sélestat

7 US ARMY

Epinal

Colmar

Gérardmer

Munster 19 ARMY

Remiremont

7 US Army Zone
1 FF Army Zone

Cernay

Mulhouse

Black
Forest

Lure

Altkirch

Bâsel

I FF ARMY

Belfort

Delle

Miles

0   10   20   30   40   50

SWITZERLAND

opposition from the 17th S.S. P.G.D. The encirclement of Metz was well under way.

This situation had been foreseen by Field Marshal von Rundstedt, and in October he had proposed that the Metz salient should be abandoned. Balck's view was that it would be better to make the Americans fight for Metz, provided the garrison withdrew in good time. However, on 7 November Hitler settled the argument by ruling that Metz was a fortress and that the garrison was to submit to encirclement and fight to the last. But we minimized the effect of these orders by only allotting second-rate troops to the Metz garrison and by not giving them any tanks or assault guns.

On the evening of 16 November Balck and I discussed the situation on the front of Army Group G. We decided that First Army should not make further sacrifices in trying to hold Metz, but should withdraw in a single bound to the line of the Nied. Our decision was influenced by the critical situation of our Nineteenth Army, which since 11 November had been under severe pressure from the Seventh U.S. Army in the Baccarat sector, and was also dealing with an offensive against the Belfort Gap, launched by the French First Army on the 14th.

Metz was an obsolete fortress, and most of the defenses were built before 1914. Nearly all the fortress artillery had been sent to the Atlantic Wall, and only thirty guns remained in the turrets. We left the 462nd V.G.D. in Metz; it numbered about ten thousand combatant troops. They were mostly elderly men, quite unfitted to stand the rigors of modern war; they did not have a single tank and were allotted only one detachment of antitank guns and one detachment of antiaircraft artillery. Ammunition was very short, but there were enough rations to last for four weeks. German civilians were evacuated from Metz on 11 November.

On the night 17/18 November First Army broke contact with the Metz garrison, and fell back to the River Nied. The move was well camouflaged and was carried out with great secrecy; it was not hampered by the XXth U.S. Corps, which closed in on Metz and had little difficulty in finding gaps in the ring of forts. On 19 November American troops entered the city of Metz from several directions, and on 21 November captured the fortress command post.[8] Most of the garrison had withdrawn into the outer forts, which continued to resist independently.

Generally speaking the Americans were content to seal off the forts and wait until starvation compelled them to surrender. The capitulation of Fort Jeanne d'Arc on 13 December marked the end of the siege.

In view of the weakness of the garrison, Metz put up a creditable resistance and played its part in tying up considerable American forces.

The Fall of Strasbourg

On 11 November the XVth Corps of Seventh U.S. Army launched an attack in the Baccarat sector south of the Marne–Rhine Canal. The new offensive was aimed at the Saverne gap in the northern Vosges—an historic gateway to Strasbourg. The blow fell on the 553rd and 708th V.G.D.'s; the former put up a magnificent fight, but the latter had never been in battle and had just arrived at the front. Moreover the American thrust was delivered along the boundary of First and Nineteenth Armies, and as we learned to our cost the conduct of operations at the point of junction between two armies is a most intricate and delicate business. On 13 November we put the 553rd Division under Nineteenth Army, but the situation remained very tense. Fifteenth Corps continued its violent attacks towards Blâmont; meanwhile the offensive of the French First Army on 14 November threatened to break through the Belfort Gap into southern Alsace.

On 14 November we ordered the right wing of Nineteenth Army to withdraw into the northern Vosges; the retreat was skilfully conducted and the American pursuit was hesitant and cautious. On the night 16/17 November the army's left wing carried out a similar withdrawal; unfortunately the commander of the 338th Division in the Belfort Gap

---

[8] General Kittel, the fortress commander, was severely wounded while fighting in the front line. As a defender of Metz, he set a better example than his predecessor, Marshal Bazaine.

had been killed in action, and the retreat in this sector was mismanaged. The rearguards were too weak, and French mobile units arrived on the new line almost simultaneously with the 338th's main body. The French armor attacked with extraordinary dash and *élan*, reflecting the temperament of the army commander, General de Lattre de Tassigny. On 19 November their tanks advanced twenty-five miles in one day to break into upper Alsace and reach the Rhine north of Basel.

Belfort fell on 21 November after fierce fighting, and on the same day French tanks entered Mulhouse. Nineteenth Army had no mobile reserves, but the 53rd Corps in southern Alsace scraped together all sorts of scratch units, including the Russians of the 30th S.S. Division, and improvised a defensive line between the Rhine and Vosges; the 198th Infantry Division, strengthened by assault guns, was ordered to counterattack from Altkirch and reach the Swiss frontier at Delle, thus cutting off the French forces at Mulhouse. Meanwhile the 106th Panzer Brigade was on its way from Lorraine to strengthen the 53rd Corps. On 20 November we appreciated at Army Group G that the enemy was developing a gigantic pincer movement, aimed at destroying Nineteenth Army. While the French First Army thrust into Alsace from the south, the Seventh U.S. Army would force the Saverne gap and advance on Strasbourg from the north.

Our problem wus complicated by the dangerous situation developing in Lorraine. Twelfth Corps on the right flank of Third U.S. Army renewed its attacks on 18 November, and the XVth Corps of Seventh Army continued to exert heavy pressure towards the Saverne gap. The weather was now clearer and the American Air Force was operating in strength. In spite of a very gallant defense the 553rd V.G.D. was driven back remorselessly towards Sarrebourg, and on 20 November more than one hundred tanks broke clean through and encircled this sorely tried division. It looked as though the division was finished, but on the night 20/21 November General Bruhn, taking advantage of the pitch dark and heavy rain, led his men right through the American lines and took up new positions blocking the way to Saverne. However, with the capture of Sarrebourg a wedge was being driven between our First and Nineteenth Armies, and the danger of Army Group G being split in two was very real.

We considered that the attack at Saverne was the more dangerous and on 20 November proposed to Rundstedt that Nineteenth Army should concentrate north of Mulhouse and abandon any further attempt to cut off the French troops on the upper Rhine. This would mean that the 198th Division and the 106th Panzer Brigade could be brought north to strengthen the Saverne gap. The plan was referred to Hitler, who totally rejected it; he ordered that "not an inch of ground" was to be yielded at Saverne, and that a counterattack by the 198th Division must go in from Altkirch towards the Swiss frontier. We had no alternative but to issue orders accordingly.

As a consolation Rundstedt let us have the Panzerlehr Division for a counterattack on Sarrebourg from the north, but it could not possibly get into action before the 23rd. In any case it was already too late to restore the situation at Saverne, for on 21 November the French 2nd Armored Division (operating under Seventh U.S. Army and commanded by General Leclerc) broke through our weak covering screens in the hills to the north and south of the town. On 22 November French and American forces of the XVth Corps enveloped Saverne; they entered the town and encircled the 553rd Division and the headquarters of the 89th Corps. However, our men did not despair and on the night 22/23 November made their way out in small groups to reassemble in the Bitche area.

Meanwhile, the 11th Panzer Division was offering a splendid resistance to the advance of the XIIth Corps from Morhange towards Sarreguemines. The division held its fifteen-mile front with a thin screen of covering troops; behind this screen groups of tanks and panzergrenadiers were placed to attack the advancing Americans in flank and rear. Thirty-fifth and 26th U.S. Infantry Divisions were attacking in the center with the 6th Armored Division on their left and the 4th Armored Division on their right. Yet in face of these odds 11th Panzer succeeded in preventing a breakthrough and inflicted heavy casualties on the enemy. Fourth Armored Division swung off towards the Saar Canal, and forced a cross-

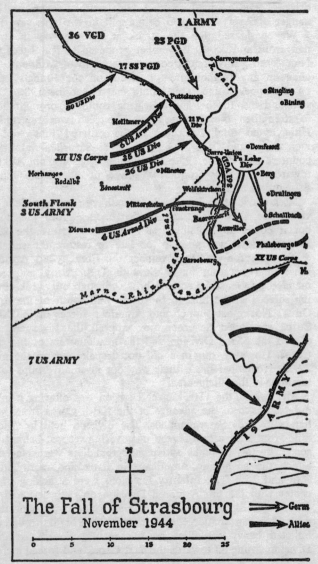

The Fall of Strasbourg
November 1944

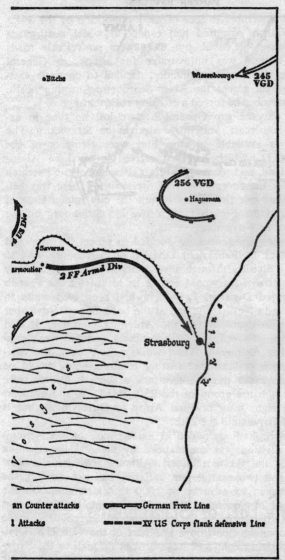

Bitche

Wissenbourg

245 VGD

256 VGD

Haguenau

US Div

Saverne

armoutier

2 FF Armd Div

Strasbourg

R. Rhine

Vosges

an Counter attacks   German Front Line

Attacks   XV US Corps flank defensive Line

ing on 22 November in face of weak opposition by the 361st
V.G.D. Fourth Armored had orders to wheel northwards
after crossing the canal, but there were no suitable roads
and the ground was unfavorable for armor, so General
Wood, the divisional commander, decided to continue eastwards and get across the River Saar before turning north.
On 24 November he forced a crossing at Fénetrange.

In the Saverne gap General Leclerc lost no time in exploiting his success, and drove straight on Strasbourg. The
only troops available to stop him were elements of the
256th V.G.D., which had just arrived in northern Alsace
from Holland, and some antiaircraft detachments and scratch
units under the commandant of Strasbourg. There was neither the time nor the means to put the city into a state of
defense, and the French tanks drove ino Strasbourg on the
morning of 24 November.

In these circumstances we decided to cancel the proposed
counterattack by Panzerlehr Division on Sarrebourg, and to
direct this division through Phalsbourg towards the Saverne
gap—a success here would enable us to cut off the French
2nd Armored Division. Panzerlehr had been bled white in
the fighting in Normandy, and at the beginning of November
was being reorganized for the Ardennes offensive. It had
thirty Mark IV's and thirty-five Panthers, and two weak panzergrenadier regiments. When we saw how weak the division was, we realized that further reinforcements would be
required to make the counterattack a success. Orders were
given for a battle group of the 25th P.G.D. to move across
from the right wing of First Army to Sarre-Union, but it
could not arrive until the 25th.

Panzerlehr had assembled at Sarre-Union on 23 November; the division was commanded by General Bayerlein, a
veteran of the Western Desert. Although two battalions of
infantry and two assault gun batteries had not arrived, the
division began its advance at 1600 that afternoon. On the
morning of 24 November, Panzerlehr ran into the flank cover
of the XVth Corps to the northeast of Sarrebourg—made
up of reconnaissance troops and part of the 44th U.S. Division. Bayerlein might well have broken through to the Sarrebourg–Saverne road, but unfortunately was taken in flank

by the 4th U.S. Armored Division, which as I have explained had forced its way across the Saar at Fénetrange. Heavy fighting developed on 24–25 November; General Eisenhower had visited the front on the 24th and consented to a proposal by Patton that the XVth Corps should discontinue its eastward advance and swing north to assist his operations along the Saar. This meant that the American forces on Bayerlein's left flank were considerably strengthened, and in fact his division was threatened with envelopment on both flanks.

On the afternoon of 25 November I went personally to Bayerlein's battle headquarters and saw for myself how precarious his situation was. Concentrated artillery fire by the 44th U.S. Division was causing considerable losses, and Combat Command B of the 4th Armored Division was fighting stoutly at the village of Baerendorff. Bayerlein advised that the attack should be discontinued, and I strongly supported his request. But O.K.W. insisted that Panzerlehr persist in its hopeless task. Anyhow, on 26 November Bayerlein was forced onto the defensive, and it was fortunate that the battle group of the 25th P.G.D. was available to sustain his eastern flank. On 27 November Panzerlehr was driven back to its original start line east of Sarre-Union; O.K.W. now recalled the division for the Ardennes operation and on the night 27/28th it was relieved by the 25th P.G.D.

Thus ended our only chance of restoring the situation in northern Alsace; it is obvious that in the face of overwhelming American superiority in artillery, armor, and aircraft, we never had any prospect of success. But Eisenhower's order that the XVth Corps should swing north to support Patton, did relieve the situation in southern Alsace and enabled Nineteenth Army to establish itself firmly in the Colmar pocket. Eisenhower says in his report that our bridgehead here afterwards exerted a "profound and adverse effect" on his operations.

Defense of the West Wall

The whole front of Army Group G was under continuous pressure. The enemy was achieving important successes, but we were keeping our forces relatively intact and falling back

slowly to the West Wall; I must emphasize that throughout
these operations our object was to fight for time and so enable O.K.W. to assemble reserves for the great counteroffensive in Belgium. I think that Patton would have done better
if the 4th and the 6th Armored Divisions had been grouped
together in a single corps, reinforced possibly by the French
2nd Armored Division. These were all very experienced
formations and were ably commanded; Wood of the 4th
Armored Division proved himself an expert in armored tactics, and Leclerc showed great dash in the advance on Strasbourg. I think the Americans made a grave mistake in cou-
pling their armored divisions too closely with the infantry;
combined as a tank army under one commander, these three
armored divisions might well have achieved a decisive breakthrough.

While great battles were raging in central Lorraine, the
XXth Corps advanced from Thionville towards the lower
Saar, and was held up by the "Orscholz Barrier." This was a
strong defensive position consisting of antitank ditches and
concrete structures; the American Intelligence knew remarkably little about it and the first attempts to force a gap
were easily repulsed. Twenty-first Panzer was in mobile reserve and counterattacked effectively. On 25 November the
XXth Corps discontinued its attacks on the Orscholz Barrier
and ordered the 10th Armored Division to thrust towards
the Saar at Merzig. The Americans had made a bad mistake
in dispersing this division in isolated attacks along the corps
front, and the order to concentrate for an advance on Merzig
was given too late to achieve any important breakthrough.

On 28 November we proposed to Rundstedt that Army
Group G should be strongly reinforced and that First and
Nineteenth Armies should deliver concentric counterattacks
toward the Saverne gap in order to regain Strasbourg, and
crush the enemy's salient in this area. It seemed a practicable
operation if three panzer divisions and two infantry divisions could be made available, but O.K.W. rejected it, as
everything was now subordinated to the great gamble in the
Ardennes.

Between 28 November and 1 December there was heavy
fighting west of Saarlautern, where the 95th U.S. Division

fought its way forward against continuous counterattacks by 21st Panzer. On 1 December elements of the 95th Division entered the western part of the town, and 21st Panzer retired to the eastern bank of the Saar. Some of our infantry still retained a small bridgehead in the western suburbs, and a single bridge was left intact. It was prepared for demolition, and engineers stood ready to blow the charges.

On the afternoon of 2 December an American observation plane reported that the bridge over the Saar was still intact, and the 95th Division prepared to capture it by a *coup de main*. In the early hours of the 3rd, American infantry and engineers made a surprise crossing in assault boats, avoided detection in the fog and rain and attacked the bridge from the rear. Our garrison was overwhelmed and the bridge was captured intact. This brilliant success was rapidly exploited; the 379th U.S. Regiment crossed the Saar on the undamaged bridge and that evening had the satisfaction of capturing the first bunkers of the West Wall.

This affair caused much excitement and a great deal of moaning in high quarters. Hitler was furious and demanded a full report; he could not understand how a section of his cherished West Wall had been allowed to fall into enemy hands. O.K.W. had entirely forgotten that the West Wall had been stripped of everything that could make it formidable in favor of the ill-fated Atlantic Wall, and that in any case its fortifications were obsolete. Antitank obstacles lay immediately in front of the main line of defense, and the emplacements were too small for the new heavy antitank guns. There was no barbed wire, telephone communications did not function, and the highly complicated firing arrangements were useless because most of the troops were quite untrained. The Führer demanded a victim and General von Knobelsdorff, the highly capable commander of First Army, was sacrificed. I personally felt much affected, because I had a high regard for this very brave and distinguished officer with whom I had shared so many experiences in Russia.[9]

Anyhow, my own tenure as chief of staff of Army Group G was about to end, for on 5 December I was ordered to

---

[9] Rundstedt himself aroused Hitler's ire by describing the West Wall as a "mousetrap."

hand over my duties to Major General Helmut Staedke. It was a bitter experience for me to terminate my long and happy association with General Balck, more particularly as I knew he had nothing to do with my removal. The fact is that at this stage of the war Hitler and his entourage were conducting a veritable witchhunt and seeking everywhere for scapegoats who could be made responsible for the blunders of the Supreme Command.

I left Army Group G with great personal regret, but I had the satisfaction of knowing that we had fulfilled our role, and delayed any serious attack on the West Wall for several months. The condition of many of our divisions at the beginning of December was deplorable, but the Americans had also suffered heavy losses, and had not achieved any vital success. The operational reserves of the German Supreme Command remained intact, and with wise strategy might still have been used with considerable effect.

General Balck did not long survive me at Army Group G. The first step was a Führer order putting Nineteenth Army under the direct control of Heinrich Himmler; this was followed by various unsavory intrigues ending in Balck's dismissal in mid-December. Fortunately Guderian intervened and arranged for Balck's re-employment as commander of Sixth Army in Hungary. But it is clear that Hitler thought that the Lorraine campaign had been badly mismanaged, and showed his displeasure by dismissing all senior officers. Balck's military reputation can well survive Hitler's censure.

band was any thing to Major General Helmut Staed... was... I either experience for... to formulate my for... type inactivity will Des of think, more particul...

22: *The Final Battles*

The Ardennes Offensive

I DO NOT PROPOSE to say much about the period immediately after my relief as chief of staff of Army Group G. I was not only dismissed from my post but I was officially removed from the General Staff—the incident was typical of the period of gloom and moral lawlessness prevailing at the end of 1944. In these circumstances I went off to my family in the Warthegau and spent Christmas with them. It was certainly no time for festivity and rejoicing; I regarded the situation on the Eastern Front with grave misgiving, for it was clear that the Russian masses were gathering in overwhelming strength for an annihilating blow. I could not bear the thought of leaving my family in Eastern Germany, and took advantage of this enforced leave to arrange a refuge for them with friends north of Berlin. Indeed my dismissal was a blessing in disguise, for within three weeks the storm broke on the Vistula; the Russians flooded into Silesia and untold horrors followed in their train.

Although General Guderian was unable to restore me formally to the General Staff, he eventually got permission to re-employ me. On Boxing Day I received orders to join the 9th Panzer Division in the Ardennes; I was to report immediately at headquarters of Army Group B somewhere west of Cologne. I got there on 28 December and reported

to General Krebs, the chief of staff to Field Marshal Model.[1]
I was excited at the thought that after long years of staff
work I was to be given command of fighting men, but my
enthusiasm diminished when Krebs explained exactly what
was happening in the Ardennes.

I had known about this operation for several months; indeed our whole strategy in Alsace-Lorraine was based on
the principle of gaining time for the Ardennes offensive.
But General Balck and I were the only officers in the army
group who knew what was being planned. On Hitler's orders
every officer in the secret had to sign a document stating
that he would face drastic penalties if guilty of the slightest
breach of security. These draconian measures certainly had
an effect and when the attack was launched on 16 December
the enemy was taken completely by surprise. I do not think
that those responsible for the detailed staff work connected
with this operation have received adequate credit. The Wehrmacht achieved a surprise every bit as staggering as the one
in the same area in May, 1940, and under normal conditions
of war and with reasonable equality of force we would have
won a very great victory. Tactically speaking the Ardennes
breakthrough was the last great achievement of the German
General Staff, a stroke in the finest traditions of Gneisenau,
Moltke, and Schlieffen.

Of course, from the strategic aspect this offensive was a
desperate gamble and proved a very great mistake. When
I was in prison camp after the war General Westphal told
me that both Rundstedt and Model were strongly opposed
to Hitler's grandiose plan for a crossing of the Meuse and
a triumphant swoop on Antwerp. They warned him that the
available forces were quite inadequate for such an operation, and submitted a so-called *kleine Loesung*, aimed at
wiping out the American salient at Aachen. Such an attack
might have "bagged" fifteen divisions and enabled us to
transfer strong reserves to the East. Hitler called this solution "pusillanimous," and however much one may condemn

---

[1] Krebs was the last chief of the German General Staff and disappeared during the final fighting in Berlin. In 1941 he was military
attaché in Moscow.

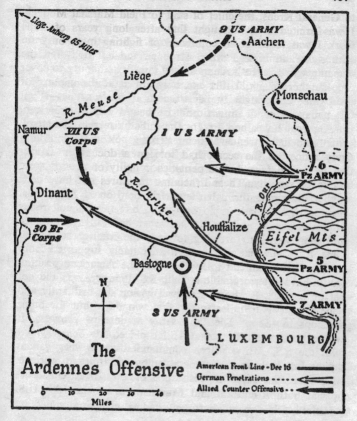

The Ardennes Offensive

American Front Line – Dec 16 ————
German Penetrations ·····
Allied Counter Offensive · ·

0   10   20   30   40
Miles

his strategy, yet it must be admitted that his will power and resolution were certainly commensurate with the magnitude of his aims.[2]

Hitler scraped together all available divisions and threw

[2] In Hitler's favor it might be said that desperate situations demanded desperate remedies, and that pure defense never won a war. But at the end of 1944 Germany had no chance of winning the war, and the only sane course was to concentrate on keeping the Russians out of our eastern provinces and to hope that even at this late hour there would be a cleavage between the United States and Russia.

them into a last gigantic effort to break the comparatively thin front held by the First United States Army from the Eifel Mountains to Monschau. Sixth S.S. Panzer Army on the right and Fifth Panzer Army on the left delivered the assault, while Seventh Army moved into Luxembourg to cover the southern flank. Hitler not only aimed at the capture of Antwerp, but sought the destruction of four armies—First Canadian, Second British, and First and Ninth American.

The foggy weather on 16 December covered the attack and blinded the tremendous air striking power of the Allies; moreover, the preparations of Manteuffel's Fifth Panzer Army had been extraordinarily thorough. His troops were brilliantly commanded and their morale could not have been higher. Sweeping through the utterly bewildered Americans, his spearheads made rapid progress along the difficult roads of the Ardennes and by 20 December had taken Houffalize and then went on thrusting towards the Meuse crossing at Dinant. If Manteuffel had been adequately supported from the north it is difficult to say how far the American position would have deteriorated, but Sixth S.S. Panzer Army did not get on so well. First S.S. Panzer Division did brilliantly and penetrated twenty miles in the first two days, but the other divisions in "Sepp" Dietrich's army made slow progress. It was a great misfortune that Hitler placed his *Schwerpunkt* with the S.S. Army, whose commander was a very gallant fighter but had no real understanding of armored warfare. Moreover, the stubborn resistance of the 101st U.S. Airborne Division and Combat Command B of the 10th U.S. Armored Division at Bastogne had a crippling effect on Manteuffel's movements.

When I reported at Army Group B, General Krebs explained that in spite of great initial success Field Marshal von Rundstedt considered the offensive a failure as early as 22 December, and Model agreed with him. Patton's Third Army had come into action on the southern flank and its vigorous attacks compelled Manteuffel to divert forces to the support of our Seventh Army. Thus the main thrust towards Dinant lost momentum. The narrow mountain roads were coated with ice and crammed with transport, and counterattacks by elements from the American Ninth Army developed on the northern flank.[3]

On 22 December Rundstedt advised Hitler to discontinue the offensive, because strong forces would soon have to be pulled out of the line in order to face the Russians in the East. Hitler would not hear of it, and heavy and resolute attacks continued for several days. But on 26 December Patton relieved Bastogne, the sky cleared over the Ardennes, and Allied air power intervened with devastating effect. On 28 December—the day I reported to Krebs—Hitler agreed to call a halt, but he would not hear of a withdrawal.

On the 29th I set off for the 9th Panzer Division, which was in the wooded hills northwest of Houffalize; the ice-bound roads glittered in the sunshine and I witnessed the uninterrupted air attacks on our traffic routes and supply dumps. Not a single German plane was in the air, innumerable vehicles were shot up and their blackened wrecks littered the roads. When I reached my headquarters I found that we were holding the most forward positions in the defensive line of Fifth Panzer Army. Looking at the situation map I noted the violent American attacks on both flanks and the grave danger facing the panzer divisions in the nose of the salient. But we were ordered to stay where we were and so we did, defending ourselvs with mobile tactics.

Most of my men were Austrians, and in spite of heavy losses their morale was still high. The panzer regiment was left with twenty tanks, and the two panzergrenadier regiments each had about four hundred men. But the artillery regiment was very strong and of high quality. We beat off the American attacks until 5 January, when orders were received to get out of this hopeless position and withdraw eastward; I was put in command of the rearguard of Fifth Panzer Army. My experiences in Russia stood me in good stead; I knew all about the problems of moving through snow and ice—a subject in which the Americans still had much to learn. By day our armored group resisted in chosen positions; all movements were carried out at night to evade

[3] On 20 December Eisenhower placed all forces on the northern flank of the salient under Montgomery's command. This wise decision was bitterly resented by many Americans.

the fighter-bombers, but even so concentric artillery fire on
our flanks inflicted considerable casualties. By mid-January the
9th Panzer Division had reached the line of the River Ourthe,
where we stood firm on the original start line of the offensive.

The results of the Ardennes fighting were more than disappointing; we had suffered excessive losses in men and
material and only gained a few weeks' respite.[4] It is true
that American forces were moved from Lorraine, and the
pressure on Army Group G slackened;[5] however, this relief
was only temporary. The same results could have been
achieved by a limited attack at Aachen, after which our operational reserves could have been switched to Poland. The
Ardennes battle drives home the lesson that a large-scale
offensive by massed armor has no hope of success against
an enemy who enjoys supreme command of the air. Our
precious reserves had been expended, and nothing was
available to ward off the impending catastrophe in the East.

Catastrophe in the East

The long-awaited Russian offensive opened on 12 January
when Koniev attacked from the Baranov bridgehead. Forty-
two rifle divisions, six armored corps, and four mechanized
brigades swept into southern Poland and headed for the vital
industrial area of upper Silesia. I remembered the bridgehead
very well, for when Balck was in command of Fourth Panzer
Army in August, 1944, he did everything possible to reduce
its size, and launched tireless and persistent counterattacks
against this most dangerous Russian lodgement. Balck fore-

---

[4] *Editor's note.* There is some uncertainty about German losses in
the Ardennes offensive. Chester Wilmot does not commit himself to
a figure, but the contemporary estimate of Eisenhower's headquarters
was 220,000. General Westphal, Rundstedt's chief of staff, estimates
25,000. *See* Siegfried Westphal, *German Army in the West* (London,
Cassell, 1952). American casualties were 77,000 including more than
20,000 prisoners. *See* John North, *Northwest Europe, 1944–1945: The
Achievement of the 21st Army Group* (London, H. M. Stationery Office,
1953), 159 and 178–79.

[5] At the beginning of January Army Group G was strong enough
to launch an offensive, which had some prospects of recapturing
Strasbourg.

saw that a breakthrough here would disrupt our entire front in southern Poland, but after our departure for the West the Russians were permitted to establish themselves permanently across the Vistula.

On 9 January Guderian had warned Hitler that "the Eastern Front is like a house of cards,"[6] but the Führer persisted in his belief that the Russian preparations were a gigantic bluff. He demanded a purely rigid defense, and removed armored reserves from Poland in a vain endeavor to relieve Budapest.[7] The result was that the Vistula front was torn to pieces in a few days; Warsaw fell on 17 January, Lodz and Cracow on the 18th, and by the 20th Zhukov's advanced columns were over the Silesian border. The frozen ground lent itself to rapid movement, and the Russian offensive was delivered with a weight and fury never yet seen in war. It was clear that their High Command had completely mastered the technique of maintaining the advance of huge mechanized armies, and that Stalin was determined to be the first to enter Berlin. On 25 January the Russians stood in front of Breslau—my native town—and by 5 February Zhukov had reached the Oder at Kuestrin, barely fifty miles from the German capital. There he was halted for a time by the skilful dispositions of General Heinrici, but in East Prussia Rokossovsky's army group smashed through to the Baltic and cut off twenty-five German divisions, while the Silesian and Hungarian fronts were kept under terrific pressure.

Like many thousands of others I followed these events with the utmost anxiety, for we all realized the horrible dangers facing our families in the East. Weeks elasped before I learned that my own wife and children had succeeded in escaping from the Soviet hordes; luckier than many, they saved nothing but their lives and a bundle of clothes they carried on their backs. Millions of Germans perished in the icy winter months of February and March, 1945; indeed a

---

[6] *Panzer Leader*, 387.

[7] On 16 January, when the whole Polish front was caving in, Hitler agreed to the transfer of Sixth Panzer Army from the West, but instead of sending it to Poland, he insisted that this army should go to Hungary. Of all his many strategic blunders, this was the most incredible.

tragedy without parallel took place. In the old German provinces of East Prussia, Pomerania, and Silesia the Russians treated the population with bestial cruelty. What happened between the Vistula and the Oder in the first months of 1945 is beyond description; nothing like it has been seen in Europe since the collapse of the Roman Empire.

Die Wacht am Rhein

On 8 February the final Allied offensive in the West opened with an attack by First Canadian Army on the Reichswald forest, in the angle between the Rhine and the Dutch frontier. This was the first phase in Eisenhower's ponderous plan for a series of blows by the various British and American armies extending down the Rhine to Strasbourg. The British 30th Corps, operating under Canadian command, smashed its way into the Reichswald under cover of the most violent bombardments ever seen in the West. Our First Parachute Army resisted with the utmost stubbornness, and for a fortnight the enemy made slow progress through this wooded and flooded country. The fighting was reminiscent of the Western Front battles of 1916–17, and just as at the Somme and Passchendaele the terrific British bombardments impeded their own advance by smashing all communications behind the German front.

On 23 February Simpson's Ninth United States Army (then operating under Montgomery's command) attacked across the River Roer in the direction of Düsseldorf and Krefeld. I was then holding an appointment as chief of staff of Manteuffel's Fifth Panzer Army, and we were in process of taking over the front from Düren to Roermond held by Fifteenth Army. Changing commands at such critical moments was a speciality of Field Marshal Model, who always wanted to have his best generals at the point of danger. Nevertheless it was a grave mistake. An army staff, and particularly the signals, must be well "run in" if it is to function with reasonable efficiency.

Ninth U.S. Army achieved an initial surprise, and on the first two days of its offensive gained numerous bridgeheads across the Roer. On 25 February a strong armored thrust

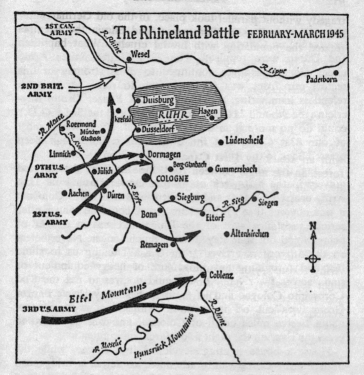

The Rhineland Battle FEBRUARY–MARCH 1945

from the Linnich bridgehead severed all contact between the 12th S.S. Corps on our right flank and the 81st Corps in our center. Twelfth S.S. suffered heavy losses, and the 338th Infantry Division, which attempted to close the gap, was caught by American tanks and flung back towards the Rhine. Panzerlehr Division from First Parachute Army was moved to München-Gladbach, and on 1 March the Americans attacked it there in great force. The town was lost that evening, and attempts to attack the American salient in flank broke down on 2 March. On 3 March American tanks broke clean through and reached the Rhine south of Düsseldorf.

Twelfth S.S. Corps had been driven into the zone of First Parachute Army; the corps passed under their command.

Meanwhile very heavy fighting was developing on the center and left of Fifth Panzer Army. At first American attempts to advance on Cologne from their bridgehead between Jülich and Düren were repulsed. The First United States Army under General Hodges continued to press strongly in this sector; our front was far too weak to stand up to such relentless hammering, and the arrival of Panzer Group Bayerlein (the 9th and 11th Panzer Divisions and the 3rd P.G.D.) could do no more than cover the retreat. By 1 March most of our 81st Corps and the 58th Panzer Corps had been pressed back to the River Erft.

Along the whole Rhine front the situation deteriorated gravely in the first week of March. On 4 March First U.S. Army crossed the Erft and smashed its way towards Cologne; it was obvious that Fifth Panzer Army could no longer offer serious resistance west of the Rhine and was in danger of being wiped out if it stayed there much longer. Nevertheless on the 5th orders arrived from O.K.W. telling us to stand fast and forbidding any movement of heavy equipment or staffs across the river. All we could do was to put the 81st Corps into Cologne and let it do its best. Bayerlein's Panzer Group was cut off in a small bridgehead at Dormagen, about twelve miles north of Cologne, and was permitted to cross the river on the night 5/6 March.

House-to-house fighting developed in Cologne, while the 58th Panzer Corps vainly attempted to retain a bridgehead south of the city. By 8 March resistance west of the Rhine had completely broken down, and the remnants of our two corps escaped across the river. As a result of Hitler's senseless orders we lost many of our remaining guns and tanks, but thanks to the initiative of local commanders a large proportion of the personnel and a certain amount of heavy equipment were saved. The army re-organized as best it could between Düsseldorf and the Sieg river; we were fortunate that the American Air Force was not very active during this period.

Meanwhile the armies on our flanks had also given way. First Parachute Army was forced back to the Rhine in the Duisburg sector, while Fifteenth Army on our left was unfortunate enough to lose the bridge at Remagen on 9 March.

The importance of this incident has been unduly magnified; the American High Command made no immediate attempt to exploit success here, and at first was content to put four divisions into the bridgehead and tell them to hang on. Moreover, at this stage it would have been easy for the Ninth U.S. Army to force a crossing north of Düsseldorf; however, Montgomery forbade it and Eisenhower supported him.[8] There is no doubt that Allied strategy was not on a high level at this period of the war; it was rigid, inflexible, and tied to preconceived plans. The whole German defense on the lower Rhine was collapsing, but the Allied leaders would not allow their subordinates to exploit success. Everything had to wait until Montgomery had prepared an elaborate set-piece attack and was ready to cross the river according to plan. Thus Field Marshal Model's Army Group B was given a new lease on life and the long agony in the West was prolonged for a few weeks.

However, on the middle Rhine the Allies got on faster, because of the initiative of Generals Bradley and Patton. The American army group commander chafed at Eisenhower's rigid control, and was inclined to let Patton have his head. On 5 March Third U.S. Army attacked in the Eifel Mountains and met with immediate and brilliant success. On 7 March Patton reached the Rhine near Coblenz; a week later he crossed the Moselle and drove through the Hunsrueck mountains into the Palatinate. His attack coincided with a heavy onslaught by Patch's Seventh U.S. Army against the West Wall between the Moselle and the Rhine. These two American armies crushed our First Army in the open plains south of Mainz, and very few survived to cross the Rhine. On the night 22/23 March Patton seized his first bridgehead on the right bank south of Mainz.

During this period Fifth Panzer Army was getting ready to meet the inevitable attack on the Ruhr. We anticipated a pincer movement, with a strong crossing between Duisburg and Düsseldorf, combined with a thrust from the Remagen bridgehead. Our sector included the city of Düsseldorf and extended along the Rhine as far as Siegburg. Twelfth S.S.

Corps was on the right, the 81st Corps in the center, and the
58th Panzer Corps on the left. All had suffered crushing
losses, and the 12th S.S. brought virtually no heavy equipment across the Rhine. Everything possible was done to fill
the gaps in the infantry units, and replacements were obtained from disbanded Volkssturm, antiaircraft, and artillery
regiments. To a certain extent our numerical losses were
made good, but the new drafts had no wish to serve as infantry, and in any case had received no training worthy of
the name. The failure of the Ardennes offensive and the
Russian invasion of eastern Germany had an adverse effect
on the morale of officers and men, although the majority
continued to do their duty loyally and the standard of discipline remained high until the final surrender.

General von Manteuffel was ordered to take over an army
on the Eastern Front, and Colonel General Harpe replaced
him; we exerted ourselves to the utmost during the fortnight's respite. Apart from filling the gaps in personnel, all
rearward services, headquarters, and antiaircraft units were
combed for weapons, and headquarters staffs were left with
nothing except a few pistols. We concentrated our defense
measures on the right flank, as a crossing was anticipated in
the Düsseldorf sector. Divisional sectors on the front of the
12th S.S. Corps were kept as narrow as possible, and the
remnants of Panzerlehr Division were kept in reserve behind
their front. We also paid attention to the left flank at Siegburg, for we had every reason to expect a thrust here from
the Remagen bridgehead. On this flank the 3rd P.G.D. was to
be in mobile reserve, but we were compelled to give up this
division on 15 March. In planning our system of defense,
we sacrificed depth in order to deploy all available weapons
to dominate the Rhine, for everyone realized that this water
barrier afforded the last opportunity for an effective resistance. The mainstay of the front was provided by the light
and medium antiaircraft guns, now withdrawn from the
Ruhr and sited in a ground role. Manned by resolute gunners
and well-provided with ammunition, they were the main factor in our fire plan.

A second line of defense was built up along the Düsseldorf–Cologne *Autobahn,* and we also pushed reconnaissance patrols across the Rhine to learn what we could of the enemy's intentions. We found that the Americans were moving their forces away from Cologne towards Bonn and the Remagen bridgehead. Attempts by Fifteenth Army to eliminate this position failed, and the Americans steadily enlarged their foothold. Strong concentrations were also evident in the Düsseldorf sector. During the period 8/23 March we were ordered to give up four divisions and a battle group of Panzerlehr, which meant that all calculations had to be adjusted, and we were forced to keep on stretching out our divisional sectors. Indeed we lost all our mobile troops to Fifteenth Army, which certainly needed them against the Remagen bridgehead. Apart from moderate artillery fire the situation on our front remained quiet.

I feel proud of the efforts made by Fifth Panzer Army during this heartbreaking period. In spite of the collapse on the Eastern Front, the hopeless strategic situation, and the breakdown of the normal system of transport and supply, yet the various headquarters and staffs continued to function with the same coolness and efficiency which distinguished the Wehrmacht in its greatest days. We felt fairly confident about holding our front, but the situation on both flanks was extremely precarious. Fifth Panzer Army had hardly any panzers under command, and virtually no reserves to protect the wings.

On 10 March Field Marshal Kesselring relieved Field Marshal von Rundstedt in the nominal post of Commander in Chief West. He greeted his staff with the remark: "Well, gentlemen, I am the new V.3."

The Ruhr Pocket

On the evening of 23 March a tremendous air and artillery bombardment descended on the front of First Parachute Army. The British Second Army forced a passage at Wesel, and the Ninth U.S. Army crossed between Wesel and Duisburg. The building of bridges went on rapidly and both armies pushed their way well across the Rhine. Indeed there was little to impede them except the wreckage created by their own bombardments.

The front of Fifth Panzer Army was not attacked, but on the 23rd General Hodges' First U.S. Army broke out of Remagen and reached the Sieg on both sides of Siegburg. On the 24th the Americans did not continue their northward advance but swung east towards Altenkirchen. We were ordered to send an infantry regiment from the 12th V.G.D. to assist Fifteenth Army, but First U.S. Army was operating in great strength and made steady progress towards the east. Meanwhile Patton's Third Army was driving forward on Hodges' right flank. Eisenhower fully appreciated the significance of this sector, and on the 28th First Army swung northeast towards Kassel and Paderborn in order to cut off the Ruhr from central Germany. On the same day Montgomery's armor was breaking out into the Westphalian plain.

So far the enemy had not attempted anything between Duisburg and the Sieg, and it was clear that he was quite content to let Fifth Panzer Army and the left wing of First Parachute Army remain in this sector. Accordingly we proposed to Field Marshal Model that only covering parties should be left along the Rhine, and that the bulk of the troops should be withdrawn in an endeavor to restore the position in the Sieg valley. Model agreed that Fifth Panzer Army should send reinforcements to the 53rd Corps then on the south bank of the Sieg in the Eitorf area, and he also ordered us to relieve First Parachute Army on the front south of Duisburg. But these measures were futile; the armored divisions of First U.S. Army were handled with great dash and confidence and covered fifty-five miles in a single day to capture Paderborn on 1 April. That afternoon First and Ninth Armies joined hands, and the encirclement of the "Ruhr pocket" was completed. More than three hundred thousand men, comprising the greater part of Army Group B, had been caught in the trap.

We pointed out to Model that supplies would not last more than three weeks, and recommended a break-out to the southeast with all available forces. But the field marshal was tied by Hitler's orders, which bade him regard the Ruhr as a fortress. During the first week of April we regrouped; the 12th S.S. Corps held the Rhine front from Duisburg to Siegburg with the 3rd Parachute Division and police and security battalions, while the 58th Panzer Corps defended the line of the Sieg with the remnants of seven divisions. All was quiet along the Rhine, but the Americans made repeated efforts to establish themselves north of the Sieg. On 3 April they gained a bridgehead at Betzdorf, but near Siegen the 12th V.G.D. drove them back across the river and captured several hundred prisoners.

The greater part of Army Group B was now pent up between the Ruhr and the Sieg, and the circumstances could not have been more depressing. The fog and cold of winter still hung over the land, and the gaunt and broken cities of the Ruhr formed a fitting background to the last act of this tragedy. The great heaps of coal and slag, the shattered buildings, the twisted railway tracks, the ruined bridges, all made their contribution to the gloomy scene. I have seen many battlefields, but none so strange as the great industrial complex of the Ruhr during the final dissolution of Army Group B.

At 0500 on 6 April the XVIIIth U.S. Airborne Corps opened a major attack across the Sieg. Our resistance was stubborn, and on the whole the Americans were contained a few miles north of the river—the 12th V.G.D. again distinguished itself. But on the eastern flank the IIIrd U.S. Corps made rapid headway against the depleted units of Fifteenth Army, and we soon lost contact with the troops on our left. Moreover, a heavy attack developed on the northern sector of the pocket, and Duisburg fell on 10 April.

On the afternoon of 9 April the Americans had entered Siegburg, and on the 11th the 13th U.S. Armored Division thrust northwards from this town. Third Parachute Division resisted heroically, and the stationary antiaircraft guns east of Cologne knocked out about thirty American tanks.[9] By

---

[9] The *Report of Operations* of First U.S. Army (p. 72) relates how our 88-mm's slowed up the advance of the 13th Armored Division. It is interesting to see how this gun continued to plague the enemy's tanks right up to the end of the war. Yet the 88 was very conspicuous and extremely vulnerable to high-explosive fire.

the evening of the 11th the Americans had reached the outskirts of Berg-Gladbach. On 13 April resistance on the southeastern sector of the pocket crumbled, and the remnants of the 183rd Infantry Division were encircled at Gummersbach. Third U.S. Corps thrust vigorously through Lüdenscheid towards Hagen, and cut the pocket in two on 14 April—Fifth Panzer Army and the 63rd Corps were isolated in the western half. Apart from holding on to particular towns and strongpoints a co-ordinated defense was becoming impossible.

During the last days of the struggle I had many private conversations with Field Marshal Model. He was an interesting character—forceful and ironical—and was well used to desperate battles; indeed his reputation had been built up by his uncanny gift for improvisation. Time and again he had succeeded in restoring apparently hopeless situations; he had pulled the Eastern Front together after the frightful collapse in June and July, 1944, and he had done the same in the West after Normandy. During April he repeatedly visited our headquarters, and I had the feeling that he was wrestling with himself to find a solution to some inner conflict. Like all senior commanders he was faced with an insoluble dilemma; as a highly qualified officer he saw the hopelessness of further resistance, but on the other hand he was bound in duty and honor to his superiors and subordinates. The German soldier went on doing his duty to the very last with inimitable discipline. During this phase I visited many units and never saw anything like dissolution or mutiny, although even the humblest private could see that everything would be over in a few days.

Model never digressed from the strict path of military discipline, but as a true servant of Germany he blunted the edge of senseless commands, and sought to minimize unnecessary destruction. Hitler had ordered a "scorched earth" policy and wanted us to wreck every factory and mining plant in the Ruhr, but Model limited himself to purely military demolitions. The field marshal was determined to preserve the industrial heart of Germany; no longer did he fight stubbornly for every building, and he disregarded the orders issued by the Führer in a last frenzy of destructive mania.

Model wondered whether he should initiate negotiations with the enemy, and put this question to me frankly. We both rejected it on military grounds. After all Field Marshal Model knew no more about the general situation than the simplest company commander in his army group. His ignorance sprang from "Führer Command No. 1" of 13 January 1940, which laid down that "no officer or authority must know more than is absolutely necessary for the execution of his particular task." Model did not know whether political negotiations were going on, and he was fully sensible of the argument that the Western armies must keep on fighting to the last in order to protect the rear of our comrades in the East, who were involved in a desperate struggle to cover the escape of millions of German women and children, then fleeing from the Russian hordes.

On the evening of 15 April orders were issued that small groups should be formed under selected officers, and should try to find a way through to the East. Soldiers without weapons or ammunition were to allow themselves to be overrun. On 17 April Army Group B ordered the discharge of the younger and older classes from the armed forces and the cessation of further fighting. On the 18th the field marshal committed suicide.

In all the remnants of twenty-one divisions were captured in the Ruhr pocket. The Americans claimed 317,000 prisoners, including twenty-four generals and one admiral; this was the largest capitulation in history with the exception of the surrender of Marshal Budenny's army group around Kiev in September, 1941.

Personally I was not prepared to be put "in the bag" if I could avoid it, and accompanied by a small group of officers I made my way eastwards. We covered more than 250 miles, lying up during the day and moving by night, but our hope of joining the Eastern armies proved vain. On 3 May we were captured by American troops at Höxter Wesel.

I have no wish to recall the circumstances of this extremely bitter episode in my life—everything that I had struggled and fought for was crumbling into dust. At the time the outlook seemed utterly black and hopeless, but I now appreciate the truth of Erzberger's remark to Foch in the railway coach at Compiègne: "A nation of seventy millions suffers, but it does not die."

23: *In Retrospect*

THE OFFICERS OF the German General Staff were not released from captivity for two and a half years, but this period behind barbed wire was not quite barren. While in prison camp I met men like General Warlimont, Keitel's deputy in the Supreme Command, Count Schwerin, the minister of finance, Backe, the state secretary for nutrition, representatives of heavy industry and senior Naval and Luftwaffe officers. I had long discussions with our famous glider pilot, Hanna Reisch, who piloted the Storch in which General Ritter von Greim flew into Berlin, when the greater part of the city was already in Russian hands. She gave me a dramatic description of the last days of Hitler in the Bunker in the Reichs Chancellery. I also talked with Hitler's private medical adviser, Professor von Hasselbach, and learned much about the personal life of the Führer. I made notes on all important points immediately after these conversations.

Not until we were behind barbed wire did we learn of the misdeeds of the Supreme Authority, deeds which shook us to the core and made our cheeks burn with shame. It was only then that I learned the truth about Rommel's tragic end.

Thanks to the numerous discussions and talks with men in Hitler's immediate entourage or with those in responsible positions in our war machine and industrial economy, I was able to form a clear conception of the general course of the struggle. After I was released, my conclusions were deepened and rounded off by the study of material from British and American sources.

During captivity one question was continually asked and constantly repeated—the opinion was voiced on many sides that treason in high circles was responsible for Germany's defeat. In my opinion we owe it to our dead comrades in arms and to those who did their duty to the last bitter end, to examine this question with the greatest care. We must decide whether Germany ever had a real chance of victory and whether treason prevented her achieving it.

On can only answer this question by taking account of the personality and character of Adolf Hitler, who as absolute ruler of the state carried the main responsibility and who in military matters exercised direct and immediate influence down to the placing of divisions, regiments, and battalions.

To glorify Hitler as an infallible genius, whose gigantic designs were frustrated by treachery, or to condemn him as the greatest criminal of all time, would be equally irresponsible and superficial.

It is an undeniable fact that Hitler was an incredibly clever man, with a memory far beyond the average. He had terrific will power and was utterly ruthless; he was an orator of outstanding quality, able to exercise an hypnotic influence on those in his immediate surroundings. In politics and diplomacy he had an extraordinary flair for sensing the weakness of his adversaries, and for exploiting their failings to the full. He used to be a healthy man, a vegetarian who neither smoked nor drank, but he undermined his constitution by taking sleeping powders and pep pills, chiefly during the later years of the war. Although his health deteriorated, his mind remained amazingly alert and active until the very end.[1] It is beyond the scope of this book to discuss the reasons for his political triumphs in the prewar period; his success was made possible by the misguided and wrongful policy adopted by the Allies after World War I; they committed

[1] See the details of his military conferences preserved in *Hitler Directs his War*.

every possible blunder from the Versailles Treaty and the occupation of the Ruhr to the incomprehensible weakness and lack of foresight in the Munich period. Extraordinary political victories completely upset Hitler's balance and judgment; he never remembered Bismarck's maxim: "History teaches how far one may safely go."

In 1939 Hitler decided on war with Poland because he was convinced that the conflict could be localized. The guarantee given by Great Britain to Poland was underestimated; indeed it was never taken seriously. Dr. Paul Schmidt has described Hitler's reaction to the British declaration of war: "Hitler was petrified and utterly disconcerted. After a while he turned to Ribbentrop and asked 'What now?'" Before the declaration of war there were no serious conversations with our one and only ally. Dr. Schmidt quotes a letter from Mussolini to Hitler written on 25 August 1939, in which the Duce pointed out that Italy was not ready for war. The Italian Air Force only had fuel for three months.

Thus the war was started, conceived, and born by the decision of a moment; Hitler had been dazzled by earlier successes and was given a misleading picture of the external situation by his amateur diplomatists. From every point of view—military, naval and economic—Germany was far from ready for total war.[2]

Although the German Army was able to cope with the tasks of 1939 and 1940, the preparations of the Luftwaffe had little relation to the realities of our position. During 1939 it was just possible to maintain the necessary front-line aircraft of the Luftwaffe, but there were no reserve stocks of any kind, and even spare parts were in short supply. These deficiencies were not apparent as long as the Luftwaffe was only faced with limited tasks. Losses incurred were replaced by the factories, although with difficulty. The gravity of the situation first became apparent after the Battle

---

[2] On 3 September 1939, Admiral Raeder, the C. in C. Navy, declared in a memorandum: "Today the war against France and England broke out, the war which, according to the Führer's previous assertions, we had no need to expect before about 1944" (*Führer's Conferences on Naval Affairs*).

of Britain, when the Luftwaffe had to cope with a two-front war.

The year 1939 ended with Germany in a very strong position politically. The military alliance with Italy and the non-aggression pact with Russia safeguarded our flank and rear. Nevertheless Britain and France could count on the support of the United States, and it was clear that the great majority of states were hardening their attitude towards Hitler and his claims. A marked deterioration became apparent in Germany's economic situation.

The year 1940 witnessed sensational military successes, but brought no improvement in the political outlook. The Tripartite Pact of Germany, Italy, and Japan, did indeed give the illusion of a world-wide alliance, but the practical aid we received from these two allies was relatively small. Italy's entry into the war was a misfortune; strategically she embarrassed Britain but economically she made innumerable demands, which Germany was in no position to meet. Russia —not a member of the Tripartite Pact—became considerably more powerful through the annexation of eastern Poland, Bessarabia, the Bukovina and the Baltic states, and her so-called sphere of interest was dangerously extended. Hitler's peace offer to Britain in July, 1940, was ignored—his promises and guarantees no longer carried any weight in the West. On the contrary, Great Britain's will to resist was immeasurably strengthened by her victory in the Battle of Britain and the fiasco of our abortive invasion. America's aid was already becoming a serious factor in the European struggle, and foreshadowed her armed intervention.

Seen from a purely military viewpoint, 1940 was a triumphant year for Germany. By occupying Denmark and Norway we forestalled similar action by Great Britain and adequately covered our northern flank; moreover, German economy was now assured of the supply of crude iron and nickel which we needed so desperately. The main offensive against France was a sensational success, staggering our own Supreme Command, but Hitler's interference with Brauchitsch's orders on 24 May halted the German armor in front of Dunkirk, and allowed 215,000 British and 120,000

French troops to escape. Chester Wilmot is quite right when he says that "Germany's defeat began at Dunkirk."[3]

An invasion of Britain was ordered, prepared, postponed, ordered again, and finally cancelled. The reasons for abandoning Operation *Sea Lion* were the absolute British naval superiority and the Battle of Britain, during which 1,733 German aircraft were lost between 10 July and 31 October, 1940. The Luftwaffe never recovered from this stunning blow. It was disquieting that our defeat was largely due to British scientific superiority in radar; we never caught up with them in this sphere, and the collapse of the U-boat campaign in 1943 was due to the same cause.

But even after 1940 there were still possibilities of ending the war if Hitler had been prepared to make some sacrifices and had demonstrated a sincere desire for peace. Instead the *Barbarossa* plan was producd, and preparations were begun for the attack on Russia. It is futile to speculate on what might have happened and how things might have developed if instead of invading Russia, we had thrown all our weight into the Mediterranean area, i.e. Malta and Africa. Hitler's continental outlook was averse to solutions of that kind.

The political balance sheet of 1941 showed a considerable deterioration in Germany's position. When Russia and Yugoslavia concluded their pact of friendship, a pact diametrically opposed to German interests, it was clearly and glaringly demonstrated that the German-Russian policy of *rapprochment* was devoid of any basis or foundation. Spain refused to come over to Germany's side, and the planned attack on Gibraltar fell away. The publication of the Atlantic Charter provided direct evidence of the closest co-operation between the U.S.A. and Great Britain. With the entry of Japan and America the war became world-wide and all hope of localizing the conflagration in Europe disappeared.

Although 1941 again brought tactical victories for German arms, the strategic situation worsened considerably. Among our military successes may be counted Rommel's victories in Africa and the rapid solution of the Balkan problem by a victory over Yugoslavia and Greece. The oc-

[3] *The Struggle for Europe*, 18.

cupation of Crete by German troops brought Great Britain's influence in the Mediterranean to the lowest level since 1797, and our U-boat operations against supplies shipped to the British Isles began to take effect.

According to the British official naval history,[4] Axis warships and aircraft sank shipping at the following rate:

    1939   222 ships comprising 755,397 tons.
    1940   1,059 ships comprising 3,991,641 tons.
    1941   1,289 ships comprising 4,328,558 tons.

The combined action of submarines and aircraft offered Germany a real chance of strangling Great Britain, but Hitler had not the patience for this sort of war. On 22 June 1941 our armies entered Russia. From that day the character of the struggle underwent a decisive change: a task had been undertaken which was beyond our available means— the two-front war had been unleashed.

It is true that at first these gigantic operations, well conceived and brilliantly executed, went according to plan, and the Russians suffered crushing defeats along the whole front from the Baltic to the Black Sea. The Red Army, crushed and decimated in the opening battles, was unable to hold all the vital points on the long front. Strong Russian forces, however, had been concentrated in the Moscow area, in order to protect the moral, economic, and military center of Russian power. Most of the German military leaders were of the opinion that it was of decisive importance to attack Moscow and defeat the Russian armies there while they were still being built up. But again at this decisive moment Hitler interfered—as he had done at Dunkirk—and decreed that the battle for Kiev must now be fought, and Marshal Budenny's army group annihilated. The aim was achieved but the continuation of the attack on Moscow was delayed for several precious weeks. When the drive on the capital was eventually resumed, it was too late: the mud and slush of autumn and an exceptionally early winter threw a

---

[4] Roskill, *The War at Sea*, 615–16. The figures include losses from unknown causes.

shield in front of Zhukov's battered armies, and stopped our advance in sight of the towers of the Kremlin. Completely unequipped for winter fighting the German troops suffered grievous and irreplaceable losses.

This was the turning point of the war; from then on victory was beyond our power.

The tragedy of the German attack on Moscow was followed by another of a different but no less decisive kind. The commander in chief of the army, Field Marshal von Brauchitsch, was dismissed from his post, and Hitler became commander in chief. From that moment no more general directives were issued to army group and army commanders, but orders were given which went into the smallest and most trifling details.

By the end of 1941 German war economy was in a serious plight. We did not have the oil supplies necessary for waging war on a world-wide scale; the Eastern campaign was making colossal demands for vehicles, armor, antitank guns, and spare parts. Moreover, the lend-lease pact was having a serious effect—Russia was receiving replacements and equipment from the inexhaustible resources of the British Empire and the U.S.A.

By the end of 1941 it had become impossible for Germany to win the war, yet diplomatic skill and wise strategy might still have achieved a "draw." The war dragged on into 1942, but the time for blitzkrieg tactics had passed, never to return. By the end of the year the initiative was in the hands of the enemy and Germany was forced onto the defensive.

Our foreign policy was cramped and restricted by events, and not even remarkable military successes could ward off Germany's fate. Rommel's attack in Africa broke down at Alamein. The Allied landings in Morocco and Algeria wrenched the initiative from German hands and gave it to the Allied leaders; by May, 1943, North Africa was lost.

In Russia the German summer offensive of 1942 might have achieved significant results if Hitler had not wavered between two main objectives—Stalingrad and the Caucasus. The result was that his armies reached the Caucasus, but not the oilfields, and got to the Volga at Stalingrad without capturing the city. So far from being defeated, the Russian armies were able to counterattack with a superiority in men and material never known before.

At the beginning of 1943 the tragedy of Stalingrad wiped out Sixth Army. The summer offensive towards Kursk failed, and the Allies landed in Sicily. The Russian counter-offensive hurled our southern armies across the Dnieper, and German strength ebbed away in bitter defensive battles. At Casablanca the Allies formulated their demand for "unconditional surrender"—diplomacy was dead, and brute force had taken over.

The year 1944 brought further crises for Germany and more successes for the Allies on all fronts. Germany's fate was sealed by the successful invasion of Normandy in June. The German front in the East was rolled up; everywhere war was carried across the German frontier and only the cautious strategy of Eisenhower and the political ambitions of Stalin delayed the decision until May, 1945. At no time during 1944 and 1945 was there the slightest possibility of ending the war victoriously.

Hitler's method of direct command hastened Germany's defeat. Orders to "fight for every foot" had disastrous effects. But apart from strategy, his methods of control affected the whole war machine. In democratic states the branches of the armed forces and the various aspects of war economy and industry were firmly co-ordinated, but in Germany there was a strange separation into independent powers. The army, the navy, the air force, the S.S., the Organization Todt, the N.S.D.A.P., the commissariats, the numerous branches of economy, all worked separately, but all received their orders directly from Hitler.

At home and on the front these branches ceased to function together and began to work on their own, the one regardless of the needs of the other. The reason for this strange and sinister phenomenon was undoubtedly Hitler's craving for power and his distrust of any independent force. The old motto, "divide and rule," was carried to its logical absurdity. To keep the army in its place the Waffen-S.S. was created.

Undoubtedly German manpower was insufficient for a world war and the numerical strength of the army began to dwindle from the winter of 1941. Replacements could not keep pace with losses.

The following figures show losses and replacements of the army groups on the Eastern Front from December, 1941, until September, 1942.

Army Groups	Losses	Replacements
South	547,300	415,100
Center	765,000	481,400
North	375,800	272,800
	1,688,100	1,169,300

Thus replacements covered only 69 per cent of requirements. In the following year the replacement situation became even more unfavorable and during the three months from July to October, 1943, losses and replacements in the armies of the East were as follows:

Month	Losses	Replacements
July	197,000	90,000
August	225,000	77,000
September	232,000	112,000
	654,000	279,000

During these months replacements covered barely 43 per cent of losses. The numerical strength of the armies in the East in June, 1941, was nearly 3,000,000 men, but by the end of the war it had dwindled to 1,500,000.

The German armament industry was not responsible for our defeat, and by superhuman efforts succeeded in increasing its output until the autumn of 1944, despite enemy air raids starting on a large scale in 1942 and continuing with mounting intensity until the end of the war. But there was too much experiment and not enough clarity in our planning. Even where German science gave us a clear lead, as in the case of high-speed submarines or jet aircraft, the advantage was frittered away by lack of co-ordination and muddled thinking at the top.

In his depositions before the international tribunal at Nürnberg, Speer, the minister for armament production, was asked when he regarded the war as lost. He replied:

From the armament point of view not until the autumn of 1944, for I succeeded up to that time, in spite of bombing attacks, in maintaining a constant rise in production. If I may express it in figures, this was so great that in the year 1944 I could completely re-equip 130 infantry divisions and 40 armoured divisions. That involved new equipment for 2 million men. This figure would have been 30 per cent. higher had it not been for the bombing attacks. We reached our production peak for the entire war in August 1944 for munitions; in September 1944 for aircraft; and in December 1944 for ordnance and the new U-boats. The new weapons were to be put into use a few months later, probably in February or March of 1945. I may mention only the jet planes which had already been announced in the press, the new U-boats, the new antiaircraft installations, et cetera. Here too, however, bombing attacks so retarded the mass production of these new weapons—which in the last phase of the war might have changed the situation—that they could no longer be used against the enemy in large numbers. All of these attempts were fruitless, however, since from 12 May 1944 on our fuel plants became targets for concentrated attacks from the air.

This was catastrophic. 90 per cent. of the fuel was lost to us from that time on. The success of these attacks meant the loss of the war as far as production was concerned; for our new tanks and jet planes were of no use without fuel.[5]

Another deposition made by Speer was also of great interest:

QUESTION: Herr Speer, how was it possible that you and the other co-workers of Hitler, despite your realization of the situation, still tried to do everything possible to continue the war?

SPEER: In this phase of the war Hitler deceived all of us. From the summer of 1944 on he circulated, through Ambassador Hewel of the Foreign Office, definite statements to the effect that conversations with foreign powers had been started. Generaloberst Jodl has confirmed this to me here in Court. In this way, for instance, the fact that several visits were paid

[5] *Proceedings International Tribunal at Nuremberg, XVI*, 484. This raises the question of what would have happened to the Red Army if Hitler had captured the Caucasus oilfields in 1942, and what might happen in the future if these oilfields are eliminated by atomic attack.

to Hitler by the Japanese Ambassador was interpreted to mean that through Japan we were carrying on conversations with Moscow; or else Minister Neubacher, who was here as a witness, was reported to have initiated conversations in the Balkans with the United States; or else the former Soviet Ambassador in Berlin was alleged to have been in Stockholm for the purpose of initiating conversations.

The continuous increase in armament production until the autumn of 1944 is indeed an amazing fact. Yet it was not enough to satisfy the requirements of the front, and every front-line soldier will confirm this sad fact. The terrific fighting in Russia and Normandy and the catastrophic retreats in the summer of 1944 led to losses which the home front could not replace. The breakdown came—according to Speer—when the supply of fuel stopped and when communications were disrupted by the devastating air attacks of the Anglo-Americans. Even though the necessary equipment was available in Germany, it could no longer reach the front line—at least in sufficient quantities.

On the other side the Allies had everything they needed, and so great were the resources at the command of the United States and British Empire, that they were able to provide immense quantities of war material for Russia. Even so, Russian production of artillery and tanks must have outstripped that of the Western Allies.

The overwhelming economic superiority of the enemy, and our inability to counter his air attacks, left us with no chance of bringing the war to a victorious conclusion. I am not blaming Germany's industry; its achievements were prodigious, but were still quite inadequate when weighed against the combined resources of the United States, the British Empire, and the Soviet Union. For Germany to challenge these three powers simultaneously was madness, and could only lead to one result.

The assertion that the war could have been won if it had not been for treason and sabotage has been disproved by the facts quoted above. If we concede that sabotage actually took place, then we must admit that this alleged sabotage may have hastened the loss of the war but was in no sense a major cause of our defeat. It is alleged that the saboteurs belonging to the resistance movement did everything in their power to bring about the defeat of Germany. They are said to have hampered the armament industry and issued false orders, to have had contact with the enemy, and to have kept back replacements from the front-line troops. But the entire literature on the resistance movement, including the productions of hostile writers, does not contain a single proof that the fighting front was ever sabotaged intentionally. There were isolated cases shortly before the war broke out, at the beginning of the campaign in France, and during the last months of the war, when members of the resistance movement made political contacts with the enemy to achieve a special aim. That was all.

General Halder says in this connexion:

My Commander-in-chief and I fought against Hitler, when it was a question of preventing him from taking decisions which, in our considered opinion, were disadvantageous for Germany and the army. But never was anything kept back or not delivered which was needed by the fighting troops in order to fulfil their difficult and heavy tasks. We never did anything—for reasons of resisting Hitler—which might have harmed the man in the front line.[6]

It has been alleged that during the last months of the war replacements did not arrive, that infantry equipment was sent to panzer divisions, and that the infantry received tanks and fuel intended for the armor. Anyone who served in the front line will readily understand the reason for this; during the last months of the war communications were entirely disrupted, so that it was virtually impossible for any replacement to reach its destination; battle group commanders laid hands on whatever came their way and numerous trains were held up. Furthermore we know very well that replacements, weapons and fuel destined for the front were held back by gauleiters who used these things for their own Volkssturm.

It remains to define our attitude towards the events of 20

[6] Peter Bor, Gespräche mit Halder (Wiesbaden, Limes Verlag, 1950).

July 1944—the attempt on Hitler's life. I personally heard of it over the wireless during the heavy defensive battles in the Lemberg area. The reaction at the front was unambiguous. We were dumbfounded to learn that a German officer had been capable of making this attempt, particularly at a time when the men on the Eastern Front were waging a life and death struggle to stem the advance of the Russian hordes. We did know of the abuses perpetrated by the "brown shirt" authorities, particularly by the "Reichs" commissars, of the arrogant behavior of these people, and of the misdeeds of the S.S. *Einsatz* commandos, although the presence of these doubtful characters was seldom felt in the vicinity of the front line. The party authorities were not very popular with the fighting troops. During quiet periods there was a lot of grumbling about these "gentlemen," and it was accepted by everyone that these things would have to be set right after the war. Nevertheless the front-line soldiers—and we officers of the *Truppen* General Staff are proud to belong to them—were disgusted to hear of the attempt on Hitler's life and indignantly refused to approve of it; the fighting soldier did his duty to the bitter end.

Not until we were behind barbed wire did we learn of the wider reasons behind this attempt on Hitler's life. I must admit that the men responsible for it were moved by the highest idealism and the deepest realization of their responsibility for the welfare of our country. Colonel Count Stauffenberg and his associates in O.K.H. realized that Hitler's regime would lead Germany to catastrophe. They sincerely believed that the elimination of Hitler would spare Germany further bloodshed. But if the attempt on Hitler's life had been successful it would have resulted in bloody internal strife with the S.S. formations. Nor would any success have been achieved in the sphere of foreign affairs. The enemy had agreed upon an "unconditional surrender" policy, quite regardless of whether Germany had a national-socialist government or not. By enunciating this policy Roosevelt strengthened the will to resist of every German, thus committing exactly the same mistake made by the German political leaders in Russia, who did not differentiate between Communism and the Russian people. Had the attempt on

Hitler's life been successful the German nation would have held the German officer corps, and in particular the German General Staff, responsible for the catastrophe.

In any case we would do well to remember that the war was not lost by the men of 20 July 1944.

Conclusion

THIS BOOK HAS been concerned entirely with war, and naturally as a German officer I am deeply concerned for the honor and prestige of German arms. Whatever the verdict of history on Nazi Germany, it will have to concede that in 1939–45 the Wehrmacht accomplished extraordinary feats, and worthily upheld the great fighting traditions of the German nation. But I have no wish to glorify the conflict, or stimulate thoughts of bitterness and revenge. On the contrary the grave problems facing the nations of Western Europe demand a realistic approach to the question of peace and war.

In this book I have attempted to set out the main tactical lessons emerging from the war of 1939–45 and in particular to stress the dangers which we all face from the immense and well-organized armies of the Soviet Union. The time has come to think seriously about the condition of Europe; indeed, if our civilization is to survive, the old enemies among the Western Powers must forget their past and look to the future. I hope most earnestly that in this book I have made some contribution to the cause of European defense and mutual understanding.

Appendix

1 April 1924—30 Sept. 1935.	Seventh Cavalry Regiment.
1 Oct. 1935—30 Sept. 1937.	War Academy.
1 Oct. 1937—31 Dec. 1939.	Third General Staff Officer (Ic) 3rd Corps; Polish Campaign.
1 Jan 1940—31 Aug. 1940.	First General Staff Officer (Ia) 197th Infantry Division; Campaign in France.
1 Sept. 1940—28 Feb. 1941.	Third General Staff Officer (Ic) First Army.
1 Mar. 1941—31 May 1941.	Third General Staff Officer, Second Army; Balkan Campaign.
1 June 1941—15 Sept. 1942.	Third General Staff Officer (as from 3 April 1942 deputy 1st General Staff Officer) Panzergruppe, later Panzerarmee Afrika.
20 Sept. 1942—31 Oct. 1942.	Military Hospital at Garmisch.
1 Nov. 1942—14 Aug. 1944.	Chief of General Staff, 48th Panzer Corps; Russian Campaign.
15 Aug. 1944—14 Sept. 1944.	Chief of General Staff, Fourth Panzer Army; Russian Campaign.
15 Sept. 1944—30 Nov. 1944.	Chief of General Staff, Army Group G; Campaign in the West.
1 Dec. 1944—31 Dec. 1944.	Officers' Pool of High Command Army; (O.K.H.).
1 Jan. 1945—28 Feb. 1945.	Attached to 9th Panzer Division; Campaign in the West.
1 Mar. 1945—May 1945.	Chief of General Staff, Fifth Panzer Army; Campaign in the West.

Index

Aachen, Germany: 381, 406, 410

Abbeville, France: 21, 24

Adam, Colonel: 211

Agar-Hamilton, J. A. I. (and L. C. F. Turner): *see Crisis in the Desert*

Agedabia, North Africa: 98-104

Air power: in Western campaign (1940), 18-19, 29-30; Battle of Britain, 31, 425-27; North Africa, 95, 99, 110, 150, 162, 175-76; Malta, 150; Russia, 185-86, 188-90, 266-68, 273, 293-95, 314, 326, 363-65; Anglo-American, 332; in Western campaign (1944-45), 380, 409; effect on German war production, 432-33; *see also* Luftwaffe, Red Air Force, Royal Air Force

Airborne landings, Russians pioneers of: 365

Aisne River: 21, 25

Akhtyra, U.S.S.R.: 287

Aksay River, Battle of: 230-38

Alam Halfa, North Africa: 170-72

Alamein, El: Rommel attempts to pierce the "Line" at, 158-62; deadlock at, 163-70

Albania, 33

Alexander, Field Marshal Earl: 173

Alexejewka, U.S.S.R.: 267

Algeria: 429

Alsace-Lorraine, military operations in: *see* West

Altenkirchen, Germany: 418

Ambrosio, General: 46

Amiens, France: 24

Antelat, North Africa: 103-104

Antonescu, Marshal: 347

Antonov, U.S.S.R.: 236-37

Antwerp, Belgium: 406, 408

Ardennes offensive: 405-10

Armored warfare: *see* tanks

Arnhem, Holland: 372

Arno River: 343

Arracourt, France: 377, 380-81

Arras, France: 22

Aslagh Ridge, North Africa: 128, 132-33

Atlantic Charter: 427

Atlantic Wall: 394, 403

Attila: 362

Auchinleck, Field Marshal Sir C. J. E.: 101n.; preparations for Cyrenaica offensive, 68-69; and Rommel's thrust to the "Wire," 90; decision to hold Benghazi, 105n.; and the Gazala battles, 113, 115, 126, 129; and the fall of Tobruk, 138-40; and the Battle of Mersa Matruh, 154, 156; and the deadlock at Alamein, 164, 168-69; relieved of command, and his achievements and faults, 173

Avranches, France: 343

Baccarat, Alsace-Lorraine: 394, 395

Backe, State Secretary for Nutrition: 423

Bagramyan, Marshal: 344

Balck, General: 333, 406; and the Battle of Sedan, 17-20; and the Greek campaign, 41-44; and the battles on the Chir River, 213-15, 218-20; and the retreat to the Donetz, 245; and the action at Manutchskaya, 246, 250; and the victory at Zhitomir, 304-305, 308; tactical ability, 304-305, 373; and the victory at Radomyshl, 312, 314-15, 318; and the withdrawal from the Ukraine, 322, 324, 326, 328-30; and the lull on the Rus-

440

Index of Army Formations